Working with Objects

Working with Objects

The OOram Software Engineering Method

TRYGVE REENSKAUG

with P. Wold and O.A. Lehne

MANNING

Greenwich

*We dedicate this book to Douglas Engelbart, because he has made
us understand that computers should be used to augment the
human intellect rather than to replace it, and because in his deep
understanding of the symbiosis between humans and information
he is still far ahead of the rest of us.*

The publisher offers discounts on this book when ordered in quantity. For more information,
please contact:

Special Sales Department
Manning Publications Co.
3 Lewis Street
Greenwich, CT 06830

Fax: (203) 661-9018
e-mail: 73150.1431@compuserve.com

Library of Congress Cataloging-in-Publication Data

Reenskaug, Trygve, 1930–
     Working with objects : the ooram software engineering method / Trygve Reenskaug with
P. Wold and O.A. Lehne.
       p.   cm.
     Includes bibliographical references and index.
     ISBN 1-884777-10-4 (hardcover : alk. paper)
     1. Object-oriented programming (Computer science)   I. Wold, P., 1957– .
II. Lehne, O.A., 1959– .   III. Title.
QA76.64.R45   1995
005.1'2--dc20   95-34774
                                                                               CIP

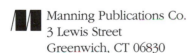 Manning Publications Co.
3 Lewis Street
Greenwich, CT 06830

Design: Frank Cunningham
Copyediting: Margaret Marynowski
Page Compositon: Lauralee Butler Reinke

Printed in the United States of America
1 2 3 4 5 6 7 8 9 10 – BB – 98 97 96 95

There are two ways of constructing a software design:

One way is to make it so simple that there are obviously no deficiencies

and the other way is to make it so complicated that there are no obvious deficiencies.

—C.A.R. Hoare

Contents

Foreword   xiii
Preface   xv
Acknowledgments   xx

Chapter 1   The Main Ideas   1

1.1   The OOram Method   2

1.2   The Technology Dimension   5

   1.2.1   Representing the Real World as Objects   6
   1.2.2   The Powerful Role Model Abstraction   7
   1.2.3   Separation of Concern and Role Model Synthesis   10
   1.2.4   OOram Implementation Links Role Models to
           Computer Programs   13
   1.2.5   OOram Reuse Technology   16
   1.2.6   Comparison with Other Methods   20

1.3   Process with Deliverables   23

   1.3.1   Introduction to the Model Creation Process   24
   1.3.2   Introduction to the System Development Process   24
   1.3.3   Introduction to the Reusable Assets Building Processes   26

1.4   Organization   28

Chapter 2   Role Modeling   31

2.1   Modeling the Real World: Human Understanding and
      Human Communication   33

2.2   Modeling Using Objects   36

2.3   Modeling Using Roles   43

   2.3.1   A Travel Expense Example   45
   2.3.2   An Internet Example   48
   2.3.3   A Sample Model Having Four Roles   50

2.4   The Model Creation Process and its Deliverables   52

2.5   Basic OOram Role Modeling Concepts and Notation   57

    2.5.1   The Object   57
    2.5.2   External Object Properties   57
    2.5.3   The Role Model   59

Chapter 3   **Role Model Synthesis   69**

3.1   Introduction to Synthesis: `DerivedTravelExpense`   71

    3.1.1   The `AirlineBooking` (`AB`) Model   72
    3.1.2   Creating the `DerivedTravelExpense` (`DTE`) Model   72

3.2   The Synthesis Operation   78

    3.2.1   Aggregation: Linking Models on Different Levels of Abstraction   86
    3.2.2   Attributes and Message Parameters   88
    3.2.3   Safe and Unsafe Synthesis of the Travel Example Models   90

3.3   Basic OOram Concepts and Notation for Role Model Synthesis   92

    3.3.1   The Inheritance and Role List Views   92
    3.3.2   Synthesis in the Area of Concern View   94
    3.3.3   Synthesis in the Environment and
           Stimulus-Response Views   95
    3.3.4   Synthesis in the Collaboration View   95
    3.3.5   Synthesis in the Scenario View   97
    3.3.6   Synthesis in the Interface View   99
    3.3.7   Synthesis in the Method Specification View   99

Chapter 4   **Bridge to Implementation   101**

4.1   Introduction to Implementation   102

    4.1.1   Object Modeling from a Programmer's Point of View   104
    4.1.2   A Simple Class Inheritance Example   108
    4.1.3   Why We Need High Level Descriptions   112

4.2   The Relationship between a Role Model and its Implementation   116

    4.2.1   Implementing the Roles   116
    4.2.2   Implementing the Ports and Interfaces   121
    4.2.3   Implementing the Methods and Actions   123

4.3   The Implementation Process   124

4.4   Choice of Programming Language   129

Chapter 5   **Creating Reusable Components   133**

5.1   Introduction to Reuse   135

5.2   Patterns   143

    5.2.1   Alexander's Pattern Language   144
    5.2.2   How to Create a Pattern   145

5.3   OOram Frameworks   153

Chapter 6   **Additional Role Modeling Concepts and Notation   157**

    6.1   Semantic View   159

    6.2   Process View   162

    6.3   State Diagram View   168

    6.4   Role List View   172

    6.5   Modeling in the Large: The OOram Module   173

Chapter 7   **Case Study: Development of a Business Information System   177**

    7.1   Objects Everywhere   178

    7.2   Enterprise Model   184

        7.2.1   Determine the Area of Concern   185
        7.2.2   Understand the Problem and Identify the Nature of the Objects   186
        7.2.3   Determine Environment Roles and Stimulus/Response   189
        7.2.4   Identify and Understand the Roles   189
        7.2.5   Determine the Work Process   190
        7.2.6   Determine the Collaboration Structure   191
        7.2.7   Determine Interfaces   191

    7.3   Information Model   194

        7.3.1   Area of Concern   195
        7.3.2   Semantic View   195
        7.3.3   Role List View   195
        7.3.4   A Hybrid Solution with a Relational Database   196
        7.3.5   Collaboration View   197
        7.3.6   Interface View   198

    7.4   Task/Tool/Service Model   199

        7.4.1   Creating Task/Tool/Service Descriptions   200
        7.4.2   User Interface Design   201
        7.4.3   A Simple Direct Manipulation Interface for Our Task Example   204
        7.4.4   A Composite User Interface for the Manager to
                Determine Travel Permission   205

Chapter 8   **Case Study: The Analysis and Design of a Real Time System   211**

    8.1   Environment Model   213

        8.1.1   Determine the Area of Concern   213
        8.1.2   Identify Environment Roles and Stimulus/Response   213
        8.1.3   Determine Typical Message Sequences   214

    8.2   Detailed Model   215

        8.2.1   Specify and Understand Objects and Roles   215
        8.2.2   Determine Typical Message Sequences   216
        8.2.3   Describe Roles as State Diagrams   216
        8.2.4   Determine the Interfaces   218

    8.3   Implementation Examples   221

        8.3.1   Bridge to C++   222
        8.3.2   Bridge to Smalltalk   223

8.3.3   Bridge to SDL   224

8.3.4   Bridge to Distributed Object Systems   226

8.3.5   OMG/CORBA   227

8.3.6   COM/OLE   228

8.3.7   OOram Executable Specifications   229

Chapter 9   **Case Study: The Creation of a Framework   235**

9.1   Step 1: Identify Consumers and Consumer Needs   237

9.2   Step 2: Perform a Cost-benefit Analysis   238

9.3   Step 3: Reverse Engineering of Existing Programs   239

9.3.1   Container-Component Hierarchy   242

9.3.2   Model-View-Controller   249

9.3.3   Mouse and Keyboard Input   254

9.3.4   Main Input Role Model   255

9.3.5   TranslatingSensor Initialization Model   255

9.3.6   The Scroller Role Model   257

9.4   Step 4: Specify the New Framework   259

9.5   Step 5: Document the Framework as Patterns
Describing how to Solve Problems   260

9.5.1   Pattern 1: The Tool   260

9.5.2   Pattern 2: Fixed Proportion Tool Layout   261

9.5.3   Pattern 3: Flexible Tool Layout   262

9.5.4   Pattern 4: The Controller   263

9.5.5   Pattern 5: The Model Object   263

9.5.6   Pattern 6: The View   264

9.6   Step 6: Describe the Framework's Design and Implementation   266

9.7   Step 7: Inform the Consumer Community   271

Chapter 10   **Organizing for Software Productivity   273**

10.1 An Industrial Approach to Software Production   274

10.2 Large-scale Production of Intelligent Network Services   281

10.3 Large-scale Production of Customized Business Information
Systems   285

Chapter 11   **Advanced Reuse Based on Object Instances   293**

11.1 Introduction to Object Reuse   294

11.2 Runtime Configuration and Object Trading   295

11.3 The OOram Composition System   298

11.3.1 The OOCS Schema Creator Layer   302

11.3.2 List of Instructions: OOCS Schema Creation   302

11.3.3 The Nature of OOCS Schemas   303

11.3.4 The OOCS Type Implementor Layer   305

11.4 Object Duplication 309

    11.4.1 `shallowCopy`—Too Simple in Most Cases 311

    11.4.2 `postCopy`—A Default Duplication Algorithm 312

    11.4.3 `structureCopy` for the General Case 314

    11.4.4 `deepCopy`—A Dangerous Operation 316

Chapter 12   **Case Study: Intelligent Network Services Organized in a Value Chain 319**

12.1 A Simple Case with an Extensible Solution 320

12.2 User Layer 326

12.3 Subscriber Layer 327

12.4 Service Provider Layer 329

12.5 Service Creator Layer 331

12.6 Service Constituent Creator Layer 334

12.7 Network Provider Layer 337

Appendix A   **The OOram Language 339**

Appendix B   **References 353**

Where to Find Definitions of Important Terms 359

Index 361

Foreword

Over the past five years, as the object orientation approach to software engineering has gained momentum in the commercial world, it has been interesting to note the increased belief in software construction as an engineering field (as opposed to the black art it has been since the dawn of the computing industry in the late 1940s). In one sense, object orientation is just another weapon in the arsenal of the programmer, to dampen complexity and restore order to large systems. Large complex systems, after all, have always been the bane of engineers, and object orientation is just another approach; not even a particularly new one.

The growing library of object technology (OT) books, however, screams out the gaping need for a new approach in software development; it also testifies to the applicability of OT for real-world problems and the efficacy of object-based solutions. After thirty years in laboratories and academe, OT has come out of the closet and is being heavily used in all phases of software development, from requirements analysis to maintenance support.

In one of my roles at the Object Management Group (OMG), I am responsible for judging application submissions to the world-wide OMG/ComputerWorld Object Application Awards program, which recognizes end-user achievement in applying OT methods to user problems. These applications are real: they represent fielded use of proven components to solve actual problems. In the last three years, I have seen these submissions move from vendors' and ISVs' attempted sales jobs, to waste management systems, airline reservations systems, insurance claim adjustment systems, governmental taxation management systems, hazardous waste management systems and property management systems (to name just a few). Clearly this technology is leading to fielded, proven applications. In most cases, these applications either replace or fully integrate existing, legacy applications, further decreasing implementation costs.

The most exciting area of this OT revolution, though not always the most obvious, is the use of OT to automate software engineering tasks themselves. OT-based analysis and design methodologies will prove the greatest leverage point for this technology. And, this book proves the point. Starting with a thorough indoctrination into the problem space and the OOram method, Reenskaug, Wold, and Lehne provide an example-filled journey through the discussion of software generation.

The role modeling approach introduced in the OOram method provides a strong basis for the modeling of interfaces, separating the implementation issues; this is an absolute necessity for implementation of distributed objects throughout the OMG approach to objects and all large-scale industrial software projects.

Practical, experience-based hints abound; you won't come away from this book without a sound understanding of OT-based abstractions for modeling programs.

Enjoy the journey.

Richard Mark Soley, Ph.D.
Object Management Group, Inc.
Framingham, Massachusetts

Preface

GOALS

The main theme of this book is to describe complex phenomena as structures of interacting objects. Object technology is applicable to a wide range of phenomena on many different levels. Examples are work procedures on the enterprise level, large scale applications on the systems level, and small, technical details on the program design level.

Real software for real users

The goals of this book are:

1 To provide a comprehensive description of the object paradigm and its applications.

2 To show how it supports a number of different views on the same model, permitting the analyst to work with a data-centered approach, a process-centered approach, or a combination of the two.

3 To show how very large and complex systems can be described by a number of distinct models.

4 To show how composite models can be derived from simpler base models.

5 To describe a number of powerful reuse techniques.

6 To describe how a systematic policy of reuse impacts on work processes and organization.

7 To show how very large systems can be described and managed in a decentralized manner.

MOTIVATION

A number of important books on object-oriented analysis and design have been published in recent years [Cox 87, Wirfs-Brock 90, Booch 94, Rumbaugh 91, and Jacobson 92]. All of these methodologies are based on the *object* as the common building block and on the *class* as a common abstraction on the objects.

There is a widespread feeling that existing methodologies could profitably be merged into a single one, and that the concepts and notation of the composite methodology could be standardized. We feel that such standardization will be premature. Objects and classes represent two different levels of abstraction; each is suited to the expression of certain properties. Static properties and relations are best expressed in terms of classes. Examples are attributes and relations, most notably for expressing the inheritance relation. Dynamic properties are best expressed in terms of objects. Examples are message interactions (scenarios), use cases, and dataflows.

The class/object duality is as essential to object-oriented programming as it is disruptive to object-oriented modeling. A future modeling standard should be built on a unified conceptual framework with sufficient expressive power to describe *all* interesting aspects of an object system within a single, integrated model.

One candidate is the OOram (Object Oriented Role Analysis and Modeling) role model. This conceptual framework combines the expressiveness of the object and the class. All information that can be expressed in a class-based model can be expressed in a role model. All information that can be expressed in an object-based model can be be expressed in the *same role model*. Furthermore, there is a synergy effect from merging the class and object properties into the same model. The result is increased leverage for the decomposition of large systems and for the systematic reuse of proven components.

The essence of the object-oriented paradigm is the modeling of interesting phenomena as a structure of interacting objects. The architecture of a home can be represented as a structure of room objects interconnected by doors and hallways. A model which says that one room may be adjacent to another room is insufficient. We need to be able to say that the dining room should be adjacent to the kitchen, and that the childrens' playroom should be far away from the master bedroom.

In an *OOram role model*, patterns of interacting objects are abstracted into a corresponding pattern of interacting roles. In our simple example, one object will play the role of dining room, another the role of kitchen, etc. The roles are interconnected to represent the layout of the home. Corresponding objects will belong to the same class if they have the same properties; they will belong to different classes if they have different properties. The role model abstraction belongs to the realm of modeling. The class abstraction belongs to the realm of implementation.

An object can play several roles. This permits a systematic *separation of concerns* by describing phenomena using different *role models*. And conversely, it permits the synthesis of a derived model by letting its objects play several roles from different role models.

This book is about the added leverage provided by *role modeling*, compared to the conventional *class modeling*. The nature of this leverage is described under the heading of *Goals* above. The added leverage motivates our introduction of a new and precisely defined set of concepts and a new notation—it motivates this book.

AUDIENCE

Familiarity with computers assumed

We assume that you are familiar with how computers and computer programming influence modern information processing, but we do not assume familiarity with a particular programming language or operating system. Most of the book is written for the manager or business person who is searching for new and better ways to produce software, for the consultant who wants to use objects to design new business organizations, and for the system creator who wants to understand how to exploit the full power of object orientation. A few sections are clearly marked as being directed at the expert computer programmer.

THE STRUCTURE OF THIS BOOK

This book is written to be read in sequence, but we suggest you skip sections which look uninteresting on your first reading. It is organized into twelve chapters as follows:

A reader's guide to this book

1 *The Main Ideas.* An overview of the OOram approach to industrial-strength software production, object orientation, and modeling. It should help you to recognize what objects can do for you and help you to set your goals. If you have some prior knowledge of the subject, you will see that the OOram ideas differ from earlier methods in important ways, and that these differences give the OOram method unique leverage for analysis, design, and reuse. If this is your first encounter with objects, you may want to skip certain parts on a first reading. Chapter 2 and other chapters offer a more gradual introduction to the same material.

2 *Role Modeling.* How to create object-oriented models of interesting phenomena. This chapter should help you create your first models and establish your work processes for analysis and design.

3 *Role Model Synthesis.* How to create derived models from simpler ones. Read this chapter to understand how you can divide your problem space and still conquer the whole. If your systems are large scale, this chapter should help you tackle them.

4 *Bridge to Implementation.* How to specify objects for implementation in different languages, how to implement specifications, how to check an implementation against its specifications, and how to analyze an existing implementation to create one or more role models describing it. This chapter ties the concepts of the OOram technology to the concepts of two popular programming languages, Smalltalk and C++. This may be the chapter which makes the OOram technology real to you if you are a programmer. If you are not, you may safely ignore the whole chapter.

5 *Creating Reusable Components.* How to create reusable components by exploiting the object inheritance properties. You cannot reuse something before you have used it. There is no snake oil that will magically give you the benefits of reuse, but we present guidelines that will help the serious practitioner gradually build a library of reusable components. Once you master the technology of synthesis, you can search for reusable components which transform your large and complex projects into small and manageable ones.

6 *Additional Role Modeling Concepts and Notation.* Presents additional role model views that have proven to be useful in certain circumstances.

7 *Case Study: Development of a Business Information System.* Stresses the work processes and the relationships between three important models: a model of the system environment, an information model, and a task/tool/service model.

8 *Case Study: The Analysis and Design of a Real Time System.* Stresses embedded systems, with their behavioral aspects described using Finite State Machines. This study exemplifies a number of different approaches to the implementation.

9 *Case Study: The Creation of a Framework.* Describes the creation of a fairly large framework supporting reuse. This study describes all of the stages in the creation of the framework, including reverse engineering of existing systems and forward engineering of the new framework.

10 *Organizing for Software Productivity.* Describes how to design a work organization in the form of a value chain, and how to select appropriate technology for the different layers. This chapter indicates the structure of a future software industry, and is written for readers who are serious about the large scale provision of customized software. It offers the greatest challenges and promises the biggest rewards. It advises you to reconsider your whole software business, to look for repeating questions which can exploit reusable answers, and to move from a job shop organization to an industrial one.

11 *Advanced Reuse Based on Object Instances.* For the specially interested reader. We describe how you can compose a system from a pool of predefined objects. This technology is an extension of the OOram role modeling technology that is the basis of the first part of this book. It is not as mature, but it can become an important supplement to OOram role modeling technologies.

12 *Case Study: Intelligent Network Services Organized in a Value Chain.* Exemplifies a complete software industry. This chapter specifies a value chain, with the actors and appropriate technology for each layer. This study shows how all the different reuse technologies have a place in a complete value chain.

USING THIS BOOK

This book helps you get started industrializing your software production

This book describes the principles behind an industrial approach to software production. We claim that the technological basis of industrial software production should be object orientation. A large part of this book is devoted to explaining all the things you can do with objects; we will also match the operations on objects to the needs of typical value chains for software production.

No viable industry was ever established on an ad hoc basis. Object orientation and industrial production of software are not some kind of magic that will produce immediate results in your next software project. You must identify your potential customers, and fully understand their current and future needs. You must identify the complete value chain, and carefully consider your place in that chain. You must devise optimal technologies and production facilities for every step in the chain. You must establish the required infrastructure for supporting the process, and staff the production facilities with people trained for their tasks. This book can help you to get started, but only your own long term dedication and investment in time and resources can lead you to the goal.

Gradual transition to full industrialization required

The software industry is still in its infancy, and it will take many years to establish an effective industrial infrastructure. We therefore recommend a gradual transition from the miserable present to the glorious future. The winners will be companies with a clear vision, an effective strategy, and the stamina needed to transform their operations from the general job shop to the industrial enterprise.

Figure P.1 illustrates our recommended progression through objects and the OOram method. We have indicated that the first step should be to implement systems using objects. If you are a programmer, this means that you should start by writing small, object-oriented programs. If you are a developer of enterprise processes, you should create some simple processes in object-oriented terms. This first step is shown dashed, because object-oriented programming is not the focus of this book. The remaining steps indicate our recommended progression into the rich world of objects.

Taskon invites cooperation

It is our hope that this book will encourage widespread adoption of the OOram method. Taskon markets OOram processes, tools, and consultancy services for a number of application areas. We invite consultants to build special method-

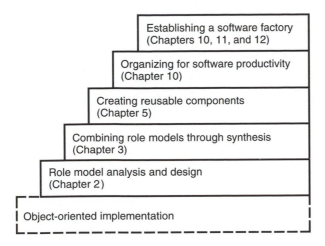

Figure P.1

Stages in the application of the OOram method

Establishing a software factory
(Chapters 10, 11, and 12)

Organizing for software productivity
(Chapter 10)

Creating reusable components
(Chapter 5)

Combining role models through synthesis
(Chapter 3)

Role model analysis and design
(Chapter 2)

Object-oriented implementation

ologies based on our products; we invite other vendors to create competing products; we invite potential competitors to cooperate with us to ensure interoperability between products to the benefit of all.

BACKGROUND

This book is based on continuous experience with objects since 1975, and practical experience in the borderland between software engineering research and the production of software for computer-aided design, production control, management information systems, and telecommunications since 1960. In all our work, the goal has been to create industrial-strength software for real users. The software engineering methodologies and tools have been created in response to our own needs and to the needs of our partners, and the success criterion has been that they enabled us to support our clients more effectively.

Our experience has clearly shown that object orientation is a powerful paradigm which is applicable to a wide range of problem areas. We have used it to design improved organizations in oil companies; to describe basic, reusable services in a distributed environment; to design client-server systems; and to specify and implement business information systems.

Object orientation is a powerful paradigm

Our most exciting experiences are with systematic reuse and an industrial approach to software production. This enables us to produce large systems in small projects, which we believe is the key to the effective production of quality software.

Large systems, small projects

Our accumulated experience also leads to a negative conclusion: there is no silver bullet that will miraculously solve all problems. The work process, the organization, and the technology have to be adapted to the problem at hand and to the people who are to solve it. We do therefore not have the audacity to present a complete methodology which will solve all problems. Rather, we present a foundation which can support many methodologies for different purposes, which we call it the *OOram method.*

Different methodologies for different problems

TRYGVE REENSKAUG
trygve@taskon.no

Acknowledgments

Trygve Reenskaug has written most of the words you find in this book, and when the pronoun I is used, it refers to him. Per Wold has been an essential partner, posing important questions and suggesting appropriate answers throughout the creation process. Odd Arild Lehne has brought his extensive teaching and consulting experience to bear on the book's structure, examples, and case studies.

Jørn Andersen, Lasse Bjerde, Jon Ola Hove, Eirik Næss-Ulset, and Carl Petter Swensson have been members of the Taskon book committee. The patience and perseverance they have shown by reading and rereading a steady stream of drafts, and their help in shaping the form and contents of the various chapters of the book, cannot be overestimated.

The development of the OOram method has taken place at the Center for industrial research (SI) in Oslo, at Taskon AS, and at the University of Oslo. We regard a good development team as a team where ideas and results flow freely, and where the success of the whole is the only measure of the success of the individual. We have always had a very good team, and the results presented in this book have been contributed by a great number of dedicated people over the past 20 years. It is impossible, in retrospect, to identify the individual contributions or even contributors, and we thank them all.

Our research in the field of applied object orientation would have died at certain critical times in the late 1970s without the wholehearted support by Bjørn Ørjansen, then director of research at SI. Important work on an object-oriented planning and control system was supported by the Aker Group in the early 1970s as part of our long cooperation on the Autokon system for the computer-aided design of ships.

The Royal Norwegian Council for Industrial and Scientific Research has given support through several grants: for the porting of Smalltalk-78 to local equipment and for creating the first Norwegian Ethernet in 1980, for the research that lead to first prototypes of our present range of products in the research and development program *Efficiency and Quality in Engineering*, and for our work with an object-oriented architecture for very large, heterogeneous systems in the Eureka Software Factory Project.

I had the good fortune to spend a year as a visiting scientist with Alan Kay, Adele Goldberg, and the Smalltalk group at the Xerox Palo Alto Research Center (PARC) in 1978–79. This was a wonderful experience, which completely changed my life, and it is impossible to fully express my gratitude for the help and inspiration I received. I particularly want to thank Adele for the support and interesting discussions that lead to the creation of the first version of the Model-View-Controller; this was probably the world's first reusable, object-oriented framework. After this visit, we got a license to port Smalltalk-78 to local equipment in Norway. This port was excellently performed by Bruce Horn, who was then a student at PARC. My colleagues and I are eternally grateful to Bruce and Xerox for giving us early experience with the world's most exciting programming environment. We are also very grateful to Bruce for permitting us to publish his work on user interface design, which you will find in Chapter 7.

We are strong believers in the axiom that programmers should take their own medicine. The authors and all members of Taskon team are heavy users of our methodologies and tools, and this book is written with our OOram documentation tools. Our own use supplies a steady stream of ideas for improvements, but feedback from other users is also crucial: they solve different problems and have different ideas about what the methodologies should do for them. We therefore thank our customers and other users of the OOram method for constructive criticisms and ideas for improvements.

Our application of the OOram method to the field of telecommunications would have been impossible without the initiative of Raymond Nilsen of Norwegian Telecom Research. We thank him, Tom Handegård, Klaus Gaarder, Bengt Jensen, and their colleagues for having taught us what we know about telecommunications and for a number of stimulating discussions in a creative atmosphere. We also thank Dag Brenna and Martha Haraldsen of Garex A/S, who gave us valuable feedback on the application of the OOram technology to the large-scale production of customized communication systems.

We express our sincere thanks to Arne-Jørgen Berre for comparing the OOram method to the currently popular methodologies for object-oriented analysis and design, and for providing important insights into the world of distributed computing. We are also grateful to Espen Frimann Koren, Magnus Rygh, and John Lakos for their preparation and discussion of the programming examples in C++. Stein Krogdahl helped create the the OOram language presented in Appendix A, but does not want to be held responsible for this first version of the language.

A number of people have contributed their time and expertise to reviewing parts or all of this book. We would like to express our sincere thanks to Ralph Johnson, Doug Bennett, Mats Gustafsson, Geir Høydalsvik, Else Nordhagen, Witold Sitek, Anne-Lise Skaar, Gerhard Skagestein, Pål Stenslet, Michael Thurell, and the anonymous reviewers who have all contributed valuable and insightful comments.

We also express our sincere thanks to Margaret Marynowski for her thorough copy editing, and to Lauralee B. Reinke for giving this book its pleasing appearance.

Finally, I would like to express my sincere thanks to a programmer and systems analyst who has been providing inspiration, unfaltering support, and valuable advice during the past 40 years: my wife Oddbjørg Råd Reenskaug.

CHAPTER 1

The Main Ideas

CONTENTS

1.1 The OOram Method   2

1.2 The Technology Dimension   5

   1.2.1   Representing the Real World as Objects   6
   1.2.2   The Powerful Role Model Abstraction   7
   1.2.3   Separation of Concern and Role Model Synthesis   10
   1.2.4   OOram Implementation Links Role Models to Computer Programs   13
   1.2.5   OOram Reuse Technology   16
   1.2.6   Comparison with Other Methods   20

1.3 Process with Deliverables   23

   1.3.1   Introduction to the Model-Creation Process   24
   1.3.2   Introduction to the System Development Process   24
   1.3.3   Introduction to the Reusable Assets Building Processes   26

1.4 Organization   28

This chapter gives an overview of object orientation as it is exploited by the OOram method, and of our general ideas about organizing software production in value chains. We recommend that you read this chapter before embarking on the details in the remainder of the book.

1.1   THE OORAM METHOD

IN A NUTSHELL

In the software engineering community, a methodology usually denotes an approach to accomplishing a task. We find it convenient to study methodologies in three dimensions: a technology dimension describing the concepts, notation, and tools; a process dimension describing the steps to be performed (mainly in parallel) together with the deliverables from each step, and an organization dimension describing the organization for effective software development.

The OOram idea is that there is no single, ideal methodology. We need different methodologies for different purposes, each tailored to a specific combination of products, people, and work environment.

The OOram method is generic: it forms a framework for creating a variety of methodologies. All will build on selected parts of the OOram technology, and each will have unique processes and organization. We will stress the common technology in this book, but we will also discuss aspects of the other two dimensions in order to help you create methodologies that are optimized for your requirements.

The software crisis

The software crisis was first officially recognized at the NATO Conference on Software Engineering in Garmisch, Germany in 1968. The conference identified the problem and started a discussion about its solution. Much has been achieved in the intervening period, but software requirements have grown at least as fast as our ability to satisfy them. Today, more than twenty-five years and many "solutions" after the Garmisch conference, we still have a software crisis and we are still searching for better solutions.

Object-oriented methods are the latest solution

The latest solution to catch the fancy of system developers is the technology based on the *object paradigm*. The first object-oriented programming language, Simula, was developed in Norway in the 1960s. The field got a tremendous boost when the Smalltalk language and development system became available in the early 1980s. The introduction of the C++ programming language made object orientation generally acceptable to the systems programming community [Birt 73, Gold 83, and Strou 86].

Books on methodologies for object-oriented analysis and design appeared in the late 1980s. The authors started out using different approaches to the common theme of describing interesting things using objects. Cox, Booch, and Wirfs-Brock based their work on the concepts of object-oriented programming languages. Rumbaugh and Jacobson started from earlier modeling paradigms, Rumbaugh from a data-centered approach, and Jacobson from a function-centered approach [Cox 87, Booch 91, Wirfs-Brock 90, Rumbaugh 91, and Jacobson 92].

Object technology has moved from the exotic to the feasible. It is now rapidly moving from the feasible into the mainstream of systems development.

A powerful paradigm merging many earlier concepts

The reason for the popularity of objects is easy to see. We have been using a number of modeling paradigms to describe different aspects of our systems. The data-centered approaches, e.g., entity-relation modeling, were excellent for modeling the static properties of information, but they were weak for modeling functionality. The behavior-centered approaches, e.g., functional decomposition or finite state machines, were great for modeling the dynamics of the system, but they were weak on modeling data.

The advantage of the object-oriented paradigm is that it neatly combines the strengths of the data-centered and the behavior-centered approaches. It is great for modeling information, and it is great for modeling behavior.

Like all previous solutions, object orientation is no panacea. It is still easy to create lousy systems and hard to create good ones. Objects offer no more and no less than an opportunity for mastering even harder problems than we have been able to master in the past.

Methodology and Method

In normal usage, a *method* is an approach to accomplishing a task, and a *methodology* is the study of a family of methods. Within the software community, the term methodology usually denotes an approach to accomplishing a task. We have therefore taken the liberty of letting the OOram method denote our strategy and technology for the creation of a family of methodologies for different purposes.

Within the software community, a methodology is taken to mean an approach to accomplishing a task. (See box.) We do not believe that we will ever find an ideal methodology that will serve all purposes equally well. On the contrary, we believe that a methodology not only has to be optimized for its goals; it should also be tailored to suit the culture, competence, and preferences of its people. It is therefore impossible to create an overall methodology which covers all needs. But we will present guidelines, examples, and case studies that may be helpful when you devise solutions to your problems in software creation, in model and software reuse, or in setting up an organization for the large-scale provision of customized software.

The OOram method is a frame of reference

The OOram method is a frame of reference for a family of object-oriented methodologies. It captures the essence of object orientation, which is to model interesting phenomena as a structure of interacting *objects*. It offers the *role model* as a powerful abstraction that supports a very general *separation of concerns*. (See Section 2.5.) The notion of *role model synthesis* supports the construction of complex models from simpler ones in a safe and controlled manner, and offers many opportunities for the systematic application of reusable components.

A methodology is usually considered to consist of the three main dimensions illustrated in Figure 1.1. The OOram method makes possible important improvements along all three dimensions:

A methodology has technology, process, and organization

1. *Technology:* the concepts, notation, techniques and tools used to describe phenomena of all kinds and sizes in terms of objects. Reuse technology offers a range of opportunities for materially reducing the size and complexity of application development projects through the systematic reuse of proven components.

2. *Process with Deliverables:* the steps to be performed and the results to be delivered from each step. Our capability for working with several models permits us to gradually zoom in on the system from its environment to its inner details in a controlled manner.

3. *Organization:* how the enterprise is organized to accommodate the operation. The OOram reuse technology permits the creation of industrial strength organizations for systematic investment in reusable components and their routine application in development projects.

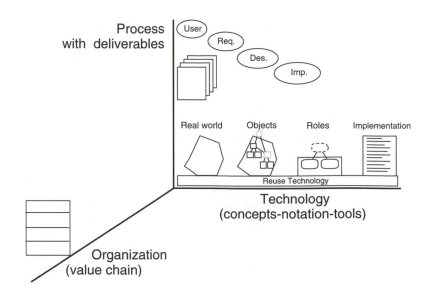

Figure 1.1

Three dimensions of system development methodologies

The OOram method widely applicable

Methodologies for a wide range of problems can be based on the OOram method. In the later chapters of this book, we will describe how OOram supports different methodologies covering the technical, organizational, and process dimensions. Our main concern will be the technical dimension, because it is common to all methodologies and a prerequisite to our proposed solutions for different processes and organizations.

The OOram method based on 20 years of experience

The OOram method traces its history to the early 1970s. One of its first applications was an object-oriented shipyard production control system [Ree 77]. The Smalltalk Model-View-Controller paradigm is another application of the OOram ideas; the senior author developed the first version in association with Adele Goldberg at Xerox Palo Alto Research Center (PARC) in 1979–80.

The driving force is need for professional software engineering

The driving force behind the development of the OOram method has been our own need for professional software engineering methodologies. Concepts, notations, and tools have been developed concurrently, because modeling concepts and notation are maximally effective when they can be supported by current workstation technology. The success criteria are:

1 The combination of concepts, notations, and tools should help a team of developers cooperate in the development and maintenance of large object-oriented systems in a way that ensures high reliability, efficiency, and stability.

2 The reuse of ideas, designs, and code should be maximized for the efficient development of a large family of related systems.

OOram is practical, sound, and useful, with or without tools

These success criteria are strongly utilitarian, and the leverage provided by tools is as important as the theoretical soundness of the technology. In particular:

1 Diagrams and tables must be informative and fit on a computer screen. We have developed the OOram method and the OOram tools concurrently, and rarely use one without the other. Other people have successfully used the OOram method without the tools. We therefore claim that the concepts and notation are suitable for manual as well as computer-assisted modes of working.

2 Software is created by people, and quality software is created by people of quality. Methods and tools cannot be a substitute for skilled people; the best we can hope for is that they will be of assistance to skilled people who will adapt them to their needs and use them with discretion.

3 Methods and tools must scale. Practical programs are often several orders of magnitude larger and more complex than typical textbook examples. Scaleability and practicability are critical to the success of software engineering methods and tools. The OOram method and tools have been created to help real people solve real problems. The goal of this book is to share our experiences with you in the hope that they will help *you* solve *your* problems in *your* environment.

1.2 THE TECHNOLOGY DIMENSION

IN A NUTSHELL

This dimension covers the concepts that form the basis of the work; the notation used for documentation; and the tools. Figure 1.1 illustrates the main ideas: We select a bounded part of the real world as a phenomenon to be the subject of our study. We choose to model the phenomenon as a structure of objects in an object model; where we distinguish between system objects and environment objects. Patterns of objects in the object model are abstracted into role models. A role model describes how a structure of objects achieves a given area of concern by playing appropriate roles. Finally, classes are defined in the implementation so that instances play a specified set of roles.

The phenomena to be described can be of any kind and any size. The technology must be selected to suit the problem; we cannot expect that the same concepts will be equally relevant to all problems.

Object technology offers several opportunities for reuse; we will discuss five of them in this book. These technologies do not in any way guarantee reuse, but they give the production engineer the freedom to select the appropriate technology for each layer in the value chain mentioned above.

Object technology is pervasive, it can be used for almost anything. We first applied it to modeling ship design processes on the enterprise level [Ree 73], when we introduced coordinated computer support for the different stages in the design process. Controlling computer-based information transfer between project stages and company divisions proved to be a serious problem, and we used objects to model the flow of information and the dependencies between divisions.

Our first object application: Enterprise model for ship design

We next applied objects to shipyard scheduling and control [Ree 77]. The yard was a heavy user of an activity planning system, but it also needed a number of specialized systems for scheduling dockside jobs, the use of the big crane, and a panel assembly line. Our idea was to replace all of their disparate systems with a single, object-oriented scheduling and control system. We represented the ship as an object, its parts as objects, the construction jobs were represented as objects. We also represented the yard, its production facilities such as dockside facilities, the big crane and the panel assembly line as objects. The objects are illustrated in Figure 1.2.

Our second object application: Shipyard scheduling

Figure 1.2

Some objects
relevant to the
shipyard
scheduling and
control operation

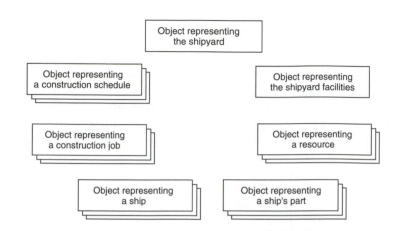

The concepts and notation of the OOram technology is common to all OOram methodologies. A specific methodology will use a selected subset, and any selection will be consistent and workable. We will here give a brief taste of its main features. You will find the complete description of the OOram technology in the main body of the book. The description is like a large salad bar; it is up to you to select the dishes you want and to ignore those that you do not like or need.

1.2.1 Representing the Real World as Objects

Objects are ideal building blocks for creating models of complex systems, because they combine information with behavior. We regard the essence of object orientation to be the modeling of interesting phenomena as structures of interacting objects, and we always consider objects in the context of their collaborators.

Objects may be defined in terms of a programming language, but we prefer a more intuitive description that highlights object collaboration and division of responsibility, and hides programming artifacts. We think of objects as being analogous to clerks: each clerk has an in-basket, an out-basket, a private data file, and a book of rules. Clerks cooperate through messages. A message consists of the named message type together with the possible parameter values. A clerk picks up a message from his in-basket and processes the message according to the appropriate rule selected from his rule book. Processing may include sending messages to other clerks, as well as reading and modifying values in the private data file.

This simple model highlights important aspects of objects and object modeling:

1 Objects, like people, have *identity*. An object (clerk) retains its identity throughout its lifetime. There has never been and will never be another object with the same identity.

2 Objects are *encapsulated*. Objects (clerks) communicate through message interaction only. The in-basket, the out-basket, the file, and the book of rules are private to the object and invisible to other objects.

3 Objects exhibit *polymorphism*. Since each object (clerk) has its own book of rules, objects may handle messages differently, according to their individual characteristics.

The clerk analogy is very useful for designing object-oriented systems: Given a task, what is the optimal organization of trusted clerks that will perform it? We endeavor to organize so as to get a clear division of authority and responsibility, to minimize duplication and communication, and to employ similar objects in different positions to reduce the need for programming (training).

So we think of the shipyard in terms of objects, as illustrated informally in Figure 1.2. The planning and control functionality is represented by the system dynamics: the objects interact according to a master strategy to produce the desired results.

All objects have certain general behavior that enable them to participate in the interaction. Each job object tries to get scheduled at the best possible time; each resource object strives for optimal utilization of its resource. But the objects also behave according to their specific nature: the big crane can handle only one ship's part at a time, the dockside facilities allocate available area to as many parts as possible, and the panel assembly line object maintains the constraint that two large panels cannot be adjacent on the line.

Objects reach their goals through interaction

1.2.2 The Powerful Role Model Abstraction

Even fairly simple systems have more objects than can be grasped by the human mind. We therefore need some abstraction to create a simple model that highlights essential aspects of the system. The common solution is to uncritically adopt the class, which is the abstraction supported by most object-oriented programming languages. The *class* is a wholesale description of a set of objects, and the *instances* of a class are the objects that have a common data structure and that share a common book of rules.

We regard the class as a powerful means for implementing objects. But programming languages focus on describing one class of objects at a time, while we always consider a structure of collaborating objects. The class abstraction is, therefore, inadequate for our modeling purposes.

The class is a powerful implementation abstraction

The *role model* is the basic object abstraction used in the OOram technology. A real world phenomenon is described as a number of cooperating objects. Subphenomena are specified by their area of concern, objects describing a subphenomenon are organized in a pattern of objects, and all objects having the same position in the pattern are represented by a role. We say they play the same role in the object structure. A role has identity and is encapsulated, and it is an archetypical representation of the objects occupying the corresponding positions in the object system. A role model describes the subject of the object interaction, the relationships between objects, the messages that each object may send to its collaborators, and the model information processes.

The role is a powerful modeling abstraction

An object can play several roles. This permits a systematic separation of concern by describing different phenomena in different role models. And conversely, it permits the synthesis of a derived model by letting its objects play several roles from different role models, as will be described in Section 1.2.3.

Objects are basically simple and controlled by rigid rules. They are mainly realized within computers, but we have also used them with success for describing the rule-based aspects of human business organizations. Each person is represented by an object, and various office procedures are described as processes of message interchange.

Even small organizations are far too complex to be comprehended as a whole. But we can select an issue or aspect and describe it to any desired level of detail. In complex systems, objects, like people, play different roles. A particular person may play the role of a `Traveler` in a `TravelExpenseAccount` model, a `Project-`

Figure 1.3
An activity
network

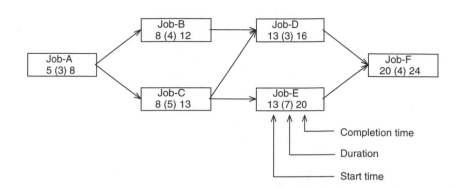

Manager in a Project model, and an Employee in the PersonnelManagement model. The roles are parts of "complete" models, each giving a full account of the relevant area of concern. The Project model could specify system roles such as ProjectManager, Consultant, Librarian, Accountant, and Secretary. Environment roles could be Sponsor and User. The role model describes the responsibility, authority, and tasks of each object, and of the model as a whole.

The total system of Figure 1.2 consists of a very large number of objects, and the object interaction processes needed to create and maintain a production schedule will be very complex. We clearly need some form of abstraction so that we can focus on one portion of the total problem at the time.

Role models invite separation of concern

The OOram method tells us to isolate an area of concern and to create a role model for it. One possible area of concern is the job scheduling activity. A simple algorithm, *activity network frontloading*, schedules all jobs as early as possible. A sample network of participating objects is shown in Figure 1.3. Given that Job-A can start in week 5, the algorithm determines that Job-F, the final job, can be completed in week 24. (The common terminology is to say that an *activity network* is a structure of *activities*. We use the the term *job* instead of *activity*, because we use *activity* for another purpose.)

A job can start when all its predecessors are completed

The frontloading algorithm states that all jobs are characterized by their duration, their predecessor jobs, and their successor jobs. A job can start as soon as all its predecessors are completed, and none of its successors can start before it is completed.

The first job, Job-A, can start in week 5; it takes 3 weeks and is completed in week 8. Job-B can start when Job-A is completed; it takes 4 weeks and finishes in week 12. Job-D can start when both Job-B and Job-C are completed; its starts in week 13, takes 3 weeks, and finishes in week 16. The project is completed when the final job, Job-F, finishes in week 24.

The class description misses the essence

A class is a popular abstraction which represents all objects that share a common implementation. For example, we can say that all job objects of Figure 1.3 are instances of the same Job class. But we will have to study this class in great detail to see the essence of the activity network. We could define DesignJob, ManufacturingJob, TransportJob, and AssemblyJob as different specializations of the Job class, but this would only clutter the issue, without aiding our basic understanding.

The role model describes a structure of objects

It is better to identify a pattern of objects which together capture the phenomenon. In Figure 1.4, we have focused on Job-E and isolated the object pattern consisting of Job-E, its predecessors (just one, Job-C in this case), and its successors (Job-F).

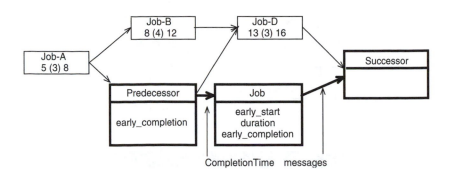

Figure 1.4

Identifying an object pattern

The object pattern is abstracted into a corresponding *role model*, where each pattern object is mapped onto a corresponding *role*. In our example, we see that this is a recurring pattern, and that any network can be constructed as a repeated overlay of these roles. (Overlaying role models will be discussed in Section 1.2.3.)

The role model, shown in Figure 1.5, captures an archetypical pattern of objects, and permits us to study its essential static and dynamic properties. A Predecessor role has one interesting attribute: its early_completion time. The Job role has three interesting attributes: its early start time, its duration, and its early_completion time.

The OOram method supports a number of different views on the role model; each view highlights some aspects of the model and hides others. For example, Figure 1.5 is a *role model collaboration* view. This view shows the roles, their attributes, and their collaboration structure.

The role model provides a more fine-grained control of message-passing than the more common class or type. The role model specifies not only the messages that must be understood by an object (role), but also which objects are allowed to send the different messages. The collaboration view may optionally show some or all of the messages that one role may send to another, or the message interfaces can be presented in an *interface view*.

The frontloading activity is specified as a sequence of messages flowing through the role model as shown in the *scenario view* of Figure 1.6. The Predecessor objects send a message, CompletionTime, to the Job role. The Job computes its own early_completion, and reports it to all its Successor roles.

If we open the Job role, we can study what takes place when it receives CompletionTime messages. This is illustrated in the *method view* of Figure 1.7. We see that the method is triggered when the Job role receives the CompletionTime message. The method computes its own early_completion when all its predecessors are ready, and it finally reports the Job's completion time to its Successors.

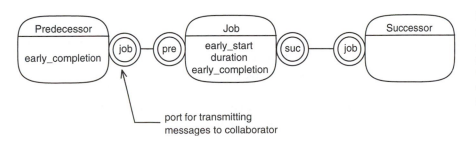

port for transmitting
messages to collaborator

Figure 1.6

Message scenario illustrating frontloading activity

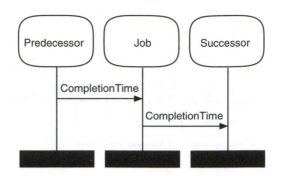

Figure 1.7

Frontloading method in Job role

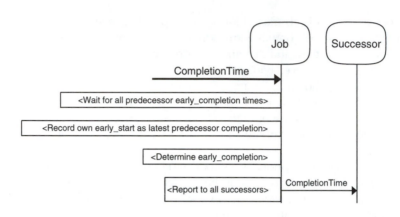

The notion of role modeling is very powerful. We have created a single role model, and the three diagrams are different views on one and the same model. The message received in Figure 1.7 is the same as the first message in the scenario of Figure 1.6. It is sent through the left port of Figure 1.5, and we could have annotated the ports with the messages that can legally be sent through them.

1.2.3 Separation of Concern and Role Model Synthesis

Divide and Conquer

Divide and conquer is an important concept in all modeling practices. In the previous section, we created a role model for an interesting phenomenon, namely, network frontloading.

The frontloading algorithm is just one of the many concerns that are relevant to shipyard scheduling and control. Another area of concern is the allocation of resources to the different jobs. One possible role model is shown in Figure 1.8. The corresponding scenario is shown in Figure 1.9, where Job asks Resource for an allocation, and Resource answers with the reserved time period.

Synthesis: Objects play multiple roles

The advantage of this separation of concerns is that we get manageable models. The disadvantage is that it can lead to a fragmented description of large problems, since each model describes only a limited aspect of the total problem. We confront the fragmentation problem via role model synthesis, where we construct *derived role models* whose objects play multiple roles from several *base role models*.

Role model synthesis is one of the most powerful features of the OOram role model. All object-oriented methods support class inheritance, where a derived class can be defined to inherit attributes and behavior from one or more base

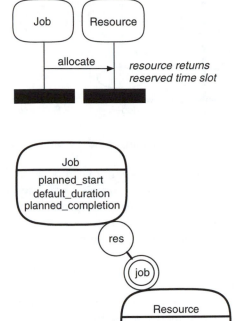

Figure 1.8

Scenario for
basic resource
allocation

Figure 1.9

Collaborators for
basic resource
allocation

classes. In the OOram method, inheritance is lifted to the model level, so that a derived model inherits the static and dynamic properties of one or more base models.

DEFINITION

> **Synthesis**
>
> The antonym of analysis is synthesis, and we use the term role model synthesis to denote the construction of a derived model from one or more base models in a controlled manner:
>
> **synthesis:** *1a: the composition or combination of parts or elements so as to form a whole... 1c: the combination of often diverse conceptions into a coherent whole.* [Webster 77].

The use of role model synthesis permits us to build complex models out of simple ones in a safe and controlled manner. Philip Dellaferra of the Deutsche Telekom Research Center first introduced the *hat stand synthesis model* of Figure 1.10. This figure, which illustrates scheduling with resources, highlights two important aspects of synthesis. First, role models are combined vertically by letting their objects play multiple roles. Second, the integration between role models is through the methods that objects use to process incoming messages.

Role model synthesis gets its leverage from always seeing inheritance in the context of a *complete* pattern of collaborating objects. We therefore inherit not only the characteristics of individual objects, but also the structure and behavior of the model as a whole. Figure 1.11 illustrates the two synthesis operations

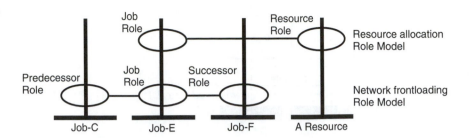

needed to create a composite scheduling model from the frontloading and resource allocation models.

Methods synthesize behavior

The dependencies between synthesized role models are expressed in the methods of the objects. The behavior of an object when receiving a message in the context of a role in one role model may be modified because it is also playing some other role. In Figure 1.12, the method for computing early completion time has been modified, from just adding the duration to asking the resource for allocation.

Safe synthesis

In the ideal case, the correct functioning of a base model will automatically be retained in a composite model after synthesis. Such *safe synthesis* is very valuable, since it permits the reuse of a correct role model with a minimum of hassle. Indeed, we would create a role model solely by safe synthesis from a number of correct base models only if we needed it for explanation purposes.

Safe synthesis is essential for designing a truly global data processing system. Ideally, we should not need to construct the overall system model with all its details. An overall model should be expressed in terms of high level base models, and a high level base model in terms of low level base models. Every base model

Figure 1.11

Composite scheduling model synthesized from two base models

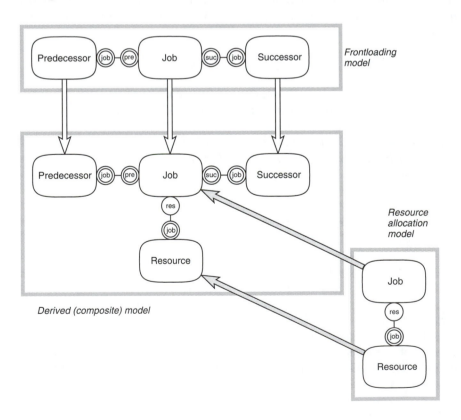

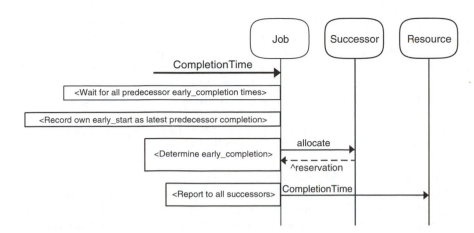

Figure 1.12

Integration though scheduling method

should be independent in the sense that its correctness will be preserved if it is applied using safe synthesis.

In *unsafe synthesis*, the composite model has to be analyzed in total before we can assume it to be correct. You might believe that unsafe synthesis is something to be avoided like the plague, but we find it useful when we analyze a limited phenomenon, to understand it and to communicate our findings. (Even if synthesizing the resource model into a wider context were unsafe, doing so could still help us create a derived model to understand the phenomenon. However, we would have to recheck the complete derived model.) In general, we permit unsafe synthesis when we analyze a relatively limited area of concern. Safe synthesis is required when we want to create models that can be reused in a general context.

Unsafe synthesis

Hierarchical decomposition is a commonly used device for dividing a complex problem into a number of simpler ones. Hierarchical decomposition is easily achieved in object systems by means of encapsulation. An object can contain any amount of complexity within itself, including a complex object structure, without exposing this complexity. But there is also a weakness associated with hierarchical decomposition: true hierarchies are rarely found in the real world.

Synthesis, a very powerful notion

Role model synthesis is a powerful notion because it facilitates the decomposition of large problems into arbitrary structures. The resource model of Figure 1.8 can in one sense be regarded as subordinate to the frontloading model of Figure 1.5. In another context, resources can be primary phenomena, and jobs may be seen as subordinate to the resources. Other superimposed structures abound in a typical enterprise. Examples are project organizations, professional structures, and various ad hoc structures. If these structures are independent, all is well. If they are interdependent, role model synthesis enables us to model the dependencies between them.

1.2.4   OOram Implementation Links Role Models to Computer Programs

This section has been written for computer programmers who are familiar with an object-oriented programming language. Nonprogrammers may safely skip it.

Any role model can form the foundation for an implementation. Real world models may be implemented as office procedures or as computer-based simulation models. Object-oriented models are implemented as programs to create executable specifications or to create application programs.

*The essence of
an object
system is not
easily seen from
the code*

In all our work with objects over the past 20 years, we have found that a programming language is ideally suited to express a detailed definition of a system under consideration. We have likewise found that a programming language is useless for expressing an overview of a system—for describing the structures of objects and their interactions. So there is nothing resembling code in the production control system of Ree [Ree 77], only attempts at expressing the static and dynamic interdependencies between objects.

The objects of Figure 1.3 play one or two roles: Job A plays the Predecessor role, role F plays the Successor role, and all the other objects play all three roles, (Predecessor, Job, and Successor).

The simplest way to implement a role model is to define a single class (e.g., Job1), that implements all three roles. We choose a programming language (e.g., C++ or Smalltalk), and implement a single class which covers all three roles. The class will have instance variables for the attributes and for the collaborators: early_start, duration, early_completion, predecessors, and successors. It will have methods to enable its instances to handle the CompletionTime message and other messages.

Since objects are meaningless when seen in isolation, we prefer to describe object types in the context of their collaborators. An *object specification model* is the role model of a structure of objects that we have implemented or intend to implement. A role in an object specification model is called an *object type*, which is a specification of a set of objects with identical, externally observable properties. An implementation of an object type is called a *class*, in conformance with common object-oriented programming terminology.

The role model of Figure 1.5 could be promoted to an object specification model. There will be three object types: Predecessor, Job, and Successor. A single class, Job1, would implement all three types so that its instances can play all three roles.

Different classes can implement the same type. The inheritance relationships between classes are implementation issues, and are immaterial in the context of types. It may be appropriate to implement two classes in different branches of the class inheritance hierarchy for the same type. In many cases, we find it convenient to create derived classes for code-sharing purposes, even if the corresponding objects have dissimilar types. Objects of the same type can, and often do, play several roles. For example, an object can be a member of a list and also the currently selected object. Therefore, many-to-many relationships exist between objects, roles, types, and classes (see Figure 1.13):

1 The object is the *is* abstraction, and represents a part of a system. An object has identity and attributes, and is encapsulated so that the messages it sends and receives constitute all its externally observable properties.

2 The role is the *why* abstraction. All objects that serve the same purpose in a structure of collaborating objects, as viewed from the context of some *area of concern*, are said to play the same role.

3 The type is the *what* abstraction. All objects that exhibit the same externally observable properties are considered to belong to the same type.

4 The class is the *how* abstraction. All objects that share a common implementation are considered to belong to the same class.

The OOram technology is independent of programming language, and most popular object-oriented programming languages may be used to implement OOram object types.

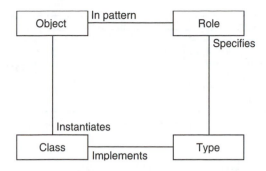

Figure 1.13

Many-to-many relationships between object, role, type, and class

OOram concepts are based on the ideas of collaborating objects and model inheritance. The concepts of the major object-oriented programming languages are based on the ideas of classes and class inheritance.

It is easy to go from an OOram model to an implementation, since the object specifications are given explicitly in the role models. A possible mapping from OOram concepts to some programming language constructs used for their implementation is shown in Table 1.1.

It is harder to derive role models from the implementation because the code reflects the complete, complex object model and some of the collaboration structure may be implicit in the details of the code.

All object-oriented programming languages support some form of inheritance. (Languages missing this feature are usually called *object-based languages.*) Some commonly used languages, such as Smalltalk, only permit *single inheritance*; i.e., a class may only have a single superclass. Other popular languages, such as C++, support *multiple inheritance*; i.e., a class may be derived from several base classes.

Single and multiple inheritance

The class inheritance structure of an object-oriented program may be designed for two entirely different and often conflicting purposes. We usually design it to reflect the structure of our concepts, so that it will map nicely onto the role model synthesis structure. But some class structures are designed just to share common code, irrespective of conceptual relationships. Both purposes are legitimate and useful; both purposes may be exploited in a well-designed program. Since our focus is on the modeling of concepts, OOram synthesis always reflects the conceptual structure.

Class inheritance used for concept specialization and code reuse

OOram	Smalltalk	C++
Role model	—	—
Role	Object	Object
Object specification, type	Class	Class
Port	Variable	Pointer data member
Interface	Protocol	Abstract class or protocol class
Message	Message	Function call
Method, Action	Method	Member function
Derived model	Subclass	Derived class
Base model	Superclass	Base class

Table 1.1

Mapping OOram models to programs

Figure 1.14

**The class
inheritance
structure can be
fashioned after
the model
synthesis
structure**

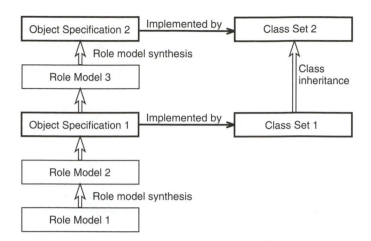

*Class
inheritance
structure may
be mapped on
the role model
synthesis
structure*

Figure 1.14 illustrates how some of the models in the role model synthesis structure are promoted to object specifications and implemented as a corresponding set of coordinated classes. `Object Specification 2` inherits from `Object Specification 1`, which indicates that `Class Set 2` may profitably be derived from `Class Set 1`.

1.2.5 OOram Reuse Technology

OOram reuse

The OOram method exploits object technology to support the controlled reuse of proven components. This facilitates the creation of work environments tailored to the needs of the particular actors (Chapter 10), reduces production costs and lead time, increases system reliability, and protects critical resources with mandatory access through proven components.

*Reusable
components
imply repeat
business*

The single most highly promoted advantage of the object paradigm is its support for reuse, but this is also the area of deepest disappointments.

Ralph Johnson has been quoted as saying that "*nothing can be reused before it has been used.*" Reuse requires repeat business so that reusable components can be identified, created, installed in a software development environment, and finally reused. An investment is needed to create reusable components, and the only payoff is through their actual use.

*Reusable
components
have suppliers
and consumers*

A reusable component has a supplier and one or more consumers. The supplier and consumers may be the same people; they must still create the reusable component before they can use it. More commonly, the suppliers and consumers will be different people, or even different organizations.

*Successful reuse
involves all
three
dimensions*

Both the creation and the application of reusable components depend upon appropriate solutions along all three dimensions of Figure 1.1 for their success:

1 *Technology.* The creator of a reusable component must choose technology that is not only appropriate for the problem, but also appropriate for the people who are going to apply it. We will here distinguish between *patterns* and *frameworks*, which are best applied by professional developers. In the advanced section, we will discuss *composition* and *duplication*, technologies that are well adapted to support nonprofessionals such as sales consultants and end users.

2 *Organization.* The benefits of reuse can be achieved only through appropriate organization. We suggest the idea of a value chain, where the people on one

level build on the results from the layer below and deliver results to the layer above. The results provided to the layer above form its production facilities, including reusable components. This is in contrast to the deliverables obtained from the various stages of the project work process; these deliverables are parts of the total project deliverables. For this reason, we regard the value chain as orthogonal to the work process on each layer.

3 *Process with deliverables.* The proper application of reusable components should be an integral part of the development work process. The success criterion for the developers must include reuse; measuring programmer productivity by the lines of code produced is finally shown to be counterproductive. The development of a reusable component is a product development that must be guided by an appropriate work process.

In the early 1970s, the architect Alexander [Alexander 79] proposed patterns as an interesting way for communicating important ideas among professionals. An enthusiastic group of computer professionals have adapted these ideas to our field, and a book on *Design Patterns* has been published [GaHeJoVli 95]. *A pattern tells the reader how to solve a problem*

In the Alexanderian sense of the word, a *pattern* is a specification of a problem and a guide to its solution. For problems in object-oriented design, the solution frequently involves an archetypical structure of objects. In these cases, the solution can often be described in terms of a role model. But this is to be construed as a communication device only, and not as a canned solution.

Some professionals use the term *pattern* in a different sense: they take it to mean an archetypical structure of collaborating objects, very similar to what Booch has called a *mechanism* and what we have formalized into the *role model* abstraction. We use the term *pattern* in the original sense to denote a guide to the solution of a problem, and we use the term *object pattern* to denote an archetypical structure of objects. We give an *object pattern* a precise meaning by defining it as an *instance of a role model.*

A *framework* is usually defined as a collection of classes that together solve a general problem, and that are intended for specialization through subclassing. The main difference between a framework and a pattern is that while the pattern tells the reader how to solve a problem, the framework provides a canned solution. *A framework is a canned solution*

Role models are admirably suited for describing frameworks. The role model defining the framework functionality can easily be synthesized into an application model. This model inherits all static and dynamic properties and possible constraints from the framework role model.

Example: The Activity Network as a Specialization of a Graph

As an example, let us return to the network planning example of Figure 1.3. The model we presented was just a small fragment of a real model. It did not include the insertion and removal of jobs; it did not include protection against cycles in the network; and it did not provide facilities for setting and modifying job attributes. All these details could probably be omitted at the analysis stage, but would have to be taken seriously at the design stage.

Most of the details are not specific to the activity network; they are common to a broad group of structures called *Directed, Acyclic Graphs (DAGs)*. An appropriate pattern would give us access to accumulated experience with these structures: *A graph pattern tells us how to design a network*

Figure 1.15

**Collaboration
view of a reusable
Directed Acyclic
Graph**

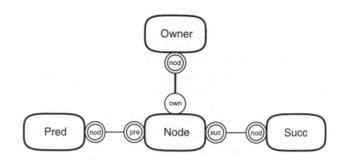

it would identify the objects, give all important algorithms, and provide practical hints as to the best solutions under different circumstances.

*A graph
framework
provides a
solution*

An alternative reusable component would be a *framework for directed, acyclic graphs*. This framework would include classes for the objects, and these classes would have programs for the insertion and removal of nodes and for protection against cycles in the network. They would probably not include facilities for setting and modifying object attributes, since this would typically be done in the derived models.

*The
component user
is fortunate*

Imagine that we are considering the activity planning problem for the first time. We would study the problem and try to identify key processes and key actors. We would study examples such as Figure 1.3 to better understand the phenomenon. We tentatively would create a role model such as the one shown in Figures 1.5–1.7. But how would we know that we have chosen appropriate roles? How would we know that we haven't overlooked some essential part of the problem? The answer is that we can hope for the best and suspect the worst, but we just cannot *know*. We must expect to revise our ideas several times as we study a problem and analyze its possible solutions.

The developer who finds an applicable reusable component is a truly fortunate person. He or she can build on the mature wisdom and experience of people who not only have solved similar problems in the past, but who have actually studied a number of different solutions and who have carefully recorded their competence.

Let us assume that we have identified our problem as being a specialization of a DAG, and that our library includes a DAG reusable component. (At this stage, it is immaterial if it is a pattern or a framework.) Let us further assume that the component suggests the roles shown in the collaboration view of Figure 1.15. We find the expected network roles of a Node with its Predecessors (denoted Pred) and Successors (denoted Succ). But we also find an Owner. The experiences of the component developers indicated that there should be an object responsible for managing the whole network. Further, they tell us that these are all the roles needed for an adequate model of a DAG.

Given this DAG reusable component, the modeling of our activity network is much simplified, and the risks are greatly reduced. All we need to do is to map the roles of the DAG model onto corresponding roles in our world of activity networks. We had overlooked the Owner role in our initial solution; however, we easily can map it onto a Schedule role (i.e., object representing a construction schedule in Figure 1.2). The full mapping between the DAG model and the Front-loading model is shown in Figure 1.16.

A good pattern explains all essentials, clearly and completely. It is also concise: the reader of a pattern is assumed to be an expert.

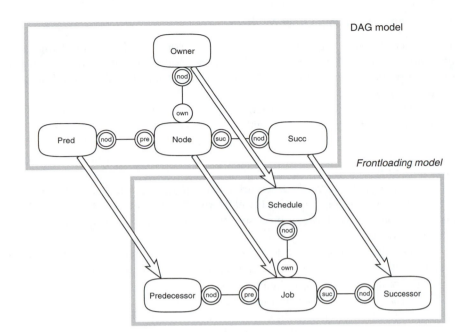

A good framework hides as much complexity as possible, making functionality visible to the application programmer on a need-to-know basis. Its visible functionality is published as a base role model to be synthesized into the application. In our example, the DAG model is synthesized into the Frontloading model in Figure 1.16, automatically giving it all the required network maintenance functionality.

The dynamic behavior exemplified by the scenario of Figure 1.6 could either be a feature of the derived model, or it could be a specialization of a general graph traversal algorithm defined in the base model.

The creation of reusable components shares many of the general properties of product development, and the life cycle may conveniently be divided into five phases:

A reusable component is a product

1 *Market analysis.* The developer must understand the needs of the potential users, and balance these needs against the costs of alternative solutions. The developer must also understand the potential users' working conditions to make the reusable component practically applicable.

2 *Product development.* The reusable component must be designed, implemented, and tested in one or more prototype applications.

3 *Product packaging.* Documentation is an important part of a packaged reusable component. The documentation includes work processes for the application of the component, installation procedures, and technical information.

4 *Marketing.* The users of the reusable component must be informed and persuaded to apply it.

5 *Application.* The reusable component must be applied, and must help its users to increase the quality of their products and reduce their expenditure of time and money.

Costs accumulate in the first four phases. The cost of the resulting assets is written off against the value created in the fifth and final phase.

1.2.6 Comparison with Other Methods

The *Object Modeling Technique* (OMT) was developed by James Rumbaugh and coworkers at General Electric Research and Development Center [Rumbaugh 91]. OMT supports three basic models: The *object model*, the *dynamic model*, and the *functional model*.

The *OMT object model* describes the actors and their relationships. It is an extended entity–relationship model, with classes that can contain attributes and operations. It is possible to describe object instances using instantiation relationships to classes. Associations between classes can be of different cardinalities and can have attributes.

The *OMT dynamic model* describes when things happen. It is based on the powerful *state charts* proposed by Harel [Harel 87]. The transitions between states take place on events, and can be associated with an action. Actions also can be associated with states.

The *OMT functional model* describes what is happening. It is based on traditional dataflow diagrams. These should be used to show transformations on values, and not to describe object interactions.

The information described in the three OMT models is almost fully described within the OOram role model. The OMT object model is best seen in the collaboration view; the OMT dynamic model is best described in the OOram state diagram view; and the OMT functional model corresponds to the process view. There are some differences, mostly due to the coherent concepts of the OOram model. The OOram state diagram is a simpler structure than the Harel state chart: all events are message interactions, and all actions are method activations. The OOram process view shows data transfer aspects of object interaction. All data are stored within objects, and are transferred as message parameters.

The *Booch method* has its basis in object-oriented design from the Ada world. However, the second edition of the book [Booch 94] is adapted to C++. The Booch method is the most comprehensive method, with respect to the modeling of language-oriented design features such as parameterized classes and public, protected, and private access.

The basic concepts of the Booch method are founded on the traditional object-oriented programming concepts: *object, class*, and *inheritance*. The logical model consists of *class diagrams, object diagrams, interaction diagrams*, and *state diagrams*. The physical model consists of *module* and *process diagrams*.

The information in the Booch class diagram can be expressed in the OOram semantic and collaboration views. There is more detail in the Booch diagrams than normally is described in the OOram view, e.g., visibility between classes, metaclasses, and parameterized classes. Instantiation of objects from classes is not described in the OOram role model; instantiation is only one of the functions of a method as seen in a scenario view.

The Booch object diagram describes a sequence of messages sent between objects. Equivalent information can be found in the OOram scenario, and message interfaces can also be found in the collaboration view and special interface views.

As was the case for OMT, the Booch state diagram is based on the Harel state-charts. The OOram finite state diagrams describe roughly the same information, with the caveat that the OOram state diagram is strictly object oriented, with all events being mapped as message interactions and all actions as (partial) method invocations.

Information that, in the Booch notation, is separated between class and object diagrams is merged within a single, comprehensive OOram role model. The role model is independent of programming language, and the views do not match the rich expression of implementation details exhibited by the Booch notation. An OOram modeler would put this kind of information into comments associated with the different model entities.

There is no direct OOram equivalent to the Booch physical model. The OOram *module* is strictly defined in terms of modeling-in-the-large: it is independent of any programming language constructs. The OOram perspective is that interfaces are associated with an object. Interfaces can be mapped directly into classes in an object-oriented programming language, or supported by a distributed object infrastructure. Such an infrastructure would support dynamic configuration at runtime.

OOSE models can be expressed as OOram views

The *OOSE methodology* has its origin in work on telecommunication applications and SDL. The initial ideas for object-oriented adaptation of the methodology was presented by Ivar Jacobson in 1986–87. The OOSE methodology [Jacobson 92] is a scaled-down version of the full methodology called *ObjectOry*.

The most famous aspect of this methodology is its reliance on *use-cases* as a glue for tying together all models. A use case (Section 2.5) is a set of interactions between the environment and the system, followed from beginning to end. A use case can be seen as a set whose members are actual sequences of interactions. A use case is thus more than a scenario (Section 2.5); it is the set of all the possible scenarios that can result from a user stimulus of the system.

The OOram method supports use-cases under the name of *OOram activities*. Activities are an integral part of the OOram role model concepts, and are supported through aggregation and other synthesis operations. Use-cases are therefore fully supported in the OOram method.

RDD models can be expressed as OOram views

Responsibility Driven Design (RDD) is one of the few published methodologies with a pure object-oriented origin [Wirfs-Brock 90]. It is based on experiences from object-oriented programming in Smalltalk done at Tektronix Labs, Software Productivity Technologies, in the period 1983–1989—while Tektronix was the only vendor of specialized Smalltalk-based workstations.

The central idea of the RDD method is to divide systematically the responsibility of the total system into responsibilities of the different classes.

Like RDD, the OOram method has a pure object-oriented origin. All concepts described in the RDD method are fully supported in the OOram method. The differences are that roles take the place of classes, and that roles are always considered in the context of their collaborators in the role model.

OOram models can replace E-R models, but we need good reasons to do so

The powerful *relational model* is well known in the database community. In this model, data are represented as *records* in *tables*. (Or more precisely, data are represented as *tuples* in *relations*.) Relational data models are often designed in terms of entity-relationship (E-R) diagrams [Chen 76 and Elmasri 94]. Most of the information shown in an E-R diagram can be shown in an OOram collaboration view.

We once did a small study to identify the benefits of the OOram role model over the traditional E-R model. We were given access to the data model of the accounting system of the University of Oslo, and began translating it into role modeling terms. We arrived at two very clear conclusions from this exercise: we could create a role model collaboration view which was very similar to the E-R diagrams; and we would never dream of creating such an object model!

There were two reasons why an analyst trained in the object paradigm would not come up with an object model resembling the existing E-R model. First, the E-R model contains a great number of details that will be the responsibility of various objects, and therefore, invisible outside these objects. Second, the scope of the E-R model is limited to static data descriptions. With an object-oriented approach, we naturally extend the scope by asking new questions: Who is interested in the data? Which operations does he or she want to perform on the data? What kind of behavior should be supported by the model?

Object identity is essential for describing dynamic behavior

One of the important characteristics of objects is that an object has *identity* (Section 2.2). An object retains its identity throughout its lifetime and regardless of changes to its data contents. Furthermore, there has never been and will never be another object with the same identity.

The notion of object identity makes it possible to reason about the dynamic aspects of system behavior, giving the object model additional leverage not available in the relational model. We can study not only the object characteristics needed to fulfill a certain purpose, but also exactly how the objects interact to achieve this purpose.

The main models of the currently popular methodologies are based on the class abstraction. The fundamental weakness of this abstraction is the same as the weakness of the relational model: it describes classes as sets of objects, and relations between objects in terms of anonymous instances.

The OOram role modeling concepts bring it all together

The OOram role modeling concepts bring all the different modeling concepts together into a coherent whole. The role model is a precise description of an object pattern whose objects are abstracted into the roles they play in the context of the pattern. Roles are archetypical objects, so the role model can combine data-centered and function-centered descriptions.

Roles have class-like properties

Like a class, a role is a description of a set of objects. But there is a crucial difference: the class describes the set of objects that exhibit common characteristics. The role describes the set of objects which occupy the same position in a pattern of objects. We can describe the semantics of the roles and their relation in the context of the role model; we can describe the attributes that must be exhibited by all objects playing the roles; we can describe how the total responsibility is allocated to objects playing the different roles; and we can describe the sets of messages one role may send to another.

Roles have object properties

Like objects, roles have identities, so we can reason about their cooperative behavior. We use *scenarios* to describe typical sequences of message flows. *Process diagrams* show how data flow between roles. *Finite state diagrams* show how each role changes its state in response to messages received from other roles.

OOram inheritance tells the complete story because it applies to complete models

There is no point in using inheritance to derive a class with added functionality if we do not at the same time derive another class which uses this added functionality. Role model inheritance not only exhibits the inheritance relationships between individual classes, it explains how the whole story told by a role model is retold by the roles of the derived model. So the OOram inheritance is done in the context of role models: a role model can inherit another role model and thus build on its functionality.

OOram technology facilitates systematic reuse

There are important practical consequences of the role model coherence. A complex reality can be represented as a complex object structure and described as a number of much simpler role models. General phenomena can be described as general role models, which can be reused as building blocks for the creation of application system models. If the general role models are implemented as sets of coordinated classes, these frameworks can be reused in a safe and controlled manner in the design and implementation of application programs.

The technology for systematic reuse provided by OOram role modeling makes it possible to organize application system development in novel ways. Extensive and systematic reuse lets us create large applications in small projects. A prerequisite is that suitable reusable components are available: systematic reuse requires investment in reusable assets.

OOram technology facilitates more effective organization

1.3 PROCESS WITH DELIVERABLES

A work process describes the steps that need to be performed in order to reach a given goal. The steps are usually described as if they are to be performed sequentially, while in reality they are performed in an opportunistic sequence and often in parallel. Documentation and other deliverables are the concrete results of the work process. It is often useful to pretend that the deliverables are the results of a rational work process, because this makes them easier to read and understand.

IN A NUTSHELL

Work processes occur on many different time scales. We have found it convenient to distinguish between three: creating a model, creating an application, and creating a reusable component.

A work process is a sequence of steps that needs to be performed to reach a specified goal. The process itself is almost invisible to all but the people who actually perform it. The process steps should therefore be intimately associated with the deliverables that constitute their concrete results. Deliverables can be computer programs, formal models, or informal descriptions.

A work process describes the steps needed to reach a goal

Processes can have different time scales, ranging from short processes for the solution of specific details to very long term processes covering the evolution of reusable assets. We find it convenient to distinguish between the following processes:

Processes on different time scales

1 The *model creation process* focuses on how to create a model or some other manifestation of thoughts for a certain phenomenon. Examples include creating a role model, performing role model synthesis, and creating object specifications.

2 The *system development process* covers the typical software life cycle, from specifying users needs, to the installation and maintenance of the system that meets these needs.

3 The *reusable assets building process* is the least mature software engineering process, but we expect it will be an essential contributor to future productivity and quality. Our focus is on the continuous production of several, closely related systems, in which we build on a continuously evolving set of reusable components. Creating a system mainly involves configuring and reusing robust and proven components, and possibly adding a few new components to complete the system.

The work processes on all three levels are iterative, and the deliverables are evolutionary. The goal is to minimize risk by focusing on the most critical parts in the early iterations.

The processes are opportunistic and iterative

Many managers dream of the ultimate work process that will ensure satisfactory solutions from every project. We believe that this dream is not only futile: it can even be harmful.

The *documentation is sequential*

Documentation is by its nature linear, and must be strictly structured. Software development processes are by their nature creative and exploratory, and cannot be forced into the straightjacket of a fixed sequence of steps. In an insightful article, Parnas et al. states that many have sought a software process that allows a program to be derived systematically from a precise statement of requirements [Parnas 86]. Their paper proposes that although we will not succeed in designing a real product that way, we can produce documentation that makes it appear as if the software was designed by such a process.

The sequences of steps we describe in the following sections and in the rest of the book are therefore to be construed as default work processes and suggested documentation structures. We also believe that you will have to develop your own preferred sequence of steps, but you may want to take the steps proposed here as a starting point.

1.3.1 Introduction to the Model Creation Process

Eight steps for developing a role model

How should you go about describing a phenomenon in a role model? In the general case, we suggest the following eight steps for creating a role model. Each step results in a deliverable, which is a view on the role model. The relative importance of these views depends on the purpose of the model.

The steps are performed iteratively until the role model is adequately defined. Steps 4 and 5 are performed in parallel. It is often easier to see what needs to be done than to identify the roles, but both need to be specified in an object-oriented model.

1. Determine the area of concern.
2. Understand the problem and identify the nature of the objects.
3. Determine environment roles and stimulus/response.
4. Identify and understand the roles.
5. Determine the message sequences.
6. Determine the collaboration structure.
7. Determine interfaces.
8. Determine the role behavior.

With the OOram method, you can describe your analysis and design in a single role model or in a number of related models. There are general process guidelines for creating the individual models, and for breaking complex situations into smaller models that "are so simple that there are obviously no deficiencies."

1.3.2 Introduction to the System Development Process

In this section, we focus on medium-term processes that cover the development of individual systems. Some important models are indicated in Figure 1.17. We step back to study the system environment at the top level; we zoom in to study implementation details at the bottom level. The relationships between models can be made formal or informal. Formal model relationships lead to a seamless system description, but it may be hard to change. Informal model relationships are easier to handle, but can hide dangerous system inconsistencies.

We consider creating five kinds of mutually dependant system modules:

1 A *system user model* describes the system environment. Most interesting systems are open systems. They will be installed in an environment that will influence the system and be influenced by it. The environment can be a human organization, as is the case for business information systems, or it can be some equipment, as is the case for embedded systems. Whatever its nature, we need to understand the system environment, and describe it in the System User model.

2 A *system requirements model* describes the system as seen from its environment. There are two important models: one of the interface between the system and its environment, and another of the system logic as perceived by its users. The relationships between these two models and the the system user model are interesting. The interface model describes the *tools* employed by the users to perform their tasks; and the system logic model describes the *subject* or *universe of discourse* of the activities described in the user model.

3 A *system design model* describes the system as seen by its developers. It elaborates the system requirements models and adds technical details of interest to the implementors. Its main features are the system components and their interaction.

4 A *system implementation model* is a precise description of the system, including all the details needed to make it operational. In the case of computer-based systems, we express this model in a programming language. In the case of human organizations, we express it as a set of business procedures.

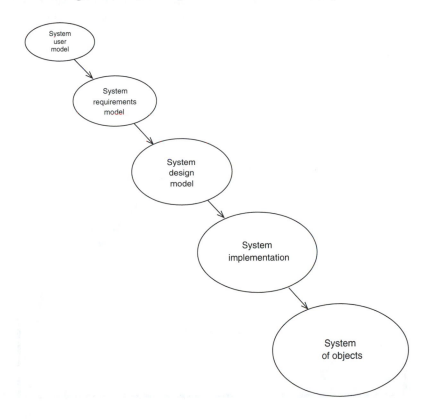

Figure 1.17

Typical descriptions on different levels of abstraction

We do not intend Figure 1.17 to suggest a classical waterfall process. The figure shows the main models and the relationships between them. The process will be opportunistic, incremental, and iterative. The four system descriptions represent four different levels of abstraction. The documentation deliverable will often be organized from the top down. The actual process will proceed from top to bottom; from bottom to top; and from the middle outwards. We call it the *yo-yo approach* to system development.

Other methodologies recommend system models resembling the four presented here. The OOram method does not enforce a particular set of models or a particular work process. On the contrary, we believe that the work process and deliverables have to be tailored to the nature of the problems, the preferred programming language, the traditions and regulations of the enterprise, the available tools and other development facilities, and the experience and preferences of the team members. If you have your own proven process, we urge you to stick to it and apply the OOram concepts and notation as a framework for your own object-oriented methodology.

1.3.3 Introduction to the Reusable Assets Building Processes

It is popular to claim that in our modern society, *change* is the only constant factor. Enterprises have to be able to adapt a continuously changing environment.

We believe this to be both true and misleading. It is true in the sense that an enterprise has to keep changing to adapt to changes in its environment. It is also true in the sense that a business has to change the core of its operations to accommodate the transition from manual to computer-based information processing; that it has to move its rule-based operations from people to computer; and that it has to cultivate the creativity, responsibility, and problem-solving capabilities of its human staff.

Figure 1.18

The Fountain Model for Reuse

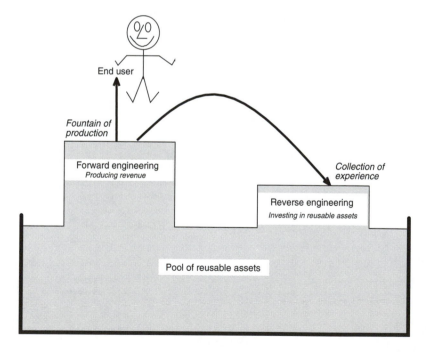

It is misleading in the sense that you cannot change everything all the time. So the challenge to the evolving enterprise is to identify what can be kept stable and what has to be kept fluid. The stable elements of a business form an infrastructure on which it can build a light and rapidly changing superstructure.

Software development is a case in point. Effective software development can be based only on extensive reuse. But reuse implies repeat business, and we never need develop exactly the same piece of software twice. So we have to identify a family of software products that we want to become our specialty, to identify common elements in this family, and to develop resuable components for these elements. This will enable us to fulfill a dream shared by many software developers: *we will be able to develop large and reliable systems in small and effective projects.*

Changing software, fixed components

Figure 1.18 illustrates that we have two kinds of activities working on two different time scales. In *forward engineering* we produce new results for the end users. The success criterion of these activities is that they satisfy user needs and thus produce value (and possibly revenue). *Reverse engineering* is an asset-building activity. It works on a longer time scale than forward engineering in that it analyzes the products produced and finds more effective ways of producing such products in the future.

The challenges to effective reuse are mainly organizational. The next section is devoted to these problems and their solutions.

1.4   ORGANIZATION

Reuse is currently applied almost exclusively to software. This section is of general interest, however, because several of the OOram reuse opportunities are applicable to all kinds of object-oriented models. We have also applied reuse technology to the design of organizations with great success.

Some people have believed that the inheritance and encapsulation properties of object orientation automatically make all objects into reusable components. This is wrong, and has caused many disappointments. Resources have to be invested in the creation of reusable components, and value is created only when they are successfully applied for a valuable purpose.

Few, if any, interesting developments are achieved by individuals working in isolation. The organization dimension is concerned with how to organize a team of people who will work together towards a common goal. Organizations come in many sizes and have widely different life spans. We may organize a few people to create a certain model, and we may organize many people to perform a complete project.

We must change from a job shop to an industrial approach to software production

The premise of this book is that we will never be able to produce high quality software efficiently in the general software job shop, just as a blacksmith will never be able to produce a high quality car in his smithy. We expect an effective car factory to turn out cars, and cars only. We should also expect an effective software production facility to turn out a particular family of software only.

We organize for reuse

We deliberately organize a number of people, called *actors*, having different resources, skills, responsibilities, and authority, for the satisfaction of customer requirements. The actors reuse concepts, designs, and software modules to enable the combination of high investment in quality and efficiency with low cost to the individual user.

Our approach is an essentially *industrial* approach to software production, even if the software industry will be materially different in culture, organization, and methods from the traditional industries. If you do not like the term *industrial* used in this context, you probably are thinking of all the negative aspects of industrialization. We prefer to focus on the positive aspects, the ability of industrial organization to consistently deliver products of high quality and low cost.

A value chain supports reuse

In a mature software industry, many different human actors will work together to provide end users with sophisticated functionality. We introduce the idea of a multilayered *value chain*, where the people in each layer build on the results from the layers below them and deliver results to the layer above them. The actors on each level have unique responsibilities, spheres of competence, and success criteria.

It is important to cast the value chain so that the actors on each level can focus on their main business and not be burdened with details that have been solved on the layer below them.

Industrial activity is a many-faceted endeavor. We will need facilities management, finance and accounting, marketing and sales, production planning and control, product specification, design, and production. Our context is the industrialized provision of software to individual users or groups of users. We will focus on the technical aspects of specification, design, and production, and put special emphasis on basic concepts and their practical applications.

The success of industrialized software production will be due to the following four key characteristics:

1 *An effective software production facility must be specialized.* An industrial facility is carefully tuned to the effective creation of its products. You would expect a group which produces compilers only to be more effective than a group which produces all kinds of software. You have to choose your specialty and stick to it.

2 *Reuse is the only known way to achieve satisfactory quality and efficiency.* Reuse permits the repeated application of proven solutions and their continuous refinement. It is an axiom that a programmer doesn't often get it right the first time; so you should observe the use of your software and give it a chance to mature through successive improvements. For mass products, this means that you should produce a steady stream of new releases; for customized software, it means that you should build an inventory of reusable components and improve them over time. In both cases, stability and your long-term commitment are essential.

3 *Work and responsibilities must be divided along a vertical value chain.* A car manufacturer designing a new car model does not start by trying to answer the question *"What is a car?"* The design team has been designing cars for years, and can concentrate on the finer details of the new model's specifications. Further, they would not worry unduly about the details of the new car's components. The engine, transmission train, electrical equipment, instrumentation, and a myriad of other details will be selected from a wide selection of available and proven solutions. The design of a new car is a question of market considerations, styling, and reuse of proven solutions. The result is a piece of equipment which is produced very cheaply and with a quality level unattainable by the best craftsmen working from scratch.

Similar vertical integration exists to a certain extent in the software industry today. An example of a value chain from the database world is: *hardware manufacturer – operating system provider – database management system provider – schema designer – fourth generation language programmer – script creator – end user.* We believe such value chains could profitably be designed for all kinds of software systems, such as intelligent network services in the world of telecommunications and work environments for professionals in the area of office automation.

4 *Matching tasks to personnel capabilities.* One of the most important characteristics of an industrial organization is that it is composed of teams having specialized goals, tasks, and competence. Teams apply different methodologies and are supported by tools tailored to their specific needs. The organization has to be carefully tuned so that each team can be made up of real people. The goals and methodologies of each team have to be adapted to the personalities and the training of its people. The successful organization of an industrial software production facility will harness a wide variety of talents to the common goals of the enterprise as a whole. If you are considering the creation of an industrial software production facility, you must choose your specialty on the basis of your people. And when you design its value chain, you must define the characteristics of the people occupying each layer as carefully as you define their responsibilities.

Industrial production is often associated with the application of unskilled labor for mindless, repetitive tasks. This is not our intention. We do not believe that good software can be produced by automata working under strictly controlled conditions according to detailed rules. On the contrary, we believe that the nature of software is such that value can be added to the product only by skilled and dedicated people. Every team in the production chain should be working in a stimulating environment which encourages creativeness and learning within the team's specialty, while permitting the team to build safely on the results of other teams without needing to understand the inner details of those results. The main part of the investment will therefore be in people, their competence, experience, and commitment to the common goal.

A corollary to this is that procedures and tools must be supportive and never be confining; they should reduce the burden of routine work that creative people have a tendency to dislike and do badly. There is no room for a tightly controlled assembly line in the software industry.

*An industrial
software
production
facility must be
designed to suit
the nature of its
products*

The tasks needed to produce software depend on the nature of that software, and we expect that different classes of products will need different organizations for their effective production. We will explore different product categories in order to understand their similarities and differences, such as a facility for the production of intelligent network services for the communications industry or a facility for the production of customized work environments for professionals in commerce and industry. In each case, we will see that we need a reference model which describes the product in general terms and which shows how we have chosen to divide the total work into manageable pieces so that each piece can be created by a team with clearly identified skills and interests.

CHAPTER 2

Role Modeling

CONTENTS

2.1   Modeling the Real World: Human Understanding and
        Human Communication   33

2.2   Modeling Using Objects   36

2.3   Modeling Using Roles   43

    2.3.1   A Travel Expense Example   45
    2.3.2   An Internet Example   48
    2.3.3   A Sample Model Having Four Roles   50

2.4   The Model Creation Process and its Deliverables   52

2.5   Basic OOram Role Modeling Concepts and Notation   57

    2.5.1   The Object   57
    2.5.2   External Object Properties   57
    2.5.3   The Role Model   59

This chapter discusses the creation of object-oriented models of a wide range of phenomena. The creation process is called role model analysis, the breaking down of a whole into a system of interacting components.

   The phenomena may exist in the real world, such as in a work organization, in some technical equipment, or may be an abstraction, such as a concept or a computer program.

The components are archetypical objects that we call roles because they represent the part an object plays within an overall pattern of interacting objects in the context of an area of concern.

Role modeling is applicable to the three higher abstraction levels indicated in Figure 2.1. Since the focus of this Chapter is on the creation of isolated models, we have not shown arrows between the levels. (The integration of multiple models into a seamless whole will be discussed in the Chapter 3.)

Figure 2.1

Typical descriptions on different levels of abstraction

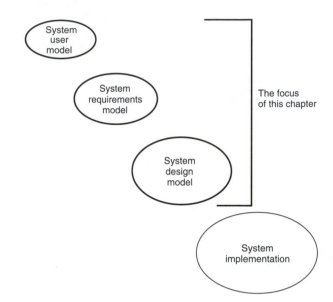

2.1 MODELING THE REAL WORLD: HUMAN UNDERSTANDING AND HUMAN COMMUNICATION

We create a myriad of mental models to help us understand phenomena of interest and to master them. A model is an artifact created for a purpose; it cannot be right or wrong, only more or less useful for its purpose. The choice of phenomena and the questions we ask about them depend on our interests, the modeling paradigms we are comfortable with, and the tools we use for expressing our thoughts. If we want to precisely communicate our ideas to a colleague, our modeling paradigm and notation must be similar to his or her paradigm and notation. If we want to communicate with a computer, our modeling paradigm must be consistent with the applicable computer language. The more expert we are in a particular modeling paradigm, the harder it may be to ask questions and appreciate answers that fall outside that paradigm.

It seems to be a deeply rooted characteristic of the human mind that we continuously try to organize and explain our impressions of the world around us. The brain specialist Michael S. Gazzaniga [Gazz 88] says that there seems to be an *interpreter* in the brain which tries to make sense out of all our varied experiences. Dreams may, for example, be explained by the mental interpreter trying to attach meaning to random events. We say that our mind creates a mental model of the world around us, which we use to explain how the world works and to predict the future—a model we use to master our surroundings.

Our mind's interpreter makes sense of our environment

Figure 2.2 illustrates that our understanding of the real world is based upon mental models which we create and manipulate within our minds, and which we try to make similar to the real world in some sense.

As an example, consider an industrial enterprise. An accountant may model the enterprise in terms of budgets and accounts, credits and debits, expenses and revenues. A production engineer may model the enterprise in terms of the flow of materials, the machining of parts, and the assembly of products. Another production engineer may model the enterprise in terms of production processes, activities and resources, and events and deadlines. An organization consultant may think in terms of actors and chains of command, or of responsibility and authority. A computer professional may model the enterprise in terms of information (its structure, sources, and sinks), and the computer-based systems used to store and process the information.

Our mental models reflect our viewpoints

This leads us to some general observations about models:

1 *A model is created for a purpose.* Suppose I wanted to describe my car. It has four wheels if I am interested in the functioning of the brakes under normal

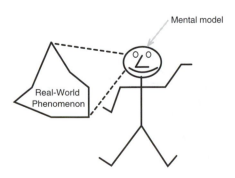

Mental model

Real-World Phenomenon

Figure 2.2

We always try to interpret our observations of the real world

circumstances. It has two wheels if I am interested in normal acceleration, because it has only two driving wheels. It has only one driving wheel if the other is spinning on an icy road. It has five wheels if I am interested in maintaining correct tire pressure, since I may get into deep trouble some day if I forget to check the spare. And finally, a particular model of Citroën cars can lift a wheel having a punctured tire and continue running on the remaining three; thus, a three-wheel model would be appropriate to study its behavior. We cannot say that any model is correct per se, only that it is more or less suited for the study of specific phenomena.

2   *A model is never complete.* We create models to simplify and generalize. For this purpose we ignore more than we include. For instance, the rims of my wheels were made by welding together a number of steel parts, they were painted with several coats of different paints, and they were manufactured in a complex production process—but I do not care about any of these details.

3   *We tend to think in hierarchical models, even though the world is rarely hierarchical.* For instance, house consists of a roof and four walls. The walls are made of bricks. But the hierarchy breaks down at the corners, where one brick belongs to two walls. Hierarchies are not inherent properties of nature, but artifacts of models that must be applied with due caution and respect.

4   *We think in multiple models, always trying to choose the best model for our purpose.* Suppose I'm driving peacefully along the road, seeing my car as part of a traffic pattern. Perhaps my mind drifts, and I see the trip in the context of a sales effort in which I am currently engaged. Suppose that suddenly, I hear ugly noises from the engine compartment. I immediately mobilize all my technical knowledge about cars and search for a model that can explain the trouble.

Our shared business models must be explicit and based on shared concepts and representations

While most of our mental models are intuitive and largely subconscious, the essence of both science and business is the creation of explicit models, called manifest models, which we can share and discuss. See Figure 2.3.

Human communication is distorted

Manifest models are really just data—patterns of ink on paper, or bits inside computers. The interpretation is in the mind of the beholder, and people may (and will) interpret the same manifest model in different ways, as illustrated in Figure 2.4.

Figure 2.4 shows a process whereby person A wants to communicate Meaning-A and codifies it according to Language-A, his personal vocabulary, to create the Data. Person B senses these Data and decodes them according to her personal vocabulary, Language-B, to get the underlying information, Meaning-B. Since Language-A is different from Language-B, Meaning-B will be different from Meaning-A.

Figure 2.3

Manifest models are concrete representations

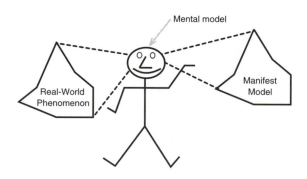

ROLE MODELING

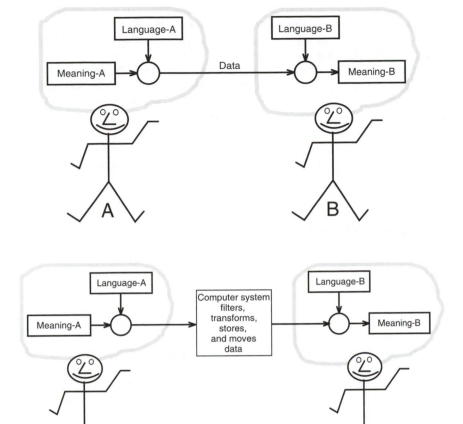

Figure 2.4

The human communication process

Figure 2.5

Human communication through a computer system

Figure 2.4 illustrates the distortion that is inherent in all human communication. The process is not improved when the data are transformed and communicated through time and space via a computer system, since many of the interpersonal adjustments developed over the millennia are lost with the removal of all personal contact between A and B, as illustrated in Figure 2.5.

The paradigms, concepts, and notation for a manifest model must be shared by the participants to make communication and discussion possible. The paradigms are usually implicit in a community of experts, which makes communication fast and efficient, and they are often subconscious. Conflicting models are rarely detected and can lead to endless discussions—such as; Is *analysis* everything preceding design, or is it the study of the current situation? Every competent systems analyst knows an answer, but different analysts give different answers, depending on their orientations.

Shared models essential for communication

In our context of system modeling, the precise communication of model information presupposes that all the communicants have a common description language. The OOram method has precisely defined concepts and notation. We suggest that you endeavor to learn and use them as consistently as possible, and that you complain bitterly to the authors if you find any inconsistencies or other imperfections.

Effective communication demands that the languages of the communicants are similar, and that all organizations invest in training and documentation. But as training is also a communication process, we can never achieve a perfect match between individual interpretations of the same data.

Any effective modeling paradigm is a good paradigm

Experts love to discuss whether one modeling paradigm is better than another. Since being an expert means that one has internalized certain ways of thinking, these discussions frequently take the form of religious wars. My view is that it is impossible to evaluate an answer without considering the question, so that a modeling paradigm has to be evaluated on the basis of its effectiveness in a certain context. The best paradigm is the paradigm which best helps me reach my goals. If my goals change, I must be willing to reconsider my choice of paradigms.

2.2   MODELING USING OBJECTS

IN A NUTSHELL

The object has three properties, which makes it a simple, yet powerful model building block. It has state, so that it can model memory. It has behavior, so that it can model dynamic processes. And it is encapsulated, so that it can hide complexity.

Object-oriented programming was invented in Norway in the 1960s

Object orientation as a programming paradigm originated with the language Simula, which was developed by a group lead by Kristen Nygaard and Ole Johan Dahl at the Norwegian Computing Center in the 1960s [Birt 73]. The widespread use of object orientation in mainstream computing is due to the success of Smalltalk and programming environment developed by Alan Kay and the Learning Research Group at the Xerox Palo Alto Research Center in the 1970s [Gold 83].

Object orientation is a powerful paradigm

Object orientation is but one of the many possible paradigms that can be used as a basis for thinking about systems. It is currently receiving a great deal of attention, because it seems to be useful in many situations and for many purposes. It has been used successfully to model human systems, such as business organizations; technical systems, such as aircraft control systems; and many different kinds of computer-based systems.

One reason for its popularity may be that it merges many earlier paradigms, such as the information models used by database designers, the behavior models dear to the hearts of communications engineers, the functional decomposition models used by many computer programmers, and the process models used in the analysis of organizations and integrated computer systems. We will see later that with object orientation, it is possible to express the information contained in all these models within a single, seamless description. (But object orientation does not replace continuous models, such as differential equations.)

The following definitions of object orientation are derived from Holbæk-Hanssen [Hol 77] and Hall [HallFagan]:

DEFINITION

System and object

A system is a part of the real world which we choose to regard as a whole, separated from the rest of the world during some period of consideration; a whole that we choose to consider as containing a collection of objects, each object characterized by a selected set of associated attributes and by actions which may involve itself and other objects.

The operative word is *choose*. We choose to regard a phenomenon as a structure of distinct objects, we choose the objects, we choose their characteristics. This choice may be "natural" if the phenomenon is discrete in nature: an organization is composed of people, and road traffic is made up of moving cars. In other cases, the choice of objects may be artificial: we think of a plant as being made up of a root, a stem, leaves, and flowers, even though there is no such distinction in nature, and it is hard to define exactly where one object ends and another begins. A corner brick could belong to either of the adjacent walls. Such difficulties should not worry us unduly, but only remind us to create precise definitions. A good model helps us understand a phenomenon of interest; a bad one does not help us and could mislead us.

Open systems are systems that interact with their environment: *for a given system, the environment is the set of all objects outside the system whose actions affect it, and also those objects outside the system whose attributes are changed by its actions.*

Open systems have environment

In Figure 2.6, the system is bounded by a heavy line: real world parts are shown as squares, objects are shown as rectangles, and environment objects are shown with gray outlines.

The definition of open systems naturally leads us to question when an object belongs to a system and when it belongs to the environment—for if an object interacts with the system as described, why not regard it as a part of the system? Following this train of thought would be inconvenient, because we then would have to consider the entire universe when studying any single phenomenon. In practice, we create a boundary around the phenomenon under study. The system objects proper are inside the boundary, while the environment objects are outside it. The system objects are fully described in the context of the phenomenon of interest, while the environment objects are only partially described.

Although the general properties of object orientation are shared by all practitioners, there are differences in the details. The differences usually boil down to differences in the semantics of the language used to express the model. Our view of object orientation is influenced by the semantics of Smalltalk, in which everything of interest is expressed in the terms of objects. Our view is also consistent with the definitions given by the Object Management Group [CORBA 91], an organization dedicated to the widespread application of object orientation in government and industry.

Many different definitions of object orientation are in use

An object is initially thought of as a black box having an inside and an outside, as shown in Figure 2.7. Looking inside, we would see that the object is capable of doing things and of storing information: it contains methods (procedures) and data. But the object cannot do anything by itself, and there is no way that we can

An object is encapsulated

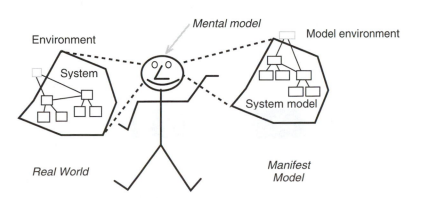

Figure 2.6

Object-oriented models

MODELING USING OBJECTS

Figure 2.7

**A simple object
by itself cannot
do anything**

deduce its internal construction from its outside. This is called encapsulation. (Some authors distinguish between encapsulation and information hiding, we do not need this distinction and will regard the two terms as being synonymous.)

*An object has
identity*

An object has an identity that it keeps throughout its lifetime, and there will never be another object having that identity anywhere in the world.

*An object can
have attributes*

An object can have object attributes that represent information associated with it. We choose the object attributes which we consider relevant in our context.

*Objects inter-
act through
messages*

An object interacts with other objects by sending and receiving messages, as illustrated in Figure 2.8. Messages do not arise by magic; every message has both a sender and a receiver.

The external characteristics of an object are described completely by its identity, the messages it understands, the messages it sends to each of its collaborators, and its apparent attributes.

A message is intention-revealing. It tells the receiving object to achieve something without telling it how to do so. The message functionality is composed of three parts:

1 A message is a trigger that causes the receiving object to select one of its methods and execute it. The resulting action may include changes in object attributes, sending messages to one or more of the object's collaborators, or the creation of new objects.

2 A message may be a forward data carrier that provides the receiver with some new information. The data are described in the message parameters that may be references to other objects.

3 After having processed a message, the receiver of a message may return resulting data to the sender.

*Messages sent
spontaneously
from environ-
ment objects*

A message received by an object triggers a method, and parts of this method may be to send further messages. The avalanche of messages flowing through the objects must start somewhere. Some objects will spontaneously send a message without first having received one. We call the initial message a *stimulus message*, and the resulting sequence of actions is called an *activity*. The object that sends a stimulus message must clearly be in the system environment.

Figure 2.8

**Objects interact
by sending
messages along
the paths
between them**

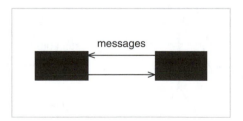

The message-passing process may be recorded by an observer in the interobject space. The observer may also deduce some apparent properties of the objects:

Object models can be observed from interobject space

1 Collaborators and message sequences. The actions performed by an object when receiving a message are defined in its *method* for that message. The method itself is invisible from outside the object, but it is possible to observe any messages the object sends to other objects, so the observer can deduce the object collaboration structure. The observer can also deduce the characteristics of the message-passing process and the identity of the stimulus messages.

2 Object attributes. An object has memory. The effect noticed by the observer is that the object may react differently when sent the same message at different times.

We find it profitable to illustrate of a pattern of *collaborating* objects as an organization of clerks collaborating in performing some common task. This way of thinking about systems is very similar to how Max Weber described *rational* work organizations 100 years ago. Weber's ideal was to populate an organization with specialists who divided the total work load among them, who had clearly defined rights and responsibilities, and who performed their work strictly according to precisely defined rules.

A structure of objects is similar to a work organization

No human organizations have been perfectly rational in Weber's sense. But if Weber had been alive today, he could have observed a perfect, rational bureaucracy as a set of collaborating objects inside a computer! An object may be considered to be a clerk having an in-basket and an out-basket. A book of rules specifies precisely the *methods*, or procedures to be followed by the clerk, for every message that he or she understands. Each clerk has his or her own book of rules, and different clerks may handle the same messages differently. This is called *polymorphism*. Finally, the clerk will have a file of folders representing the current values of the *attributes* for which he or she is responsible.

Most life cycle models distinguish between the analysis of an existing organization along with its problems; the specification and design of a system that should solve these problems, and the implementation of the new system. Different modeling paradigms have often been used for the different stages, and there has been no guarantee that information gathered in one stage was faithfully carried over to the next stage.

Analysis and design

We shall see that the object-oriented approach is equally applicable to all stages of the life cycle and to all levels of abstraction. We can create object models of an existing organization or system, object models of a proposed future organization or system, object models of an application program, and object models of reusable program libraries. In all cases, we use the term *analysis* to denote the modeling of a phenomenon as a structure of interdependent object parts. This is in conformance with the common definition of the term:

analysis

1: *separation of a whole into its component parts* 2a: *an examination of a complex, its elements and their relations* 2b: *a statement of such an analysis ...* [Webster 77].

DEFINITION

(We also support the opposite operation, and use the term synthesis to denote the composition of derived models from simpler ones.)

There is still a distinction between the study of an existing phenomenon and the creation of a new artifact. This distinction is not in the concepts and notation we use to describe the models, but rather in the work processes we follow to create them. The study of an existing phenomenon is a reverse engineering operation, while the creation of a new system is a forward engineering operation.

Is the postindustrial society an object-oriented society?

As an aside, we may suggest that this indicates why some large, bureaucratic organizations seem to be getting into trouble in our postindustrial society. The bureaucratic organization is tuned to let people behave only in a precisely prescribed and predictable manner, but computers perform this kind of behavior much better than people.

The successful postindustrial enterprise seems to be organized as a structure of autonomous units collaborating towards a common goal. In contrast to the bureaucratic model, this market model for organizations is harder to manage and harder to populate. Individual creativity, responsibility, understanding, and independence of thought are harnessed to the common good. All behavior that can be formally described is pushed down into a computer-based support system.

You can observe the contrast by comparing a large department store with a shopping mall, or a large integrated factory with a network of cooperating smaller companies. The depth and importance of this transition was brought home to me once when I was giving a seminar in object-oriented programming. During a recess, a man came up to me showing all signs of being deeply moved. He told me that he had been an ardent communist for more than fifty years. Gorbachov's revelations and the demise of the Soviet empire had been hard to swallow, and he was now learning that even computer programs were moving from a centralized model, in which all power and wisdom emanate from a main program, to a decentralized model of cooperating objects!

Create systems that fit existing environments

We frequently find it convenient to combine the two modes of operation, because we frequently want to create new systems that will fit into an existing environment.

A company organization example

As an example, suppose we wish to create a model of an enterprise from the perspective of its formal organization. We have chosen this domain to illustrate that objects have a wide application area, and to avoid all the technical details of computing which could easily obscure the inherent simplicity and common sense of object-oriented modeling.

We defined a *system* as a part of the real world that we choose to consider as containing a collection of objects. We want to study how people interact to handle a travel expense account, so we choose our system to be the enterprise and the objects to be its people, because the actors involved in this procedure are people. We elect to ignore concepts like departments and groups, since they are mere abstractions which do not actually *do* anything. It seems natural to represent each person as an object, as shown in Figure 2.9.

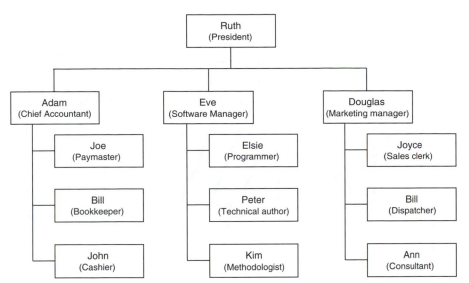

Figure 2.9 could, of course, be interpreted as a conventional organization chart, decomposing the business along lines of authority and responsibility. But we choose to interpret it differently: the rectangles in this figure denote *objects*, and the lines denote a particular set of *relations* between the objects. In this model, every rectangle represents a person object and every line represents a *works for–reports to* relation. In a more general model, objects could represent different kinds of entities, and there could be different kinds of relations between them.

Object identity

The object identity property is evident in our example. A person can be one of a pair of identical twins, change his or her name, amputate arms and legs, install a new heart, have a face lift, even change his or her sex—his or her identity remains the same. All the atoms of a person's body are replaced several times during his or her lifetime, and thoughts and feelings change, and yet, the person is the same; there has never been and will never be another person having the same identity. In our example, there are two persons named Bill. They are modeled as different objects, so we know there are two employees having the same name.

Object attributes

We could choose to consider the following person object attributes: name, job position, address, telephone number, salary, age, and competence. The attributes can be simple, such as name, or complex, such as competence.

Due to the object encapsulation property, we cannot know which form an attribute takes within the object. The age attribute could be explicitly stored in an instance variable (Section 2.5) within the object, or it could be computed whenever it was needed from an instance variable containing the birth date and a generally available current date.

Message interaction

As an example of message interaction, let's describe what happens when Peter wants to travel somewhere at the expense of his company. A possible process is illustrated in Figure 2.10:

1 Peter sends a travelPermissionRequest message to Eve, his manager.

2 Eve checks her budget and plans, and sends a travelPermission message to Peter.

Figure 2.10

Messages arising
from the expense
report process

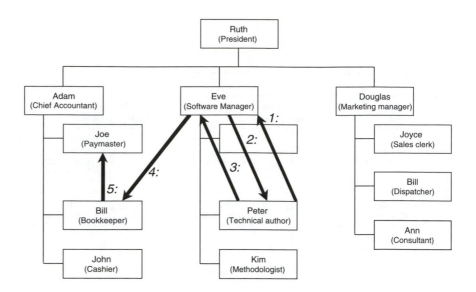

3 Peter purchases the necessary tickets, travels, prepares an expense report, and sends an expenseReport message to Eve.

4 Eve checks the expense report, adds her authorization, and sends an authorizedExpenseReport message to Bill, the bookkeeper.

5 Bill updates his accounts and sends a paymentRequest message to Joe, the Paymaster.

6 Joe notes the request and records the need to pay Peter sometime in the future.

2.3 MODELING USING ROLES

The role model is an abstraction on the object model where we recognize a pattern of objects and describe it as a corresponding pattern of roles.

The role model supports separation of concern and describes the static and dynamic properties of a phenomenon in a single, coherent model.

Object models, as described in the previous sections, provide powerful constructs for describing a wide range of interesting phenomena. Even though we have only outlined descriptions of very simple examples, we hope you appreciate that we could have chosen more complex phenomena and augmented the models with additional information.

We need abstractions

Real cases are rarely simple. A real organization could consist of a hundred employees, and we would probably want to study dozens of different procedures. The object model would then be too complex to be studied as a whole, and we would need additional abstractions to highlight interesting aspects to enable us to think about them in a meaningful way.

One popular abstraction of object orientation is the concept of class; which defines the attributes and behavior of a set of similar objects. The inheritance relation permits a derived class to be defined as an extension and modification of a base class.

Figure 2.11 indicates a possible structure of capabilities of the people that populate our sample organization. `Ruth`, `Adam`, `Eve`, and `Pete` are managers—these roles could be played by any person having the required capabilities. Observe that the capabilities of the people populating an organization do not help us understand how the organization operates. We similarly find that understanding the object class structure does not help us understand how the structure of objects operates.

The classification abstraction is not very helpful for understanding object structures

It is as if we want to build a new home, and the architect has shown us the specifications of the doors, windows, walls, and sanitary fittings. It may be useful to the builder to know that he can use the same window design in many places, and that all windows may share some of the same production processes, but we want to know how the house will function as a home

Object-oriented programming languages focus on the *class*, which describes isolated objects. We feel that while this may be reasonable for the programming phase of system development, it does not reflect the way we want to *think* about objects. We want to model structures of objects that interact to achieve some purpose. A class will describe the method its instances will use to service an incoming message. It does not tell us if the sender of the message is using the service correctly; nor does it tell us what happens to the messages that are sent from its

We need to see objects in context

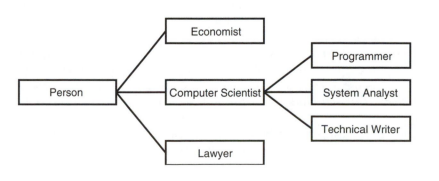

Figure 2.11

A specialization–generalization hierarchy of the Expense-Account objects

Figure 2.12
**Manifest Role
Models**

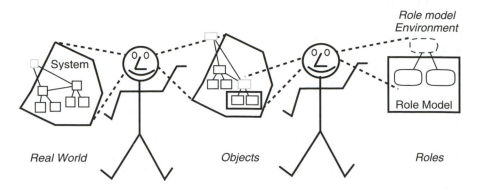

instances. We want to understand the activity as a whole, but all we see is a short time slice taken out of context.

A role focuses on the position and responsibilities of an object

The notion of a class focuses on the *capabilities* of the objects; while the notion of a role focuses on the *position* and *responsibilities* of an object within the overall structure of objects. Training people is costly and time consuming, and we strive to give people general training which makes them capable of filling a variety of positions. Programming is also costly and time consuming, and we strive to program objects that can serve in different positions in a variety of object structures.

In role modeling we always consider objects in context

We want to see an architect's plan and leave it to the builder to exploit component commonality. Later on, we shall see that the powerful notion of specialization is retained in the form of specializing patterns of interacting roles through a process called *synthesis*. Right now, we will study individual role models and see how they represent phenomena of interest.

The OOram technology focuses on how interacting roles achieve their goals

In the *OOram Role Model*, we isolate interesting functions and study how they are realized in general patterns of interacting roles. Beck and Cunningham are quoted as saying "no object is an island" [Helm 90]. A highbrow version of this refers to the classical Greek philosopher Plato, who described the philosopher as "a man who insists on seeing things together, who refuses to consider the parts out of their relation to the whole whose parts they are; and who is therefore the inexorable foe of crude and premature generalizations from whichever department of investigation happens at the time to be most in evidence."

The OOram Role Model

The *role model* is the basic abstraction used in the OOram technology. A role model is a description of a structure of cooperating objects along with their static and dynamic properties: What are the subjects of the object interaction, the relationships between the objects, the messages that each object may send to its collaborators, and the information processes?

The role model is an object-oriented model of an object structure, and represents a bounded part of the real world or of an interesting concept. It models patterns of collaborating objects as a similar structure of collaborating roles. This is illustrated in Figure 2.12.

A role model is a part of a structure of objects which we choose to regard as a whole, separated from the rest of the structure during some period of consideration. We choose to consider the whole as a collection of roles, each role being characterized by attributes and by actions which may involve itself and other roles.

Figure 2.12 illustrates how the role model describes a pattern in the system of objects. The system and the role model are bounded by heavy lines, objects are shown as rectangles, and environment objects are shown with gray outline. Notice how role modeling is an additional abstraction step from the modeling illustrated in Figure 2.6.

OOram Analysis is the breaking down of the whole problem area into separate *areas of concern,* and the description of each area in a role model shows interesting views of the phenomenon of interest. A phenomenon is described by a number of cooperating objects. Subphenomena are specified by their areas of concern. Objects describing a subphenomenon are organized in a pattern of objects, and all objects having the same position in the pattern are represented by a *role,* we say they *play the same role* in the object structure. A role has identity and is encapsulated, and it is an archetypical representative of the objects occupying the corresponding positions in the object system. We can therefore say that *a role model is an object-oriented model of an object structure.*

Role model is an object-oriented model of an object structure

The role model is therefore an abstraction:

- We *suppress irrelevant objects,* representing only the objects that participate in the activities.
- We *suppress irrelevant aspects,* representing only the aspects that are relevant in the context of the activities.
- We *suppress irrelevant details,* using the object encapsulation property to hide details considered uninteresting in the context of the activities.
- We *generalize object identity,* representing patterns of interacting objects performing the activities by a similar, archetypical pattern of roles performing these activities.

The role model is the abstraction. Any pattern of objects which enacts the roles is a *role model instance;* the objects themselves are *role instances.*

2.3.1   A Travel Expense Example

Important roles in our travel expense example could be Traveler, Authorizer, Bookkeeper, and Paymaster, as illustrated in Figure 2.13. A role model describes these roles, their responsibilities and rights, their static relationships, and their dynamic behavior.

Figure 2.14 is a role model collaboration view that shows the roles and message communication paths. The figure says that the participants in the handling of a travel expense report are playing the roles of Traveler, Authorizer, Bookkeeper, and Paymaster. The Traveler and the Authorizer know about each other and exchange messages. The Paymaster does not know about the Bookkeeper and cannot send messages to it, similarly the Bookkeeper does not know about the Authorizer. This is true in the context of the current area of concern. Other role models might show close interaction between them.

Two roles are marked as belonging to the environment—the Traveler because it initiates a model activity by sending the first, unsolicited message, and the Paymaster because it is the final recipient of the completed expense report.

Associated with the line from the Traveler role is a *port,* a small circle that represents the messages that the Traveler role may send to the Authorizer role in the context of this model. Other small circles are similarly interpreted.

A role model can be viewed from many different viewpoints (Section 2.5) and in many different ways, with each view highlighting certain aspects and hiding others. We can look inside individual roles; we can study messages passing be-

Role models may be viewed in different ways

Figure 2.13

An object
pattern is an
instance of a role
model

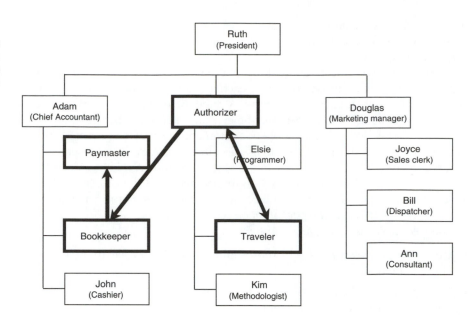

tween roles; and we can study the system as seen from its environment. We can
take a data-centered approach and study the roles, their semantic interpretation,
their responsibilities, and their attributes. We can take a process-centered approach and study the message paths between the roles, the messages permitted
sent along each path, typical message sequences, and the role methods that are
triggered by these messages.

It is important to note that the views are artifacts of our modeling process; we
choose to view the phenomena under study in certain ways because they help
clarify our ideas and communicate them to others. Our choices can be neither
right nor wrong, but they may be more or less suitable for our purpose. The
views are supplementary; and we select the combination that best suits our
needs.

One view is the *area of concern view*, which is a free text description of the
subject described by the model. Another view is the *collaboration view* of Figure

Figure 2.14

Sample OOram
role model

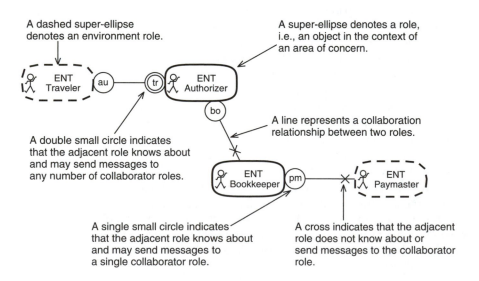

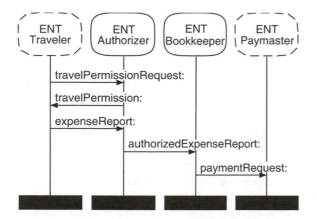

Figure 2.15

Travel Expense procedure— typical message scenario

2.14, which shows the roles and the message paths between them. A third view is the *scenario*, which shows a typical sequence of messages that flows through the model. The message flow starts with the *stimulus message*, which is an external event that triggers an activity in the model. There are many other views, and they will be discussed as we need them.

In this example, we would like to augment the static collaboration view of Figure 2.14 with a dynamic view. Our example has one activity. This activity starts with a stimulus message when the `Traveler` asks the `Authorizer` for permission to travel. The activity includes all actions resulting from this stimulus; a typical example is shown in the scenario of Figure 2.15. This scenario is a formal description of the message interaction given earlier:

1. The `Traveler` sends a `travelPermissionRequest` message to the `Authorizer`.
2. The `Authorizer` sends a `travelPermission` message to the `Traveler`.
3. The `Traveler` sends an `expenseReport` message to the `Authorizer`.
4. The `Authorizer` sends an `authorizedExpenseReport` message to the `Bookkeeper`.
5. The `Bookkeeper` sends a `paymentRequest` message to the `Paymaster`.

The scenario shows a sequence of messages as observed in the interobject space. It does not describe the methods (i.e., how the objects handle their incoming messages). We can shift our point of observation to the inside of a role and describe the method that is triggered by an incoming message. Figure 2.16 is a

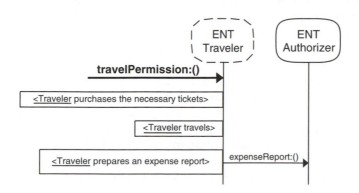

Figure 2.16

The `travel-Permission` method

method view. It shows the `Traveler` method that is triggered by the `travelPer-mission` message:

1 The `Traveler` purchases necessary tickets.

2 The `Traveler` travels.

3 The `Traveler` prepares an expense report and dispatches it to the `Autho-rizer`.

Divide and conquer Role model analysis is a powerful extension of the object orientation paradigm because it permits us to identify different kinds of phenomena and to study them in isolation without losing the benefits of objects.

This capability to divide complex systems into any number of simpler ones enables us to describe any particular phenomenon within a huge system of objects. Role model synthesis enables us to study the subsystem interdependencies by creating derived models. (See Chapter 3.)

We will give two additional role model examples. The first example models the transfer of files between two computers on the Internet. It is simple in the sense that it involves only two objects, but it illustrates how separation of concern can materially simplify the models and highlight important aspects. In the second example, we use role modeling to describe how several objects play their roles to achieve some purpose.

2.3.2 An Internet Example

Systems consisting of relatively few objects may often be described in a single role model, but many practical object structures will be too large and complex to be comprehended as a single model. We must identify different concerns which are covered by the system, and analyze each of them separately. We divide the whole into manageable parts and conquer each part with an appropriate model. If the whole is simply the sum of its parts, we have thereby conquered the whole. If not, we may use OOram *synthesis* to create derived models which describe the dependencies. OOram synthesis will be the theme of Chapter 3. For now, we will continue our studies of the use of isolated role models.

The Internet as a huge structure of objects We will use the Internet as an example of a large object structure. The Internet connects several million computers. As is typical of its distributed nature, nobody knows the exact number. As seen from the Internet, the connected computers appear as objects: they have identity, they are encapsulated, and interact only by sending messages to each other.

The Internet is used for a wide variety of purposes. Some are well known, and some are only known within their user communities. We believe the Internet to be a prototype of the information systems of the future; it is not a designed system, but has evolved as many different people have made their contributions. The whole is not known to anybody, and would exceed our mental capacity even if we had access to all relevant information. We can, however, select any activities in which we may be interested, identify the objects that take part in these activities, idealize them into roles, and describe the activities to any desired detail.

Concern: FTP As an example, let us select the well-known network *File Transfer Program* (FTP). The interaction between FTP participants is based on the Arpanet standard *File Transfer Protocol*, which allows the transfer of files between two remote computers. Two objects are involved as indicated in Figure 2.17a. The first takes the initiative and controls the activities; this object plays the `Client` role. The other is

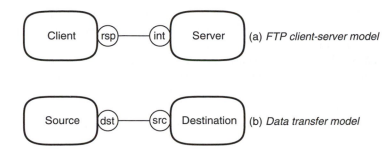

(a) *FTP client-server model*

(b) *Data transfer model*

a provider of services; this object plays the Server role. Some objects (computers) are able to play only the Client role; other objects are able to play only the Server role; and some objects are able to play both roles. The abstraction from object to role permits us to ignore these complications and create a "pure" model in which each role has a single purpose. The role model is illustrated in Figure 2.17a.

Client-Server activities

Given the Client and Server roles, we can now study how they perform various activities. In one activity, the Client identifies itself by name and password to the Server so that the Server can establish the appropriate privileges. Another activity permits the Client to navigate in the Server's file directory hierarchy. A third activity permits the Client to specify operations on the *current file directory.*

The FTP standards for these activities do not interest us here. The point is that we can describe each activity as an interaction process involving the Client and Server roles. Each activity will start with a stimulus message from the Client, and will result in a response in the form of appropriate changes in object attributes or some final termination message. For Example a change directory stimulus message results in a change in the Server's currentDirectory attribute. A list directory stimulus message results in a termination message to the Client that contains the list.

Concern: Transferring a file

The main purpose of FTP is to transfer files between the connected parties. Files may be transferred from the Client to the Server or from the Server to the Client. We combine these two cases by defining file transfer as being the transfer of a file from an object playing the Source role to an object playing the Destination role. This is illustrated in Figure 2.17b.

We normally want to be able to transfer files in both directions; the Client and Server objects then need to be able to play both the Source and Destination roles. We could alternatively define a system of objects that permitted file transfer only in one direction; a Client which could only play the role of Destination would be more secure than the general Client, since it would be unable to export files to other destinations.

The initiative for a file transfer is taken by the object playing the Client role, and the choice of roles actually played at any given time by that object depends on the direction of the desired transfer.

File transfer activity is fairly complex

The transfer of a file causes a fairly complex interaction between the Source and the Destination. The Source has to split the file into transferable chunks that have to be reassembled in correct sequence in the Destination. The Source has to add redundant data to the chunks so that the Destination can check that each chunk has been transferred correctly. Protocols have to be established between the Source and the Destination to control the flow of data, and to ensure retransmission of incorrect chunks. All this can be studied in the role model independently of which objects play the roles of `Client` and `Server`, and which objects play the roles of `Source` and `Destination`.

Separation of concern is a powerful simplifying device

This example illustrates two points about role modeling. The first is that we need to see the involved objects if we want to describe how a structure of objects performs its duties. The second is that separation of concern is a powerful way of breaking a complex situation into simple components. We could have created an object model having two objects: one playing the roles of `Client`, `Source`, and `Destination`, the other playing the roles of `Server`, `Source`, and `Destination`. This derived model would be more complex and harder to understand than the two simple models of Figure 2.17, and the combination of the two essentially separate functionalities would not in any way add to the value of the model.

2.3.3   A Sample Model Having Four Roles

Concern: The purchase of goods

The last example we have chosen is that of a company buying something from a supplier. The company pays for the goods by instructing its bank to transfer the required amount to the supplier's bank and to credit the supplier's account. This example is designed to illustrate that it may be convenient, and even essential, to study several objects together to give an adequate description of an activity.

The problem is simply modeled by four roles as shown in Figure 2.18. The company is represented by the `Company` role, the supplier by the `Supplier` role, and the two banks by the `PayerBank` and the `PayeeBank`.

Alternative mapping between roles and objects

The simple model of Figure 2.18 suggests that four objects could be involved, each playing one of the roles. But this is only one of the possible mappings between roles and objects. The company and the supplier might use the same bank: the `PayerBank` and `PayeeBank` roles would then be played by the same object. Or the company could actually be a bank: the `Company` and `PayerBank` would then be played by the same object. Many other mappings are conceivable. The role model permits us to concentrate on the essence of the phenomenon, disregarding the mapping to actual objects.

Many views are supported

The scenario of Figure 2.19 shows a typical message sequence for a purchasing activity.

Interfaces show messages sent

A third view is shown in Figure 2.20; this is a collaboration view annotated with the messages interfaces for each of the ports. The `Company` role can receive two messages from the `Supplier` role: bid and goodsAndInvoice. No messages are sent from the `Supplier` role to the `PayeeBank` in this model. The `Supplier` role is therefore marked as not knowing the `PayeeBank`. (This is in the context of this role model only, since the `Supplier` object is very likely to know its bank!)

Figure 2.18

The collabo-rating roles

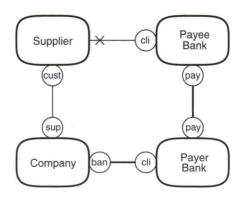

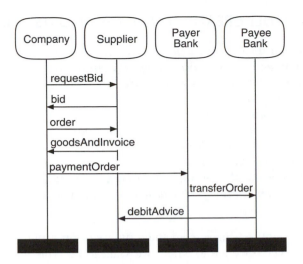

Figure 2.19

A scenario shows a typical message sequence

The Company role can send the requestBid and order messages to the Supplier. It can also send the paymentOrder message to the PayerBank. The PayerBank can send transactionReceipt messages to the Company, and transferOrder messages to the PayeeBank. Finally, the PayeeBank can send transferReceipt messages to the PayerBank, and debitAdvice messages to the Supplier.

Notice the fine-grained control of message interaction provided by the role model. For instance, the PayerBank understands the paymentOrder message, but that message can only be legally sent from an object that plays the Company role.

Many views give expressive power to the analyst/designer

Combined with the separation of concern exemplified in the previous section, the appropriate selection of views gives the analyst a powerful means for reducing complex problems to a number of simple descriptions.

This example also illustrates the advantages of roles having identity: We not only can check that some supplier will be paid; we can actually check that the supplier who delivered the goods is also the supplier that ultimately gets paid.

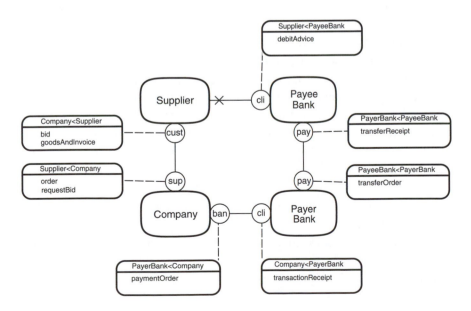

Figure 2.20

Interfaces specify messages that may be sent from a role to a collaborator

2.4 THE MODEL CREATION PROCESS AND ITS DELIVERABLES

IN A NUTSHELL

Work processes must be tailored to the task at hand and to the people who are going to do it. Further, no work process magically ensures a successful modeling operation; quality results can only be produced by skilled people. The deliverables from a work process are more concrete, and we suggest a list of deliverables that can be taken as a starting point.

Finding the objects in a model is considered a hard problem for novices, and fairly straightforward for experienced analysts. We suggest a few hints to help you in finding objects, but suggest that the most important source is to be found in reusable components. Such components package accumulated expert experience and provide excellent starting points for novices and experts alike.

Work processes tailored to tasks

Whenever we want to achieve something, we perform a number of operations that lead from where we are to where we want to be. This sequence of operations is called a *work process*, and the operations called *process steps*. There is no single work process that covers all needs. We have to tailor our own process, based on where we are, where we want to go, and the available technology.

OOram role model analysis is appropriate for a great variety of different work processes. Each process will apply the views that are most informative. It is unlikely that any process will ever need all of them.

It is important to note that these views are artifacts of the modeling process. We choose to view the phenomena under study in certain ways. Our choices can be neither right nor wrong, but they may be more or less suitable for our purpose.

The sequence of steps we suggest in the following is therefore to be construed more as a suggested documentation structure than as a default work process. You may want to develop your own preferred sequence of steps, taking the steps proposed here as a starting point.

The model creation process introduced in Chapter 1 consisted of the following eight steps:

1 *Determine the area of concern.* Write a free form (prose) description of the issue under consideration.

2 *Understand the problem and identify the nature of the objects.* For each area of concern, identify the nature of the objects that will be involved.

3 *Determine environment roles and stimulus/response.* Describe the messages that are sent from environment roles and cause an activity in the described system. Also describe the response, which is the overall effect of the activity.

4 *Identify and understand the roles.* Separate and idealize the tasks and responsibilities of the objects and describe them as the roles they play in the system.

5 *Determine the message sequences.* Create scenarios showing the activities performed by roles in response to stimulus messages.

6 *Determine the collaboration structure.* Show the roles in a structure of collaborating objects.

7 *Determine interfaces.* Determine the messages that each role may send to each of its collaborators.

8 *Determine the role behavior.* Describe interesting methods triggered by messages for the key roles.

These steps provide you with an object-oriented model of the phenomenon under study. This model provides a static description defining the roles, their characteristics, and their collaboration structure, and it provides a dynamic description defining the message processes.

Novice analysts frequently struggle with finding objects or roles. This is a symptom of a deeper problem, namely that the analyst has not yet internalized the object paradigm.

Finding the objects

There is, unfortunately, no known procedure which will always yield suitable objects or roles up front. But it may be a comfort to know that once you have mastered the object paradigm, your intuition will usually provide good initial choices. In a contribution to the Internet, Ward Cunningham suggests that most objects in any big system are obvious and easily found by examining the vocabulary of anyone familiar with the domain. Most of the remaining objects can be found by pooling the wisdom and experience of interested parties. A possible technique is to use the CRC cards described below. Finally, according to Cunningham, there are a few objects that can only be found by living and working with the system over an extended period of time. These few objects are often crucial, and make accumulated complexity melt away.

It is thus easy to find most of the objects up front, but there is really only one way to find all of them: study a similar system that has had the benefit of a long history of evolution and improvements. This is one of the most compelling reasons for applying reusable patterns and frameworks: they provide mature solutions to known problems.

Objects found by combination of personal creativity and study of existing systems

Below, we endeavor to give a few general hints to help the novice find the initial objects.

What is a good object?

1 A good object has a clearly defined role in the overall structure of objects. (An object cannot be good per se, only in the context of the purpose and structure of the role model!)

2 A good structure of objects represents the area of concern described by the model in an intuitively pleasing manner.

Where should one look for objects?

1 Study the problem domain:
   • Consider general domain aspects.
   • Consider the users' expressed needs.
   • Consider any other available source.

2 Study any available text:
   • Nouns are candidates.

3 Study any available drawings and overview diagrams:
   • Entities are candidates.

What is often a good object?

1 A model of a part of the real world.

2 A thing to which thought or action is directed.

3 Something which would be described as an entity in an entity-relation model.

4 Something which has identity and exists over time.

What is often not an object?

1 A *value.* A value is something without interesting internal structure or behavior in the context of the role model. A value may then be represented as a role attribute.

2 A *process.* If the process can be adequately represented as a sequence of messages flowing in the model, it is modeled as role model activity and described by an appropriate dynamic view, such as a scenario or a state diagram.

3 *Time.* Time is usually implicit in the model. (But a timer is concrete and may be a good object.)

CRC cards support working in groups

A good technique for finding objects and roles is to use class-responsibility-collaborator cards (CRC cards) as the focus points of group discussions. CRC cards are adapted from Cunningham and Beck [Wirfs-Brock 90].

CRC cards are index cards, with each divided into three areas, as shown in Figure 2.21. One card is created for each role, and the group discusses how the roles interact to achieve the response specified for each stimulus. Individual group members should claim ownership of one or more roles (cards). This makes it much simpler to check that each role has the necessary information to take responsibility for its own part of the activities:

1 CRC cards support the decomposition part of the design and help assign responsibility to the constituent roles.

2 Objects collaborate through *intention-revealing* message sends.

3 An attractive characteristic of index cards is that they are *concrete*: they can be owned, pointed at, and moved about.

4 The technique gives the group the impression (illusion) of *completeness* when they are done with the design.

Notice that when a group works with CRC cards, they study the roles and messages simultaneously. The technique therefore tends to be effective both for finding "good" roles, and for finding simple, but adequate, model behavior by enacting the scenarios (even if the dynamics of messages passing are not recorded on the cards). The CRC technique supports role modeling directly, since it focuses on object responsibility and object interaction.

Figure 2.21
CRC card for the
Authorizer
role

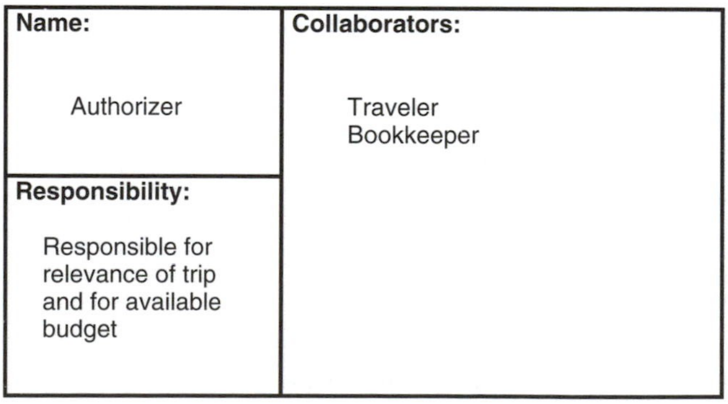

Name:	Collaborators:
Authorizer	Traveler Bookkeeper
Responsibility:	
Responsible for relevance of trip and for available budget	

The creation of a structure of collaborating roles is, in many ways, similar to creating an organization of people collaborating in performing some common task.

Role structures similar to work organization

We have earlier mentioned Max Weber's dream of a rational work organization. The following literal excerpts from Etzioni [Etzioni 64] form a beautiful description of this "perfect bureaucracy": logical, rational, extremely efficient, and extremely rigid. Applied to the computer system, it is perfect. Applied to the human organization, it can become a nightmare (my comments appear in parenthesis):

Max Weber's rational work organization was object-oriented

1 "*Emphasis of structure.* 'A continuous organization of official functions bound by rules.' Rational organization is the antithesis of ad hoc, temporary, unstable relations; hence the stress on continuity. Rules save effort by obviating the need for deriving a new solution for every problem and case; they facilitate standardization and equality in the treatment of many cases." (In the travel expense case, we focus on the actors and their formal responsibilities. We ignore all informal contacts and interactions.)

2 "*A specific sphere of competence.* This involves (a) a sphere of obligations to perform functions which have been marked off as part of a systematic division of labor; (b) the provision of the incumbent with the necessary authority to carry out these functions; and (c) that the necessary means of compulsion are clearly defined and their use is subject to definite conditions. Thus a systematic division of labor, rights and power is essential for rational organization. Not only must each participant know his job and have the means to carry it out, which includes first of all the ability to command others, but he also must know the limits of his job, rights, and power so as not to overstep the boundaries between his role and those of others and thus undermine the whole structure." (In the travel expense case, we focus on the formal object attributes and actions. We ignore all *soft* aspects such as the personal characteristics, motivations, benefits, and social aspects.)

3 "*Hierarchy.* The organization of offices follows the principle of hierarchy; that is, each lower office is under the control and supervision of a higher one. In this way, no office is left uncontrolled. Compliance cannot be left to chance; it has to be systematically checked and reinforced." (Well, we are not quite so rigid, but we carefully control the collaborators of an object and the messages it may send to them.)

4 "*Norms of conduct.* The rules which regulate the conduct of an office may be technical rules or norms. In both cases, if their application is to be fully rational, specialized training is necessary. It is thus normally true that only a person who has demonstrated an adequate technical training is qualified to be a member of the administrative staff...." (This is strictly true; the system is completely defined by the program.)

5 "*Independence.* In order to enhance the organizational freedom, the resources of the organization have to be free of any outside control and the positions cannot be monopolized by any incumbent. They have to be free to be allocated and reallocated according to the needs of the organization. 'A complete absence of appropriation of his official positions by the incumbent' is required." (This is the principle of object encapsulation. An object should influence other objects only through their official interfaces.)

6 *"Documentation.* 'Administrative acts, decisions, and rules are formulated and recorded in writing....' Most observers might view this requirement as less essential or basic to rational organization than the preceding ones, and many will point to the irrationality of keeping excessive records, files, and the like, often referred to as 'red tape'. Weber, however, stressed the need to maintain a systematic interpretation of norms and enforcement of rules, which cannot be maintained through oral communication." (A trivial fulfillment of this rule is through the program source code. We read the rule to mean that we also want higher level documentation describing goals, specifications, architecture, and design.)

Weber's rules for a rational organization and Etzioni's comments are almost uncannily appropriate for the design of object-oriented systems. Admittedly, we cannot construct a complete system as a rigid hierarchy of objects. But if we consider individual activities, each of these activities can be designed as a distinct role model according to rules which are very similar to the rules formulated by Weber. We propose the following *OOram rules for rational object-oriented design*:

1 *Emphasis on structure.* The relations between participating roles in a rational design of a role model are bound by a *specification* that is part of the design, not just the implementation.

2 *A specific sphere of competence.* For each role, this involves the duty to react appropriately to messages received, which have been marked off as part of the systematic division of responsibility, and the right to delegate work to collaborators by sending messages to them at times clearly described in the design, as well as the duty not to send any other messages.

3 *Hierarchy.* In every role model, each lower level role is under the control and supervision of a higher level one. In this way, no role except the top one is left uncontrolled. Specifically, this means creating a role, initializing it, connecting it with its collaborators in the overall structure, and removing it at the appropriate time. (This is the weakest rule, and is not always relevant.)

4 *Norms of conduct.* For a given role model, the behavior of a role is regulated by rules or norms. By rules, we mean precise statements about the behavior. By norms, we mean general guidelines. The distinction relates to the responsibilities of the designer versus the implementor. Rules put more constraints on the implementor than do norms.

5 *Independence.* An object may play a role in several role models. The collaborators of an object in the context of one role model do not know about its other roles, and thus cannot infringe on its behavior in other contexts.

6 *Documentation.* Each role model must be fully documented on the design level. It is particularly tempting to let the norms of conduct for a role model be an informal part of the programming team's culture—"the way we do it here". This is guaranteed to eventually cause you trouble. Most real systems are so complex that we can only trust their correctness if they are constructed from well-documented models, each of which "is so simple that it is obviously correct."

7 *Reusability.* While this rule has no counterpart in Weber's rules, it certainly has a counterpart in real organizations. We continuously search for generally useful role models, and we reuse an existing role model whenever appropriate. In some cases, we can also reuse the code; in other cases, just the pattern. Either way, reuse improves system reliability and reduces the work involved in understanding programs developed by other people.

2.5 BASIC OORAM ROLE MODELING CONCEPTS AND NOTATION

OOram role model analysis helps the developer master object structures of any size. The object structure may already exist. The purpose is then to understand it. Alternatively, the purpose may be to design a new object structure. The objects are then imaginary. In both cases, the OOram approach is to identify different concerns which are represented in the object structure, and to create idealized object models, called role models, which focus on the selected area of concern and ignore everything else.

The essence of role modeling is that we always consider objects in context. An isolated object cannot do anything because a message must have both a sender and a receiver. It is only when we consider structures of collaborating objects that we can study cause and effect, and reason about the suitability and correctness of objects and their structures.

2.5.1 The Object

We have defined objects as being *encapsulated*. This is illustrated in Figure 2.22. It means that we can observe some of an object's properties from the outside, while other properties can only be seen from inside.

External and internal observation

2.5.2 External Object Properties

Observed from the outside, objects appear as indivisible *atoms*. Each object has its own unique identity, and is characterized by its *behavior* and *attributes*.

The behavior of an object is characterized by the messages it can receive, and also by the messages it can send to other objects. Many different message seman-

Messages

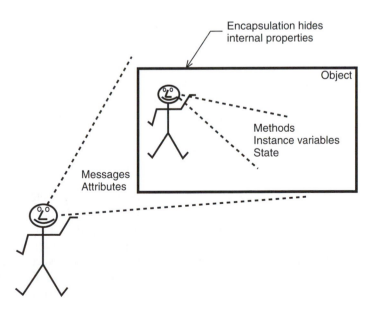

Encapsulation hides
internal properties

Object

Methods
Instance variables
State

Messages
Attributes

Figure 2.22

External and internal object properties

tics have been proposed. Our selection is adopted from the Object Management Group [CORBA 91]:

1 Synchronous. Only one object can be active at any time, and the sender's actions continue only after the receiver's actions are completed. The receiver may return a result to the sender.

2 Synchronous deferred. Before a message can be transferred, the sender object must be ready to send it and the receiver object must be ready to receive it. The sender and receiver objects are synchronized at the time of message transfer. The sender's actions continue after the receiver has accepted the message. A return value could confirm the receipt of the message.

3 Asynchronous. The sender can transmit a message at any time, and the sender's actions continue immediately. The receiver manages a queue of incoming messages, and may need to wait for an acceptable message to arrive in the input queue. A return value to the sender could confirm that the message has been put into the receiver's input queue.

An Interface is a set of messages
The number of different messages understood by an object may be very large, and we find it convenient to group them: an OOram interface is a named set of messages, or more precisely, of message types. This use of the term conforms with CORBA [CORBA 91], but some professionals use the term *interface* to denote signals going in both directions, i.e., messages sent and received by an object. The OOram technology uses two interfaces to describe this: one for messages it sends and another for messages it receives.

At least two roles needed
A role model consisting of at least two roles is needed to describe an object's interaction with other objects in space and time.

Attributes
An object may store information. To the outside observer, this information is described by the object's named attributes. Attributes are *virtual* in the sense that they do not say anything about how the object represents information internally in the *instance variables* described below.

Attributes are visible to the outside observer only through messages whose behavior depends on the current value of one or more attributes (usually, but not always, through a value returned from the receiving object).

Internal Object Properties

As seen from the inside, the object realization is described by its *methods*, its *instance variables*, and its *state*.

Methods
A *method* defines the action taken by an object when receiving a message. The method may cause the object to send messages to one or more of its collaborator objects. It can create new objects, and it may have the side effect of causing a change to one or more of the object's instance variables.

The distinction between a message and a method is essential because it permits different objects to handle the same message using different methods; each object can "do the right thing" when it receives a message. This feature of object orientation is variously called *polymorphism* or *late binding* in the literature.

The fancy names are unimportant, the ability to hide the details of an operation inside an object is essential. For example, different graphical objects can respond to a `display` command according to their individual characteristics; different bank account objects can compute accumulated interest according to the nature of the account; individual `TravelAuthorizer` persons can follow different rules when they determine their responses to travel permission requests.

Instance variables represent attribute information. An instance variable may hold the value of an attribute directly, or the object may have a method that enables it to compute the value of an attribute from the values of one or more instance variables.

Instance variables

The distinction between an attribute and an instance variable is essential because it permits the analyst to think in terms of information without considering its representation. The attribute could, for example, be a person's age. The instance variable could hold the person's birth date, so that the object could compute the age whenever needed. The object could even delegate the responsibility for maintaining information to some other object: an instance variable could hold a reference to the other object and a method could know how to retrieve the required information from it. This possibility will be discussed in depth in Section 3.2.1.

The internal conditions of an object which affect its behavior are abstracted into its possible states, where a state determines which messages the object is ready to receive and how it will process them. When the object receives a message, it performs an action that depends on the current state, and enters a next state which may be different from the current state.

State

If the actions taken when the object receives a message are different in different states, the corresponding method will be a composite with different action branches for the different states.

Some practitioners use the terms *instance variable* and *state* interchangeably. We find it useful to distinguish between these two terms in order to cater to the relatively few situations where it is necessary to study objects with state-dependent behavior. More details appear in Section 6.3.

2.5.3 The Role Model

OOram *analysis* is defined as the description of some interesting phenomenon as a system of interacting objects. In data processing, *analysis* is commonly used to denote the study of what is visible to the user community, while *design* is used to denote the description of the internal construction of a new system. OOram *analysis* covers both these interpretations: we *analyze* the world as perceived by the user community, and we *analyze* a system as perceived by its creators. The antonym is *synthesis*, the composition of a whole from its constituent of parts.

OOram analysis

The OOram role model supports *separation of concern*. A large and complex phenomenon, which we think of as a large and complex structure of interacting objects, may be split into a number of subphenomena. Each subphenomenon is described by its own *role model*.

Separation of concern

A role is an idealized object in the sense that it is an archetypical example of the object within the pattern, and that the role's characteristics form a subset of the object's characteristics that are of interest within the limited scope of the subphenomenon.

An object model is a structure of objects representing an aspect of a phenomenon. A role model is a structure of roles representing an aspect of an object model; it is an object-oriented model of an object structure. In simple cases, the role model is identical to the object model and there is exactly one role for each object.

Definitions

A role model is a part of a structure of objects that we choose to regard as a whole, separated from the rest of the structure during some period of consideration. It is a whole that we choose to consider as a collection of roles, with each role being characterized by its attributes and by the messages it may receive from and send to other roles.

For a given system of roles, the environment is the set of all roles outside the system that send messages to the objects of the system, and also those roles outside the system that receive messages from the roles of the system.

Roles have all the properties of objects: they have identity and attributes; they are encapsulated; they interact by message-passing, and their actions are defined by their methods. Inheritance is supported by a process called *synthesis* that will be described in Chapter 3.

There is a many-to-many relationship between objects and roles: an object may play several different roles from the same or different role models; and a role may be played by several different objects.

A role model may be observed in different perspectives

We may observe the system of interacting roles from different observation points. OOram supports three points of observation, called perspectives:

1 *Environment perspective*, where the observer is placed in the system environment so that he or she can observe the system's interaction with its environment roles.

2 *External perspective*, where the observer is placed between the roles so that he or she can observe the messages flowing between them and indirectly deduce the role attributes.

3 *Internal perspective*, where the observer is placed inside a role so that he or she can observe its implementation.

The analyst observes only views of the underlying model

When thinking about some interesting phenomenon, the OOram analyst creates a mental object model of the phenomenon. This model can only be captured on paper or a computer screen as one or more *views*—these views are different presentations of an underlying *OOram model*. In the case of a paper report, the underlying model is abstract in the sense that it has no explicit representation. In the case of a computer-based system, the underlying model can be represented in an object database. See Figure 2.23.

Ten different views on the same model

Systems of interacting objects may be studied in different views, with each view expressing certain aspects of the system of roles while suppressing others. OOram analysis supports ten different views on a role model:

1 Area of concern view. This view is a textual description of the phenomenon modeled by the role model.

2 Stimulus-response view. This view shows how environment roles may cause some activity in the system of roles by sending a stimulus message, and the overall effect of the activity, called the response.

Figure 2.23

The analyst can only see and manipulate views of an underlying model

Mental object model

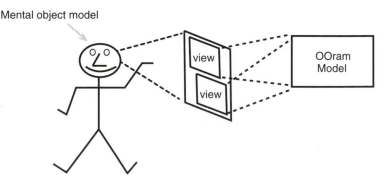

3   Role list view. This view shows a list of all roles with their explanations and attributes.

4   Semantic view. This view shows how we attach meaning to the roles and the relationships between them.

5   Collaboration view. This view shows the pattern of roles and the message paths between them.

6   Interface view. This view defines all messages that may be sent along each of the message paths.

7   Scenario view. This view shows sample time sequences of messages flowing between the roles.

8   Process view. This view shows how data flows between the roles, and the actions taken by the roles to process the data.

9   State diagram view. There may be one state diagram for each role. This view describes the possible states of the role, the signals that are acceptable in each state, the action taken as a result of each signal, and the next state attained after the action is completed. The only kind of signal possible in our model is the receipt of a message.

10 Method specification view. When an object receives a message, the message triggers the execution of a method within it. The method specification view describes the messages to be sent from the method with the corresponding receiving roles. It may also include a more or less formal description of the procedure.

The views are meaningful only in certain perspectives, as shown in Table 2.1. The basic views are described in the following; the views marked with an asterisk (*) are described in Chapter 6

Important notes:

1   The views are different presentations of the same model for the purposes of documentation and user interaction.

2   A subset of the views should be selected to suit a particular modeling process. It is unlikely that anybody will ever need them all.

Table 2.1   Applicability of the views in different perspectives

	Environment perspective	External perspective	Internal perspective
Area of concern view	Applicable		
Stimulus-response view	Applicable		
Role List view (*)	Applicable	Applicable	
Semantic view (*)		Applicable	
Collaboration view		Applicable	
Scenario view	Applicable	Applicable	
Interface view		Applicable	Applicable
Process view (*)	Applicable	Applicable	Applicable
State Diagram view (*)			Applicable
Method Specification view			Applicable

3 The views are *not* orthogonal. Their mutual consistency should preferably be enforced automatically, but it is also possible to do so by manual means.

Six of the views are described in the following subsections using a notation appropriate for documentation; the rest are described in Chapter 6. The OOram language notation given in Appendix A is more formal. It is harder for a human to read, but more appropriate for automatic information interchange between OOram systems.

Area of Concern View

Area of Concern view describes the model as a whole

The area of concern view (Figure 2.24) is a free text describing the phenomenon modeled by the role model. The text should indicate the purpose of the model and be sufficiently precise to enable a reader to determine which phenomena are covered by the model, and which are not. The description must be precise because it will be used to determine which objects belong to the system and which objects are outside it.

Stimulus-Response View

A stimulus is a message that triggers an activity

Stimuli are defined as messages sent spontaneously from an environment role to one of the system roles. The sequence of actions taken by the system is called an *activity*. The response involves one or more messages sent from the system to one or more environment roles, or some other changes that are described as a free text, such as changes to object structure or attributes. The stimulus-response relationships are tabulated in Figure 2.25; an example is shown in Figure 2.26.

Alternative is to show system as virtual role

An alternative presentation of the stimulus-response view is to use a collaboration view where all the system roles are shown as a single virtual role. This view is annotated with the stimulus and response messages.

Figure 2.24
Area of Concern example

This role model describes how an enterprise purchases goods and pays for them.

Figure 2.25
Graphical notation is in the form of a table

Stimulus message	Response messages	Comments
environment role >> message name	{environment role << message name}...	Free text description of other results

Figure 2.26
Stimulus-response example

Stimulus message	Response message	Comments
Enterprise >>requestBid	Vendor << creditAdvice	The enterprise has received and paid for the desired goods

Collaboration View

The Collaboration view shows the roles and the message paths between them. Our notation is shown in Figure 2.27 and illustrated in Figure 2.28.

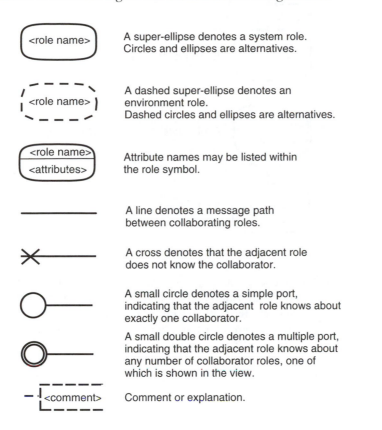

A super-ellipse denotes a system role.
Circles and ellipses are alternatives.

A dashed super-ellipse denotes an environment role.
Dashed circles and ellipses are alternatives.

Attribute names may be listed within the role symbol.

A line denotes a message path between collaborating roles.

A cross denotes that the adjacent role does not know the collaborator.

A small circle denotes a simple port, indicating that the adjacent role knows about exactly one collaborator.

A small double circle denotes a multiple port, indicating that the adjacent role knows about any number of collaborator roles, one of which is shown in the view.

Comment or explanation.

Figure 2.27

Collaboration view notation

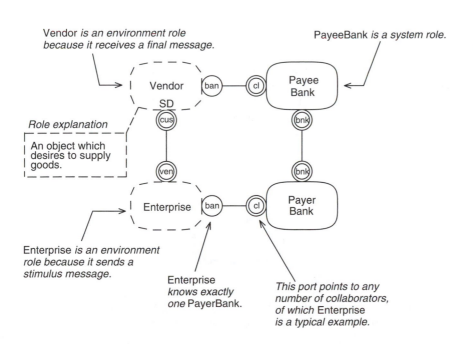

Vendor *is an environment role because it receives a final message.*

PayeeBank *is a system role.*

Role explanation

An object which desires to supply goods.

Enterprise *is an environment role because it sends a stimulus message.*

Enterprise *knows exactly one PayerBank.*

This port points to any number of collaborators, of which Enterprise *is a typical example.*

Figure 2.28

Collaboration view illustration

Figure 2.29

**Examples of
decorated role
symbols**

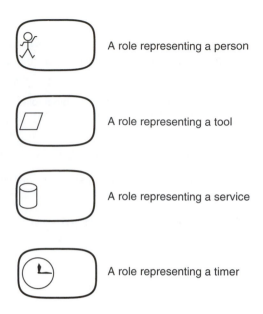

A role representing a person

A role representing a tool

A role representing a service

A role representing a timer

Martin recommends that data be represented with square-cornered rectangles, while activities be drawn with round corners [Martin 87]. Roles (and objects) combine data and activities. We have, therefore, searched for representative shape that is neither round nor square. A super-ellipse seems to satisfy our needs. Its shape is shown in the figures.[1]

*Role symbols
may be
decorated*

Role symbols may be decorated to indicate the nature of the object. Figure 2.29 illustrates some possibilities, but the analyst is free to define his or her own symbols.

*Virtual roles are
arbitrary
clusters of
concrete roles*

Roles may arbitrarily be lumped into *virtual roles* for convenience. A virtual role is a role that represents a cluster of objects rather than a single object. Virtual roles are denoted by a super-ellipse with a shadow, as shown in Figure 2.30. Note that virtual roles are artifacts of the presentation and do not exist in the underlying role model.

A virtual role is one of the OOram constructs for representing aggregation. In the other constructs, there is an object which acts as an interface to a cluster of other objects. (Aggregation will be discussed in more detail in Chapter 3.)

*External
Collaboration
view*

The external collaboration view shows the system as a single virtual role together with its environment roles, as illustrated in Figure 2.31.

Virtual roles and their associated virtual ports must be resolved into concrete roles. Figure 2.31 can, for example, be resolved into Figure 2.28.

Figure 2.30

**Virtual role
notation**

Virtual
role

---

1. (The formula of the super-ellipse is $(x/a)^{**}4 + (y/b)^{**}4 = 1$. We recommend that you use circles or ellipses if your tools do not support super-ellipses).

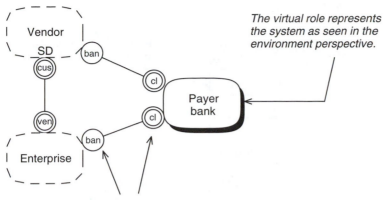

The virtual role represents the system as seen in the environment perspective.

These virtual ports represent all message paths between the environment role and the system roles.

Scenario View

A *scenario* is a description of a specific, time-ordered sequence of interactions be-tween objects.

An *interaction* represents the event of transmitting a message from a sender object to a receiver object. Both the sending and the receiving objects must be represented as roles in the role model. Interactions are assumed to be atomic and strictly ordered in time.

The scenario thus shows a *sample* sequence of messages as they flow through the structure of objects. The first message must be one of the role model's stimu-lus messages. Scenarios may be created in the environment and external perspec-tives.

The OOram scenario is adapted from the Message Sequence Chart defined in the standard [CCITT Z120]. Our notation is shown in Figure 2.32 and illustrated in 2.33.

In his book on object-oriented software engineering, Jacobson uses the term *actors* to denote a system's environment objects [Jacobson 92]. An OOram stimu-lus message is an operation initiated by an actor, and a use case is an OOram ac-tivity, i.e., the system actions that result from the stimulus. We propose that scenarios are admirably suited to describe use cases. A single scenario, as de-scribed here, will be sufficient for simple use cases, and the aggregation and syn-

A scenario exemplifies a message sequence

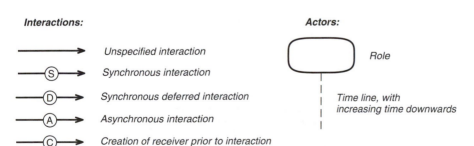

Figure 2.32

Scenario notation

Figure 2.33

Scenario illustration

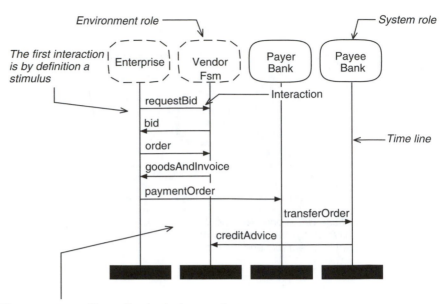

Message name with or without actual parameters

thesis operations discussed in Chapter 3 enable us to dissect a use case down to any desired detail.

The three different semantics of messages were defined on page 57.

Interface View

Interfaces define messages that may be sent

An interface view defines a set of messages that may be sent from one role to another. Interfaces are usually specified textually, but may also be shown in an annotation in the collaboration view shown in Figure 2.34.

Textual form more useful

We find that we can use the graphical form of Figure 2.35 only in simple cases, such as in very high level overviews, trade show demonstrations, and tutorials. Real world models are too complex for the graphical presentation to fit on a computer screen or a sheet of paper, and we prefer a textual form. As with the role list view, the textual form of the interface view may be written informally or in the formal OOram language. The full language syntax is discussed in Appendix A; we give a simple example of the formal textual notation in Figure 2.36 and an informal form in Figure 2.37.

A comment is associated with every message definition. Use it to describe the functionality of each message as clearly as possible. Focus on the *intent* of the message without saying how the receiver is to perform the operation. Try to keep the interfaces lean and powerful. Watch for nearly identical messages, and try to merge them.

Figure 2.34

Graphical interface notation

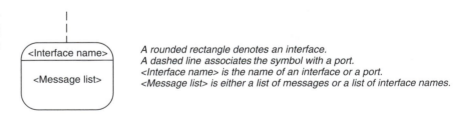

A rounded rectangle denotes an interface.
A dashed line associates the symbol with a port.
<Interface name> is the name of an interface or a port.
<Message list> is either a list of messages or a list of interface names.

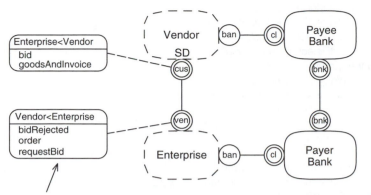

Figure 2.35
Graphical interface illustration

*An interface named Vendor<Enterprise
(Vendor-from-Enterprise)
defines the messages that may be
sent to Vendor from Enterprise.*

interface 'Vendor<Enterprise'
    message synch 'requestBid'
        explanation *"Request bid for delivery of specified goods"*
    message synch 'order'
        explanation *"Order goods"*
    message synch 'bidRejected'
        explanation *"Reject bid"*
interface 'Enterprise<Vendor'
    message synch 'bid'
        explanation *"Submitting bid"*
    message synch 'goodsAndInvoice'
        explanation *"Sending goods together with invoice"*
interface 'PayerBank<Enterprise'
    message synch 'paymentOrder'
        explanation *"Order to transfer money"*
interface 'Enterprise<PayerBank'
    message synch 'transactionReceipt'
        explanation *"Acknowledging order to transfer money"*
interface 'PayeeBank<PayerBank'
    message synch 'transferOrder'
        explanation *"Order to transfer money"*
interface 'PayerBank<PayeeBank'
    message synch 'transferReceipt'
        explanation *"Acknowledging order to transfer money"*
interface 'Vendor<PayeeBank'
    message synch 'creditAdvice'
        explanation *"Advising that money has been received on behalf of vendor"*

Figure 2.36
Textual specification of interfaces in the OOram language

Figure 2.37

Informal textual specification of interfaces

interface 'Vendor<Enterprise'
       'requestBid' *"Request bid for delivery of specified goods."*
       'order' *"Order goods"*
       'bidRejected' *"Reject bid"*
interface 'Enterprise<Vendor'
       'bid' *"Submitting bid"*
       'goodsAndInvoice' *"Sending goods together with invoice"*
interface 'PayerBank<Enterprise'
       'paymentOrder' *"Order to transfer money"*
interface 'Enterprise<PayerBank'
       'transactionReceipt' *"Acknowledging order to transfer money"*
interface 'PayeeBank<PayerBank'
       'transferOrder' *"Order to transfer money"*
interface 'PayerBank<PayeeBank'
       'transferReceipt' *"Acknowledging order to transfer money"*
interface 'Vendor<PayeeBank'
       'creditAdvice' *"Advising that money has been received on behalf of vendor"*

The example is clearly from an early stage of the analysis process, since the message parameters have not yet been specified.

Method Specification View

The Method specification view is similar to a scenario view. The main difference is in the perspective; the scenario observes the message flow from interobject space, and shows a specific sequence of message transmissions. The method specification view observes the processing of a message from within a specific role. It shows the message reception, the method which it triggers, and the messages sent from that method.

The semantics and notation should be clear from Figure 2.38.

Figure 2.38

Sample method specification view

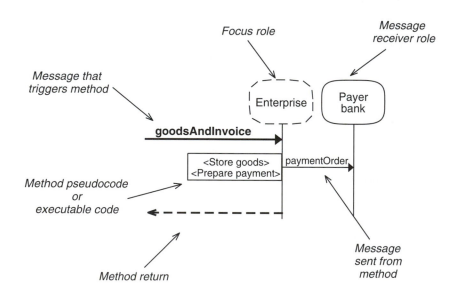

CHAPTER 3   ✧   ✧   ✧   ✧   ✧

Role Model Synthesis

CONTENTS

3.1   Introduction to Synthesis: `DerivedTravelExpense`   71

     3.1.1   The `AirlineBooking` (AB) Model   72
     3.1.2   Creating the `DerivedTravelExpense` (DTE) Model   72

3.2   The Synthesis Operation   78

     3.2.1   Aggregation: Linking Models on Different Levels of Abstraction   86
     3.2.2   Attributes and Message Parameters   88
     3.2.3   Safe and Unsafe Synthesis of the Travel Example Models   90

3.3   Basic OOram Concepts and Notation for Role Model Synthesis   92

     3.3.1   The Inheritance and Role List Views   92
     3.3.2   Synthesis in the Area of Concern View   94
     3.3.3   Synthesis in the Environment and Stumulus-Response Views   95
     3.3.4   Synthesis in the Collaboration View   95
     3.3.5   Synthesis in the Scenario View   97
     3.3.6   Synthesis in the Interface View   99
     3.3.7   Synthesis in the Method Specification View   99

This chapter tells you how to achieve separation of concern while retaining control of the overall system.

Divide and conquer is an important concept in all computing practices. If a problem is too large and complex to be handled as a whole, we divide it into a number of manageable subproblems and model each of them as a role model. A role model is complete in the sense that it represents its whole area of concern. We may use it to analyze the described phenomenon to any desired detail.

Several base models may be combined into a composite, or derived, model by the synthesis operation. The phenomenon covered by the derived model is some combination of the phenomena described by the base models, and the derived model is complete in the sense that it represents a whole phenomenon. Synthesis is called safe when the static and dynamic correctness of the base models is retained in the derived model, and unsafe if we retain only the static correctness and have to study the derived model to determine its dynamic correctness.

Some useful base models are illustrated in Figure 3.1.

Figure 3.1

Models on all levels may be synthesized from simpler base models

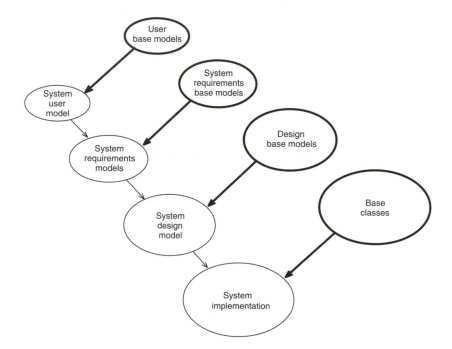

1 The system user model may be composed from more general base models, which we may create as part of our current project or which we may find in a library of reusable components.

2 The system requirements model also may be composed from more general base models, which we may create as part of our current project or which we may find in a library of reusable components.

3 The system design model describes the system components and their interaction. We would expect that a number of critical design details may be found in a library of reusable design base models (frameworks).

4 The system implementation is a specialization of reusable base classes expressed in library frameworks.

3.1 INTRODUCTION TO SYNTHESIS:
DerivedTravelExpense

We will illustrate the concept of synthesis through a concrete case. You will see that you can master a complex phenomenon by dividing it into manageable subproblems, and that you can retain control of the whole system using synthesis. We would like to challenge you to imagine how you could employ this technology to model your own complex of computer-based systems.

IN A NUTSHELL

We have chosen to illustrate synthesis by extending the `TravelExpense` enterprise (ENT) model to include a model of airline ticket booking. We laid a good foundation for this in Section 2.3 when we created a `TravelExpense` model. In this model, the purchasing of airline tickets appeared as a small comment in the method definition of Figure 2.16. We have several options now for expanding the operation `<Traveler purchases the necessary tickets>`, as illustrated in Figure 3.2:

Travel-Expense case extension

a **Extend the `TravelExpense` model.** We can extend the `TravelExpense` model, as shown in Figure 3.2a by adding messages and methods that describe the airline booking operations.

b **Synthesize a new `AirlineBooking` model into the `TravelExpense` model.** We can create a separate `AirlineBooking` model and synthesize it into the `TravelExpense` model, as shown in Figure 3.2b. The `TravelExpense` model is then extended as in alternative (a), but the `AirlineBooking` issues are also described in a separate base model.

3 **Create a new `Derived TravelExpense` model synthesized from a new `AirlineBooking` and the old `TravelExpense` models.** We can create a new `AirlineBooking` model and then successively synthesize it and the `TravelExpense` models into the derived model, as shown in Figure 3.2c. We then retain both base models, which can be studied and modified independently, but we also get the derived model, where we can study the interdependencies between the base models.

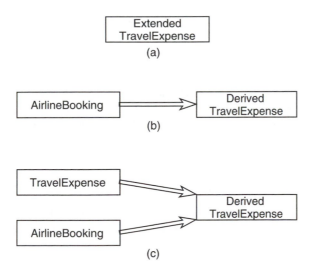

Figure 3.2

Alternative synthesis strategies

The first alternative is perfectly viable in this case, since even the extended model will be quite simple and manageable. However, we will not follow this alternative, because it does not illustrate the issues we want to discuss.

The second alternative is often selected when one wants to base one's model on a general mechanism. This is not the case here, and we will postpone the discussion of alternative (b) to Chapter 5.

The third alternative seems best suited to our purpose. We will create two base models, `TravelExpense` and `AirlineBooking`, and then combine them into a `DerivedTravelExpense` model that gives an overview of the total solution: we will develop the `AirlineBooking` model in Section 3.1.1, and then combine it with the existing `TravelExpense` model in Section 3.1.2.

Synthesis is often the best alternative. Consider that you have created a model that gives a nice, clean solution to a certain problem. You don't want to clutter it with all the details of error handling. It is much better to create a separate model of your error-handling mechanism, and use synthesis to create a third model that combines the two while retaining the original, clean models for later use.

3.1.1   The `AirlineBooking` (AB) Model

The area of concern is shown in Figure 3.3.

This problem has one activity, and thus one stimulus message: the `ABTraveler` begins the activity by sending an `orderTicket` message. The normal response, i.e., the final result of the activity, is that the traveler receives the tickets and records the ticket costs for later use. See Figure 3.4.

The essence of this model is the office procedure for handling tickets. We describe it in the scenario of Figure 3.5.

The collaboration view may be deduced from the scenario view, and is shown in Figure 3.6.

The precise definitions of interfaces and roles are important, but boring. We hide them within our computer-based OOram tools, where the analyst can browse them as needed. The interfaces are shown textually in Figure 3.7.

3.1.2   Creating the `DerivedTravelExpense` (DTE) Model

Let objects play multiple roles

We will now compose a derived model from the `AirlineBooking` (AB) and `TravelExpense` (TE) models using *synthesis*. We will call the new model `DerivedTravelExpense` (DTE).

Figure 3.3

AB Area of concern

> Airline tickets are ordered by a booking clerk and paid directly to the travel agent. The traveler must show the cost of the tickets on the expense report as an expense, and as an advance, since he or she did not pay for them.

Figure 3.4

AB Stimulus-response view

Stimulus	Response	Comments
ABTraveler >> orderTicket	ticketWithCost >> ABTraveler	Ticket cost retained in attribute of ABTraveler role

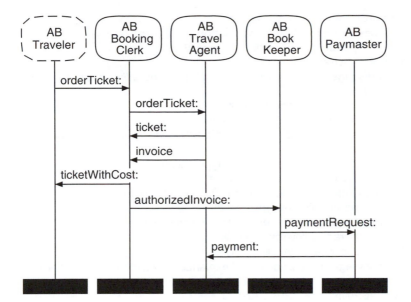

Figure 3.5

AB Airline-
Booking scenario

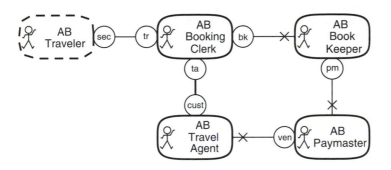

Figure 3.6

AB Collabor-
ation view

The essence of synthesis is that we *let objects play multiple roles*. So we first create an empty DerivedTravelExpense model, and then successively *synthesize* the TravelExpense and the AirlineBooking models into it. The area of concern for the derived model is given in Figure 3.8.

The environment roles are still the Traveler who wants to travel, and the Paymaster who must arrange for the remuneration of the Traveler. The system itself is represented by a single, virtual role, as shown in Figure 3.9.

As in the TravelExpense model, a travel activity starts with the stimulus message travelPermissionRequest: from the Traveler (Figure 3.10).

The ordering of a ticket is part of the TE-Traveler action. The AirlineBooking stimulus orderTicket is thus part of the travel preparations, and has become an internal message in the derived model.

The synthesis operation is illustrated as a synthesis collaboration view in Figure 3.11. The first step is to synthesize the TravelExpense model into the derived DTE model. The bordered arrows denote the synthesis relation; they go from the base roles of a base model to the corresponding derived roles of the derived model.

Figure 3.7

AB message
interfaces

interface 'ABBookingClerk<ABTraveler'
    message 'orderTicket:' **explanation** *"Purchase ticket(s)."*
        param 'ticketSpecification' **type** 'String'
interface 'ABTraveler<ABBookingClerk'
    message 'ticketWithCost:' **explanation** *"Transmitting the ticket(s) together with
cost information."*
        param 'package' **type** 'String'
interface 'ABTravelAgent<ABBookingClerk'
    message 'orderTicket:' **explanation** *"Reserve specified passages and issue
ticket(s)."*
        param 'ticketSpecification' **type** 'String'
interface 'ABBookingClerk<ABTravelAgent'
    message 'ticket:' **explanation** *"Transmittal of ticket(s)."*
        param 'aTicket' **type** 'String'
    message 'invoice:' **explanation** *"Transmittal of invoice."*
        param 'anInvoice' **type** 'String'
interface 'ABBookKeeper<ABBookingClerk'
    message 'authorizedInvoice:' **explanation** *"Pay this authorized ticket invoice."*
        param 'anInvoice' **type** 'String'
interface 'ABPaymaster<ABBookKeeper'
    message 'paymentRequest:' **explanation** *"Pay this invoice."*
        param 'anInvoice' **type** 'String'
interface 'ABTravelAgent<ABPaymaster'
    message 'payment:' **explanation** *"Transmittal of payment."*
        param 'aCheque' **type** 'String'

Figure 3.8

DTE Area of
concern

The area of concern is the procedure for travel management, including the purchase of tickets.

Figure 3.9

DTE
Environment
collaboration
view

Figure 3.10

DTE Stimulus-
response view

Stimulus	Response	Comments
DTE-Traveler >> travelPermissionRequest	Reimbursement will be added to the next salary payment.	

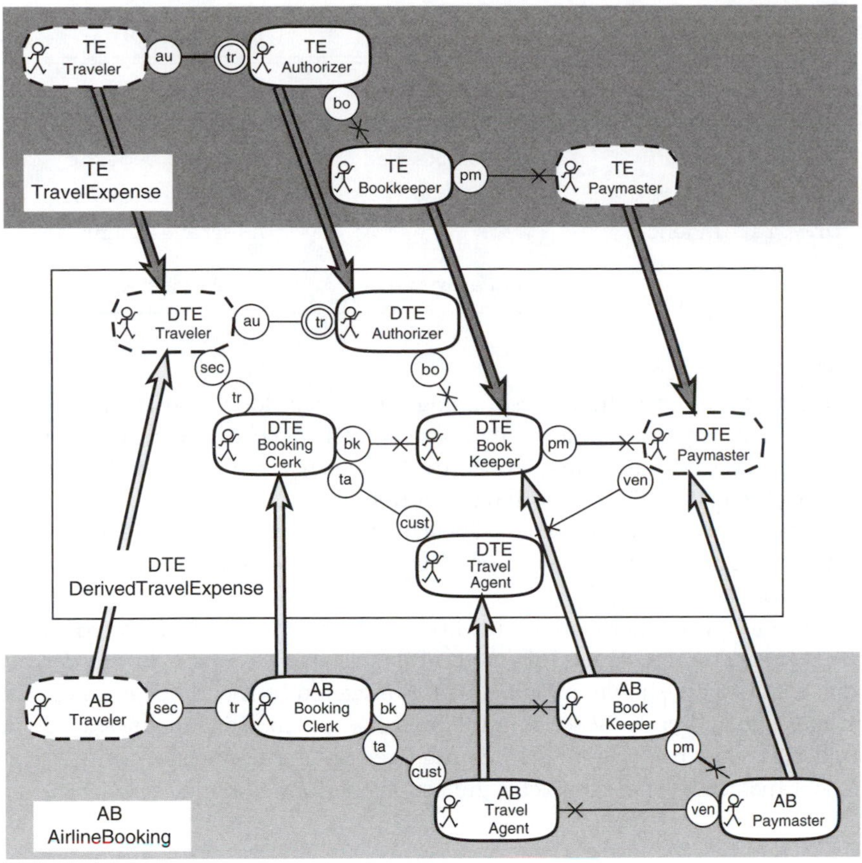

Figure 3.11

DTE synthesis
collaboration
diagram

The basic principle of OOram role modeling is that we consider an object in the context of its collaborators; we describe both the sender and the receiver of every message. The derived model must, therefore, at least have one role corresponding to each of the roles of its base models.

The synthesis relation specifies that the derived role should *play* the base role. The derived role should fulfill the base role responsibilities and is granted its privileges: the DTE-Traveler plays the role of the TE-Traveler, the DTE-Authorizer plays the role of the TE-Authorizer, etc.

We similarly bind each role of the AB model onto a role in the DTE model. We must add the DTE-BookingClerk and the DTE-TravelAgent to match the corresponding roles in the AB model, but we can reuse existing DTE roles to match the remaining AirlineBooking roles. The DTE-Traveler, DTE-Bookkeeper, and DTE-Paymaster now play two roles, and must conform to both specifications.

Even in this very simple example, the graphical synthesis collaboration view is cluttered and hard to read. The compact tabular presentation view of Figure 3.12 is usually better for professional system documentation.

The table has one row for each role in the derived model. The first column contains the names of the derived roles. There is an additional column for each

*Tabular
synthesis
notation more
useful*

Figure 3.12

DTE Synthesis
Table

Derived model DTE	Base model **TE**	Base model **AB**
DTE-Traveler	TE-Traveler	AB-Traveler
DTE-Authorizer	TE-Authorizer	
DTE-Bookkeeper	TE-Bookkeeper	AB-Bookkeeper
DTE-BookingClerk		AB-BookingClerk
DTE-TravelAgent		AB-TravelAgent
DTE-Paymaster	TE-Paymaster	AB-Paymaster

base model that shows the corresponding base role. Model consistency is preserved by mapping each role of the base models onto a role in the derived model. The derived model may contain roles which are not mapped from any base model role; this is not shown in the current example.

*Airline-
Booking
activity spliced
into Expense-
Account action*

A scenario view of the derived model activity is shown in Figure 3.13. It shows how the `AirlineBooking` activity from Figure 3.5 is merged into the `TravelExpense` activity of Figure 2.15.

The key to this merger is in the method of Figure 2.16 that is triggered by the `travelPermission` message. This method is split into two parts in the derived model: the first part, shown in Figure 3.14, is triggered by the old `travelPermission` message and ends by sending the `AirlineBooking` stimulus message. The second part, shown in Figure 3.15, is triggered by the termination of the `AirlineBooking` activity and completes the actions performed by the `Traveler`.

Figure 3.13

DTE scenario

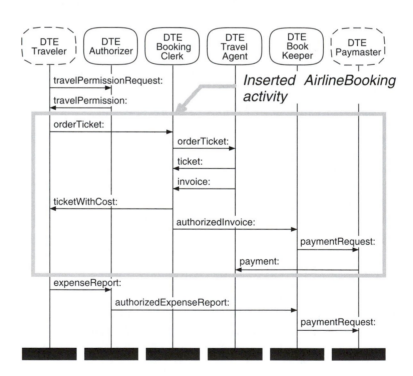

76   ROLE MODEL SYNTHESIS

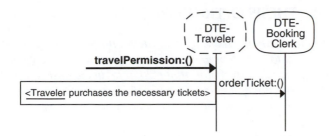

Figure 3.14
First part of `Traveler` method

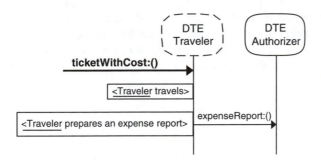

Figure 3.15
Second part of `Traveler` method

3.2 THE SYNTHESIS OPERATION

We always seem to extend the scope of our systems, and even object models are frequently too complex to be comprehended by our limited brain capacity. The OO-ram technology provides abstractions that help us to divide and conquer, enabling us to handle complex phenomena in a controlled manner. We analyze different parts of a phenomenon to create simple role models, and understand each of these models separately.

Complex models are constructed from simpler ones in a controlled and consistent manner. This construction, called synthesis, *permits us to reuse proven models in a variety of contexts. The advantages of reuse are threefold. First, reuse reduces development cost and lead time. Second, the reuse of tested models in a controlled environment increases total quality. Third, critical phenomena can be protected by mandatory access through validated models; thus ensuring system integrity. The main disadvantage is probably the danger of blindly building on old models, thereby loosing the fresh outlook and creativity needed to discover new insights.*

We may create solution islands

As we have stressed earlier, our first approach to a new problem is to focus on its essential aspects, and to postpone all the trivial parts to later stages in the development. The principle of minimizing risk (Section 4.3) suggests that we start with the parts we expect will be the hardest to get right, and continue with other parts as the harder ones get resolved. We might begin by sketching out the work flow in the organization, creating a high level model of the information requirements, making a small user interface prototype, or studying high level state machine models showing essential states and transitions in critical processes.

We think in a number of distinct models, each having its own unique area of concern and representing a part of the whole.

Many authorities recommend an orderly progression from the abstract to the concrete: create the first models on a high level of abstraction and then fill in details as work progresses. We find that this excellent advice is not always easy to follow, because we often have to start with some low level problem due to its high risk.

Whatever our work process, we will end up with many different models describing different aspects of the problem and its solution. There will be overview models on a high level of abstraction, and low level models showing the details of bounded parts of the problem. We do not want to extend an overview model with more and more details until it becomes a huge model containing everything; we want to retain the overview model and to supplant it with auxiliary descriptions of the various details.

We need seamless model inter-dependencies

Each of our models shows a different aspect of the same overall phenomenon; i.e., they are strongly linked to this common phenomenon. The models are not orthogonal, but are highly dependent because the same objects often appear in several of them. We support the ideas of traceability and seamless descriptions, so that whenever we observe some information in one model, we will be able to link it to any other description of the same thing—whether in a different model on the same level of abstraction, or in another model on a different abstraction level.

Subclassing is used for concept building and for code sharing

Inheritance is used in object-oriented programming for two different purposes: concept building and code sharing.

When concept building, we subclass a given superclass because the concept represented by the subclass is a specialization of the concept represented by the superclass. Instances of the subclass will have all the attributes of the superclass, and will understand all the messages understood by the superclass, in addition to possibly having attributes and messages defined in the subclass.

In Objectworks/Smalltalk for example, the class `VisualComponent` defines objects which can be made visible on the computer screen. The `VisualComponent` subclass `TextLines` represent lines of stylized text; instances of `TextLines` understand all the `VisualComponent` messages, in addition to messages which manage their text attributes.

When code sharing, we subclass a given superclass quite simply because it contains useful code. The messages defined in the superclass need not all be meaningful in the context of the subclass. For example, the Objectworks/Smalltalk class `Collection` defines a message (`at: index`) which gives indexed access to its contents. The class `Set` is a subclass of `Collection`. An instance of class `Set` contains an unordered collection of unique elements. Indexed access to sets is meaningless and therefore prohibited. Most of the `Collection` code is useful in `Set`, and the decision to make `Set` subclass of `Collection` was one of expedience rather than a consideration of abstract concepts. We regard code sharing as a useful and legitimate use of class inheritance in programming, as long as we make it quite clear what we are doing.

We could similarly synthesize an OOram base model into a derived model because the base model contained useful constructs. But the purpose of OOram models is to enhance our understanding of a phenomenon, and we insist that synthesis be used for the synthesis of concepts.

Synthesis only used for concept building

An object model is a *simulation* of the phenomenon it represents; its objects *enact* the phenomenon. It is common sense that if we want to isolate certain aspects of the phenomenon, we correspondingly must isolate the relevant aspects of the objects which enact them, and we must describe their *roles* in the context of the studied aspects.

Role modeling and synthesis apply common sense to objects

It is also common sense that if we want a structure of objects to simulate several phenomena simultaneously, we must let its objects play the roles which describe these phenomena.

Analysis and synthesis are the two operations which enable us to zoom in and out in our study of the complex world around us.

Separation of concern and multiple role playing by synthesis make it possible to describe systems of any size using OOram role models.

OOram models describe systems of any size

Consider an extremely complex system having an enormous number of objects, such as the total system of an enterprise integrated with the systems of all its suppliers and customers. We can still isolate any phenomenon and study it as a role model, and we can still describe any composite phenomenon by creating a role model synthesized from the models of its parts.

We might be tempted to consider all our interdependent models as being parts of a single, global model. We could create this global model by starting with any model and recursively adding all models that are related to it. The global model would in many ways resemble the global conceptual schema used in database technology, and the individual models would be similar to the external schemas.

No global model needed

We do not believe that the idea of a global model is a fruitful one. We believe that everything in the real world somehow depends on everything else, so that a truly global model would be very large indeed, and impossible to create or manage. Our definition of a *system* in Section 2.2. reflected this: a system is something we choose to consider as a whole during some period of observation, and it has an environment which links it with the rest of the world, without including the rest of the world in itself. Remember that we could not include all environment objects in our system, without modeling the whole universe.

Finding the models

We will end this introduction to synthesis with the $64,000 question: How do we find the models; i.e., how do we determine that we should factor out a base model or merge several models into a larger one?

There are no hard and fast rules, but we will endeavor to give a few loosely formulated guidelines. Behind these guidelines is the fortunate fact that this is an area where the good systems analyst can demonstrate his or her excellence.

It is commonly believed that our short term memory can manage 7 ± 2 notions at the same time. So we suggest the guideline that a role model should consist of 7 ± 2 roles. We should search for subphenomena to be factored out from models that are substantially larger than this. We should also search for common base models that can be synthesized into several derived models, or several times into the same model.

Conversely, we should consider merging models which contain fewer than 5 roles. Models that are used several times are exceptions to this rule—such as the client-server models which contain just two roles in their basic form but which may be synthesized into many different derived models.

Many different model relationships

A model may depend on other models in many different ways. Generalization-specialization is an important model relationship: one model describes a general phenomenon, while other models describe its specializations. A general model could, for example, describe how we make important decisions in our organization. Two different specializations of this model could describe how we create a budget or how we establish a major project. (The creation of different kinds of reusable components will be discussed in Chapter 5.)

Another important model relationship is aggregation: what is described as a single role on one level of abstraction is expanded on the next level of detailing into a model having several roles.

A third, very interesting model relationship is the object-subject relationship: the universe of discourse (object attributes and message parameters) in a role model may be specified as the roles of another role model.

DEFINITION

> **OOram synthesis**
>
> The Webster dictionary defines synthesis in the following way: *"synthesis 1a: the composition or combination of parts or elements so as to form a whole...c: the combination of often diverse conceptions into a coherent whole."*
> [Webster 77]

We represent model relationships using the very general notion of role model synthesis, whereby we specify that individual objects should play several roles, possibly from different role models.

We say that the base model is synthesized into the derived model. This is achieved by synthesizing every base role in the base model into a corresponding derived role in the derived model.

The concept of synthesis is as important to OOram role modeling as the concept of inheritance is to object-oriented programming. In both cases, we specify that some objects should, in some sense, be similar to other objects. The main difference is that while object-oriented programming focuses on the relationship be-

ROLE MODEL SYNTHESIS

tween individual classes of objects, OOram synthesis focuses on the relationships between complete patterns of objects.

The idea of objects playing multiple roles has a clear parallel in the theory of organizations: a person typically plays multiple roles, such as a subordinate in a department, a member of a project, and a traveler.

Consider the file transfer protocol example of Figure 2.17. The figure describes two models: a Client-Server model and a Source-Destination model. *Objects play multiple roles*

We are now in the position to design three different systems by using these two models as base models and synthesizing them into three different derived models. Figure 3.16 shows a system in which the Client can send files to the Server; Figure 3.17 shows a system in which the Client can retrieve files from the Server; and Figure 3.18 shows a system in which the Client can send files to and retrieve files from the Server.

A base model may be repeatedly synthesized into a derived model. Figure 3.19 shows a role model for a tree structure. The base model (a) describes a minimal tree consisting of a Mother role and a Child role. A Child has one and only one Mother, while a Mother can have any number of Child objects, even none. *Base models may be applied repeatedly*

The Mother may ask her Child to execute a block of code recursively, either executing the code before traversing the subtree (preorderTraverse) or after (postorderTraverse). The Mother may also ask her Child for all tree leaves (getLeaves). The Child may ask its Mother for the root of the tree; in this case, it is the Mother herself.

Figure 3.19 (b) shows a three-level tree having roles Root, Node, and Leaf. This is a derived role model; it is created by synthesizing the basic tree model twice. First, the Root and Node roles are specified to play the Mother and Child roles, respectively. Second, the Node and Leaf roles are specified to play the Mother and Child roles. A Root object will now play the Mother role; a Node object will play both the Child and the Mother roles; and a Leaf object will play the Child role.

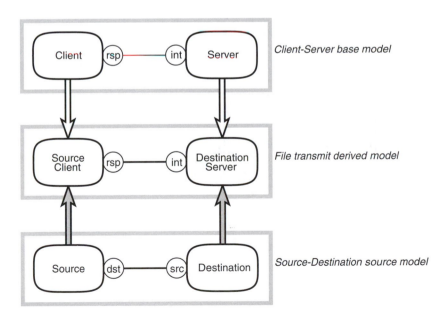

Client-Server base model

File transmit derived model

Source-Destination source model

Figure 3.16

A system in which the **Client** can send files to the **Server**

Figure 3.17
A system in which the `Client` can retrieve files from the `Server`

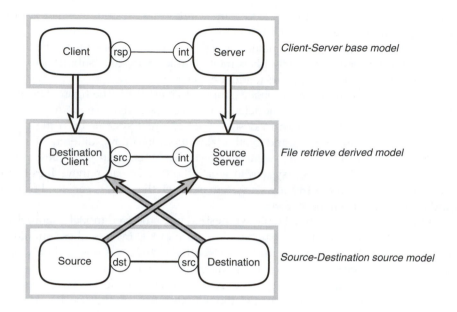

Client-Server base model

File retrieve derived model

Source-Destination source model

Figure 3.18
A system in which the `Client` can send and retrieve files

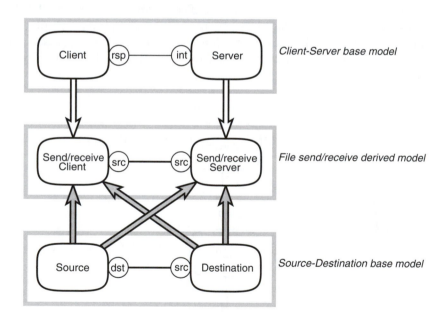

Client-Server base model

File send/receive derived model

Source-Destination base model

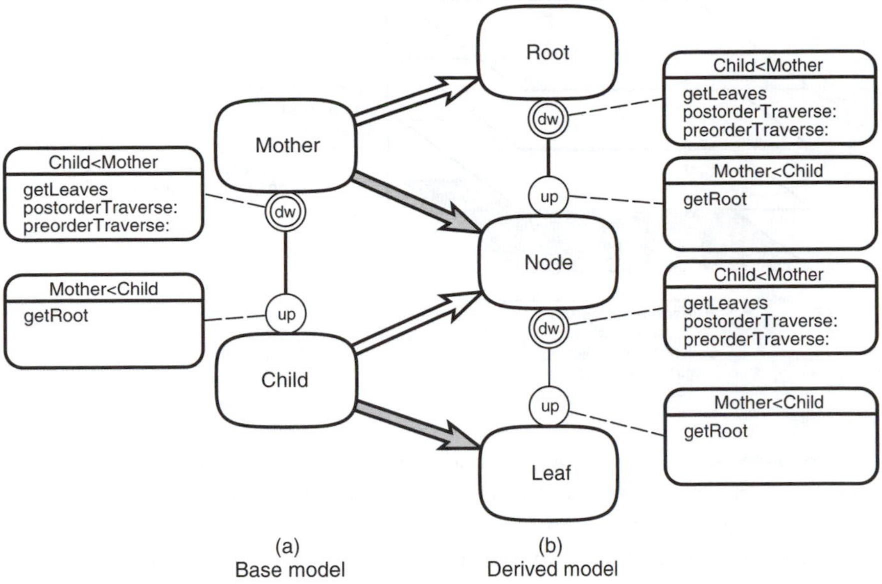

Figure 3.19
Creation of a
composite tree

(a)
Base model

(b)
Derived model

We see that the interfaces of the derived model are simply inherited from the base model, and it is not necessary to repeat the specification in the derived model. Further, if the base model had been implemented as the classes Mother1 and Child1, the implementation of the derived model could exploit this by deriving its classes from the base classes.

Synthesis is an operation on role models, not on single roles. The argument is that if we extend the services offered by one object, we must also extend some other object, to make it utilize the new functionality. We do not know the exact nature of these objects; but we do know that they will play the appropriate roles. So when we specify that Root plays the role of Mother, we immediately ask: "Who plays the corresponding role of Child?" Figure 3.19 shows two synthesis operations, not four.

Synthesis applies to whole role models

The notation for synthesis is a set of bordered arrows connecting base roles to corresponding derived roles. The first synthesis operation is marked by white arrows in Figure 3.19, and the second is marked by colored arrows.

The ideas of role model analysis and role model synthesis give us two independent dimensions in the description of systems of interacting objects, which are illustrated abstractly in Figure 3.20:

Two-dimensional modeling

1 Integration within a role model is achieved through collaborator interaction.

2 Integration between role models is achieved by letting an object play several roles. An interdependency between two roles played by the same object is described in a *method*. The method is triggered when the object receives a message in the context of one role; it may send messages and thus trigger activities in the context of another role. The method could also change an attribute which is defined in the context of another role.

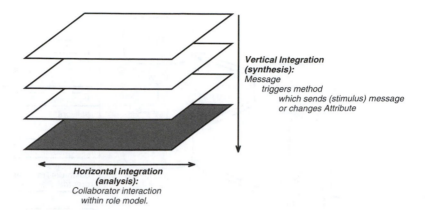

Figure 3.20
Two-dimensional
modeling

Vertical Integration
(synthesis):
Message
*   triggers method*
*   which sends (stimulus) message*
*   or changes Attribute*

Horizontal integration
(analysis):
Collaborator interaction
within role model.

We want to retain base model correctness in the derived model

The purpose of role model analysis is to understand a phenomenon and to specify its possible implementation. We spend considerable effort to persuade ourselves and others that a model is a faithful and correct representation of the phenomenon, and that the implementation will fill our needs and be without serious flaws.

Assuming that a base model is correct in all the aspects we care to consider, we would like this correctness to be retained in a model that is derived from it using synthesis so that we do not need to repeat the correctness considerations. We will distinguish between three kinds of correctness:

1　That the derived model conserves the static correctness of the base model.

2　That the derived model conserves the dynamic correctness of the base model.

3　That the derived model correctly reflects the semantics of the base model.

Static correctness can be retained automatically

It is fairly easy to create an OOram tool that conserves static correctness through a synthesis operation. Specifically:

1　All roles in a base model are mapped onto corresponding roles in the derived model.

2　The attributes of the base roles are retained as attributes of the corresponding derived roles.

3　All ports in a base model are mapped onto corresponding ports in the derived model. The cardinalities of the ports in the derived model must be consistent with the cardinalities of the corresponding ports in the base model: the minimum cardinality of a derived port must be equal to or greater than the minimum cardinality of the corresponding base port, and the maximum cardinality of a derived port must be equal to or less than the maximum cardinality of the corresponding base port.

4　All interfaces defining the messages that are permitted to be sent from a base port are retained as identical interfaces defining messages that are permitted to be sent from the corresponding derived port (except for possible renaming of messages).

Due diligence required to retain dynamic correctness

Dynamic correctness means that the base model message sequencing specifications are retained in the derived model. We have defined a method as the action taken by a role in response to a received message, and an activity as the sequence of actions taken by a structure of roles in response to a stimulus message. The dynamic correctness of a role model is closely linked to the dynamic correctness of its activities, and the preservation of dynamic correctness through a synthesis operation means the preservation of the integrity of the activities.

Figure 2.3 illustrates how a manifest model, in some way, is a representation of a mental model. We cannot automatically check that this representation is correct; the correspondence can be checked only through mental processes. For example, consider that we have a general `Tree` model with a `Root` role collaborating with any number of `Leaf` roles. Further, assume that we want to model a mother-child relationship, and decide to derive the `Mother-Child` model from the `Tree` base model. We can formally check that the `Mother-Child` model has the properties of the `Tree` model, but we cannot formally check that either model corresponds to our mental ideas of mothers and children.

Base model semantics shall be retained in all derived models

For all proper applications of the OOram synthesis operation, the analyst must make sure that the meaning of the derived model is consistent with the meanings of all its base models.

Static correctness guarantees that we send messages only through ports for which they are defined. But it does not prevent us from specifying a method, in the context of one of the object's roles, that sends an arbitrary message associated with another of its roles. We may, therefore, break into the middle of a base activity and play havoc with any argument about its dynamic correctness, causing the time sequences of messages observed in a derived model to violate the base model activity specifications. This may be acceptable. It could be that we want to specify a new activity in the derived model that merely uses some of the base model functionality. We call this unsafe synthesis, since we have to recheck the dynamic correctness of the derived model. The antonym is safe synthesis, synthesis where we can trust that the dynamic correctness of the base model is retained in the derived model.

Safe and unsafe synthesis

Else Nordhagen and Egil Andersen of the Department of Informatics at the University of Oslo are both exploring different formal foundations for role modeling. Parts of their work are concerned with describing the synthesis of dynamic behavior, which is a deep research topic. It would be premature to report their results here, so we refer the reader to their preliminary publications [E. Andersen 92, Nordhagen 89, Nordhagen 95].

Safe synthesis

The essence of safe synthesis is that the integrity of the base model activities must be retained in the derived models. An activity must be started by its stimulus message and then permitted to run its course, without interference, to its completion. The key to the success of safe synthesis is that it does not matter what other activities the objects perform before, during, or after a base model activity, as long as they do not interfere with it in any way.

Safe synthesis preserves integrity of base activity

Summing up, all base model roles are mapped onto derived model roles in the synthesis operation.

In safe synthesis, the integrities of the base model activities are retained in the derived model. This means that a base model activity can be triggered only by its stimulus message. The stimulus message can either become a stimulus message in the derived model, or it can be sent from one of the methods in the derived model.

Environment roles may become system roles in derived model

In the first kind of safe synthesis, an environment role of a base model is synthesized into an environment role of the derived model, and the stimulus messages of the base model becomes stimulus messages of the derived model.

In the second kind of safe synthesis, an environment role in the base model is synthesized into a system role in the derived model. A base model stimulus message is sent from a method in the derived model, and becomes part of its normal message flow.

We claim that these two synthesis constructs retain activity integrity, but stress that further research may reveal anomalous cases which render the constructs unsafe. The constructs have been formulated for synchronous message semantics, and further work is needed to identify safe constructs for parallel processes. We also believe that there are a number of other safe constructs, so do not take this list as being final:

1   *Activity superposition* is a kind of safe synthesis in which a base model stimulus messages is retained as a stimulus message in the derived model. The base model activity is retained unchanged as a derived model activity, independent of all other activities in the derived model.

2   *Activity aggregation* is a kind of safe synthesis in which a base model activity details a method in the derived model. It is very similar to a closed subroutine: the method sends the base model stimulus message, and the corresponding base model activity is permitted to run to completion without interference. The method continues after the base activity has terminated.

3.2.1   Aggregation: Linking Models on Different Levels of Abstraction

Aggregation is an important modeling idea

The principle of hierarchical decomposition is important in the study of complex systems. Indeed, some authors hold it to be a fundamental principle of nature itself [Booch 94]: A plant consists of three major structures (root, stems, and leaves), and each of these can be decomposed into its own substructure.

While we agree that hierarchical decomposition is important and useful, we cannot agree that it is a part of nature. The plant does not know about roots, stems, and leaves; these ideas are useful to the botanist and the schoolteacher, and have been so widely published so as to become an established truth.

The idea of hierarchical decomposition belongs to the world of models rather than to the real world. More specifically, we regard hierarchical decomposition to be one of the principles for organizing role models. Looking at it this way, we can get the benefits of hierarchical decomposition within the scope of some role models. We do not insist that the hierarchy be pervasive, it may not be visible if we study the object structure from some other perspective.

Let us return for a moment to Figure 2.3. Like any other model, a hierarchical model can neither be right nor wrong, just more or less useful for a given purpose. The distinction between a root and a stem is useful if I want to cook carrots for dinner. It would be useless if I wanted to study the flow of nutrients through a plant, and I would do better to select a more appropriate model highlighting a plant's vascular system.

Hierarchical decomposition and aggregation, often called the *consists of–part of* relationship, is an artifact of our thoughts: we choose to consider certain objects as being the parts of another object in the context of certain role models. This is illustrated conceptually in Figure 3.21a. (Aggregate objects are shown as gray, while other objects of the outer system are shown as white, and other part objects are shown as black.)

There are two criteria that should alert you to the possibility of factoring out subphenomena from a model on any level. One is when a model gets overly complex. We prefer a model to have somewhere between 5 and 9 roles; it will then fit nicely in our short term memory and on a computer screen. Another crite-

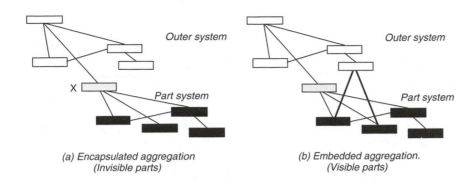

Figure 3.21

**Considering
certain objects to
be parts of
another object**

Outer system

Outer system

X

Part system

Part system

*(a) Encapsulated aggregation
(Invisible parts)*

*(b) Embedded aggregation.
(Visible parts)*

rion is that if the model displays repeated patterns of similar structures, these patterns should be described in separate models and removed from the main model.

Good choices of areas of concern, and thus of models, are usually found in an iterative process. If a model gets too complex, we split it up into smaller models. If we get too many very simple models, we combine them into larger ones.

We represent the idea of aggregation as a pair of role models: When considering the *outer system*, the aggregate is represented as a single role. When considering the *part system*, the aggregate is represented as a role model showing its parts. The single role in the outer system is found as the environment role of the part system.

The OOram technology supports three different kinds of aggregation: encapsulation, in which the parts are invisible from outside the aggregate role; embedding, in which some parts are visible; and virtual, in which the aggregate role is an artifact of thought not represented as an object in the object structure. All three kinds imply that different models have common objects, as we shall see in the following.

A role in the outer system may completely encapsulate the roles of the part system. The part roles then will be invisible in the external perspective of the outer system. This is called encapsulated aggregation. There is one shared object, as can be seen from the object model of Figure 3.21a and the corresponding role models of Figure 3.22a.

*Encapsulation
hides the parts
within a single
role*

We see that the object marked X plays two roles: it is a system role of the outer system and an environment role of the part system. We could use synthesis to create a derived model covering both, but this composite would be quite complex. We would create it only in the rare cases where it gives us important new insights. We usually prefer to keep the two models separate, using the safe synthesis construct *activity aggregation* to combine them in the implementation.

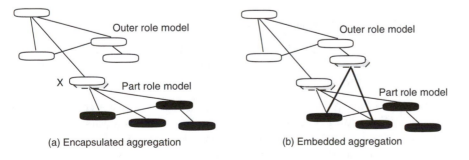

Figure 3.22

**Representing an
aggregate as a
structure of
collaborating
roles**

Outer role model

Outer role model

X

Part role model

Part role model

(a) Encapsulated aggregation

(b) Embedded aggregation

Figure 3.23

Virtual roles group a cluster of roles as a single aggregate

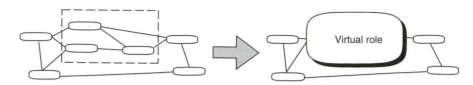

Some of the part roles may be visible to some of the roles of the outer system.
The objects corresponding to these outer roles then play environment roles in the
part system. Embedded aggregation is the name we give to this open kind of aggregation. The outer system can see several of the objects in the embedded system, as illustrated in the object model of Figure 3.21b and the corresponding role
models of Figure 3.22b.

The characteristic feature of embedded aggregation is that it is open. The outer
system has references to the objects of the embedded system so that they can interact with it. This is a potentially unsafe situation, and the derived model may
have to be created and analyzed for correctness.

In our illustration, we have assumed that each role maps onto a separate object. The separation of concern between role models permits mapping, however.
The roles of the outer role model and the roles of the part role model may be
mapped onto common objects in any way we please. The overall system will still
behave as specified, as long as we follow the rules of safe synthesis and preserve
activity independence.

A number of roles may be grouped and presented as if they were a single
role—without this single role representing an object in the object structure. This is
called *virtual aggregation*, and is illustrated in Figure 3.23.

Many words have been written and many pictures flashed on overhead projec-
tors to describe the notion of a *client-server* system architecture. Clients are typically personal computers or workstations running the user's software, while the
servers are background computers that are linked to the clients through communication channels and that manage shared data via their associated programs. We
recognize the client-server architecture as an essentially object-oriented architecture; role modeling is ideally suited for describing both the client and the server
parts, and encapsulated aggregation is the composition construct which will
safely combine the two and permit us to change focus between the client and the
server as needed.

There is still no consensus as to the best division of responsibility between the
client and the server. We see that *any* case of encapsulated aggregation can be
implemented in a client-server architecture. The positioning of the communication path within the overall system is an engineering decision. We will describe
our proposal in Section 7.3.

3.2.2   Attributes and Message Parameters

A role model describes how objects interact to achieve some purpose. The subject of their interaction is represented as message parameters and object attributes.

Message parameters may be grouped as follows:

1   *Nonobject values.* A parameter may represent something we consider to be
    outside our world of objects. It can be concrete, such as a paper form. Or it
    can be abstract, such as a value in a relational database. We also consider basic
    data types, such as *Integer* and *String*, to belong to this group.

Sidenotes (left margin, top to bottom):

Embedding makes parts visible to several roles in the outer system

Embedded aggregation

Any role-to-object mapping permissible

Virtual roles hide details

Client-server architecture

Attributes and parameters represent the subject of object interaction

2 *References within current role model.* A parameter may reference a role in the current role model. An example would be *Eve* in this message to Peter: *Your travel authorizer will be Eve.* The receiver will normally use the parameter to update the value of one of its ports. The interaction with these roles is described by the role model views discussed at length in Chapter 2.

3 *References within another role model.* A parameter may reference a role in another role model. This other role model then defines part of the universe of discourse for our current role model. The receiver will normally use the parameter to update the value of one of its attributes.

Role attributes can be defined in the same way. References to roles in the current role model are represented as *ports*, and other attributes are either nonobject values or role references to another role model.

The third group of parameters provides an interesting relation between role models: the objects of the parameter role model constitute (part of) the subject of interaction of the current role model.

An interesting relationship between role models

Messages carry the parameter values from one role to another, and it is only possible to send messages to a parameter role from one of the current roles. This current role must have a port referencing the parameter, or the parameter role must be encapsulated within the current role, as illustrated in Figure 3.24a.

The current role model may sooner or later want to send a message to trigger an activity in the parameter model. This message must be a stimulus message to keep the synthesis safe. Its sending role must, therefore, be an environment role in the parameter model.

It is important to realize that the objects of the current role model and the objects of the parameter role model all exist in the same world of interacting objects. The distinction between the role models is an artifact of our choice of role model abstractions and is a result of our separation of concern. The object marked X in Figure 3.24 plays two roles: one in the *current role model* and one in the *subject role model.* The two role models are integrated through the methods of object X which send stimulus messages to the subject role model. The role models are otherwise independent.

The *parameter* and *attribute* relationships link a model with its universe of discourse. We will use it in the case study in Chapter 7 to link a model of a human organization to a model of its information base, but the concept is recursive and can be applied on as many levels as you can manage.

Object-subject relationship very general

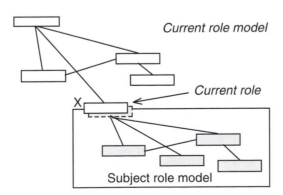

Current role model

Current role

Subject role model

X

Figure 3.24

Representing an attribute or a parameter as an encapsulated role model

Figure 3.25

Simple synthesis example

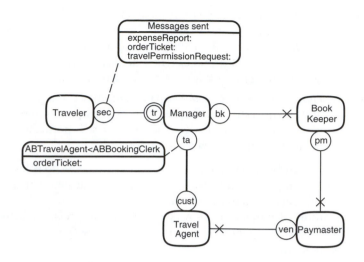

3.2.3 Safe and Unsafe Synthesis of the Travel Example Models

Let us illustrate safe and unsafe synthesis using an example. We will slightly modify the DerivedTravelExpense model so that the Authorizer and the Booking-Clerk are played by the same derived role, called the Manager. The role model and a few critical interfaces are illustrated in Figure 3.25.

There are two activities in this example: the TravelExpense activity describes the overall management of a business trip, and the AirlineBooking activity describes the booking and payment of airline tickets. These activities may be combined in different ways:

1   *Activity superposition* (Figure 3.26). The Traveler could order tickets independently of the authorization process, for example, because it would be too late to wait until the travel was authorized, or because there are many other situations where tickets need to be ordered. (The base models would have to be

Figure 3.26

Activity superposition illustration

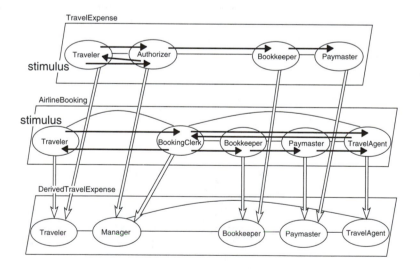

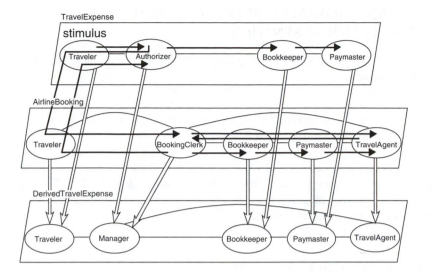

Figure 3.27

Activity aggregation illustration

extended to include travel cancellation capabilities to cater to the case when travel permission is refused.)

2 *Activity aggregation* (Figure 3.27). The synthesis described in the previous section was an example of activity aggregation: the AirlineBooking activity was started from an action in the TravelExpense activity.

3 *Unsafe synthesis* (Figure 3.28). The Manager in the role of Authorizer receives a travelPermissionRequest message. She could decide to grant the permission and also—to be extra helpful—don the hat of BookingClerk and order the required tickets. The AirlineBooking model assumed that the initiative was with the Traveler; therefore we have to reconsider the dynamic behavior of the derived model to protect ourselves against surprises.

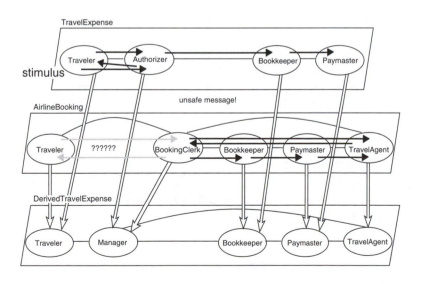

Figure 3.28

Unsafe synthesis illustration

3.3 BASIC OORAM CONCEPTS AND NOTATION FOR ROLE MODEL SYNTHESIS

Here, we will give a technical description of the synthesis operation as seen in each of the OOram views.

Synthesis affects all views and perspectives

We focus on Safe Synthesis

The OOram technology offers a large number of different views on the role models, as described in Section 2.5. All of the views are somehow affected by the synthesis operation, and we will discuss each of them in the following sections.

As discussed in Section 3.2, the static and semantic correctness of the base models can be carried over to the derived model automatically. We suggested two constructs that preserve the dynamic correctness of the base models. These two constructs, called *activity superposition* and *activity aggregation*, will be the focus of this Section.

3.3.1 The Inheritance and Role List Views

The purpose of the inheritance views is to show the base-model–derived model relationships between role models.

Three inheritance views

There are three views showing the inheritance (export–import) relationships between role models:

1 The *synthesis view* shows any number of role models and the inheritance relationships between them without giving any internal details.

2 The *inheritance collaboration view* shows two or more role models and the inheritance relationships between their roles.

3 The *inheritance table* gives the same information in tabular form.

4 The *OOram language inheritance specification* gives the same information in textual form.

Synthesis view

In a synthesis view, role models are shown as rectangles. *Base-model–derived model* relationships are shown as bordered arrows. Derived models are shown to the right of the corresponding base models, as illustrated in Figure 3.29. Figure 3.30 shows some of the the role models used in this section, together with their synthesis relationships.

Inheritance collaboration view

The notation for individual role models follows the notation given in Section 2.5. The *inheritance collaboration view* shows several, related role models. All base model roles are mapped to the corresponding derived model role by a bordered arrow, as illustrated in Figure 3.31.

Figure 3.29

Synthesis view notation

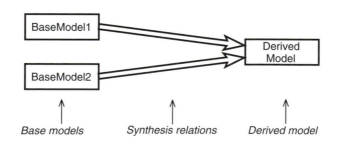

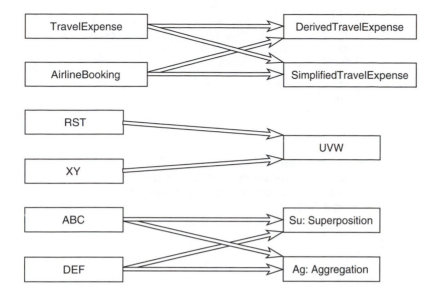

Figure 3.30

Synthesis view of example models used in this section

An inheritance table is shown in Table 3.1. It has one row for each role in the derived model. The first column shows the roles of the derived model, while the other columns show the corresponding roles in the base models. Note that all the roles of the base models must be accounted for in the derived model, but the reverse need not be true.

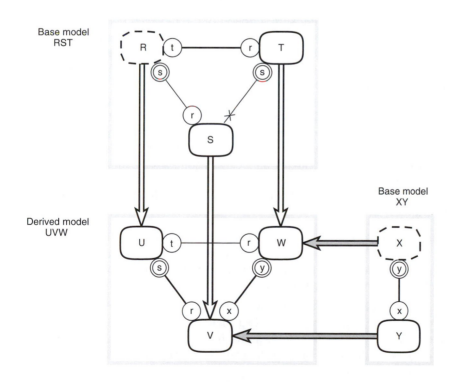

Figure 3.31

Sample Inheritance collaboration view

Table 3.1

Sample
Inheritance Table

	Derived model UVW	Base model RST	Base model XY
	Role U	R	
	Role V	S	Y
	Role W	T	X

Figure 3.32

Example OOram
language
inheritance
specification

role_model 'RST' **explanation** *"Example three-role base model."*
role_model 'XY' **explanation** *"Example two-role base model."*
role_model 'UVW' **explanation** *"Example 3-role derived model."*
base_model 'RST'
   'R' -> 'U'
   'S' -> 'V'
   'T' -> 'W'
base_model 'XY'
   'X' -> 'W'
   'Y' -> 'V'

The inheritance mapping can be specified as an OOram language inheritance specification as part of the definition of the derived role model. The full language is defined in Appendix A; an example of inheritance specification is shown in Figure 3.32.

3.3.2 Synthesis in the Area of Concern View

No automatic composition of area of concern

An area of concern is a free text description of the modeled phenomenon. Automatic synthesis of the derived area of concern is not possible (except for a simple concatenation of the constituent texts). It is the analyst's responsibility to specify the area of concern for the derived model and to ensure that it is semantically consistent with the areas of concern of the base models.

Manual composition of area of concern

The synthesis operation is very general, and may support many different relationships between the derived model and its base models, but the phenomena described by the base models will always, in some sense, be parts of the phenomenon described by the derived models. The area of concern of the derived model will, therefore, explicitly or implicitly encompass the areas of concern for the base models.

The synthesis of the areas of concern for our two safe synthesis constructs are as follows:

1 *Activity superposition.* The derived model's area of concern includes the area of concern of its base models. For example, we could have two different `TravelExpense` models for national and international travel. We could use synthesis to derive a model that covers both cases.

2 *Activity aggregation.* A base model elaborates an action (method) in the derived model. As an example, consider that our `AirlineBooking` model elaborates one of the `Traveler` role's actions in the `TravelExpense` model. The area of concern of the detail base model may be invisible in the area of concern of the derived model.

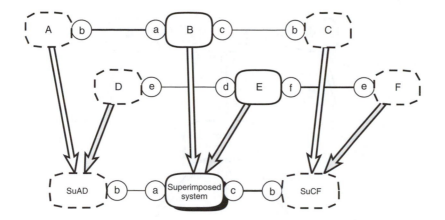

Figure 3.33

Superposition
environment
view

3.3.3 Synthesis in the Environment and Stimulus-Response Views

A stimulus message from an environment role in the base model may be handled in one or both of the following ways in the derived model:

Retain or explain base model stimuli

1 *Superposition*. A stimulus message in a base model may become a stimulus message in the derived model. The corresponding base environment role must then be mapped onto a derived environment role.

2 *Aggregation*. A stimulus message in a base model may be sent from one of the methods of the corresponding role in the derived model. The derived role can in this case be either a system role or an environment role; the base model environment role sending the stimulus message must have been mapped onto it.

Activity superposition is illustrated in Figure 3.33. The stimulus and response messages of the base models are retained as stimulus and response messages of the derived model. The base model environment roles have here been mapped onto common derived environment roles, but they could alternatively have been mapped onto different derived environment roles.

Activity aggregation is illustrated in Figure 3.34. The DEF model is hidden within the AggregationSystem, where its activity is part of a method in a derived role.

3.3.4 Synthesis in the Collaboration View

There are no formal relationships between the responsibilities of the roles of the derived model and the roles of the base models, but the analyst should ensure that they are consistent. The general restrictions on roles, ports, and cardinalities mentioned previously also hold for the collaboration views:

Formal collaboration view dependencies between synthesized models

1 All *roles* in the base models should be mapped onto roles in the derived model.

2 The *attributes* of the base model roles should be included in the attributes of the corresponding derived model roles.

3 The *collaborators* of the derived model roles should include the collaborators of the corresponding base model roles.

Figure 3.34
Aggregation
environment
view

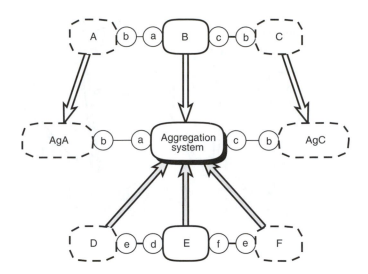

4   All *ports* in the base models should be mapped onto corresponding ports in the derived model. The cardinalities of the ports in the derived model must be consistent with the cardinalities of the corresponding ports in the base model. Specifically, the minimum cardinality of a port in the derived model must be equal to or greater than the minimum cardinality of the corresponding ports in the base models, and the maximum cardinality of a port in the derived model must be equal to or less than the maximum cardinality of the corresponding ports in the base models.

Notation   The graphical notation for the inheritance collaboration view is described in Figure 3.31. The inheritance table in Table 3.1 is used to describe the inheritance relationships in most practical work; the collaboration view of the derived model then looks just like any other collaboration view.

Figure 3.35 illustrates activity superposition in the collaboration view. The base model environment roles have been mapped onto common derived environment roles, but they could have been mapped onto different roles in the derived model.

Figure 3.35
Superposition
collaboration
view

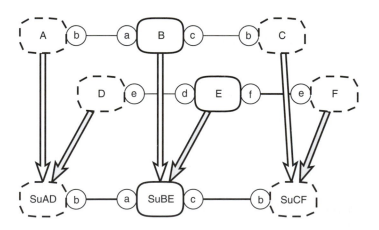

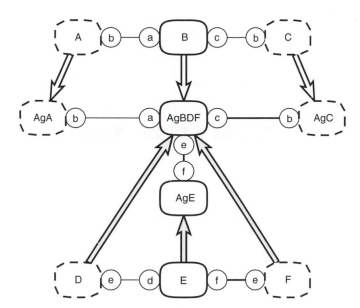

Figure 3.36

Aggregation
collaboration
view

The base model system roles have been mapped onto a common role in the derived model, but they could have been mapped onto different roles.

Figure 3.36 illustrates activity aggregation in the collaboration view. The derived model constitutes the base model environment: the derived system role Ag-BDF plays the environment roles D and F. It sends the stimulus message of the DEF model from one of its methods, and receives the response message from the DEF activity.

3.3.5   Synthesis in the Scenario View

We will illustrate the safe synthesis of scenarios by assuming the pair of extremely simple activities for the base models shown in Figures 3.37 and 3.38.

In activity superposition, the base model activities become derived model activities. The corresponding scenarios are simply carried unchanged into the derived model, as illustrated in Figure 3.39.

Scenario superposition

In activity aggregation, a base model stimulus message is sent from within a derived model method. We have illustrated this by sending the DEF stimulus message from the derived method for message ab1. The corresponding scenario is shown in Figure 3.40.

Scenario aggregation

Figure 3.37

ABC Scenario

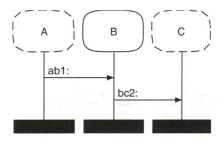

Figure 3.38
DEF Scenario

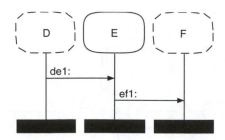

Figure 3.39
Scenario superposition

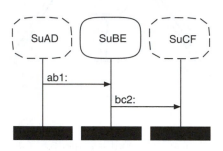

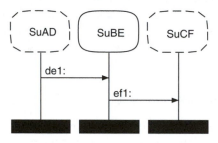

Figure 3.40
Scenario aggregation

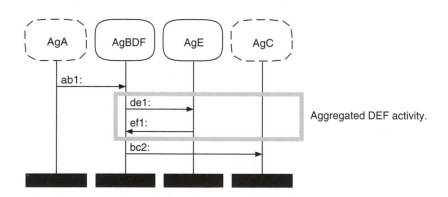

Aggregated DEF activity.

ROLE MODEL SYNTHESIS

The DEF stimulus message is sent from within the derived model method for message ab1: in role AgH. The DEF activity is thus completely embedded in this method.

3.3.6 Synthesis in the Interface View

The interfaces associated with a port in the derived model include all interfaces associated with the corresponding ports in the base models.

All base model interfaces included

Base model interfaces are immutable in the derived model: messages may neither be added nor removed. It is possible to rename the derived interfaces and messages; but this adds to the confusion and should be avoided if possible. (The exception is when there are name conflicts between base models which are synthesized into a common, derived model.)

Base model interfaces immutable

New messages can be added only to interfaces which are defined in the derived model.

Messages added only in new interfaces

It is usually not necessary to repeat the specification of the imported interfaces in the documentation of the derived model, but they may be included if this improves readability.

Imported interface documentation optional

3.3.7 Synthesis in the Method Specification View

When a base role is synthesized into a derived role, all its collaborators and the corresponding message interfaces are synthesized correspondingly. The derived role has to provide a method for every message understood by the base role. The default is to retain the base role methods; the behavior of the derived model will then correspond to the behavior of the base model.

Default: Base method becomes derived method

The derived role may redefine one or more methods, causing the derived model to behave differently from the base model. In principle, the derived method can do anything. For example, it can send any message on any port regardless of where that message was originally defined. This leads to unsafe synthesis, where our understanding of the base model behavior does not help us understand the behavior of the derived model.

Unsafe method override possible

The *activity superposition* safe synthesis construct is illustrated in Figure 3.26. The stimulus messages of the base models become stimulus messages of the derived model, and the activities of the base models become activities of the derived model. No method override is required in the derived model, but certain kinds of overrides are permissible and may be desirable.

Activity superposition

The detailed method logic may be influenced by the combination of roles played by the object. The procedure followed by a travel Authorizer who is a department head could, for example, be different from the procedure followed by a travel Authorizer who is a project manager.

The detailed behavior often depends on the value of an attribute belonging to another role played by the same object. The Traveler stores the cost of the airline ticket as part of the AirlineBooking role model. When filling in the expense account, the Traveler adds this amount as an expense and deducts it as an advance.

The activity aggregation safe synthesis construct is illustrated in Figure 3.27. The activity of the second base model should be part of a method in the first model. This method must be modified in the derived role to send the required stimulus message and to wait for its completion. In addition, the overrides permissible in the superposition construct are also permissible here.

Activity aggregation

CHAPTER 4   ✧   ✧   ✧   ✧   ✧

Bridge to Implementation

CONTENTS

4.1   Introduction to Implementation   102

    4.1.1   Object Modeling from a Programmer's Point of View   104
    4.1.2   A Simple Class Inheritance Example   108
    4.1.3   Why We Need High Level Descriptions   112

4.2   The Relationship between a Role Model and its Implementation   116

    4.2.1   Implementing the Roles   116
    4.2.2   Implementing the Ports and Interfaces   121
    4.2.3   Implementing the Methods and Actions   123

4.3   The Implementation Process   124

4.4   Choice of Programming Language   129

This chapter has been written for computer programmers. It tells you how to create an implementation having the functionality specified in one or more role models.

Implementations may be created by different technologies: Business processes may, for example, be manual or computer assisted, and computer programs may be specified in a variety of different programming languages. The OOram method is basically independent of the implementation technology, but the shrewd analyst will let the intended implementation technology color the details of the analysis.

We will not attempt to cover all possible implementation technologies here, but will focus on computer implementation in an object-oriented programming language. The presentation covers implementation in Smalltalk and C++. The OOram method has also been used successfully to specify programs written in other languages, such as C and Eiffel, and also to specify manual business processes in large organizations.

4.1 INTRODUCTION TO IMPLEMENTATION

IN A NUTSHELL

We have stressed the value of the divide and conquer strategy. Objects play many roles, and our descriptions are materially simplified when we focus on one function at a time. We now consider the stage where we have created the role models and want to combine them in an implementation. This is also the time for filling in the details. In the role models, we reason about overall functionality. We are now allowed to focus on one class at the time and to get its details right.

The implementation stage is the acid test for our separation of concern: successful role models interact only at a few easily controlled points. There is something suspicious with our role models if we need to reconsider the whole when we implement the details.

Transition between design and implementation

The art of computer programming is outside the scope of this book. Our interest focuses on the transition between the abstract design descriptions and the implementation, with special emphasis on how one can maintain consistency between the different levels of description, as illustrated in Figure 4.1.

Simple solutions to simple problems

A simple problem often can be solved using simple means. If we want to build a birdhouse, we take a few pieces of wood and nail them together. If we need to count how many times different characters occur in a text file, we write a simple program to do the counting.

Complex problems may have equally simple solutions. A builder can create temporary living quarters for his crew by stacking a number of prefabricated huts. A UNIX expert can specify very powerful functionality by linking a number of existing programs through a shellscript. Programmers routinely invoke proven library functions to reduce the apparent complexity and improve the quality of their programs.

Figure 4.1

Typical models on different levels of abstraction

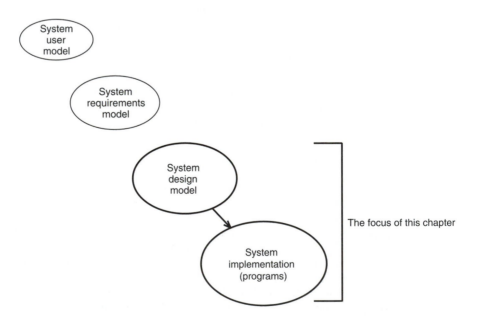

BRIDGE TO IMPLEMENTATION

The top-down approach for hierarchical decomposition was introduced by Wirth [Wirth 71] and has since been advocated by many methodologists. (Aggregation and hierarchical decomposition were discussed in Section 3.2.1). Hierarchical decomposition has had a long history of success, because hierarchical models are easy to understand and help one to partition large problems into smaller ones.

Hierarchical decomposition for simple solutions to complex problems

The main difficulty with hierarchical decomposition is that there are many problems that are not amenable to it. On the human level, we have studied an object pattern that describes the handling of travel expense accounts. Other models would be needed to describe the myriad of other functions in an enterprise. A few examples are design, production, budgeting, accounting, and materials management.

Horizontal decomposition splits complex problem into several simpler ones

All of these models belong on the same level, so they cannot be organized into a hierarchy. However, each model can be described as a role model, and they can be implemented together as a structure of objects in which each object plays a number of roles. In principle, we can create a derived model combining all the functions. In practice, we rarely do so at the level of these examples. The reason is that we define the functions to be reasonably independent, so that the derived model does not provide new insights.

The OOram program design philosophy follows similar lines. We create different role models for important aspects of the problem. The program objects play multiple roles from these models, and we fill in role model dependencies and other details in the program implementation.

One program— many models

All real development work is iterative, so we also need a smooth reverse transition from the implementation to the role models, because we want to maintain consistency between the two.

We will illustrate horizontal decomposition using a simple example. Consider that we want to write a simple text editor which permits the user to open several windows simultaneously on the same text. We need to create a number of (nearly) independent models:

1   The `TextEditor` model describes how we represent text and how we edit it.

2   The `Model-View-Controller` describes how we manage the representation of information (*model*), the presentation of information (*view*), and user input (*controller*). The details appear in Chapter 11.

3   A `Transaction manager` lumps a number of operations into a single, indivisible transaction.

4   A `Persistent object store` ensures that the textual information is maintained between program executions.

The objects of the `TextEditor` program are described in part by the `TextEditor` role model, which describes the text aspects of the program; in part by the `Model-View-Controller` (MVC) role model, which describes the synchronization between text objects and one or more editors; in part by the `TransactionManagement` role model which describes how complex functions are encapsulated into atomic operations; and in part by the `PersistentObjects` role model, which describes how objects are made permanent so that they survive individual program executions.

An interesting observation is that while the `TextEditor` role model is specific to the current problem, the other three models are general in scope, and could be found in a library of reusable components.

Figure 4.2

OORam models
describing
different aspects
of the same
program

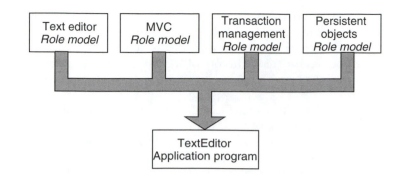

Figure 4.2 illustrates how we merge the role model functionalities in the implementation. It is neither necessary nor useful to create the derived model if the four base models are almost independent, which could easily be achieved in this example.

Bridge from role model to implementation

In the remainder of this chapter, we will discuss how to create a program that satisfies the specifications in one or more role models. But first we will say a few words about object-oriented programming and the reasons for creating higher level models.

4.1.1 Object Modeling from a Programmer's Point of View

Brad Cox has suggested an explanation of object orientation in terms of the implementation [Cox 87]. According to Cox, there is a small, but significant, difference between the way data are stored in a procedure-oriented program and the way they are stored in an object-oriented program.

Client must know the types of its data

In procedure orientation (Figure 4.3), the `Client` must carefully match operations and data. The programmer can do this by *importing* the type definitions into his or her program.

Data know their types

In object orientation (Figure 4.4), each data storage area is augmented with a pointer to the data type. Different data can therefore react differently to the same operation, according to the information stored in the data type.

Figure 4.3

Procedure
orientation,
according to Cox

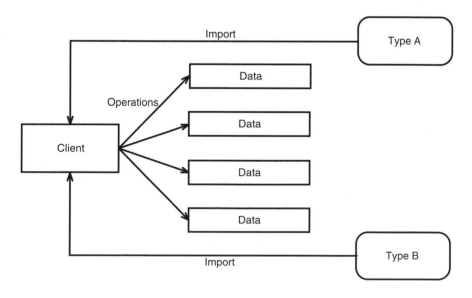

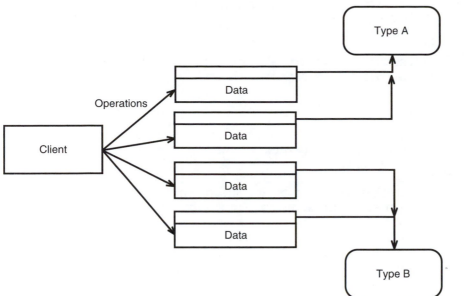

Figure 4.4

Object orientation according to Cox

As an example, we will show how to write a program to draw the simple house facade shown in Figure 4.5. We will outline programs in the procedure-oriented language FORTRAN and in the object-oriented languages C++ and Smalltalk. If your expertise is in some other language, you may benefit from the advice that we were given at a seminar by Gerald Weinberg: we were finding it hard to read programs in an unfamiliar language because we unconsciously were focusing on the parts we did not understand. Weinberg's advice was that we consciously should ignore the unfamiliar parts and focus on the parts we understood. This made the going much easier.

The following is an outline of the FORTRAN program:

Procedure-oriented program for drawing a house facade

```
C      NOTICE THAT THE CLIENT, I.E., THE CALLING
C      PROGRAM, HAS TO KNOW THE TYPES OF THE DATA
C      ITEMS AND SELECT THE APPROPRIATE SUBROUTINE.
       SUBROUTINE DRAWWALL(IXMIN,IXMAX,IYMIN,IYMAX)
```

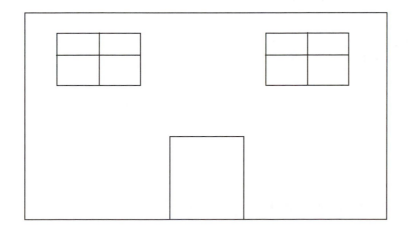

Figure 4.5

A simple house facade

```
C     STATEMENTS FOR DRAWING A BLANK WALL
C     CODE OMITTED
      END
C
      SUBROUTINE DRAWWINDOW (IXMIN,IXMAX,IYMIN,IYMAX)
C     STATEMENTS FOR DRAWING A WINDOW
C     CODE OMITTED
      END
C
      SUBROUTINE DRAWDOOR (IXMIN,IXMAX,IYMIN,IYMAX)
C     STATEMENTS FOR DRAWING A DOOR
C     CODE OMITTED
      END
C     DECLARE ARRAYS KIND, X0, XM, Y0, YM,
C     AND FILL THEM WITH DATA. CODE OMITTED
      DO 1000, I=1, MAX
      IF (KIND(I).EQ.1) CALL DRAWWALL(X0(I),XM(I),Y0(I),YM(I))
      IF (KIND(I).EQ.2) CALL DRAWWINDOW(X0(I),XM(I),Y0(I),YM(I))
      IF (KIND(I).EQ.3) CALL DRAWDOOR(X0(I),XM(I),Y0(I),YM(I))
 1000 CONTINUE
```

A C++ program for drawing the facade is given below. The knowledge about how to draw a particular element has been delegated to the element itself. This polymorphism simplifies program extension and facilitates reuse.

```cpp
class Figure {
public:
  virtual ~Figure() {};
  virtual void draw() const = 0;
protected:
  Figure(const Point& topLeft, const Point& bottomRight);
private:
  Figure(const Figure&);          // Avoid copy
  Figure& operator=(const Figure&); // Avoid assignment
  Point topLeftPoint;
  Point bottomRightPoint;
};
Figure::Figure(const Point& topLeft, const Point& bottomRight) :
  topLeftPoint(topLeft),
  bottomRightPoint(bottomRight)
{}
class Wall : public Figure {
public:
  Wall(const Point& topLeft, const Point& bottomRight);
  virtual void draw() const;
};
Wall::Wall(const Point& topLeft, const Point& bottomRight) :
  Figure(topLeft, bottomRight)
{}
void Wall::draw() const
{
  // code omitted
}
class Window : public Figure {
```

```
public:
  Window(const Point& topLeft, const Point& bottomRight);
  virtual void draw() const;
};
Window::Window(const Point& topLeft, const Point& bottomRight) :
  Figure(topLeft, bottomRight)
{}
void Window::draw() const
{
  // code omitted
}
class Door : public Figure {
public:
  Door(const Point& topLeft, const Point& bottomRight);
  virtual void draw() const;
};
Door::Door(const Point& topLeft, const Point& bottomRight) :
  Figure(topLeft, bottomRight)
{}
void Door::draw() const
{
  // code omitted
}
class Facade {
public:
  Facade() {}
  void draw();
  void add(Figure* f);
private:
  List<Figure*> list;
};
void Facade::add(Figure* f)
{ list.append(f); }
void Facade::draw()
{
    for(ListIter<Figure*> it(list); it.isMore(); it.next())
    it.item()->draw();
}
```

A Smalltalk program for drawing the facade is shown below. The syntax is different, but the logic is roughly the same as in the C++ example.

```
Object subclass: #Figure
    instanceVariableNames: 'topLeftPoint lowerRightPoint '.
Figure methodsFor: displaying
draw
    self subclassResponsibility.
Figure subclass: #Window
    instanceVariableNames: ''.
Window methodsFor: displaying
draw
    " Define method for drawing a window. "

    ⋮

Figure subclass: #Door
    instanceVariableNames: ''.
```

Door methodsFor: displaying
draw
 " *Define method for drawing a door.* "
⋮

Figure subclass: #Wall
 instanceVariableNames: ''

Wall methodsFor: displaying
draw
 " *Define method for drawing a wall.* "
⋮

Figure class methodsFor: testing
drawFacade
 | elements |
 elements := OrderedCollection new.
 " *Add elements and set their attributes.* "
⋮

 elements do: [:elem | elem draw].
 " *Evaluate the statement* **Figure drawFacade** *to test the program.* "

4.1.2 A Simple Class Inheritance Example

Classes, base classes, and derived classes

In most object-oriented programming languages, all objects sharing the same implementation are said to belong to a common *class*, and the class defines the program controlling these objects. A class can create new objects; this is called *instantiating* the class. All objects created by a given class are called *instances* of that class.

The object specification defines the attributes, while the class defines the *instance variables* as the designer's choice of internal representation. Some instance variables contain pointers to the object's collaborators; other instance variables represent its attributes. The class also defines a *method* for each message that the object must understand. The method is the code describing the actions to be taken by the object when it receives the corresponding message.

A class may be defined as being similar to another class with given modifications and extensions. This is called *programming by difference*, and the class is said to be *derived* from its *base class* or to be a *subclass* of its *superclass*. The *derived class* will inherit all instance variables and methods from the *base class*. In addition, it may:

1 Add instance variables to the object.
2 Add new methods making the object understand additional messages.
3 Override methods in the base class so that the object's behavior is modified for the corresponding messages.

Example: Modeling a Point

As an example, we will define a class for objects representing points in a two-dimensional coordinate system. The point object should know its coordinates in both the Cartesian and the polar coordinate systems, so we will give it four attributes: X, Y, radius r, and angle t (for *theta*). We define messages to set and read these attributes:

1 SetXY. Set the point's coordinates to the given X and Y values.

2 SetRT. Set the point's radius and angle to the given values.

3 GetX, GetY, GetR, GetT. Four messages that return the current values of the point's attributes.

We can also define operations on points. For example, the function vectorAdd returns a new Point, which is calculated as the vector sum of the receiving object and the point given as a parameter.

We now have to define instance variables to hold the attribute information. Should we store the Cartesian coordinates, the polar coordinates, or both? All three solutions are possible; the best choice will depend on how we expect the point objects to be used. We could store the full, redundant information if we frequently need all the attributes and rarely set their values; otherwise, we could store the information in its most frequently used form. The most interesting solution would be to define two classes, CartesianPoint and PolarPoint. Instances of these classes could be used interchangeably, and they could even be mixed. Objects referring to the point objects would see only a difference in performance.

We first define Point in C++ as an *abstract class*, which is a class that should not be instantiated:

The Point class

```
class Point {
public:
  virtual ~Point() {};

  virtual void   setXY(double, double) = 0;
  virtual double  getX() const = 0;
  virtual double  getY() const = 0;

  virtual void   setRadiusAndAngle(double, double) = 0;
  virtual double  getRadius() const = 0;
  virtual double  getAngle() const = 0;

  virtual Point&  vectorAdd(const Point& delta) = 0;

protected:
  Point() {};              // Abstract class

private:
  Point(const Point&);          // Avoid copy
  Point& operator=(const Point&); // Avoid assignment
};
```

We define the abstract class Point in Smalltalk:

```
Object subclass: #Point
     instanceVariableNames: ''

Point methodsFor: accessing
setX: x setY: y
     self subclassResponsibility
getX
     self subclassResponsibility
```

```
getY
        self subclassResponsibility
setR: rVal setAngle: angVal
        self subclassResponsibility
getR
        self subclassResponsibility
getT
        self subclassResponsibility
vectorAdd: aPoint
        ^self class new
                setX: self x + aPoint x
                setY: self y + aPoint y
```

The symbol ∧ in the Smalltalk `vectorAdd:` method causes it to return the value of the expression. The expression is read as follows: Create a new instance of the same class as the receiver. Send the message `setX:setY:` with parameters (the receiver's x attribute + the parameter point's X attribute) and (the receiver's y attribute + the parameter point's y attribute). Finally, return the value of the expression to the sender.

The Cartesian-Point class

We next define in C++ a subclass, `CartesianPoint`, to hold the Cartesian coordinates. The methods involving X and Y are simple, while the methods involving polar coordinates involve computations:

```
class CartesianPoint : public Point {
public:
  CartesianPoint(double x, double y);
  ~CartesianPoint() {}
  void   setXY(double nx, double ny);
  double getX() const { return x; }
  double getY() const { return y; }
  void   setRadiusAndAngle(double r, double a);
  double getRadius() const;
  double getAngle() const;
Point& vectorAdd(const Point& delta);
private:
  double x;
  double y;
};
CartesianPoint::CartesianPoint(double nx, double ny) :
  x(nx),
  y(ny)
{}
void CartesianPoint::setXY(double nx, double ny)
{
  x = nx;
  y = ny;
}
void CartesianPoint::setRadiusAndAngle(double r, double a)
{ setXY(r * cos(a), r * sin(a)); }
double CartesianPoint::getRadius() const
{ return hypot(x, y); }
double CartesianPoint::getAngle() const
{
  double t = atan2(y, x);
  if(t < 0.0) t = 2 * PI + t;
  return t;
```

```
}
Point& CartesianPoint::vectorAdd(const Point& delta)
{
  x += delta.getX();
  y += delta.getY();
  return *this;
}
```

The following code defines CartesianPoint in Smalltalk:

```
Point subclass: #CartesianPoint
    instanceVariableNames: 'x y '
Point methodsFor: accessing
setX: xFloat setY: yFloat
    x := xFloat.
    y := yFloat.
getX
    ^x
getY
    ^y
setR: rVal setAngle: angVal
    x := rVal * angVal cos.
    y := rVal * angVal sin.
getR
    ^((x * x) + (y * y)) sqrt.
getT
    ^(y / x) arcTan
```

We define the class `PolarPoint` in C++ in a similar way. All methods involving polar coordinates are now simple, while the methods involving Cartesian coordinates are more complex:

The PolarPoint class

```
class PolarPoint : public Point {
public:
  PolarPoint(double r, double a) ;
  void   setXY(double x, double y);
  double getX() const;
  double getY() const;
  void   setRadiusAndAngle(double r, double a) { radius = r; angle = a; }
  double getRadius() const { return radius; }
  double getAngle() const { return angle; }
  Point& vectorAdd(const Point& delta);
private:
  double radius;
  double angle;
};
PolarPoint::PolarPoint(double nr, double na) :
  radius(nr),
  angle(na)
{}
void PolarPoint::setXY(double x, double y)
{
  double a = atan2(y, x);
  if(a < 0.0) a += 2 * PI;
  radius = hypot(x, y)
  angle = a;
```

```
}
double PolarPoint::getX() const
{ return (radius * cos(angle)); }
double PolarPoint::getY() const
{ return (radius * sin(angle)); }
Point& PolarPoint::vectorAdd(const Point& delta)
{
  setXY(getX() + delta.getX(), getY() + delta.getY());
  return *this;
}
```

The following code defines PolarPoint in Smalltalk:

```
Point subclass: #PolarPoint
       instanceVariableNames: 'r t '.
Point methodsFor: 'accessing'
setX: xFloat setY: yFloat
       r := (xFloat squared + yFloat squared) sqrt.
       t := arcTanY: yFloat andX: xFloat.
getX
       ^t cos * r.
getY
       ^t sin * r.
setR: rVal setAngle: angVal
       r := rVal.
       t := angVal.
getR
       ^r.
getAng
       ^t.
```

The power of object-oriented programming

These simple examples illustrate some points about object-oriented programming:

1 Encapsulation. Objects hide their implementation. It is not possible to observe from outside an object how its attributes are represented or how the messages it receives are handled in its methods.

2 Configurability. All objects that behave properly toward a given collaborator with respect to messages sent and received, may replace each other with respect to that collaborator irrespective of their classes. This property follows from the encapsulation property.

3 Polymorphism. Different objects may treat the same message in different ways, depending on the methods they use to process it.

4 Inheritance. A class can be derived from another class, the derived class need only specify how it is different from the base class.

4.1.3 Why We Need High Level Descriptions

A program is defined by its executable code

Why should we ever want to create higher level models of an object-oriented program? The binary executable code is the only representation that gives a precise definition of what the program will actually do under all possible circumstances. The source code contains equivalent information—assuming that the compilers and loaders do what we expect them to do. But we have also added embellishments that have no effect on program execution: comments and names of program entities convey meaning to a human reader, but have no effect on program execution. Most of us still prefer to study the program in its source code form, even if we are occasionally mislead by improper comments and entity names.

Office procedures are very similar in that they are defined by procedure texts, and there are no high level descriptions. We will later show that higher level, object-oriented descriptions of office procedures give important benefits, but we will now restrict our arguments to computer programs.

While we try to create a program structure which clearly separates different concerns into distinct classes and methods, we still end up having to satisfy several requirements in the same unit. Consider a method that changes the state of a persistent object. The primary function of this method is to change the state. In addition, it must raise an exception if the specified change is inappropriate. It must update all dependent objects, such as visual presentations on the screen. It must ensure that the new state of the object is reflected in its persistent form (e.g., on disk). If the state change is part of a transaction that is canceled, the method may have to undo the change. *The binary executable code mixes all system functions*

If the code is simple and readable, we need nothing else. In practice, the program code usually is not as simple and readable as we could wish, and we have four excellent reasons for wanting to create higher level models: *Why high level models?*

1 *Simplification.* We want a *simplified description* which can be grasped by the limited capacity of our brains. We use such abstract descriptions to reason about the system before diving into its details, and to provide a clear documentation of its overall features.

2 *Evolution.* The more details we put into our descriptions, the harder it will be to change them. The original rationale for introducing a design stage in the program life cycle was that it is much cheaper to change a design description than it is to change a complete program. But this is true only to the extent that the design description really *is* smaller and simpler than the program code.

    A viable alternative is to describe the essential aspects as a *simplified program*. This *incremental programming approach* is often more productive than a prolonged period of high level (and abstract) analysis and design.

3 *Emphasis.* The program code is an explicit representation of the program logic, while the source code may also exhibit the data structures. Important static and dynamic program properties are specified implicitly, and are not always easy to fathom. Many OOram views explicitly express aspects of the program which are not immediately apparent from the program code.

4 *Documentation* (Human-to-human communication). A successful program will have a long life. Many people will try to understand it in order to fix bugs and modify its functionality, usually under great time pressure. Good documentation will help them understand the underlying architecture and constraints, and thus maintain system integrity.

All four considerations have proven to be important in our practical work. Making changes to an isolated role model is trivial, as is making changes to the details of an isolated method. But due to the ripple effect, changing a role model which depends on other role models is harder. In general, we can say that the work involved in making a change depends on the number and nature of its dependent parts, be they state diagrams, method definitions, or dependent models. Large systems need another abstraction layer to keep things simple. We advocate a clear, modular architecture for this purpose, and keep low level modules stable *Simple models are easy to change* while the high level modules are being developed. (We will describe OOram modules in Section 6.5.)

Simple models may hide ugly details

Our experience has also provided counterexamples to these observations. Simple role models are excellent for providing the answers to critical questions, but we may fail to find the most critical questions. Our understanding of the issues may be incomplete, problems we deem to be important may evaporate under close scrutiny, and problems we believed to be trivial may turn out to be really mind-boggling. We therefore need to go all the way and describe the solution as a program before we can be sure that our original questions were the right ones. In the normal software life cycle, in which the design stage is separate from the implementation stage, deficiencies in the design which are discovered during implementation cause costly rework.

Some description methodologies, notably in the field of database systems, follow the *100% rule. The high level description should include sufficient detail for the automatic generation of the application program.* We then regard this description as a program, and the description language (which may be graphical) as a very high level programming language. The whole argument repeats itself: Can we manage with this program as the sole description of the application, or do we need simplified and more abstract models?

Executable specifications are simplified programs which combine the best from both worlds

We often find it convenient to introduce an intermediate stage between design and implementation which we call the *executable specifications.* The specifications are implementations in the sense that they can be executed as programs, but they have neither the efficiency nor the robustness required of a finished program product. Their aim is to highlight deficiencies and details in the system logic; they are abstractions in the sense that they suppress many aspects of the target program and hide trivial details.

The ultimate consumer of a manifest model is human

Some computer professionals may tend to associate system description paradigms with the internal workings of the computer. But the computer hardware does not *know* about FORTRAN and C, entities, relations, objects, or messages. A computer is just a piece of electronic hardware, performing its operations according to the programs represented as bit patterns in its memory. So the audience of a high level description is a human being, not a computer.

Many years ago, we attended a seminar given by M. A. Jackson which profoundly changed our attitudes to programming techniques. The following is a description of the result of this experience. (Apologies to Jackson if he should be misrepresented.)

We permit only systems we understand

In Figure 4.6, the top line symbolizes all programs that a given computer may perform. These programs are generated by systematically loading the computer's memory with each possible bit pattern, and then, in turn, asking the computer to start executing from each possible starting point. The number of different programs that can be executed by a personal computer is on the order of 10 raised to the power of many million, a truly staggering figure. Most of these programs will come to an abrupt halt; some of them will never terminate. To the computer, they are all legal programs. What most of them have in common is that they do nothing that we, as humans, regard as useful or even meaningful.

The middle line in the figure illustrates the almost infinitesimal subset of these programs that do something that we find meaningful. Jackson's insight was that even these programs are not acceptable, because the functioning of most of them will be outside the grasp of the human mind. Jackson's thesis was that of all the meaningful programs, we should limit ourselves to the small portion of them that we can understand. This is illustrated as the bottom line of the figure.

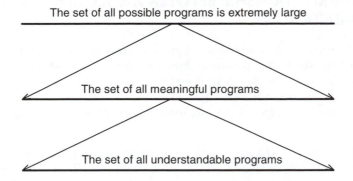

The set of all possible programs is extremely large

The set of all meaningful programs

The set of all understandable programs

Figure 4.6

Our methodologies are designed for people— computers will accept anything

According to Jackson:

"For any given problem, there is one and only one correct solution. The tragedy of computing is that there are so many other solutions which also work."

Our first line of defense is to create programs that are within the grasp of the human mind—programs that are "so simple that there are obviously no deficiencies." We believe that such programs should be our ideal. No other representation can beat the simple program text for precision, clarity, and completeness.

Simplicity is a goal

The need for high level representations arises when the problem is too complex to yield simple code in its solution—when the structure of objects gets too large to be readily grasped by the human mind. OOram role modeling was created to answer this need and to provide a model of the program that is simple and easy to understand.

4.2 THE RELATIONSHIP BETWEEN A ROLE MODEL AND ITS IMPLEMENTATION

IN A NUTSHELL

The OOram role model describes the static and dynamic properties of a pattern of collaborating objects. The program classes specify the exact static and dynamic properties of their instances. Both descriptions define the objects, and there is a clear relationship between them. We will see that it is easy to transform the information in the role model into corresponding information in the classes.

Any role model can be implemented

An OOram role model can be promoted to an *object specification* model, in which the roles are promoted to object specifications. The object specification roles are shown in heavy outline, as illustrated in Figure 4.7. A virtual role has to be resolved into concrete roles before being promoted, since a virtual role represents a cluster of objects rather than a single object.

OOram concepts mapped on to the programming language

Role models specify the static and dynamic properties of object patterns, and thus of object-oriented programs. The concepts of the role models map onto the concepts of the programming language. We indicated some possible mappings in the *Main Ideas*, and repeat them in Table 4.1 for your convenience. The map is meant to help a programmer understand the OOram terms, but the terms are not equivalent since the OOram method focuses on roles, and a programming language focuses on classes.

4.2.1 Implementing the Roles

An object specification is a partial description of an implemented object

A role is an idealized description of an object in the context of a pattern of collaborating objects. Through our policy of divide and conquer, we focus on the object aspects that are relevant for the role model's area of concern.

The object specification describes an object which will actually be implemented. The role is made more concrete when we promote it to an object specification. The programming language concept corresponding to an object specification is a class.

The default is that there is a one-to-one relationship between object specifications and classes, but in general, there is a many-to-many relationship between them.

The simplest situation is if we create a complete object specification model for the set of classes we want to implement. In Figure 2.17, we defined a `Client-Server` model and a `Data transfer` model. In Figure 3.18, we used these models as base models and derived a `File send/receive` model. In Figure 4.8, this model has been promoted to an object specification model ready for implementation in two classes, one for each role.

Figure 4.7

Roles specifying implementation are drawn with heavy outlines

System role   Environment role

System object specification to be implemented as a class

An environment object specification is sometimes implemented as an incomplete class

OOram	Smalltalk	C++
Role model	—	—
Role	Object	Object
Object specification, type	Class	Class
Port	Variable	Pointer data member
Interface	Protocol	Abstract class or protocol class
Message	Message	Function call
Method, action	Method	Member function
Derived model	Subclass	Derived class
Base model	Superclass	Base class

Table 4.1

Mapping OOram models to programs

We may choose to program different classes that implement the same object specification. The classes may have different space/speed tradeoffs, or different functionality, even if their instances play the same role in the current role model. For example we can implement a dummy class for the `Client` role which can later be replaced by a selection of different product implementations for simple and sophisticated end user file manipulation systems.

Many classes may implement the same role

The different subclasses of `Point` for Cartesian and polar coordinates given in the example of Section 4.1.2 also illustrate several implementations of the same object specification.

We want to stress that the OOram method does not insist that we create a complete set of derived models and object specifications. On the contrary, the OOram method specifies that we create only the models needed for our understanding of the system, and that models and source code together constitute the system documentation. Most well-defined models should be sufficiently independent to render a formal synthesis operation superfluous. The programmer implements the classes directly from the several base models so that the class instances will play all the required roles.

A class may implement many roles

One example is the activity network model of Section 1.2.2. The role model is quite sufficient to specify the single class that plays the roles of `Predecessor`, `Job`, and `Successor`.

Another example is the two base models for the FTP file transfer. These models can be promoted to object specifications as shown in Figure 4.9, leaving it to the implementor to make the two classes play the roles of (`Client`, `Source`, `Destination`) and (`Server`, `Source`, `Destination`), respectively.

Our naming convention is that role names are alphabetic, and classes are given the names of the primary role followed by a numeric suffix. The class for the `Client` role would be named `Client1`, and the class for the `Server` role would be `Server1`.

We name classes using numeric suffixes

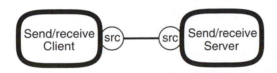

Figure 4.8

File send/receive object specification model

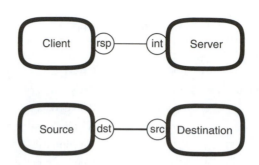

The object specifications of Figure 4.8 and 4.9 both lead to the following class definitions:

```
// Class: SendReceiveClient1
class SendReceiveServer1;
class SendReceiveClient1 {
public:
  SendReceiveClient1();
  ~SendReceiveClient1();
private:
  SendReceiveClient1(const SendReceiveClient1&);          // Avoid copy
  SendReceiveClient1& operator = (const SendReceiveClient1&); // Avoid assignment
  SendReceiveServer1* server;
};      // end of SendReceiveClient1
// Class: SendReceiveServer1
class SendReceiveServer1 {
public:
  SendReceiveServer1();
  ~SendReceiveServer1();
private:
  SendReceiveServer1(const SendReceiveServer1&);          // Avoid copy
  SendReceiveServer1& operator=(const SendReceiveServer1&); // Avoid assign-
ment
  SendReceiveClient1* client;
};      // end of SendReceiveServer1
```

Similarly, in Smalltalk we would have:

Object subclass: #SendReceiveClient1
instanceVariableNames: 'server '.
Object subclass: #SendReceiveServer1
instanceVariableNames: 'client '.

Synthesis can be mapped onto class inheritance

A class may be derived from a base class, and a group of classes may be derived from a group of base classes.

An object specification model can be derived from a base object specification model. This is an open invitation to let the derived classes be derived from the corresponding base classes. We could, for example, define base classes for the Client and Server roles and augment them with send/receive functionality in the subclasses. In Smalltalk, this is accomplished by the following code:

Object subclass: #Client2
instanceVariableNames: 'server '.
Object subclass: #Server2
instanceVariableNames: 'client '.

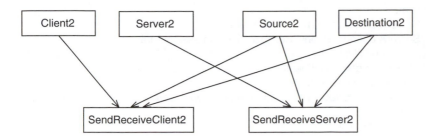

Figure 4.10
Possible multiple
inheritance
hierarchy

Client2 subclass: #SendReceiveClient2
        instanceVariableNames: ''.
Server2 subclass: #SendReceiveServer2
        instanceVariableNames: ''.

If our programming language includes facilities for multiple inheritance, we could implement classes for the Client, the Server, the Source, and the Destination roles. We could then implement the different combinations described in Figures 3.16–3.18 by suitable derivations. An example for the file send/receive case is shown in Figure 4.10.

The following C++ code uses multiple inheritance to implement the class structure of Figure 4.10. You may find that it is more interesting than it is practicable:

```cpp
// Class: Client2
class Client2 {
public:
  Client2();
  ~Client2();
private:
  Client2(const Client2&);         // Avoid copy
  Client2& operator=(const Client2&); // Avoid assignment
};      // end of Client2
// Class: Source2
class Source2 {
public:
  Source2();
  ~Source2();
private:
  Source2(const Source2&);         // Avoid copy
  Source2& operator=(const Source2&); // Avoid assignment
};      // end of Source2
// Class: Destination
class Destination {
public:
  Destination();
  ~Destination();
private:
  Destination(const Destination&);         // Avoid copy
  Destination& operator=(const Destination&); // Avoid assignment
};      // end of Destination
// Class: Server
class Server {
public:
  Server();
  ~Server();
```

```
  private:
    Server(const Server&);          // Avoid copy
    Server& operator=(const Server&); // Avoid assignment
  };        // end of Server
// Class: SendReceiveClient2
class SendReceiveServer2;
class SendReceiveClient2 : public Client2, public Source2, public Destination {
public:
  SendReceiveClient2();
  ~SendReceiveClient2();
private:
  SendReceiveServer2* client;
};        // end of SendReceiveClient2
// Class: SendReceiveServer2
class SendReceiveServer2 : public Server, public Destination, public Source2 {
public:
  SendReceiveServer2();
  ~SendReceiveServer2();
private:
  SendReceiveClient2* client;
};        // end of SendReceiveServer2
```

Automatic code generators are useful, but less flexible than human programmers

When we use automatic program generators, we find it convenient to distinguish between the automatically generated code and the manual extensions. We let the tools create (abstract) classes with a zero suffix, e.g., Client0, The programmer extends and modifies this code in a subclass, e.g., Client1. The advantage is that we can regenerate the superclass when the models are modified without interfering with the manually prepared code. The disadvantage is the added complexity caused by doubling the number of layers in the class structure; see Figure 4.11.

We have been using automatic code generators for Smalltalk and Eiffel, and find them very useful for creating executable specifications and prototypes. We usually remove the abstract layer from the final production code to avoid the unnecessarily deep class hierarchy, and use checking programs in the maintenance phase to maintain the correspondence between the object specification and the code.

Figure 4.11
Automatically generated superclasses, manually prepared subclasses

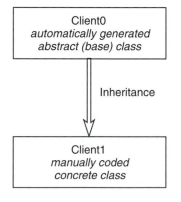

Client0
automatically generated abstract (base) class

This class may be updated automatically at any time ...

Inheritance

Client1
manually coded concrete class

... without destroying the manually created code in this class.

4.2.2 Implementing the Ports and Interfaces

A *Port* is an abstraction of a variable. The default is to map the port onto an instance variable, but it may be mapped onto any kind of variable. In Smalltalk, it could be a *global, instance, class,* or *temporary* variable; in C++ it could be *private* or *public*.

A port describes a variable

The implementation of a port will depend on its cardinality. A ONE port will be represented as a pointer variable. A MANY port will be represented as some kind of collection such as Set, Array, or LinkedList. The role model does not formally specify the kind of collection to be used. The choice is left to the implementor, but the analyst can indicate his or her preference in a comment associated with the port.

A multi-port is implemented with a collection

The default name of the variable is the name of the port. We usually follow the naming conventions for variables in our programming language when we name our ports.

The port is not necessarily implemented as an instance variable; a local method could compute the pointer whenever needed. The message interaction between collaborators could also be taken care of by a special program. In the case of the FTP file transfer implementation, the messages will be transmitted through a communication path according to the Internet Transmission Control Protocol (TCP). The operating system is likely to support some kind of *socket* that facilitates this communication, and our methods will use these facilities to transmit messages.

Such program details are immaterial for the role models at the analysis level. They can be described in design-level role models or can be left to the discretion of the implementor.

The important principle is that while a role model may give a simplified view of the program, it should be given a true representation of the collaboration structure in the context of its area of concern. There must be a port for every message sent. You cannot say that a particular port is unimportant because it only lasts for a few microseconds. You either need it, in which case it should be shown, or you do not need it, in which case you should not send messages along it.

The role model should never lie

If we find that the collaboration view gets too complicated when we show *all* the relevant interaction paths, we must simplify the program logic rather than cheat ourselves and others by falsifying the view.

An OOram interface is a named collection of messages that may be sent from one role to another. Popular programming languages such as Smalltalk and C++ define all messages that are to be understood by the instances of a class; they do not check that the messages originate from an authorized sender. The reason for the mismatch is that in OOram we focus on patterns of collaborating objects, while the popular languages focus on the capabilities of individual classes.

OOram controls the messages sent

This apparent mismatch is easily bridged: The set of messages to be understood by a class is the union of all the messages sent to it from its collaborators. If we implement role B in Figure 4.12 as class B1, we give it two variables ba and bc, and create methods for all the messages sent from its collaborators, as indicated. We similarly create classes A1 and C1, which implement roles A and C, respectively. Class A1 will define a variable ab and methods which send messages messAB1 and messAB2 to this variable. Class C1 will define a variable cb and methods which send messages messCB1 and messCB2 to this variable.

It would be nice if the compiler could check that our implementation actually conforms to the object specification. In Smalltalk, we can implement the named

Checking implementation onformance

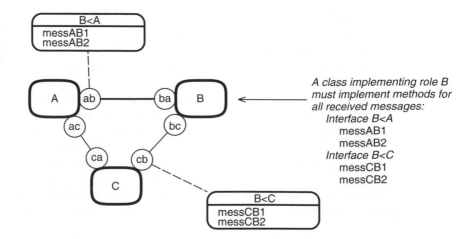

Figure 4.12

A rudimentary object specification example

interfaces as Smalltalk *protocols*. A Smalltalk compiler does not enforce the OO-ram specifications since it does not support static type checking. The type system of statically typed languages does not readily support our notion of giving different message privileges to different collaborators (see the box). Neither Smalltalk nor C++ guarantee that a value has been assigned to a variable before it is used. (Some Smalltalk compilers do a partial check.)

Once we know the classes that implement given roles, it is easy to check that they understand all the messages they are supposed to receive. It is harder to check that objects will send only the messages they are supposed to send. We can rely on *manual checking*, which is error-prone and tedious; *static code checking programs*, which are hard to make; or *monitored execution programs* for dynamic testing, which can test only specific cases. Monitored execution will be described in Section 6.5.

4.2.3 Implementing the Methods and Actions

OOram supports different levels of method detail

A *method* specifies the work to be done by an object when it receives a message. Methods (or *member functions*) are defined explicitly by their code in the class; message sends appear embedded in the code. OOram role models can include method specifications that can be defined on four different levels of detail:

1 By the name of the message and a comment describing its intention. The programmer has to create the code from his or her general understanding of the designer's intentions.

2 By a free text (comment) describing the method's operation, together with a specification of the messages sent from the method and their receivers.

3 By pseudo code describing the method's operation, together with a specification of the messages sent from the method and their receivers.

4 As code in a programming language, such as C++ or Smalltalk.

The first level is an integral part of the message interface view, and the remaining levels are seen in the method specification view described in Section 2.5.2. Figure 2.38 is an example of a method specified as pseudo code.

Depending on the details included in the method specifications, automatically generated methods can be more or less complete. In the simplest case, the method (procedure) header may be generated automatically, with the message explanation in the form of a comment. Formal parameters and their type will be included, if this information is in the role model. The method bodies will be generated as completely as possible from the specifications.

Automatic code generation

An unsuccessful attempt at supporting OOram specifications using a language-type system:

A fine point for the specially interested: when developing a bridge between OOram object specifications and the programming language Eiffel, we tried to define deferred Eiffel classes for the ports. Classes ab and cb defined the respective interfaces, and class B1 was made a subclass of these classes so that it supported both interfaces. The advantage was that the compiler checked the interfaces against the OOram object specification. The disadvantage was that we got a very large number of classes and spent much time in compilation.

The scheme was torpedoed by its handling of object references in message parameters, however. Consider the role model in Figure 4.12. Assume that the computation process starts with anA1 (an instance of A1) creating aB1, storing a pointer to this object in its variable ab. It then creates aC1, and sends the message setB, with aB1 as parameter, to aC1. The variable ab in aB1 is typed with the ab interface. The object aC1 receives the setB message and tries to store the parameter in its cb variable. But cb is typed differently from ab, and we get a type error. Changing the type of variable cb does not help, because the object aC1 then cannot send the required messages to aB1.

This experiment confirms Bjarne Stroustrup's assertion mentioned earlier: *If you don't like the basic type system of a language, use another language with a type system that suits your taste better.*

4.3 THE IMPLEMENTATION PROCESS

The yo-yo approach to computer programming is an opportunistic, risk-reducing strategy. As usual, we recommend that you develop your own implementation process, which will be uniquely adapted to your own requirements.

Your implementation processes must be tailored to your needs

Like all other work processes, you will have to tailor your implementation processes to your specific applications and your own work situation. Your previous experience with systems development in general and object-oriented development in particular, is of crucial importance, as are the facilities available to you and the kinds of systems you want to develop. This section may give you a useful starting point if you are relatively new to object orientation.

OOram supports many different work processes

The OOram perspectives and views are designed to support a wide variety of work processes and implementation styles: they support many different abstractions, and the freedom to choose the detailed syntax and message semantics supports different programming styles.

The top-down approach is powerful, but the devil may be in the details

The idea of top-down development was introduced in the 1960s. Oxford gives the following description [Oxford 86]: *"an approach to program development in which progress is made by defining required elements in terms of more basic elements."* The trouble with the top-down approach is that the devil is often found in the details: the early assumptions prove to be inadequate and the top level design has to be modified.

The pure top-down approach seemed very rational, and we advocated it in several seminars and university courses in the 1970s. We also asked a number of graduate students to use the approach in their work and to report on their experiences. Much to our chagrin, we found that none of the students were able to follow our sound advice. We then monitored our own work, and found that we regularly broke the rules ourselves. Further observation told us that a prerequisite to following the top-down approach was that we knew at least one and preferably several ways of implementing the lower level details. This was rarely true for the students, with their limited experience, and often was not true for us when we were exploring new application technologies.

We encounter the same problems when we teach object orientation and the OOram method to programmers. It is hard to relate to abstract concepts, and the only way to make them real is to actually write concrete, object-oriented programs. We advise a concrete-to-abstract approach to learning object orientation: begin by writing simple programs, and introduce the OOram method only when the basic concepts are well understood through real programming experience.

Bottom-up approach: The parts may not fit together

An alternative is the bottom-up approach, which Oxford describes as follows [Oxford 86]: *"an approach to program development in which progress is made by composition of available elements."* The trouble with the bottom-up approach often appears in the final system integration stage. The system components may be excellent in themselves, but this does not guarantee that they can be composed into the required system.

The principle of minimizing risk

We call our current approach the *yo-yo approach,* because it combines the top-down and bottom-up approaches according to *the principle of minimizing risk.* We identify the part of the problem that we believe will be the hardest to get right, and experiment with possible solutions. When we feel that we have mastered this part, we identify the next-hardest part, and so on. This principle corresponds in many ways to the principles advocated by Boehm [Boehm 88], where you will find many more details.

An alternative to the principle of minimizing risk is to solve the simple problems first so as to get early tangible results. This is often good for morale, and may even help clarify the hard problems by removing extraneous details.

The nature of the critical part will vary from case to case. In some cases, we may not know which functionality the users will actually need. It is then a good idea to start with the user interfaces, and support them with dummy data representations. The users get hands-on experience with the proposed system at a very early stage, and can provide valuable feedback.

Identify critical uncertainty

In other cases, we may suspect that we do not understand the users' mental models. It can then be appropriate to start with a collaboration view, possibly making it appear concrete to the users by providing appropriate user interfaces.

The critical problems can also be on a lower level. Will we really be able to create the algorithm for a required function, or do we need magic to solve the problem? Can we create a program that satisfies the speed requirements? Practical experiments can give the answer.

The yo-yo approach implies that we want to be able to cross the bridge between OOram models and implementation in both directions: we may have created a design and want to implement it, or we may have created a prototype implementation and want to extract the design information from it. Good processes, with their associated tools, should support both directions.

Cross the implementation bridge in both directions

We are programmers at heart, and we rarely find that we fail to notice woolly details. The danger is rather that our vision of our work is too narrow. We guard against system integration problems by creating the top level program as early as possible—inserting dummy methods for the details. We then fill in programs for the critical parts as they are created. In this way, we create an operational program at a very early stage, and we keep improving it until it is ready for delivery. Whenever possible, end users are involved in the prototype testing, so that they can have maximal influence on the final product.

Keep an eye on the total problem!

We are constantly trying to be conscious of our own mental blocks. We may, for example, work on the high level aspects of a distributed system, and find that our thoughts keep wandering off to the problem of program-to-program communication. We then digress and work with a small distributed program until we have removed the block. Once the problem is cleared, we can continue the high level considerations and base them on a solid foundation.

Beware of mental blocks!

There is one caveat to the principle of minimizing risk: most development projects have limits on time and resources. It is indeed a sad situation if essential functionality is still missing when the ax falls and a project has to be terminated.

Identify essential functionality!

There are great benefits to be gained if we manage to stimulate the creativity of the users and everybody else around us: such interaction improves the final product and its acceptance, and it is great fun. But beware of escalating specifications! Some functionality may have to be postponed to a later project, or the scope of the current project may have to be expanded to take the users' increased appetites into account.

Beware of escalating specifications!

As a general rule, we do not cross bridges until we get to them. We try to make the system architecture expandable, and we regard the users' expressed requirements as examples rather than the whole story. But we keep the code consistent with the architecture and as simple as possible. We do not complicate it to provide hooks for extensions. The following guidelines are inspired by the excel-

Postpone program optimization!

lent book by Kernighan and Plauger on programming style [KerPla 74], which should be required reading for all programmers. The guidelines apply not only to programming, but to all levels of analysis and design:

1 *Make it right.* Our first concern is to create a program that reflects the users' requirements.

2 *Make it clear.* Our second concern is to make the program simple—"so simple that there are obviously no deficiencies." Initial program versions are often dirty: the division of responsibility between the objects is not optimal; the same logic is repeated in several locations when it could be replaced by a single occurrence in the right location. We use reverse engineering to extract the design from a running program. We then clean up the design before reimplementing a cleaner version of the program.

3 *Make it fail-safe.* The encapsulation property makes it fairly easy to protect objects from all kinds of abuse by their collaborators. If we take this principle too far, we end up with schizophrenic objects that spend most of their time checking each other. It is a good idea to draw boundaries around groups of objects; we call them *fire walls.* We carefully check all messages passing a boundary and trust all messages flowing within it. The role model is an alternative unit for fire wall protection: all stimulus messages are treated with suspicion, while all internal interactions are assumed to be in order.

4 *Instrument the programs. Measure before making efficiency changes.* There is no point in optimizing code that has but a small contribution to the overall running time of the program. We find that our intuition about where the program spends its time is unreliable. We postpone making efficiency changes until the program execution time proves to be a problem, and then only after careful and detailed performance measurements. (This applies to code details. It is usually more important to design an efficient architecture than to optimize the code.)

The iterative development process

To sum up, the development process can start with a prototype implementation or with an abstract analysis. In either case, the process is iterative, moving between the abstract and the concrete until the system is complete (or until the available time and budget have been exhausted). See Figure 4.13.

Exploratory programming is powerful

Notice the bottom loop in the figure. Modern programming environments with source code browsers and incremental compilation make exploratory programming really attractive, because we can express our ideas directly in a programming language and test them immediately. Exploratory programming is particularly powerful for the make-it-right phase. In one session where we monitored our work, we created a first prototype in just under three hours. The measured average cycle time (think-edit-compile-test) was 2.5 minutes.

Create your own process!

We do not expect that this process is quite right for you, but it may give you ideas that could be useful when you create your own processes. You will also want to add further steps for product implementation, testing, installation, and maintenance. Do not expect your first process to be ideal, but observe how you actually work, and improve the process description as you gain experience.

Exploratory programming may play havoc with software reliability

Back in 1980, our group at the SINTEF-SI research institute had already logged twenty years of FORTRAN software product development, and considered itself pretty professional. We followed a waterfall life cycle model and used techniques such as careful design and peer reviews to produce reliable code. We believed, as we still believe, in Dijkstra's dictum that the only way to produce software with-

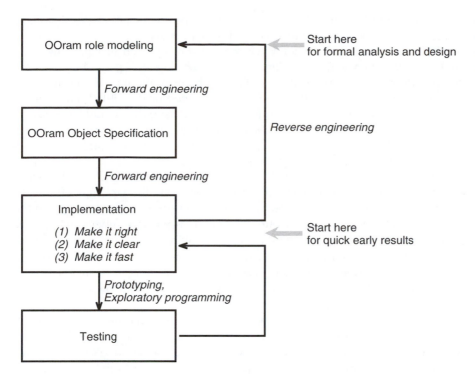

Figure 4.13

Simple
implementation
process

out errors is to avoid introducing them in the first place; the number of errors remaining in the programs is likely to be proportional to the number of errors found and removed during testing. In one monitored case we did in 1976, we found no errors in two out of three subroutines during unit testing, and no errors at all during system testing. (This was a 2,000-line preprocessor for object-based FORTRAN programming.)

Exploratory programming seems to be the antithesis to this careful approach to software development. While the group immediately recognized its clear benefits, there was strong opposition to introducing such a haphazard technique into our tidy development process. The solution we have ended up with is the double loop approach shown in Figure 4.13, in which exploratory programming is considered a specification activity. The final program is created from the top down according to the established principles.

Our message to users and management is that *a nice-looking prototype or demonstration program can be created in no time, but it takes real time to create a real program.* An early prototype looks good to users and management, and it is sometimes hard to persuade them that the main part of the work remains to be done. We are still searching for software metrics which can make this main part visible, so that it will be properly appreciated by managers and clients. (This section is written for programmers, but you may want to show this paragraph to your manager!)

Development of real software takes real time

Significant systems are developed by groups of people working together in teams. In the Middle Ages, there were *polymaths*, geniuses who knew everything that was worth knowing. Geniuses have always been in short supply, and the current body of knowledge is too large to be mastered by a single person. But a balanced team can possess a polymathic knowledge within its area of responsibil-

System development requires teamwork

ity, and the symbiotic intelligence of a closely cooperating team can exhibit many of the characteristics commonly associated with a genius.

Egoless teamwork

Our view on the ideal system development team has been strongly influenced by Gerald Weinberg's epoch-making book on *The Psychology of Computer Programming* [Weinb 71]. The success or failure of a team member is closely linked to the success or failure of the team: we all succeed or we all fail. Ruth cannot claim that the project's failure was caused by Stupid Sam; she should have discovered the difficulties and taken corrective action in time. Open communication channels, mutual respect, and acceptance of individual strengths and weaknesses are essential properties of a good team.

Common language essential

A common language is essential for effective communication channels. Object orientation and the OOram method constitute our common language on the abstract level. Our programming rules and conventions provide the language on the concrete level. The intention of our conventions is what Weinberg calls *egoless programming*: any programmer in the team should be able to read any piece of code and work with it in an effective manner. There is no such thing as component ownership—only component responsibility, which may be reassigned to other team members. We recommend that you establish your own conventions, adapted to your team's requirements.

Process depends on problem

We tend to get suspicious when we meet someone who claims to have the ultimate work process that will work with all kinds of people for all kinds of problems. We find that our optimal work process depends on the kind of problem we are going to solve, its position on a sophistication scale from routine to research, the availability of reusable components which are applicable to the problem, the time available, the number and qualifications of people we are going to work with, and a host of other factors. To us, industrial production of software implies that all these factors are kept reasonably fixed to permit the evolution of an optimal work process.

4.4 CHOICE OF PROGRAMMING LANGUAGE

No programming language is ideal for all purposes. Yet many programmers feel very strongly about their language, and are personally affronted if somebody dares to propose that another language could be superior for some purposes.

It is therefore with some hesitation that we suggest that Smalltalk is a higher level language than C++. We believe that C++ is the better language for many purposes, because it gives the programmer complete control of low level computational details such as memory allocation. We also believe that Smalltalk is better for other purposes, because it invites the programmer to ignore low level computational details such as memory allocation.

Role models are used to model a wide range of phenomena within computers and in the world around us. The appropriate implementation technologies will depend on the nature of the phenomenon and the purpose of the implementation. The processes used to create the human objects of a travel expense model are very different from the processes used to create the computer-based objects of a file transfer program. Even if we confine ourselves to the creation of computer-based systems, the ideal implementation process will depend on the problem and the selected programming language.

Different implementation technologies for different phenomena

In an ideal world, the implementation would be written in an OOram programming language, which would reflect the concepts of the OOram method. For example, a variable would be typed to ensure that it can point to any object that is capable of playing the specified role or roles, regardless of the object's implementation.

In the real world, we have to use one of the standard programming languages that have been developed without regard to any specific modeling technology. The final choice of programming language may be based on technical considerations, on total life-cycle costs, on strategic considerations such as training requirements, or even on apparent popularity.

We focus on Smalltalk and C++

The main vendors of object-oriented program development systems do not publish their sales statistics, but C++ and Smalltalk seem to be the most popular languages, followed by Eiffel and Objective C. C++ is currently by far the most widely accepted language. Smalltalk seems to be increasingly accepted, particularly in the business information system community.

There are many C programmers in the world, and many people believe that it is easier for a C programmer to make the transition to object-oriented thinking through C++ than through Smalltalk. We believe this to be a fallacy. The very similarities between C and C++ can make the essential paradigm shift harder, because the programmer is permitted to continue thinking along an old track. We believe that it is much better to make a clean break and create one's first object-oriented implementations in a pure object-oriented language such as Smalltalk, even if the final products are to be written in a hybrid language such as C++.

The hard part of learning object orientation is to internalize the mental model, not to learn the language syntax

It is hard to compare the productivity of a Smalltalk programmer relative to a C programmer. A few studies that have been mentioned on the electronic bulletin boards seem to indicate that Smalltalk is six times more productive than C. But the samples used in the studies have been small, and the effects of different people, development processes, and program libraries have not been considered. Smalltalk is a higher level language and *should* be more productive, but we cannot claim that this is borne out by conclusive observation.

Smalltalk may appear more productive

Static and dynamic typing

C++ is a statically typed language. Variables are typed on the class of the permissible objects, and the compiler ensures that the object receiving a message will also have a method which can handle it. The programmer can override this discipline using *type casting*, and can then specify messages which cause catastrophic termination of the program.

The Smalltalk language is untyped in the sense that a variable may point to any object. It is dynamically typed in the sense that all objects will handle any message in a defined way: if an object does not have a method for the received message, a `Message not understood` exception is raised, and the programmer can decide on the proper action to take.

Typing systems are beneficial

We have no doubt about the benefits of a typing system. It prevents a certain class of runtime errors and enforces a precise documentation of the variables. We are more doubtful about the wisdom of typing a variable on the implementation (class) of the objects to which it refers, because the implementation descriptions include all details about the internal construction of the object. Typing on implementation thus breaks the object encapsulation, and we lose the valuable flexibility and generality that enable us to create objects having identical external characteristics, but different implementations.

For example, we have a Smalltalk implementation of a rudimentary relational database; we use it for prototyping and demonstration purposes. A separate set of classes implement clients for remote access to popular database servers. All these database classes implement interchangeable objects, but they need not have a common base class.

Our systems evolve over the years, and we sometimes want to replace an old class hierarchy with a new and better one. We want to introduce the new hierarchy gradually as our confidence in the new solution grows and as time permits. Both the old and the new class hierarchies, therefore, have to coexist in the system for a considerable period of time.

Abstract classes are artificial

While it is possible to use the notions of abstract or virtual classes to fake a type system in the statically typed languages, we would prefer to use a language with an explicit type system that supported the OOram notion of roles, collaborations, and interface definitions.

Garbage collection

Some languages, such as Smalltalk, Eiffel and Objective C, have automatic garbage collection. This means that objects are retained in memory as long as they are reachable from the root of the object structure. When the object is no longer reachable, its memory space is automatically released and can be reused by other objects.

Other languages, such as C++, have manual garbage collection. It is the responsibility of the programmer to know when an object is no longer needed and to explicitly free its memory space. It is both hard and important to get this memory management right. If object space is not freed, the memory will gradually be filled with garbage. If an object is freed prematurely, the system will crash catastrophically. We recommend that if the target language does not support automatic garbage collection, the creation and destruction of objects should be clearly described in appropriate role models.

Do not violate the intentions of your programming language

All complete programming languages are in some sense equivalent, and any computation may somehow be realized in any language. Languages differ in how directly the programmer's ideas may be expressed. It has been said that a real programmer can write FORTRAN in any language. Bjarne Stroustrup, the inventor of C++ once said "*C++ is not a very good Smalltalk; it was not meant to be. Similarly, Smalltalk is not a very good C++; it was not meant to be.*"

This means that if we use C++, we should adapt to the C++ way of thinking. Similarly, if we use Smalltalk, we should adapt to the Smalltalk way of thinking. One of the goals of the OOram method has been to make its notions adaptable to the programming styles supported by the different programming languages, but its actual use should be colored by the philosophy of the target programming language.

Smalltalk is a higher level language than C++. A number of data representation and memory management issues have been automated and made invisible to the programmer. This, combined with its English-like syntax and uniform use of objects, has empowered us to create user interfaces, system architectures, and reusable programs which would otherwise have been outside our intellectual grasp.

Smalltalk higher level than C++

There is no such thing as a free lunch. Smalltalk has acquired a reputation for being inefficient. There are several reasons for this. One is that Smalltalk pioneered sophisticated user interfaces which consume vast amounts of computer power. Such programs were bound to lose when they were compared to C programs implementing traditional command-line interfaces.

C more efficient than Smalltalk

Another reason could be that the typical Smalltalk programmer may be more inclined to reuse existing code, even if specialized code could be made more efficient.

A third reason is that the high level, dynamic nature of the Smalltalk language makes it harder to create efficient compilers and runtime systems. When we began using Smalltalk at the end of the 1970s, we estimated that a Smalltalk program could be up to 40 times slower than a comparable C program. There have been impressive improvements in compilers and run-time technology since those early days. Chambers reports a factor of 10 between an early Smalltalk and plain C [Chambers 89]; the current releases of Smalltalk are significantly faster. It is also possible to call low level, optimized C procedures from a Smalltalk program.

We believe that a rational (as opposed to strategic) choice of programming language should be made on the basis of total life- cycle costs. Smalltalk is fast enough on current hardware for most applications, but in some cases we may have to use more expensive hardware to attain satisfactory performance. This has to be offset against faster response to changing requirements, reduced development and maintenance costs, and more direct modeling of the users' mental models.

Rational choices should be made on total life-cycle costs

Our arguments give C++ an edge for heavily used, stable systems. Smalltalk is the preferred language for customized and adaptive software installed in relatively small numbers. Smalltalk is also the preferred language for custom-made software, as well as the language of choice for the rapid creation of executable specifications and for prototyping.

The technological optimum could well be a combination of the two. In a client-server solution, Smalltalk could be the best choice for the client part, while C, C++, or Eiffel could be the best choice for the server part.

CHAPTER 5

Creating Reusable Components

CONTENTS

5.1   Introduction to Reuse   135

5.2   Patterns   143

    5.2.1   Alexander's Pattern Language   144
    5.2.2   How to Create a Pattern   145

5.3   OOram Frameworks   153

This chapter is primarily written for suppliers of reusable components, but will also help discerning consumers become better buyers. You will find that object-oriented technology offers many opportunities for reuse, and that some of them are more demanding than others as to maturity and product stability. You will also find that reuse is no silver bullet. Reuse has great potential, but your benefits will be closely related to your investment in competence, time, money, and dedication.

We distinguish between incidental and planned reuse. *Incidental reuse* means that you happen on some recurring pattern of objects during analysis or design, isolate this pattern, and describe it as a separate role model. *Planned reuse* is much more. In planned reuse, the reusable component is a planned product created by a supplier for the benefit of a number of consumers. Its development is based on a deep understanding of the problems it addresses and the way it will help the consumers. A reusable component is an asset, and the cost of its development is written off against future benefits.

A profound statement about reuse is attributed to Brad Cox: "Before you can reuse something, you must use it." Similar sentiments have been expressed by other authorities. We believe that Ralph Johnson or Brian Foote is the originator of this one: "Reusable frameworks are not designed; they are discovered." So the paramount condition for planned reuse is that you have something that has been used a number of times and that can be generalized into something reusable by you or by somebody else.

5.1   INTRODUCTION TO REUSE

Reuse is hard to achieve, but well worthwhile, because it enables us to create big systems in small projects. Reusable components are products created by a supplier and applied by a number of consumers. The success criterion for a reusable component is that it is actually being used. The key to success is the effective communication between the supplier and the consumers.

IN A NUTSHELL

Large projects are notoriously hard to get right. They are difficult to plan and control; they are expensive in time and resources; and we all know numerous disaster stories. In contrast, small projects are simple to plan and control; they are usually successful; and the possible failures are cheap and easy to rectify.

Evolution is easier than revolution

But how can small projects produce big results? An important answer is *reuse*. If 99% of the solution can be created from proven components, a 100-month programming activity can be reduced to just 1 month.

Some of the greatest successes of object-oriented technology are based on reuse, and we will discuss no less than five interesting reuse technologies in this books. But some of the saddest failures are also from the field of reuse, and the main thrust of this chapter is to put reuse in its proper perspective: it is wonderful, but it is not a trivial task to harvest its benefits.

All successful business operations rely heavily on reuse. Our first reaction when asked to solve a problem or produce a result is to search our accumulated experience for applicable solutions. If we need to produce a project proposal, we start from an old proposal for a similar project. If we need to produce a new piece of code, we search for proven solutions to similar problems. We all rely heavily on such *incidental reuse* as a matter of course. Its benefits are undisputable and its arch enemy is the *not invented here* syndrome.

Many kinds of reusable things

Business people do not like the arbitrariness of incidental reuse. They want to formalize their experience and package it in such a way that it can be reused reliably and consistently. They create business procedures which describe proven ways of performing critical operations; they standardize tools and techniques which will help them reach their goals; they establish libraries of proven ideas, models and program components. Experience may even be embodied in a computer program: a project proposal can be generated automatically from parameters provided by the user.

Planned reuse

Our theme is the *planned reuse of object components*. By this we mean reusable components that are created with the same care and dedication as end user applications. A reusable component is a product that solves a specified class of problems for an identified consumer community. Like any other product, the creation of a reusable component takes a significant investment in time and money which must be written off against future benefits.

There are several advantages to planned reuse. We have already mentioned reduced cost and lead time. The reusable components are carefully checked and thoroughly tested, so their use will improve software quality and consistency. We often need to protect critical resources, such as important business data and access to shared systems. The mandatory reuse of proven components can help maintain system integrity, if they include mechanisms ensuring their correct application.

Figure 5.1

Reusable components occur on all levels of modeling

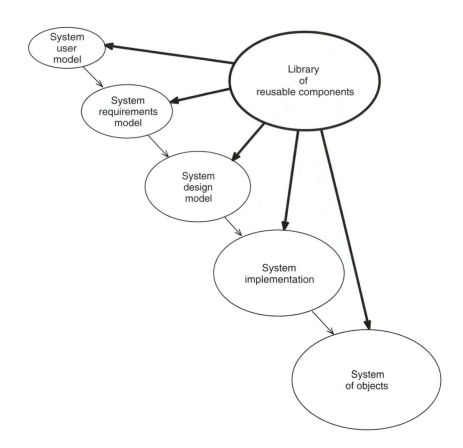

Reuse technologies applicable on all levels

Figure 5.1 illustrates that we can employ reusable components on all levels of abstraction; ranging from the system user model to the system of objects running in a computer. Reusable components can materially reduce the required effort on all levels, and it may even be possible to avoid the design and implementation stages altogether.

Figure 5.1 illustrates a number of opportunities for planned reuse:

1 A *system user model* can be composed from more general patterns, which we may create as part of our current project or which we may find in a library of reusable components.

2 A *system requirements model* can be composed from more general patterns, which we create as part of our current project or which we find in a library of reusable components.

3 A *system design model* can be based on a number of patterns or frameworks found in a library of reusable components.

4 A *system implementation* can be derived from one or more framework classes found in a library of reusable components.

5 A *system of objects* can be composed from predefined library objects, as described in Chapter 11.

Understand the consumers' business

The specification of a reusable component must be based on careful analysis of existing solutions created by the consumer community. We try to identify recurring problems and to be reasonably sure that similar problems won't arise in the future. (We do not necessarily want to retrofit a reusable component into an existing solution, because "if it works, don't fix it".) The existing instances of the problem solutions are taken as examples. We try to understand the tradeoffs involved and create a general solution. Last but not least, we try to understand the consumers' work situation and make sure that the new component will be acceptable and truly useful to them in their work.

The creation of a reusable component is not a one-time effort. We create an initial solution, use it, and continue honing it as we gain more experience. The first release may be clumsy, inefficient, and unreliable. But the beauty of reusable components is that we can afford to improve them over time, so that we ultimately end up with components which are elegant, efficient, and highly reliable. This alternation between use and asset building is illustrated in Figure 5.2.

Reusable components must evolve over time

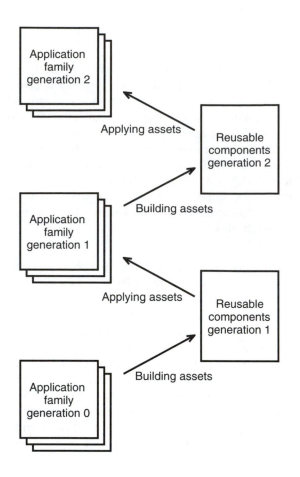

Figure 5.2

Alternate use of applications and improvement of reusables

The success criterion for a reusable component is that it is actually being used!

I have lost count of all the wonderful reusable components I have created over the years that either have been lost or reside quietly in some out-of-the-way library. Measured as entertainment, their development was great fun. Measured as business propositions, their development was a dead loss because we have not recovered their cost through their use.

My colleagues and I have also written many successful reusable components. They constitute the very foundation on which we build all our software; they enable us to build customized software in days that otherwise would take weeks or months.

The success criterion for a reusable component is that it is actually being used. Why is it that some reusable components are highly successful while others fail? It does not seem to have anything to do with their technical excellence; I have seen sophisticated solutions fail where mediocre components are embraced by everybody. It does not seem to be a question of documentation. I have tried writing short instructions: they failed because they did not enable the reader to use the components effectively. I have tried writing long and detailed instructions: they failed because nobody could be bothered to study them. Could it be that the problem is essentially human rather than technical? See the sidebar boxes for two experiences from different fields of endeavor; they may hold clues to the answer.

Let humans do what humans do best!

The North Sea oil production platforms are very large, very complex, and very costly. Time is at a premium, and concurrent engineering is used extensively to minimize the design period. This means that each of the thousand designers builds his work on preliminary results that somebody else may be in the process of modifying. My son is employed in this work, and I tried to sell him a project to develop computer-assisted coordination. Wouldn't it be nice if a designer could point at a drawing detail on his computer screen and immediately get access to all other drawings covering the same area? My son was not impressed. All he needed was to be able to point at a detail on a drawing and find the names of the two or three other designers working in the same area. He could then contact them on the phone and coordinate the work quite easily.

My mistake was to think in terms of an automatic system, while my son knew that real designs are created by real people. Computers can support them but never replace them. My advanced data processing problem had evaporated, and the researcher in me lost interest. You may draw your own conclusions as to the relevance of this example to my wonderful reusable components which nobody uses.

Complex products are created by competent people

An example which I believe is relevant to our discussion is taken from the shipbuilding industry. In the early 1970s, I was working in close cooperation with a Norwegian shipyard to develop a novel system based on object-oriented concepts for the planning and control of shipbuilding operations. Then came the oil crisis, and the bottom fell out of the market for large tankers. The yard survived because at the time oil was found in the North Sea, and they switched their operation almost overnight from constructing ships to building oil production platforms. The planners worked overtime to remold their plans for the new products, but the production problems proved more formidable than they had imagined in their worst case scenarios.

A harassed chief of planning later gave me this valuable insight: "*I thought we controlled our production through our formalisms and beautifully detailed plans, but I was wrong. What we did have was a crew of highly skilled people who knew how to build ships. Our plans were a kind of varnish on top of this, only giving marginally improved effectiveness. We got into trouble because our collective competence had not prepared us for the challenges of the new products.*"

This kind of experience is bad news for the manager who is tired of being dependent on his professional staff and who wants to formalize its knowledge and competence so as to make software production into a mechanical operation which can be performed by obedient slaves. It is good news for the professional who likes to view himself as being indispensable—he is.

Formal methods cannot replace humans, but they can be helpful. The reuse technologies we will present in the following chapters are all useful for creating concrete representations of ways to do things so that they can be reused by others. But I would like to state loudly and clearly that we cannot replace human cooperation, creativity, and competence; we can only augment these qualities, and help the competent become more effective.

I believe the little stories in the boxes hold the key to why some reusable components are successful where other components fail. I am a programmer at heart, and tend to act as if the creation of a good reusable component is the hard part. It isn't. The hard part is to create a component that people not only need, but that they will actually want to use. The successful component is in harmony with its consumers, and their goals, working habits, and competence.

The critical part of a successful reusable component is the successful communication between its supplier and its consumers. Consider the simple communication model in Figure 2.4. A UNIX manual, like most other technical documentation, is a kind of binary dump of the supplier's mind. (*See sidebar "Focus on consumer" on page 137.*) It is a description of the solutions; the consumer must map these solutions onto his or her problems.

Writing for the consumer is much harder. It requires the writer to understand the consumer's tasks, mental models, and vocabulary. It requires *communication*.

Personal contact is the supreme medium for communicating technical know-how. Professionals who possess complementary competence and who work closely together experience a continuous learning process. If managers want to encourage learning, they will form and reform teams for the purpose of knowledge transfer, and they will reward team performance rather than individual achievements. (Read [Weinb 71] and learn!)

Even if word of mouth is the best communication channel, it is by no means sufficient. Carefully conceived documentation helps the consumer correctly and effectively apply reusable components.

Linguists distinguish between a person's active and passive vocabulary. Your active vocabulary consists of the words you use. Your passive vocabulary consists of the words you understand when other people use them, even if you do not use them yourself. I believe it is fruitful to similarly distinguish between a person's active and passive competence. Your *active competence* consists of all the things you know how to do. Your *passive competence* consists of all the things you understand when you see other people do them, even if you could not easily do them yourself.

It is clear that a consumer must possess the necessary active competence to apply a reusable component successfully. It is equally important that the consumer possesses a passive competence that gives the necessary context to the component's application. We recommend that the component documentation be layered, so that a reader will find information for his or her active competence on the top layer and information for his or her passive competence on the layers below it.

We suggest that the following three layers may be useful: *list of instructions, logical map,* and *implementation description.* We will discuss them briefly below.

A list of instructions gives the consumer the essentials for applying a component. It is like road directions: "Go South on 280 until you hit the Page Mill Road exit. Turn left. Turn right at the first traffic light, then, take the first left. It is the first building on your left after the first intersection." These directions are great if they are right, if the consumer has the expected background knowledge, if he or she wants to go from somewhere up north, if he or she wants to go to the designated destination, and if he or she doesn't try to be smart. But the consequences could be catastrophic if he or she tries a slight variation, since he or she could easily get hopelessly lost.

The list of instructions should be sufficient for the consumer who has the active competence to apply it. It is intended to jolt one's memory, not to teach new skills. The consumer's passive competence should include a logical map that gives context to the work and protects against component misuse.

When the supplier gives a consumer freedom to reuse a component in many different ways, there is a danger that the consumer will use it incorrectly. A reusable component should include a description of constraints, which may be compulsory or may just be warnings about possible dangers. It is preferable if the constraints can be enforced by automatic tools; otherwise check lists should be provided to help the consumer use the component correctly. (Quality assurance procedures based on the ISO9000 standard are heavy users of check lists [ISO9000]. The lists are filled in and signed by the developers, and archived for future reference.) *Specify constraints*

A *logical map* is a high level description of a component and its structure. It is like a road map which gives sufficient information to enable an automobile driver to get his or her bearings, but where a great deal of information is suppressed because it is considered irrelevant or not timely. *Logical map*

The consumer will study the logical map if it isn't already part of his or her passive competence. He or she will have to study it more carefully if it is necessary to specialize the component. His or her active competence will include the logical map, and his or her passive competence will include the implementation description so that he or she can specialize the component in ways that were intended by its creators.

An *implementation description* is a description of the component's implementation written for the consumer. It includes a description of the specification, design, code (for programs), and tests. *Implementation description*

A provider of reusable components needs to include the implementation description in his or her active competence for component maintenance and evolution. A sophisticated consumer needs to include the implementation in his or her passive competence.

Object-oriented technology has two properties which make it especially suitable for creating reusable components: inheritance and encapsulation. We exploit these properties in five distinct and independent OOram technologies for component reuse: *OOram reuse technologies*

1   *Reuse based on inheritance.* Inheritance and polymorphism permit objects to be defined as being similar to other objects with specified points for modifications and addition. Reuse based on inheritance will be discussed in detail in the following sub-sections.

    a   A *pattern* describes a general problem and gives directions for its solution. Patterns can be used in many disciplines and for many purposes. We use them to describe and reuse base structures and activities in the areas of *system user*, *system requirements*, and *system design* modeling. Patterns are excellent for transferring reusable competence.

    b   An OOram framework represents a generally useful structure of objects. It is packaged as a reusable object specification model together with the corresponding class implementations. Frameworks are mainly used to describe and reuse low level design constructs, but may also be used to capture and reuse the basic constructs of an application domain. Frameworks are excellent for transferring solutions to hard problems in the form of classes designed for specialization. The main difference between a pattern and a framework is that the pattern explains the solution to a hard problem, while the framework hides it.

2   *Reuse based on encapsulation.* Object encapsulation separates the object's externally visible properties from their internal realizations. It enables us to replace one object with another as long as the latter behaves properly, and to bind different objects into a variety of structures. Reuse based on encapsulation will be discussed in detail in Chapter 11.

   a   An OOram composition system (OOCS) is an extensible system for composing object structures from predefined building blocks. The composition is controlled by a conceptual schema called an *OOCS schema.* The building blocks are reusable components specified by *OOCS types.* The OOCS is excellent for enabling analysts to compose complex systems without a programming stage.

   b   *Runtime configuration and object trading* is a technique for matching and linking objects at runtime. It is primarily used to select and attach suitable editors to objects representing user information. Runtime configuration and object trading is excellent for the automatic or semiautomatic selection of applicable classes in a dynamic environment.

   c   *Object structure duplication* is a technique for copying an existing master structure. This is trivial in simple cases, but we shall see that the duplication of arbitrary parts of an object structure is far from trivial. Object structure duplication is excellent for distributing objects, when combined with a gradual binding of their attributes.

Reuse based on encapsulation is particularly interesting. As computer programmers, we tend to focus on the creation of new programs. But we should not forget that the cheapest and safest way to produce new object structures is to create new configurations of objects from existing classes or to copy a validated master structure.

5.2 PATTERNS

IN A NUTSHELL

In this section we will illustrate how to describe object modeling know-how in terms of a pattern language, and how this idea helps us build concrete solutions on the best available practices. A pattern is a fixed-format description of how to solve a certain class of problems. A pattern language is a collection of patterns. A concrete problem is solved by decomposing it into subproblems and applying an appropriate pattern to each of them. Pattern languages can be made for many different disciplines, they originated for the purpose of capturing "the quality without a name" in architecture. We apply patterns to capture and document the essence of good object modeling practices.

Patterns are as applicable on the detailed programming level as they are on the organization level. The goal is always to communicate the solution to a problem; an appropriate notation and conceptual foundation must be chosen to support this goal. Role models are often appropriate if the solution involves patterns of interacting objects. General role models can be promoted to become library patterns. They must then be packaged for reuse; their existence must be published. If they express enterprise standards, their application must be enforced.

When we create object models of phenomena of interest to us, we frequently find it useful to factor out general features and create more abstract base models. This gives us the opportunity to partition the solution into general and special models, and helps us understand the phenomena on different levels of abstraction. (We discussed the technology of model separation and composition in Chapter 3.)

Divide and conquer

Some role models capture the essence of a solution to a general class of problems. Such models may be applicable to a broad range of specializations, and can profitably be packaged and added to the reusable assets of the enterprise. An OOram *pattern* is a fixed-format package consisting of a role model together with documentation describing when and how it should be used. The documentation can also specify constraints that ensure the correct functioning of a concrete application.

Package valuable solutions

Each pattern solves a clearly specified problem. A pattern can solve a complex problem; it can then reference other patterns for the solution of subproblems. A concrete problem is solved by applying a string of patterns. The collection of patterns is called a *pattern language*, and the series of patterns used to solve a specific problem is a sentence in this language.

Patterns can be created for a wide variety of purposes, ranging from abstract business procedures and information structures, to system architecture guidelines, and general ways of solving basic program design problems. This range is illustrated in Figure 5.3. The library of patterns constitutes part of the information assets of the enterprise.

The object community uses the term *pattern* in two senses. Some people use it to denote a specific object pattern: "*When several classes cooperate closely on a given task, we say the classes form a mechanism or pattern, with each pattern representing a dependency cluster*" [Soukup 94]. We use it in a more abstract sense, as a description of how the reader can solve a problem. This use of the term *pattern* originated with the architect Christopher Alexander, who said that "*Each pattern describes a problem which occurs over and over again in our environment, and then describes the core of the solution to that problem, in such a way that you can use this solution a million times over, without doing it the same way twice.*" [Alexander 77]

Patterns tell you how to solve problems

Figure 5.3

Patterns can be applied on all levels of modeling

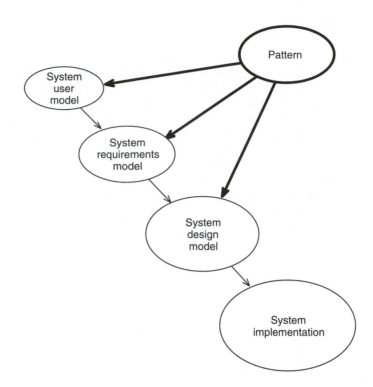

Alexander's quest for communicating good architectural practices in many ways parallels our quest for communication between the supplier of a reusable component and its consumers. The applicability of Alexander's patterns to objects was first recognized by Ward Cunningham while the latter was at Tektronix, and patterns now have a profound influence on the thinking of leading software engineers. For further details and an example, we refer you to Johnson [Johnson 92].

We expect to see many publications of patterns describing *best practices* in object-oriented software engineering. A high standard for quality and lucidity has been set in Gamma et al. [GaHeJoVli 95]. This book describes simple and elegant solutions to twenty-three problems in object-oriented software design. It should be required reading for all object-oriented programmers.

5.2.1   Alexander's Pattern Language

Alexander's pattern language captures the "quality without a name"

There are many similarities between the work done by an architect and the work done by a system designer, and we may have something to learn from the ways architects have attempted to solve the communication problem.

The architect Christopher Alexander has searched for a way to capture the essence of good architecture and to describe solutions to architectural problems in such a way that it will help other architects produce consistently good results. [Alexander 77, 79]. His idea was to build a collection of *patterns*, each pattern stating some problem and describing its solution. Some patterns describe high level problems such as "the distribution of towns" or "the countryside," which need more detailed patterns such as "country towns" and "cities" for their solution. The more detailed patterns build on patterns for "the family" and "house for a small family," down to details such as "alcoves," "dressing room," and "child caves."

Alexander's vision was that he should be able to formalize the "quality without a name" which separates good architecture from bad architecture, and communicate it to other architects. He called his scheme a *pattern language*, because any specific solution should be created by selecting the appropriate patterns and composing them into an organic whole.

What strikes us most forcibly when reading *A Pattern Language* is what it leaves unsaid. The problems are described under the assumption that the reader is as familiar with them as the writer, and the solutions are more in the nature of hints than of detailed instructions. Alexander assumes that the architect knows how to design and that the builder knows how to build. There is nothing about architectural notation, structural engineering, sound building practices, production control, or economy. *Alexander presupposes strong common culture*

Let us refer back to the shipyard planning example of Chapter 1. The common competence of the group is the main factor; the plans, patterns or reusable components comprise a varnish on top of this common culture. These constructs may be highly valuable, but cannot replace the human qualities of the practitioners.

Our suggestion for a three-level documentation of reusable components has been strongly influenced by Alexander's patterns. The *list of instructions* could profitably be in the form of a pattern, it should be brief—bordering on the cryptic. It should give the reader a sudden insight, an *aha!*, which starts him or her on the right track for a good solution. The pattern should not bind the details of the solution; they are well within the competence of the reader and have to be adapted to the concrete problem. The pattern helps the knowledgeable reader see the important points to consider, but does not provide all the details of the solution.

The pattern can be augmented with a *logical map*, giving background information to the less competent reader, so that he or she may fully appreciate the practical implications of the pattern. If all readers are expected to be fully competent, the logical map can be omitted.

Alexander's books, which inspired the pattern movement, date back to 1977 and 1978. Alexander later tried out his theories in practice, but he was sadly disappointed. The "quality without a name" has proven to be more elusive than expected, and he now finds that the creative process is as important as the patterns. We refer you to Gabriel's excellent columns in the *Journal of Object-Oriented Programming* for more details: [Gabriel 94a] is a summary of the good news, and [Gabriel 94b] summarizes the bad news.

I must admit I am quite pleased that Alexander's original vision did not materialize. It makes me uneasy when people try to isolate the soul and dissect it. I trust they will never succeed, and I base this trust on the systems theorem that the whole is more than the sum of its parts. I believe the "quality without a name" is intimately associated with the whole: analyze it to find its constituent parts, and it's gone. The pleasing practical consequence is that it still takes people of quality to create products of quality. But the parts are also valuable, and emerging libraries of patterns will help quality people create better systems. *Pattern languages very useful, but no panacea*

5.2.2 How to Create a Pattern

Our interest focuses on problems which are concerned with choosing appropriate objects, deciding on their attributes, and determining their essential behavior. We achieve pattern generality by describing solutions in terms of role models.

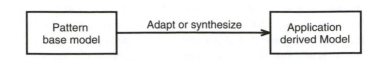

These models can be used directly by synthesis, but they can also be used to communicate a general idea, such that concrete solutions will be variants of the general pattern role model. (See Figure 5.4.)

When to package a pattern

It is appropriate to create a pattern if the following conditions are satisfied:

1 The phenomenon and the possible models describing it are well understood.

2 The investment will be amortized because the problem will be recurring in the future and the pattern will actually be used by the consumers. The primary motivation may sometimes be a desire to ensure a uniform solution to a common problem; economic considerations will then be secondary.

How to do it

You can create a new pattern by following these operations (not necessarily in this sequence):

1 Identify consumers and their goals, needs, competence, working habits, and preferences.

2 Perform a cost-benefit analysis to estimate return on a possible investment in a new pattern.

3 Perform reverse engineering on existing instances of the phenomenon to understand all the issues and possible solutions.

4 Specify the new pattern in general terms, highlighting the core of the problems to be solved and the goals to be reached.

5 Create a pattern describing how to solve the problem.

6 Describe the background of the new pattern and the rationale for the choices made in its creation.

7 Inform the consumer community about the new pattern, motivate them to use it, train them, and make the pattern available to them.

Implementation

Our patterns are implemented as a role model together with the appropriate documentation. The role model will be described in the documentation, but should preferably also be stored in the reuse library in electronic form, to simplify its synthesis into derived models.

A simple adaption of Alexander's pattern language gives us the following suggested contents of a pattern:

1 Pattern title.

2 Conditions for using the pattern.

3 Brief problem description.

4 Stepwise description of work process when applying the pattern.

5 Description of the base model, using the appropriate views and explanatory text to show its main features.

6 Required and recommended constraints. The consumer is not permitted to violate the required constraints. Recommended constraints may be violated, but

it is usually wrong, meaningless, or dangerous to do so. The consumer must understand the issues and take full responsibility.

7 Checklist for quality assurance of the consumer's use of the pattern.

8 Related patterns.

The book by Gamma et al. [GaHeJoVli 95] gives more details including programming hints and examples.

Example: A Decision Model and Project Portfolio Management

One of our clients is a large enterprise that organizes its major investments as projects. We have worked with a branch of this enterprise that is responsible for defining and managing such projects.

Project portfolio management

The client's projects vary in size from a few million dollars to a few billion dollars, and are performed by other parts of the enterprise or by outside contractors. Large projects are typically subdivided into smaller ones. Project coordination is typically performed by our client.

Traditional project management methods address the needs of the project contractor: how to split the total project into manageable activities, and how to plan and control the activities in time and resources.

Our client's problems were on the next higher level: how to decide on a project and define its scope; how to select a contractor; how to negotiate and enter into a contract; and how to maintain control so that the contractor really does the job allocated to him. To complicate matters, our client was supervising a large number of projects simultaneously.

Our task was to help our client improve and formalize the work procedures, and to create and install effective computer support for these procedures.

One of our senior consultants worked with a representative user group to establish a formal model of their work with project portfolio management. It turned out that this formal model could profitably be made object-oriented because the clients needed to determine the *who, what, when,* and *how* of project portfolio management.

Requirements analysis

Further, the client did not want to model the *who* part onto named individuals or positions in the organization, but onto roles that people play. Role modeling was, therefore, a natural choice.

The discussions in the group were not all smooth and to the point. The initial discussions were particularly confused; members of the group had clearly different perceptions about the essence of the problem (which is the main advantage of working with a group rather than with an individual).

Divide and conquer

The main breakthrough came when our consultant discovered that they were discussing two issues simultaneously: How do we, in general, make and implement decisions in our enterprise? And how do we, specifically, make and implement decisions regarding projects?

The decision-making process was recognized as being a very general one. It was decided to create a separate model for decision-making; and to derive the portfolio control model from it.

A model for making important decisions

The decision-making process is applicable in many contexts outside the area of project portfolio control, and is a clear pattern candidate. We will here sketch out such a pattern. It is intended as an illustration only, and many details essential to decision-making have been omitted.

This pattern is applicable in all situations where the enterprise is to make a major decision. A major decision is defined as a decision where premises and consequences have to be studied in the organization prior to the decision being made by the proper authority.

Problem

In a rational organization, there is a systematic division of authority and responsibility between its members. A major decision will be made by somebody (or some body). Prior to this, proposals have to be written and studied by the relevant personnel to ensure that the best efforts are applied to making a good decision in a timely manner.

Solution

The basic collaboration diagram is shown in Figure 5.5. This diagram shows one level in a hierarchical organization, and it can be used to compose a model with any number of levels. The core of the solution is to harness the efforts of as many organizational levels as required:

1 Write a careful description of the decision to be made.

2 Identify the people to be involved, either as individuals or as roles in the organizational structure. Apply the role collaboration diagram of Figure 5.5 on as many levels as required. This diagram defines the roles you will need to map onto real people in organizational units.

3 Identify the work procedure and document it. The skeleton scenario of Figure 5.6 will help you get started.

4 If the pattern model is adequate for your purposes, you can derive your application model from it. Otherwise, you can edit a copy as required.

This is a recursive model: My chief may be somebody else's subordinate, and my subordinate may be somebody else's chief. The basic message interaction scenario is shown in Figure 5.6. The diagram shows the interaction across a single level. Multilevel interaction can be derived by synthesis.I, the DecisionMaker, receive a proposal from my superior; my staff studies it and splits it into more detailed proposals for my subordinates. When I get their response, my staff merges

Figure 5.5
Decision Maker:
collaboration
diagram

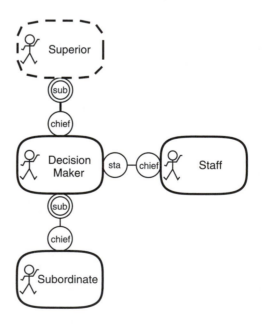

CREATING REUSABLE COMPONENTS

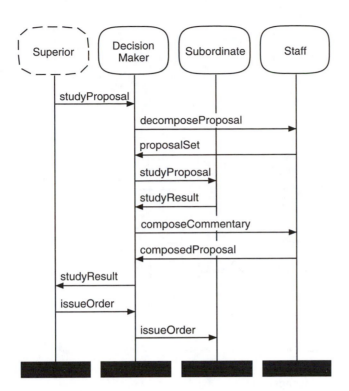

Figure 5.6
**Decision Maker:
typical scenario**

their results so that I can send a consolidated proposal to my superior. The decision is made and is communicated down the command chain. (We have omitted the details of the required staff work from this pattern.).

The processes for making important decisions must be carefully documented. The documentation should include references to the generic decision maker pattern and carefully explain any deviation from it.

The Decision Maker pattern can be specialized for making many different kinds of decisions. As an example, we have sketched out solutions to four different kinds of decision problems in an oil production operation. We applied the Decision Maker model twice and renamed the roles to get the head office decision model shown in Figure 5.7. We applied it once and renamed the roles to get the general model for local operational decisions in Figure 5.8. Certain decisions need the advice of experts; the model in Figure 5.9 takes care of that. Finally, important decisions can be made only by the home office; Figure 5.10 shows the decision structure.

Application example: An organization for oil production

The synthesis view of Figure 5.11 shows the synthesis relationships between these models. Their details do not concern us here. The point is that patterns permit us to factor out common features and create a structure of reusable base models. The large body of possibly unrelated procedures becomes unified and consistent. We try to push the stable parts of our procedures up toward the base models, while the variable aspects are pushed down toward the derived models. If we do it right, we get an organization in which it is easy to create new procedures and modify old ones, because the complex parts of the procedures are in the stable models, while the variable parts are in small and simple derivations.

A powerful tool for simplifying and unifying procedures

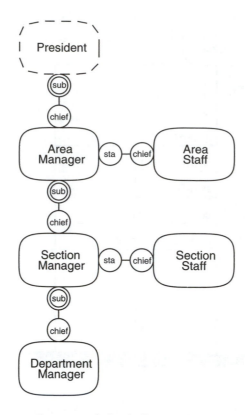

Figure 5.7 The head office organization

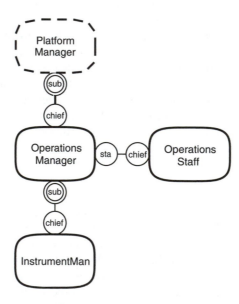

Figure 5.8 Organization for decisions that can be made locally on an oil production platform

CREATING REUSABLE COMPONENTS

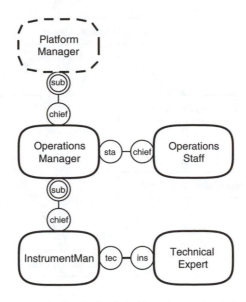

Figure 5.9   Organization for local decisions that need technical expertise

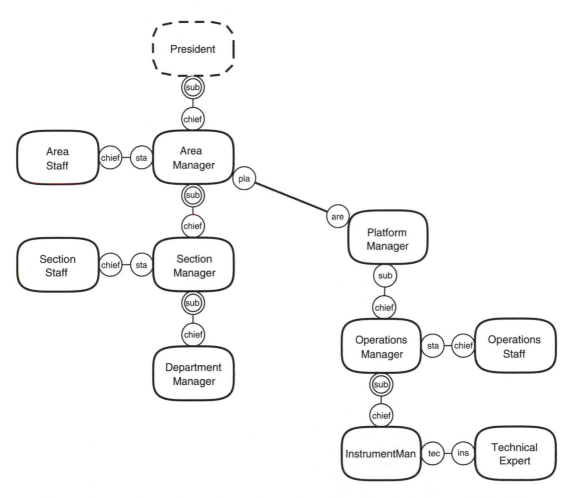

Figure 5.10   Organization for major decisions that need technical expertise and involvement of head office

Figure 5.11
Synthesis view
showing
relationships
between
example models

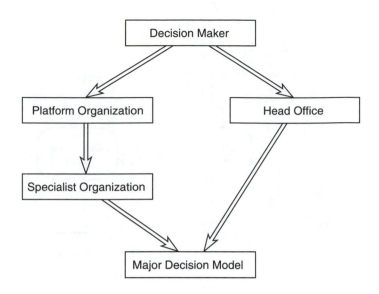

5.3 OORAM FRAMEWORKS

This section is written for programmers, and you may safely skip it if you are not interested in programming.

An OOram framework *is a reusable component containing a role model describing a general solution, a correlated set of base classes implementing its roles, and possibly descriptions of applicable constraints. We discuss the nature of an OOram framework and then give hints as to an appropriate development process.*

The creation of an OOram framework is illustrated through an extensive case study in Chapter 9.

IN A NUTSHELL

Safe role model synthesis provides a nice, powerful way of specifying and using reusable class structures. A *framework* is an object specification model which is created for the express purpose of being generally reusable through synthesis; together with a corresponding cluster of classes which has been designed for subclassing. The framework is a packaged product that solves a specific problem; it includes instructions for when and how to use it safely.

A framework is a problem solution

Figure 5.12 illustrates that OOram frameworks provide the application programmer with solutions for the design and implementation stages. System design is simplified because the programmer can build on proven solutions by synthesizing the appropriate role models into his or her design. System implementation is simplified because the programmer can build programs by inheriting from the corresponding base classes.

Frameworks support design and implementation

Figure 5.12

OOram frameworks support design and implementation

In general, a framework is a reusable module

When we study solutions to a number of different, but related, problems, we often find common subproblems which are costly to implement and hard to get right. We solve such subproblems once and for all, so that application programmers in the future can build on the common solution and inherit its functionality and correctness.

In the software engineering community, a framework is commonly defined as a software module which facilitates the development of applications. A framework can provide functionality such as operating system utilities, network communications, or interface development facilities.

Object-oriented framework is a set of coordinated classes

An *object-oriented framework* is usually defined as a set of base classes that together describe a generally useful object structure. Application programmers use this object structure by deriving specialized classes from the framework's base classes.

OOram framework is a product

An *OOram framework* is a product designed for planned reuse. Insights into the best ways of solving given programming problems are captured in a collection of interdependent classes that are prepared for subclassing. These classes are described by a role model which specifies the framework's essential functionality and hides all unnecessary details.

Patterns and frameworks are reusable components that describe solutions to general problems. The difference is on the abstraction level: the pattern describes how the reader can solve a problem, while the framework provides a concrete solution. The pattern is tutorial in nature, it explains the essential components of the solution so that the reader can apply them. A framework takes care of many solution details so that the application programmer need not see them or worry about them.

The application programmer inherits the solution by deriving his or her design model from the framework base model. At the implementation stage, he or she derives application classes from the corresponding framework classes.

The core concepts of an OOram framework are illustrated in Figure 5.13. (This is a semantic view; its concepts and notation will be fully described in Section 6.1.) It shows how the framework role model consists of roles which are implemented as base classes. The application program is specified by a consistent mapping of the framework elements onto corresponding elements in the application.

Synthesis can be implied when the derived model gets uncomfortably complex without giving new insights. It is often sufficient to create a role model for the application that follows the object structure of the framework without actually performing the synthesis operation.

The OOram framework should be developed under stringent quality requirements, so that the application programmer can rely on its correctness. It may also be beneficial to provide automated tools that help the application programmer conform to the framework's inherent constraints.

Improving frameworks is a two-edged sword

We have learned the hard way that deriving our own software from somebody else's framework is a two-edged sword. We have achieved the expected gain in productivity and quality in our initial development, but we have also experienced chaotic situations when the framework provider improved the framework classes in new releases. The *surface area* between the frameworks and our derived classes was large and undefined, and it was very hard to determine the consequences of framework changes.

Even the vendor's bug fixes can cause catastrophies, because we are likely to have fixed the bugs in our subclasses. Just consider what happens when a framework method returns a count which is 1 too large. Our subclass will have sub-

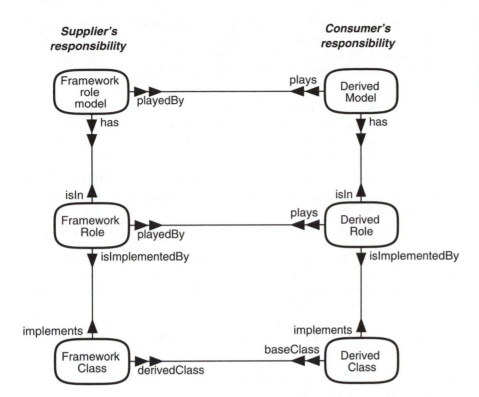

Figure 5.13

Semantic
relationships
between
framework
concepts

tracted 1 from the returned count, which is okay until the framework is fixed. We will then use a count which is 1 too small. Or consider that the new version of the framework has made a subtle shift in the responsibility between some methods. We may have created an override for one of the methods in our subclass, and this method will now have the outdated responsibility.

We have tried, without success, to persuade various framework providers that they under no circumstances can modify a framework once it is published, but we must admit that their desire to improve their products is understandable. There is clearly a dilemma here. One of the great selling points for a framework is that it can be steadily improved over the years to the benefit of all consumers. But our experience indicates that such improvements can cause much rework and introduce subtle bugs in the derived applications.

The framework provider cannot modify the frameworks at will

Brad Cox defines the *surface area* of a component as all the things that must be understood and properly dealt with for one component to function correctly in combination with another [Cox 87]. Examples are class names, data names, message names and parameter types; time sequence constraints, garbage collection requirements, protection domains, and concurrency considerations.

We believe that the solution to the maintenance dilemma is to reduce and carefully define the surface area between a framework and its derivatives. The surface area of a good framework should be kept as small as possible. The framework provider is obliged to keep the surface unchanged, but is free to improve any of the hidden parts. Similarly, the framework consumer can modify only designated, visible parts of the framework. These are two of the main motivations for our insistence that an OOram framework must be much more than a collection of classes; it must include firm rules for its proper use. The optimum solution depends on the circumstances and the tools available—if the supplier can make it

Specify and reduce surface area

impossible to violate the rules, if there is an automatic rule checker, or if rule conformance is a manual operation. The main thing is that the rules are clearly expressed and that the consumer abides by them.

When to create a framework

It is appropriate to create an OOram framework when the following conditions are satisfied:

1 The investment will be amortized because the problem will be recurring in the future and the framework will actually be used by the consumers. The primary motivation may sometimes be a desire to ensure a uniform solution to a common problem; economic considerations will then be secondary.

2 The phenomenon and the possible models describing it are well understood.

3 Several implementations that include the phenomenon exist and are available for analysis.

4 The requirements for a generally applicable framework are well understood.

It may also be appropriate to create frameworks under less than ideal conditions. The motivation could be that it is often better to dive into a problem and then improve the solution as we learn and gain experience, than it is to wait for the ideal conditions to materialize.

How to create a framework

We suggest a possible list of operations for creating a framework. You will not necessarily perform them in the given sequence, and you may want to add or remove some operations:

1 *Identify consumers and consumer needs.* Consumer goals, needs, competence, working habits and preferences.

2 *Perform a cost-benefit analysis* to estimate the pay-back of the investment in a new framework.

3 *Perform reverse engineering* of existing programs to understand all the issues and possible solutions. The devil is often in the details. Reverse engineering is a powerful method for identifying details that can play havoc with an otherwise pleasing architecture.

4 *Specify the new framework* in general terms, highlighting the problems to be solved and the goals to be reached.

5 *Document the framework as a pattern, describing how to use it to solve problems.* This pattern enlarges the consumers' active vocabulary. We strongly recommend that this part be created before the framework is designed and implemented. This is because a successful framework must be easy to understand and safe to use, and we rely on our inborn laziness to ensure that the interface to the consumer will be as simple as possible. (You might enjoy reading the user manual for your favorite program and highlighting all sentences that couldn't possibly have been written before the program.)

6 *Describe the framework's design and implementation* for the consumers' understanding and passive vocabulary.

7 *Inform the consumer community* about the new framework, motivate them to use it, train them, and make the framework available to them.

Chapter 9 presents a case study that illustrates the creation of a major framework.

CHAPTER 6   

Additional Role Modeling Concepts and Notation

CONTENTS

6.1   Semantic View   159

6.2   Process View   162

6.3   State Diagram View   168

6.4   Role List View   172

6.5   Modeling in the Large: The OOram Module   173

This chapter is intended as a reference, to be read on a need-to-know basis. Its sections can be read in any sequence.

The role model may be observed from a number of perspectives and manipulated in many different views. The large number of views offered by the OOram method does not complicate it, because any given work process applies only the small selection that carries the most useful information.

Some central role model views were presented in Section 2.5; we will here describe some additional ones:

1 The *semantic view* describes the meaning we associate with the roles and their relationships.

2 The *process view* describes the flow of data between the roles and the processing of the data in these roles.

3   The *state diagram view* describes the legal states of a role and the messages that trigger a transition from one state to another.

4   The *role list view* gives an overview of the roles, their names, purpose, and attributes.

5   The *OOram module* encapsulates a number of models and controls high level export and import of models.

6.1   SEMANTIC VIEW

*The semantic view describes the meaning we associate with the roles and their re-
lationships. We rarely need the semantic view, since the collaboration view usually
contains sufficient information.*

*Three basic
concepts in
traditional
semantic
modeling*

The purpose of traditional semantic modeling is to create a representation of concepts and ideas along with the relationships between them. A common expression of semantic models is the *entity-relationship* (E-R) model [Chen 76, Elmasri
94]. The two basic notions of E-R modeling that are of interest to us are the following:

1 *Entity.* An entity represents the set of all instances of the same thing, idea, or
   concept that we want to think about. An important attribute of an entity is a
   description of the meaning we attach to the entity instances. Entities are commonly denoted by a rectangle in E-R diagrams.

2 *Relation.* The entities of a problem domain are somehow related to each other.
   A relation is a representation of the meaning we attach to the relationship between entities. A relation is bidirectional. It describes what a first entity is in relation to a second one, as well as what the second is in relation to the first. A
   relation is commonly denoted by a line connecting the entities. The line may
   be annotated with text describing the relationships. Four different kinds of relations are commonly recognized:

   • *Aggregation.* The two directions of the aggregation relation are commonly
     called *consists-of* and *part-of.*

   • *Use.* The two directions of the use relation are commonly called *uses* and
     used-by.

   • *Subtype.* The two directions of the subtype relation are commonly called *is-
     a* and *kind-of.*

   • *Association.* The two directions of the association are given names to de-
     scribe the nature of the relationship.

The different kinds of relations are handled as follows:

1 *Aggregation* can be modeled by structures of interacting objects in several
   ways. We gave a detailed discussion of this topic in Section 3.2.1.

2 *Use relation.* In an object model, this relation implies that an object sends messages to (uses) another object. This relation is shown explicitly in the collaboration view that was described in Section 2.5.2.

3 *Subtype relation.* This is the base–derived model relation that was described in
   Chapter 3.

4 *Association.* This is the relation shown in the OOram semantic view. It describes the *meaning* we attach to the relation.

The semantic view is designed to capture E-R kind of information for a system
of interacting roles. We describe the *concepts* that the analyst associates with the
roles and the relations between them. The notation is shown in Figure 6.1. Figure
6.2 is a semantic view of the Purchasing model of Section 2.3.2.

*The semantic
view describes
the meaning of
the roles and
their relations*

Figure 6.1
Semantic view
notation

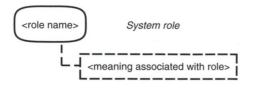

<role name>　　　System role

<meaning associated with role>

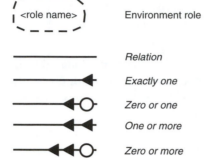

<role name>　　　Environment role

―――――――　　　*Relation*

―――――◄　　　*Exactly one*

―――――◄O－　　　*Zero or one*

―――――◄◄　　　*One or more*

――――◄◄O　　　*Zero or more*

The symbols are drawn close to the source role. They are annotated with a text describing the meaning of the relation in the direction of the arrowhead.

Figure 6.3 shows an E-R diagram which corresponds to this example. The important difference is that the entities are *types*: the diagram says that the Enterprise *is client of* some Bank, and the Vendor *is client of* a possibly different Bank.

Roles are like objects in that they have identity. If we should interpret Figure 6.3 as a semantic view, it would mean that the Enterprise and the Vendor are both clients of the same Bank; and that the Bank cooperates with itself. Notice that Figure 6.2 does not say they must be different; the same Bank object could play both roles.

The E-R model is on a higher abstraction level than the role model, and E-R diagrams can be more compact than the corresponding semantic views. We need the concrete aspects of the role model because we want to reason about its behavior. In our example, we want to be able to analyze the model to convince ourselves that the Vendor who delivers the goods will also be the Vendor who receives payment. We can make this kind of arguments on the role level, but not on the type (or entity) level. (This problem is often called *the equivalence of path problem* in the E-R community.)

Figure 6.2
Semantic view of
Purchase
model

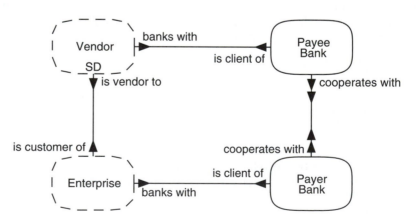

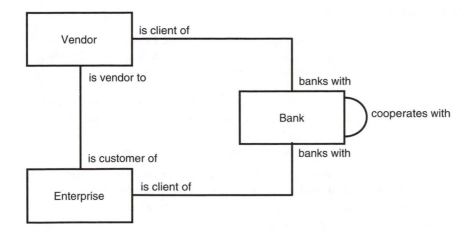

Figure 6.3
Corresponding
E-R diagram

There is a strong correspondence between the semantic view and the collaboration view. The semantic view describes how we think about the concepts and their relationships. The collaboration view shows how the objects collaborate in order to provide a faithful representation of our thoughts. A relation represents a conceptual relationship, and a port represents the object's knowledge about one or more collaborators. The diagrams will have similar topologies, except that all relations need not be represented as message paths if there are no messages flowing between the associated objects. Furthermore, the cardinalities of the ports may be more restricted than the cardinalities of the relations, since an object may not need to know all the associated objects at any given time.

Collaboration view and semantic view—different meaning!

We rarely need the semantic view, since the collaboration view in most cases contains much the same information.

The synthesis operation does not lead to semantic relations between the base model and the derived model. The reason is that there is no formal relationship between the *meaning* a human observer associates with the roles and relations in a derived model and the *meaning* he or she associates with the roles and relations of the base models. The analyst must ensure that they are semantically consistent.

Structural relationship between base and derived semantic views

There are formal relationships between the structures (syntax) of the derived and base models; the general restrictions on roles, ports, and cardinalities hold for the systems seen in the semantic views:

1 All *roles* in the base model must be mapped onto roles in the derived model.

2 Every *relation* in all base models must be mapped onto a corresponding relation in the derived model.

3 The *cardinalities* of the relations in the derived model must be consistent with the cardinalities of the corresponding relations in the base models. Specifically, the minimum cardinality of a derived model relation must be equal to or greater than the minimum cardinality of the corresponding base model relations; and the maximum cardinality of a derived model relation must be equal to or less than the maximum cardinality of the corresponding base model relations.

The notation for the semantic view of the derived model is the same as the general notation described above. Inheritance relations may be added as shown in Figure 3.31, but this is rarely of interest.

No new notation

6.2   PROCESS VIEW

A Process view describes the flow of data between roles, and the processing of these data in the roles. We find the process view particularly useful for describing the flow of data and work procedures in human organizations.

IDEF0 is a well-known standard for Process analysis

Process analysis is a well-established and powerful technique for describing how a system processes data. The OOram process view is based on the ideas of the IDEF0 standard [IDEF0 93], and has been adapted to our general object model. The basic IDEF0 concepts, illustrated in Figure 6.4, are as follows:

1   *Mechanism.* The actor (person, role, machine, resource, competence, software system, etc.) that deals with *how*, or the means by which the process is done— e.g., which people, machines, programs, etc., are required.

2   *Input.* Data or *raw materials* undergo a process or a series of activities, and are transformed into output.

3   *Process.* A series of operations contributing to a specific purpose. In the IDEF0 technique, a process is described by a verb or verb phrase and is represented graphically by a rectangle.

4   *Control.* Data controlling or influencing the way in which the process converts its input into output. The control affects the mode of activities, and may be in the form of parameters and rules to be used by the mechanisms, such as deter- mining which output is produced, how much, and when it is produced (e.g., directions, standards, purposes, timing, quantities, etc., which control or direct the way in which an activity is performed).

5   *Output.* Data or *products* are produced by, or result from, the process.

Mapping IDEF0 and OOram concepts

The IDEF0 concepts can be mapped nicely onto the concepts of the OOram method:

1   *IDEF0 mechanisms* are the actors that perform actions. In our object model, all actions are performed by an object. The actor must, therefore, be an object. This is represented by a role in our model.

Figure 6.4

The IDEF0 ICOM concept (input, control, output, mechanism)

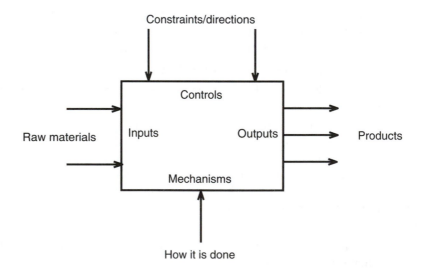

2 The *IDEF0 input* constitutes the input data to the object. The only way to carry data to an object is through a message, and the input data must be carried as message parameters or return values. Several inputs can be grouped as parameters to the same message—if they have the same sender, the same receiver, and are sent at the same time. There are no unsolicited messages in our object model. Initial data are represented as the parameters of a stimulus message from an environment role.

3 An *IDEF0 process* is defined as a series of operations contributing to a specific purpose. The corresponding OOram concept is the execution of a method.

4 *IDEF0 control* is a trigger releasing an action. In our object model, actions are released only when the object receives a message. The action is defined by a method, and the trigger is a message. This message can be received only after all necessary data have been received, and it could be the last data-carrying message. The data carried by the other data-carrying messages must be stored in the object's attributes so that they are ready when the trigger message arrives. (Asynchronous data-carrying messages can be stored in the object's input queue until the trigger message arrives.) The choice of solution is not part of the process view; it could be described in a state diagram view, or it could be postponed to the implementation stage.

5 *Output.* Data or *products* are produced by, or result from, an action. The output from one object must be input to another, and must be transmitted from the data source as a message. This message will be received by some other object as described under *Input.*

The notation for a Process view is shown in Figure 6.5. Roles are shown as super-ellipses, actions as rectangles, data as parallelograms, and dataflow as arrows.

The use of the process view is illustrated in Figure 6.6. Since objects are the only possible actors in an object-oriented system, every action has to be associated with a role. The role responsible for an action is indicated by its column. The responsibility for the data being transferred is undefined.

Most process analysis methods support composite actions, which are actions that are later decomposed into a number of smaller actions, with data flowing between them. This is easily supported by the process view with one caveat: if the composite action is performed by several roles, a corresponding virtual role must be defined to maintain the one-to-one relationship between process actors and roles. The decomposed process view will begin with a single action and will end with another action, both being parts of the composite actions.

The OOram process view

Composite actions supported

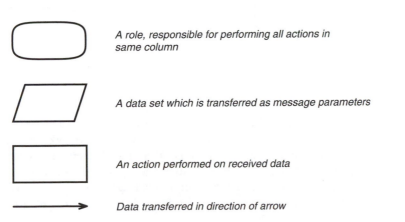

Figure 6.5
Process view notation

A role, responsible for performing all actions in same column

A data set which is transferred as message parameters

An action performed on received data

Data transferred in direction of arrow

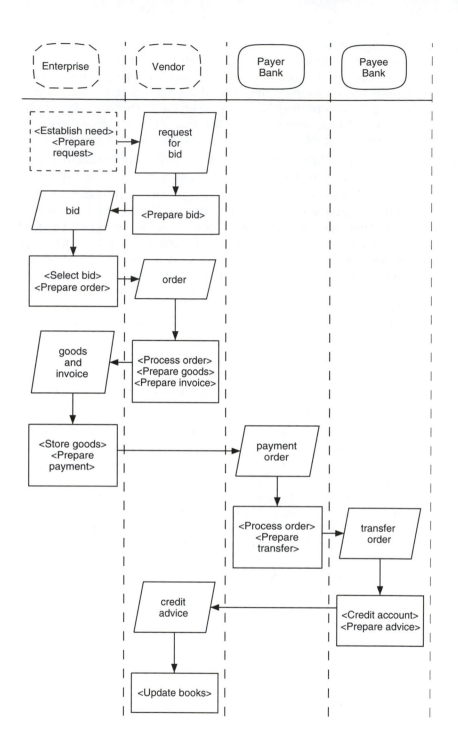

Figure 6.6
Process view of
Purchase
model

Data stores are
special objects

Conventional dataflow analysis represents data stores as special elements. The only way to store data in our object model is as object attributes. We must, therefore, represent a data store as a role in a column in the diagram. The data store object receives and transmits data through messages, and the data stored at any time may be derived from the data store's input data. Data store objects will normally be persistent: their contents will survive individual program executions.

A process that is described in a role model cannot, in general, be assumed to be valid in a derived model. The reason is that in the general, unsafe synthesis, the base model activities are not preserved in the derived model.

Processes lost in unsafe synthesis

The essence of safe synthesis is that the base model activities are preserved in the derived model. In these cases, the processes of the base model are preserved in the derived model. We have suggested two safe synthesis constructs where the destiny of a process after a synthesis operation corresponds to the destiny of the stimulus message that starts it:

Processes inherited in safe synthesis

1 *Activity superposition.* The base model stimulus messages become derived model stimulus messages. The base model activities become independent derived model activities. The base model processes become independent derived model processes. This is a trivial case that will not be discussed further.

2 *Activity aggregation.* The base model stimulus message is sent from one of the derived model methods. The base model activity becomes a subactivity, and the base model process becomes a subprocess under this method in the derived model.

We will illustrate activity aggregation by an example from the `DerivedTravel-Expense` model.

Activity aggregation means that we splice a base model process into a derived model process

Figure 6.7 shows a process view corresponding to the scenario for the `TravelExpense` model in Figure 2.15. Similarly, Figure 6.8 shows the process view corresponding to the scenario for the `AirlineBooking` model in Figure 3.5.

When we synthesize the two models into the `DerivedTravelExpense` model, the `AirlineBooking` activity is spliced into the method for the `travelPermission` message. Compare the scenario of Figure 3.13 and the method views of Figures

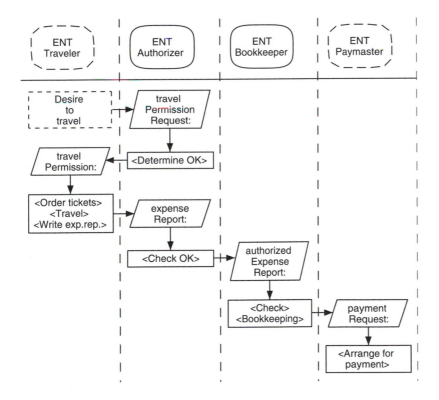

Figure 6.7

Expense-Account process view

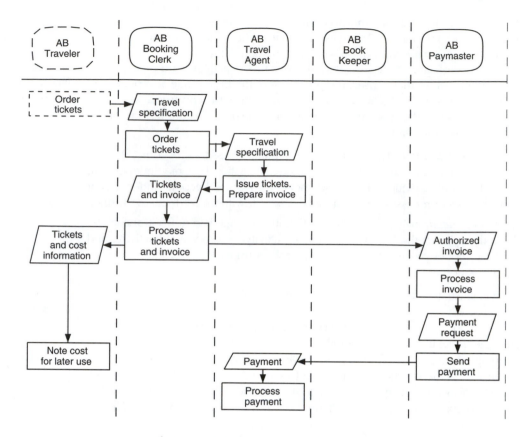

Figure 6.8 **AB (Airline-Booking) process**

3.14 and 3.15 with the combined process view of Figure 6.9. You will appreciate that different views highlight different aspects of a common model, and that you can select the views that are most convenient and informative for your purpose.

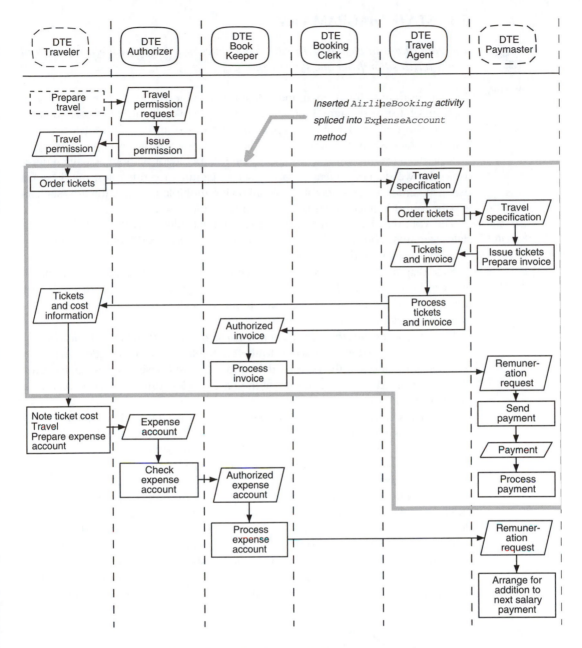

| DTE
Traveler | DTE
Authorizer | DTE
Book
Keeper | DTE
Booking
Clerk | DTE
Travel
Agent | DTE
Paymaster |

Prepare travel → Travel permission request → Issue permission → Travel permission

Inserted `AirlineBooking` *activity spliced into* `ExpenseAccount` *method*

Travel permission → Order tickets → Travel specification → Order tickets → Travel specification → Issue tickets Prepare invoice → Tickets and invoice → Process tickets and invoice → Tickets and cost information

Process tickets and invoice → Authorized invoice → Process invoice → Remuneration request → Send payment → Payment → Process payment

Tickets and cost information → Note ticket cost Travel Prepare expense account → Expense account → Check expense account → Authorized expense account → Process expense account → Remuneration request → Arrange for addition to next salary payment

Figure 6.9   **Derived-Travel-Expense** process view

6.3 STATE DIAGRAM VIEW

The state diagram view describes the legal states of a role and the messages that trigger a transition from one state to another.

State diagrams belong to internal perspective

We can zoom in to focus on an individual role or object, and study its behavior in the form of a state diagram. In a state diagram, the overall pattern of collaborating roles in the role model has disappeared; all we see are the messages received from the object's environment. The sending of these messages is kept out of sight.

State diagrams are suitable for specifying role behavior without actually writing the code. We do not generally specify state diagrams for our roles, but they are useful in certain cases—notably cases involving multiple message threads, such as is often found in telecommunications and real time systems.

Use state diagrams sparingly, and late in the process

The volume of a description increases dramatically with the introduction of state diagrams. You should only use them if you really need them, and then only at a late stage in the design process.

State diagrams are omitted if the design can be made so simple that the problem can be postponed to the implementation stage. The main advantage is that the volume of the models is drastically reduced, so that they are easier to create, easier to check, and easier to modify.

We *cannot reason about the dynamic correctness by studying a single state diagram.* We must extend our scope to the complete role model to determine the dynamic correctness of the base models, and we must consider the state diagrams of all synthesized roles to determine if the base model correctness is preserved in the derived model.

The theory and usage of state diagrams is a specialized subject which we will not attempt to cover adequately in this book. We will content ourselves with indicating how state diagrams may be defined in the context of a role in a role model, and refer you to the literature for further details [Bræk 93].

State diagram view

In conventional state diagrams, actions are triggered by signals. The only possible signals in our object model are the receipt of messages, and actions are defined as methods. There can be at most one state diagram for each role. It describes the possible states of the role, the messages that are acceptable in each state, the action taken as a result of each message, and the next state attained after the action is completed. The OOram notation is shown in Figure 6.10.

Figure 6.11 shows the collaboration view of the Purchasing model from Figure 6.2. Figure 6.12 shows the state diagram for the Vendor role in this model.

Figure 6.10

State diagram graphical notation

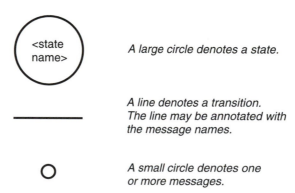

<state name>   *A large circle denotes a state.*

_____   *A line denotes a transition. The line may be annotated with the message names.*

O   *A small circle denotes one or more messages.*

Collaboration view

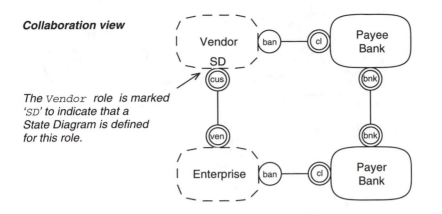

The `Vendor` role is marked
'*SD*' to indicate that a
*State Diagram is defined
for this role.*

Figure 6.11

Purchase model collaboration view

We shall now discuss how we can preserve a successful state diagram through a safe synthesis operation. Note that we restrict our arguments to sequential message semantics. The safe synthesis of state diagrams for parallel processes is a research topic, but we expect that the preservation of the activity integrity will hold the key to success.

Compose the derived state diagram in safe synthesis

The state diagram of a derived role will in some sense be a product of the state diagrams of its base roles. If a base role M has states m1, m2, and m3; and another base role, N, has states n1 and n2, the derived role may have the states m1n1, m1n2, m2n1, m2n2, m3n1, and m3n2. This is illustrated in Figure 6.13.

General synthesis leads to state space explosion

Our two safe synthesis constructs are much simpler. We start with activity superposition. We notice that the base model activities are to be retained as independent activities in the derived model, and that at most one activity can be performed at a time. The effect is that the initial state of *all* derived roles will be the combination of the base model initial states, and rest of the base model state diagrams will appear as separate structures with no transitions between them. This is illustrated in Figure 6.14 for role MN, which is derived from roles M and N.

Activity superposition

In activity aggregation, the activity of one base model is triggered as a subactivity in one of the methods of another model. Figure 6.15 illustrates an example in which the state diagram of role N is encapsulated within a single state in the state diagram for role M.

Activity aggregation

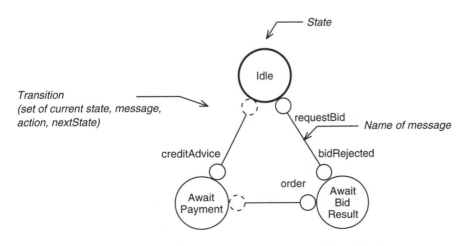

Figure 6.12

Vendor state diagram

Figure 6.13
General state
diagram synthesis

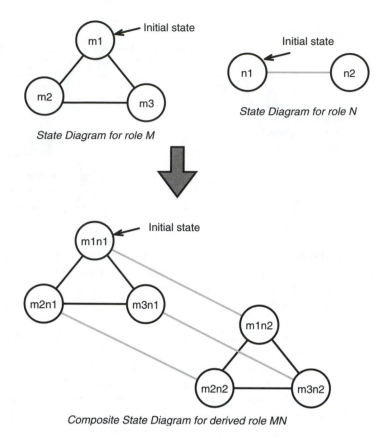

State Diagram for role M

State Diagram for role N

Composite State Diagram for derived role MN

Figure 6.14
Activity
superposition

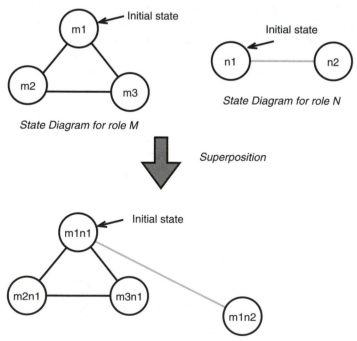

State Diagram for role M

State Diagram for role N

Superposition

Composite State Diagram for derived role MN

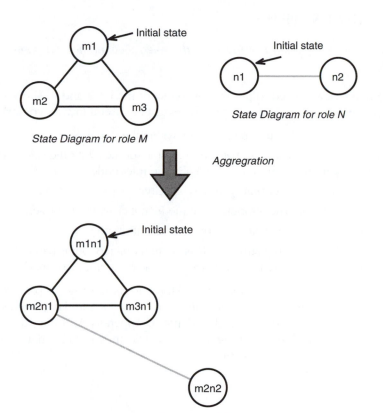

State Diagram for role M

Initial state

State Diagram for role N

Figure 6.15

Activity
aggregation

Aggregration

Composite State Diagram for derived role MN

Notice that the state diagrams of all other derived roles are copies of their respective base model state diagrams. The interdependence between base model state diagrams is allowed only in the triggering role.

Also notice that attributes may not be modified by an action method if this causes a state change in a different base model, because such change modifies base model behavior.

6.4 ROLE LIST VIEW

IN A NUTSHELL

The role list view gives an overview of the roles, their names, purposes, and attributes.

Many data items associated with roles

The role list view is used to give an overview of the roles and to show some of their properties. You should select the ones that are useful in your context:

1 *Role name.* The role's unique identifier within the role model.

2 *Explanation.* The meaning that the analyst associates with the role and its responsibility in the community of roles in the role model.

3 *Attributes.* For each attribute you may specify:

- *Attribute name.* The attribute's unique identifier within the role.

- *Explanation.* A free text description of the attribute.

- *Type.* The type of the attribute. This is often omitted, but is particularly interesting if the attribute is a reference to a role in another role model.

Formal language is defined, but an informal report is often easier to read

The form of the role list should be adapted to its purpose. If precision is of paramount importance, write the specification in the OOram language as exemplified in Figure 6.16 and discussed in depth in Appendix A. If the purpose is to communicate your ideas to colleagues and clients, an informal variant, as exemplified in Figure 6.17, may be better.

Figure 6.16

Specification example, written in the OOram language

role 'Vendor'
    explanation *"An object which desires to supply goods."*
    attribute 'accounts'
        explanation *"To keep track of outstanding accounts with customers."*
role 'Enterprise'
    explanation *"An object which desires to purchase goods."*
role 'PayerBank'
    explanation *"The bank of the Enterprise."*
role 'PayeeBank'
    explanation *"The bank of the Vendor."*

Figure 6.17

Specification example, written informally

role 'Vendor' *"An object which desires to supply goods."*
    attribute 'accounts' *"To keep track of outstanding accounts with customers."*
role 'Enterprise' *"An object which desires to purchase goods."*
role 'PayerBank' **explanation** *"The bank of the Enterprise."*
role 'PayeeBank' *"The bank of the Vendor."*

6.5 MODELING IN THE LARGE: THE OORAM MODULE

Working with a large number of interdependent models can be confusing. Arbitrary synthesis relationships may lead to complex structures that are hard to manage. OOram Modules provide a way to group role models, hide details, and declare certain models to be visible and available for import into other modules.

IN A NUTSHELL

The development of a large system will often be distributed among several teams, who are separated in space or time. It is an administrative goal to keep the dependencies between the teams as small and simple as possible to reduce the need for coordination and the danger of undetected inconsistencies.

Modeling in the large

As mentioned earlier, Brad Cox defines the *surface area* as everything that is visible at the interface between a supplier and a consumer [Cox 87]. This interface includes everything the consumer needs to know and understand, such as data element names and types, function names, number of parameters and their types, restrictions on the time sequences of operations, concurrency, and protection domains. Techniques for reducing the surface area between programming packages are called programming in the large. We similarly define modeling in the large as techniques for packaging models and minimizing the surface area between model packages.

The synthesis operation establishes a dependency between the base model and the derived model. Ad hoc synthesis between a large number of models can easily lead to a chaotic structure that is hard to create, and even harder to modify. We want to group role models, and encapsulate each group, so that we can control the features that should be visible to other groups.

The OOram module is an encapsulation of OOram models. The OOram module supports modeling in the large by exporting one or more carefully contrived models, and hiding other models and model details which are deemed internal to the module.

An OOram module is a package

An important application of modules is to package reusable components. The work process will then be somewhat different, this was discussed in Chapter 5. It is appropriate to create an OOram module if the following conditions are satisfied:

1   The total set of role models gets too large to be easily manageable.

2   The models can be arranged into distinct groups.

3   There are details in the models of the group that need not be visible to the derived models outside the group. Encapsulation and information hiding are then appropriate.

4   The exported models are reasonably stable.

A module may import role models from other modules and synthesize them into its own models. Imported object specifications specify classes that have been implemented and that may be subclassed in the importing module. A selected subset of the information defined in the module may be declared as export features and thus made available to other modules, as illustrated in Figure 6.18.

An *export model* is a model which is designed to be reused through synthesis into another model. It consists of the following parts:

1   A role model or object specification.

2   A coordinated set of classes that implement the model. The classes are designed to be subclassed in a controlled manner (optional).

Figure 6.18
The OOram
module

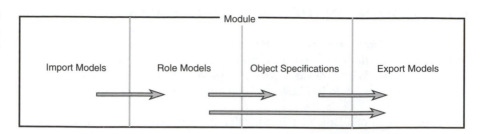

3 Rules for the import of the model, blocking the subclassing of some classes, and restricting the modifications permitted in the subclasses of others. The rules should be designed to ensure the static and dynamic integrity of the export model. Many different rules can be contemplated; they should preferably be automatically enforceable or checkable (optional).

Module
structure
expresses
system
architecture

Modules support concurrent engineering of large systems. A team can encapsulate a system within a module, declare the role models it imports from other modules, declare details as private and thus hide them within the module, and declare certain models as export models and thus make them available to other teams.

Modules support division of authority and responsibility between development teams, and are used to express the high level system architecture. The following operations may be used to determine the modules and create the top level architecture, they are not necessarily performed in this sequence:

1 System characterization. Write a short, free form (prose) description of the system, its purpose, and main features.

2 Identify and understand the modules. Factor the information requirements of the total system and assign them to modules. Similarly factor the processing requirements of the total system and assign them to modules. Iterate to make modules represent "natural" entities of a reasonable size and complexity.

3 Determine interdependencies. Determine the information transfer requirements between modules. Initially, this is done by specifying the nature of information transferred (role model, object specification, etc.) and its area of concern. The models are later augmented with more detailed information as needed.

  Iterate Steps 2 and 3 to minimize intermodule dependencies.

4 Assign the detailing of each module to a developer or development team.

  Iterate Steps 2, 3, and 4 to revise export/import information, and to maintain simple intermodule dependencies.

Programming
in the small is
relatively
simple

Programming a small system in an incremental programming environment such as Smalltalk is relatively simple. Using exploratory programming techniques, a satisfactory set of classes and methods will usually evolve naturally, and the system source code will usually provide adequate documentation.

Medium pro-
grams described
by role models

When programs grow so that their logic is not immediately apparent from the code, a logical layer is added in which the systems are described by one or more role models.

Programming
in the large is
another matter

For very large systems, the number of role models makes it hard to manage them and keep track of their interdependencies. We then need a methodology that helps us separate the total system into understandable parts and manage their integration. We add the rigor of a systematic design methodology to control the development process and to document its results. We get a structure of related modules, each containing a number of related models. Each model is presented through a number of different and overlapping views. These modules, models, and views must be made consistent in all their details.

The role models prescribe permissible message sends; these must be consistent with the messages actually sent by the programs. Role models build on other role models through synthesis. If a base model is changed, the derived models must all be updated accordingly. Tools can be provided to check and help the programmer in the updating tasks, but hard work is still involved, and it is easy to get lost in the petty details.

The good news is that the discipline, modularity, and precision provided by a good analysis and design methodology make it easier to scale to real-sized projects. The structure that modularization imposes on the design gives other people a chance to understand what has been done and why it was done. Quality checks can be applied at different levels of abstraction by independent auditors. The logical descriptions make it possible to apply automated tools to check that the programs actually conform to the designer's intentions. *The good news*

We offer the following advice for good working habits:

1 It is crucial to design the architecture right, which means that the choice of modules and their exported functionality should be stable, and their surface areas should be minimized. The hassle involved in system updates is immensely reduced if one can get this right.

2 Keep modules and role models brief and sketchy until the architecture and all naming conventions are stable.

3 Exploratory design and implementation of modules is a powerful idea that yields good results in a short period of time. But keep the architecture stable! Exported models should be changed infrequently, and only after careful consideration.

4 Keep it lean and mean. The models exported from the modules should be simple—easy to understand and easy to apply.

Two modules may be related in three different ways as follows: *Different module relations*

1 *Peer-to-peer module relation.* The two modules represent phenomena on the same abstraction level, and each is responsible for a part of the total system. A typical application is when the functionality of a domain is to be made available to another domain in a controlled manner. This is illustrated in the example below.

2 *Aggregation relation.* The two modules belong on different abstraction levels. What appears as a single object on one level appears as structure of objects on the next level down, and what appears as single operations on one level are expanded into complete activities on the next level down.

The server in a client-server combination will typically be packaged in a module. It will export one or more descriptions of the service as seen from the clients, and will hide all details about its realization.

3 *Generalization-specialization.* A module may define the solution to a general problem; another module may import this solution and specialize it.

We could, for example, create a general module for making minor expenditure decisions in our company. The TravelExpense model could then import and specialize its export model. Other examples are given in Chapter 5.

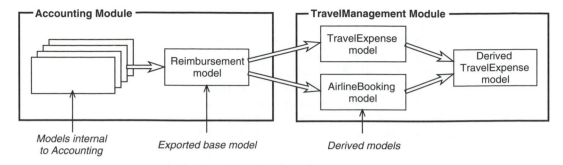

Figure 6.19   Full graphical module notation

The `TravelExpense` and `AirlineBooking` models described in Sections 2.3 and 3.1 both included facilities for reimbursing someone: they were slightly different for the reimbursement of the traveler and the travel agent. It might be better if we had standardized the reimbursement procedure and applied it consistently in all cases. A possible solution would be to create an `Accounting` module, a module that includes a great deal of financial and accounting details. This module would *export* a `Reimbursement` model that would be *imported* by the `TravelManagement` module. The `TravelExpense` and `AirlineBooking` models would be derived from the common `Reimbursement` model. This solution is shown in full graphical notation in Figure 6.19, and in an abbreviated form in Figure 6.20.

Module
architecture
case study
In Chapter 12, we will present an extensive case study describing a possible commercial organization for creating, deploying, and using advanced telecommunication services. The notion of modules is an important part of its technological foundation, facilitating the transfer of technology between different operators and protecting critical resources which need to be controlled by the technology supplier.

Modules make
OOram
technology
scale to very
large systems
Modules provide system organization and information hiding facilities that make it feasible to manage very large systems. A bank may create a *customer module* that exports certain models which its customers can import into their own systems and thus integrate banking with other operations. The customer module will also be part of the bank's system architecture and can be integrated with other modules through a different set of export models.

This is an enormously important result. A customer designs, implements, and understands its information systems, just as the bank designs, implements, and understands *its* system. The two system worlds are integrated through shared models so that they technically constitute a coherent whole, yet no single person or group of persons need have an overview of the total system.

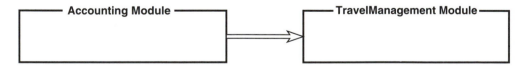

Figure 6.20   Abbreviated graphical module notation

CHAPTER 7 ✧ ✧ ✧ ✧ ✧

Case Study: Development of a Business Information System

CONTENTS

7.1 Objects Everywhere 178

7.2 Enterprise Model 184

    7.2.1 Determine the Area of Concern 185

    7.2.2 Understand the Problem and Identify the Nature of the Objects 186

    7.2.3 Determine Environment Roles and Stimulus/Response 189

    7.2.4 Identify and Understand the Roles 189

    7.2.5 Determine the Work Process 190

    7.2.6 Determine the Collaboration Structure 191

    7.2.7 Determine Interfaces 191

7.3 Information Model 194

    7.3.1 Area of Concern 195

    7.3.2 Semantic View 195

    7.3.3 Role List View 195

    7.3.4 A Hybrid Solution with a Relational Database 196

    7.3.5 Collaboration View 197

    7.3.6 Interface View 198

7.4 Task/Tool/Service Model 199

    7.4.1 Creating Task/Tool/Service Descriptions 200

    7.4.2 User Interface Design 201

    7.4.3 A Simple Direct Manipulation Interface for Our Task Example 204

    7.4.4 A Composite User Interface for the Manager to Determine Travel Permission 205

This case study describes three interrelated models critical to a full understanding of business information systems: The enterprise model, the information model, and the task/tool/service model.

7.1 OBJECTS EVERYWHERE

IN A NUTSHELL

We use objects to model the organization of the enterprise and the computer system architecture. We use objects to model the human work procedures and the symbiosis between humans and their personal computers. We use objects to describe the user interfaces.

We suggest that business information processing can be represented conveniently by three interrelated role models: the first is a model of the human work processes; the second is a model of the human tasks with the corresponding computer tools, and the third is a model of the shared information. This model triad is illustrated by a case study of the travel expense system mentioned earlier.

An enterprise is a work organization

Enterprise is the term commonly applied to all kinds of work organizations. We find enterprises in the public sector ranging from the offices of central government to the local fire brigade. We find enterprises in trade and industry, and we find them in voluntary organizations. Their common characteristic is that they provide a stable framework to support people working together in an organized manner toward a common goal.

Work processes result in value creation

Value is created when a person performs some useful task. This task will be part of a work process that may involve other people as well, as indicated in Figure 7.1.

The professional needs consistent and integrated information

Professionals performing the tasks will be supported by a combination of methods, procedures, and tools which we will call their *information environments*. A personal information environment is an integrated and unified interface to the world of computer-based information. It is customized to its owner's tasks and designed to be an effective aid in *all* his or her information-processing activities—the retrieval of information; the creation of new information based on his or her skills, experience, competence; and on cooperation with teammates as well as with other people within and outside the organization. This symbiosis between a person and his or her information environment is illustrated in Figure 7.2.

The system architecture should support cooperation on all levels

People do not work in isolation, and our symbiosis of people and information systems could be repeated on all levels of the organization such as the team, the department, and the division as illustrated in Figure 7.3. In this model, every organizational unit is modeled as an object which is implemented as a combination of humans and computers. Interaction between these objects can take place on the human or computer levels, as appropriate. This system architecture could implement new and powerful ways of organizing a business.

A two-dimensional client-server architecture

We believe that the person-oriented approach is valuable, and may indeed be the driving force behind the personal computer revolution. It is distinct from the traditional function-oriented approach, but does not replace it. One consideration is that a person needs to integrate all his or her information-processing facilities. Another consideration is that a company needs integrated functions. For example,

Figure 7.1

A work process consists of a sequence of tasks

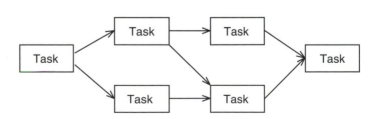

A BUSINESS INFORMATION SYSTEM

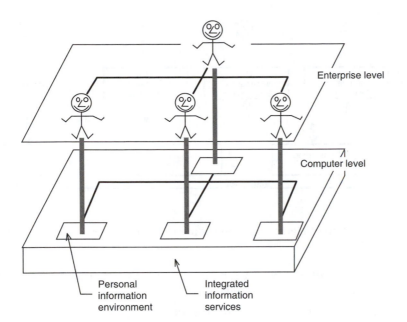

Figure 7.2

Personal information environments support the members of the organization in their individual work and their cooperative efforts

Enterprise level

Computer level

Personal information environment

Integrated information services

a company needs integrated systems for computer-aided design, for materials management, for project control, and for economic management. A project manager performing the task of assigning people to the project's activities needs a tool that provides simultaneous access to the personnel function, the manpower loading function, and the project control function.

We clearly need an overall system architecture which combines both approaches. We advocate the specialized client-server architecture that is illustrated in Figure 7.4. The client parts provide task-oriented information environments tailored to the needs of the individuals, and the server parts provide the functional integration. The name we have chosen for this architecture is the *task/tool/service* architecture, because it describes how an individual's *tasks* are supported by customized *tools* that access common information *services* on his or her behalf.

We have chosen the term *tool* to denote an artifact that a person employs to perform a task, and the term *user information environment* to denote the integrated set of tools employed by a person. We have chosen the term *information service* to denote a service object which is responsible for managing certain information, such as for accounting or materials management. An information service object will typically encapsulate a database or an old application system (frequently called a *legacy system*).

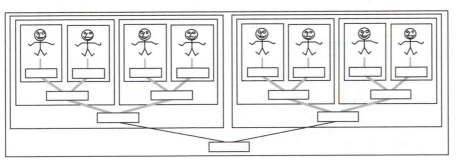

Figure 7.3

Multilevel man–machine symbiosis

Figure 7.4

Task/tool/service system architecture

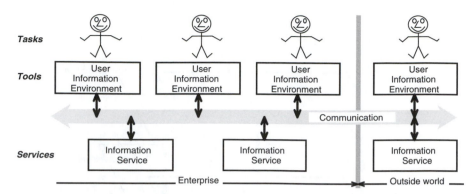

Tasks

Tools

Services

The architecture of Figure 7.4 supports many levels of integration, as illustrated in Figure 7.5.

1   *Integration within a service.* A service may encapsulate a database, which is used to integrate all functions pertaining to the domain served by the service.

2   *Direct integration between services.* One service may call upon another; it then becomes a client of that service. This level of integration should be used with discretion, because it can make the total system very difficult to change. One viable discipline is suggested in Figure 7.3, where team services may be clients of department services, which in turn may be clients of division services.

3   *Integration of services via tools.* A tool may be the client of several services, and may be used to move information between them. This kind of integration is very flexible, since tool programs should be much smaller and simpler than service programs. It is easier to maintain system flexibility through evolution.

4   *Integration between tools.* In principle, a tool may be the client of another tool, so that information may be transferred between them. Tools should be created and phased out fairly rapidly to reflect changes in work procedures and personal preferences. Tool–tool integration makes the total system more rigid and harder to change. We recommend that you avoid this kind of integration.

5   *Integration between people.* Even in a computer-intensive environment, people must still be encouraged to communicate both formally and informally. This communication can be person-to-person, through telephone, by fax, or through an electronic message system.

Figure 7.5

Levels of integration

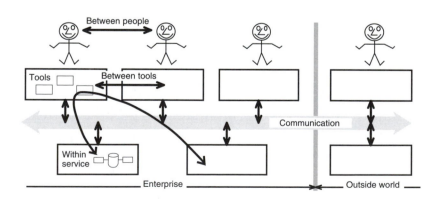

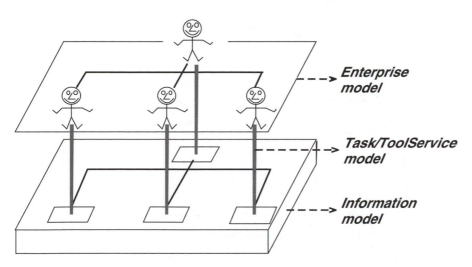

Figure 7.6

Personal information environments support the members of the organization in their individual work and in their cooperation

Enterprise
model

Task/ToolService
model

Information
model

The *task/tool/service* architecture tells us that we have to perform analysis and design on three levels. The levels will be represented by three distinct, but interdependent models, each of which offers its own insights into the problem and its solution. The levels are illustrated in Figure 7.6, and described in detail in the following subsections.

Three levels of information system modeling

1 The *enterprise model*, describes how people work and interact to achieve a given goal. This corresponds to the *system user model* of Figure 1.17.

2 The *information model*, describes the *subject* of the work detailed in the enterprise model. The data will ultimately be handled by an appropriate information service. This is one of the *system requirements models* of Figure 1.17.

3 The *task/tool/service model*, describes the tasks and the interfaces between the people and the information model. This is another *system requirements model*.

The task/tool/service and the information models can be elaborated on several levels of abstraction.

The three models are interrelated as illustrated in Figure 7.7. The enterprise model defines the tasks for the task/tool/service models and the information that needs to be represented in the information model. Each task/tool/service model defines a number of operations that have to be supported by the information model.

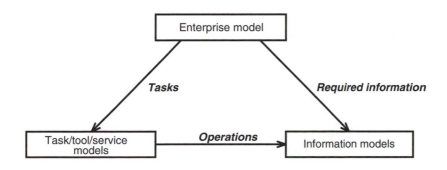

Figure 7.7

Relationships between the three models

Figure 7.8
A development
process

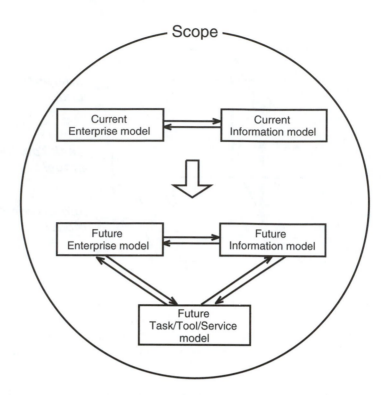

Analysis and design are opportunistic

We begin by modeling the current situation, and usually create the enterprise and information models in parallel. We next develop a corresponding pair of models for the desired, future situation as illustrated in Figure 7.8. Purists may want to keep the current and the future models distinct; in practice, we often permit the former to gradually evolve into the latter. We continually iterate between the future enterprise and information models because new ideas for organizing the enterprise lead to new demands on information, and insights into possible information structures suggest opportunities for improved organizations.

The scope of the project should be under continuous scrutiny. The scope may be expanded to incorporate new ideas for increased functionality, or it may have to be reduced because some of the original ideas may prove impractical or infeasible.

Once the future enterprise and information models begin to stabilize, we introduce the task/tool/service level modeling. We continue to iterate between the enterprise, information, and task/tool/service models until analysts and users agree they have reached a satisfactory solution.

We will later stress the importance of user participation in these early stages of the development process. We recommend that you consider using early prototyping to ensure that the users fully appreciate the consequences of the proposed specifications.

The task/tool/service architecture described in this section may be studied on two levels. It may be taken as a proposed solution to an important set of problems, or it may be taken as an example of three very interesting relationships between models: the *actions* of the *enterprise model* define the *activities* of the *task/tool/service model*; the *data* of the *enterprise model* define the *objects* of the *information model*; and the *actions* of the *task/tool/service model* define the *operations* of the *information model*.

We will now create the three models for the travel expense example introduced in Chapter 2. We will create enterprise, information, and task/tool/service models that focus on the needs of the Authorizer role.

7.2 ENTERPRISE MODEL

IN A NUTSHELL

We create an object model of an organization in the context of a certain work procedure. The case we have chosen is a possible work procedure for the management of travel expense accounts. This problem was introduced in Chapter 2. We will give it a more detailed treatment here.

Business process reengineering

The essence of business process reengineering is to reevaluate the goals of an enterprise and the means it employs to reach them. Of prime importance is looking at the enterprise in a new light, getting new insights, and finding new ways to reach old and new goals.

It has been said that invention consists of 5% inspiration and 95% perspiration. The perspiration part of business process reengineering is to design the new organization, its procedures and its information systems. It is usually appropriate to create two sets of models: *as is* models describe the current way of doing things, and *reengineered* models describe the future organization and its systems.

Based on the idea of business reengineering presented in Hammer [Hammer 93], we will consider a procedure in the light of the overall goals of the enterprise. Is the procedure really necessary? If the answer is "yes," could we achieve the required results in a more effective manner? Is it really necessary to assume that everybody wants to cheat the system, or can we trust people to do the right thing? In this case study, we will assume that the inspiration part is completed, and that we now want to create a detailed description of the new organization and the appropriate computer support.

Modeling process must be adapted to our needs

Some authors of papers on object-oriented modeling of enterprise information systems express strong views on the optimal sequence of steps in the analysis and design process. Some, such as Rumbaugh and Wirfs-Brock [Rumbaugh 91, Wirfs-Brock 90], advocate that we should identify the objects before identifying the behavior, while other authors, such as Rubin [Rubin 92], advocate the opposite sequence. We believe that the optimal process is opportunistic: we should at all times work on the model and the view that offer the best opportunities to improve our insights. The path will be twisted, but the job will be completed when all the chosen models and views are consistent and faithfully resolve the requirements.

The enterprise modeling process we follow in this presentation consists of seven steps:

1 *Determine the area of concern.* Write a free form (prose) description of the issue under consideration.

2 *Understand the problem and identify the nature of the objects.* Identify the user community and understand their requirements. Identify the nature of the active participants; they could be concrete entities, such as people or equipment, or they could be abstractions, such as departments. In our example, they are the people involved in the issue under consideration; understand their duties and how they perform them.

3 *Determine environment roles and stimulus/response.* Describe the messages that are sent from environment roles and cause an activity in the described system. Also describe the response, which is the overall effect of the activity.

4 *Identify and understand the roles.* Separate and idealize the tasks and responsibilities of the actors as the *roles* they play in the process.

5 *Determine the work process.* Create a model showing the tasks performed by the actors, and the corresponding process.

6 *Determine the collaboration structure.* Show the roles in a structure of collaborating objects.

7 *Determine interfaces.* Determine the messages that each role may send to each of its collaborators.

These steps will provide you with an object-oriented model of the process under study—a static description defining the objects, their characteristics, the collaboration structure; and a dynamic description defining the processes under study. We will now describe these steps in detail for our sample process, and also give some hints to help you create descriptions for your own application areas.

7.2.1 Determine the Area of Concern

Our first step is to identify the bounds of our study. The *area of concern* is a textual (prose) description. It may describe a broad problem, such as the administrative procedures of an organization, or it may describe a narrow problem, such as the handling of travel expense reports.

The area of concern is probably the most important step of all. Which part of the complex world surrounding us do we want to consider, and which aspects of this part do we consider sufficiently important to merit inclusion in the model? If we choose too wide an area, the model will become intractable ("so complicated that there are no obvious deficiencies"). If we make the area too small, we may get lost in the large number of models needed to describe everything we are interested in. (Programmers often like to compare an overly complex program to a bowl of spaghetti. The object-oriented equivalent is noodle soup.)

The requirements specification is a good starting point for defining areas of concern. In simple cases, you will need just one model, and the area of concern will be the area covered by the requirements. In more complex cases, you may still find it useful to start constructing a model of the overall system. However, it is also often possible to identify important subphenomena up front and to model them before embarking on an overall model. In extreme cases, it may be possible to partition the requirements into independent parts that can be modeled separately; the overall model then becomes superfluous and can be omitted.

In my own practical modeling work, I almost invariably believe that the *area of concern* is so obvious that I do not need to write it down. In every case, this has proven to be an illusion. In fact, it has always been surprisingly hard to write down a precise area of concern. My advice is that you start by defining the area of concern in writing, and that you make it as complete and succinct as you possibly can. Return frequently to this description and improve it to reflect your increased understanding of the area under consideration. We will try the description shown in Figure 7.9 for our expense account example.

> The area of concern is the handling of travel expense accounts. We focus on the expense account itself, and do not model details about why the trip was made, or how the traveler is reimbursed for his expenses.

Figure 7.9
Area of concern

7.2.2 Understand the Problem and Identify the Nature of the Objects

The next step is to identify the people we want to help. We call them the *actors*. The actors may be the members of one or more departments, or the people involved in certain operations. Our initial selection of actors will be an intelligent guess. We may later find that other actors have to be included and that some of the initial ones may be ignored.

Who are the actors, and what are their roles in our example? As a starting point, we consider the company organization, which was shown in Figure 2.9 and is repeated in Figure 7.10 for your convenience. (We show the organization relationships as a guide, even if they have little bearing on the current problem.)

We seem to have two possibilities when selecting the actors of our model: either to model the organizational units, such as *company* and *departments* as objects, or to model the people populating the company. The choice seems simple in this case, since companies and departments are abstractions, which cannot do anything by themselves. We will formulate a model whose objects represent the people involved in creating and processing travel expense accounts.

We often find that the community of actors is too large for us to relate to every one of them personally. We have to select a smaller number of *typical actors* as representatives of the whole. It is important to include all kinds of actors in this smaller set. It is a grave mistake to focus on the managers, or on those who are most forward and outspoken, or on those who are enthusiastic for new ideas. If we are to be of any help, we must understand our future users, their goals and concerns, and their areas of competence and interests.

Be aware of people's different perceptions

In her insightful doctoral dissertation, Elanor Wynn found that there are basically three ways of finding out what happens in an office [Wynn 79]: we may ask the managers, we may ask the workers, or we may observe the work as it actually happens in the office. Each of these approaches gives important insights, but they will all yield different results. The manager and the workers will tell you how

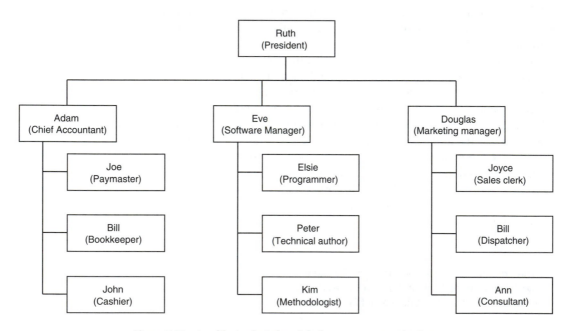

Figure 7.10   An object-oriented model of a company organization

A BUSINESS INFORMATION SYSTEM

they perceive the workplace; these perceptions will differ from person to person. But some of the most important aspects of the work will be so obvious to the participants that they will never think of mentioning them. You must consciously search for such "obvious" aspects through observation and through asking numerous questions.

It is also important to be alert to all aspects of the work processes. Wynn found that almost all communication between office workers had several distinct, but interwoven aspects—a work aspect ("order 5 boxes of copy paper"), a social aspect ("how is your cold?," "why can't you learn to look up the reference number before you call me?"), and a training aspect ("always remember to send a copy of these invoices to Pete"). Introducing a new system for the work aspect may play havoc with essential processes in the organization. The head of a university computer center got fed up after observing that there was always a large group of happy people around the coffee machine, which was next to the printer. He removed the coffee machine, and ended up having to hire three more advisors to help students solve their problems [Weinb 71].

Be aware of the "soft" aspects

Be aware of the tendency many of us have to consider people stupid because they do not have *our* deep understanding of the concepts or do not use the terminology of *our* specialty. At the bottom of such impressions, we frequently find our own complete ignorance of *their* competence, concepts, and terminology! Our goal is to be at one with the user community, so that we understand the details of their work and the nature of their goals, ambitions, and cooperative culture. Empathy is more important than precision; communication is more important than following some fixed methodology. Looking back on Figure 2.4, we realize that the professional analyst is a person who is able to learn the language of the users to communicate with them and avoid misunderstandings. Communication is perfect when the participants interpret the data in the same way. No harm is done if we do not understand each other and know it: we can then continue the discussions until everything is clear. The real danger arises when the participants interpret the data differently without realizing it. We claim that misunderstanding is the mother of the most gigantic failures in information systems development.

Be aware of your own perceptions

We strongly recommend that systems analysts approach the user community with due respect and humility. Use any fair means known to you to establish communication: if the users are trained in some formal notation, use it even if you consider it inferior to *your* notation. For most users, free text and informal diagrams are better than any formal notation. Use your notation to translate your understanding into precise and unambiguous descriptions. Use those descriptions as your background information, and check your understanding against the users in the users' language. We do not mean that you cannot show your beautiful diagrams to the users. But your responsibility is to communicate with them—not to trap them as hostages for your pet projects.

Communicate!

The success criterion of any project should be that the users get exactly what they expected. It is easy to see that they have reason to be upset if the project has been oversold and they get less than they expected. But should we applaud the pleasant surprises of results exceeding expectations? My answer is "no." If you were developing a system commercially, you could have asked a higher price if the users understood its full value. Such surprises are a result of poor specification or communication, and the results probably would have been even better if the users had been aware of the system's full potential.

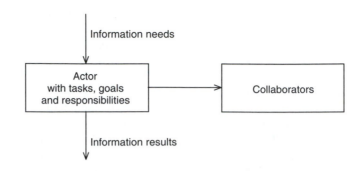

Figure 7.11

What we need to understand about each actor

In our example, we identify all the people who are in any way involved with the travel expense account process. We cannot do so without considering the process, so the analysis must by its nature be iterative. We identify some people and learn about their involvement in the process. This points us to other people and other parts of the process, and so on. A useful way of thinking about the individuals is to consider them as information-processing entities. Through conversation and observation, we build our understanding of the actors, their responsibilities, their collaborators, and their information processes, as illustrated in Figure 7.11. (But do not forget the other aspects which we discussed above!)

Figure 7.11 is also an illustration of the relationship between the enterprise and information models discussed earlier; here, the information is the subject of the object interaction.

I did my first study of this kind in an engineering company. I spent a couple of weeks interviewing various people, and collected a great deal of data. Back in the office, I tried to create a process diagram, linking people through their information interchange. To my chagrin, I discovered that almost none of the information people created was ever used, and almost none of the information people used was ever created. The thing was a complete mess, and my first thought was that the company was a mess as well. On second thought, I realized that the company in fact produced complex and working designs, so there had to be some other reason for the discrepancies. I found the following (this was many years ago, and I am sure most companies have cleaned up their acts by now):

1 *Synonyms.* People from different disciplines used different names for the same information.

2 *Information Packages.* Somebody produced a named package of information containing many information items. Nobody used the full package, but all the items were used by somebody.

3 *Homonyms.* The trouble caused by homonyms showed its ugly head later in the study. Different people using the same term for different concepts cause no trouble until these people try to communicate. In the engineering company, this happened when we first tried to create information processing systems spanning several disciplines.

My wife recently worked at creating a multidisciplinary database for the management of hydroelectric resources. To some, a dam is the thing you put across a river to trap the water; to others it is a body of water together with all the installations around it. The difficulty in such cases is that we generally do not distinguish between terms and concepts. People get very upset when their well-established terminology is "misused" by somebody else, and religious wars may ensue if different interpretations of the terms are well-entrenched in the terminology of both parties.

Ask one computer expert: "What is a system?" and you will get an answer. Ask a group of experts, and you will get a discussion.

7.2.3 Determine Environment Roles and Stimulus/Response

An environment role is a role that triggers some activity in the system, or a role that receives a trigger for some unspecified activity in the environment. In our case, the Traveler takes an initiative; the cause of this initiative is outside the scope of this model. The Traveler is, therefore, an environment role. When the travel is completed and the travel expense report has been processed, the Paymaster is asked to arrange for reimbursement. This model does not describe how this is done; the Paymaster is therefore an environment role.

The stimulus messages and the corresponding system responses are conveniently presented as shown in Figure 7.12. The system is shown as an unspecified cluster of roles called a *virtual role*. The system input and output ports are annotated with the stimulus and response messages.

7.2.4 Identify and Understand the Roles

It is customary in organization development to consider people's *roles* in the enterprise processes. A person may play many roles, and a role may be played by several people. We want to create a *role model* of the travel expense report process. A role model is a stylized object model:

1 *Identify object patterns*. Identify a pattern of interacting objects, and represent it as a corresponding pattern of interacting roles.

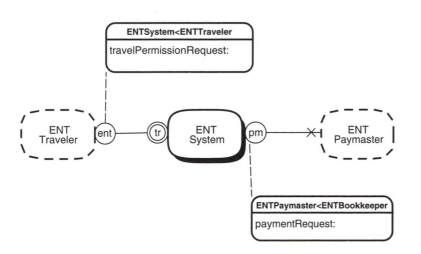

Figure 7.12

Stimulus/ response

Figure 7.13
The roles

role 'ENTTraveler' **explanation** *"The person who travels"*
role 'ENTAuthorizer' **explanation** *"The person who authorizes the travel."*
role 'ENTBookkeeper' **explanation** *"The person responsible for bookkeeping."*
role 'ENTPaymaster' **explanation** *"The person responsible for reimbursement."*

2 *Suppress aspects irrelevant to the current topic,* and represent information only about the objects that you *choose* to consider as relevant. In our example, we consider only travel accounts and suppress related phenomena, such as budgeting and reimbursement.

3 *Generalize object identity,* and represent all objects serving the same purpose within the structure of objects as a single role. Think of this role as *a typical object* in the context of the area of concern. In our example, we let a `Traveler` role represent any person who travels, and an `Authorizer` role represent any person who authorizes travel.

4 *Suppress irrelevant detail,* using the object encapsulation property to hide details that do not help you understand the phenomenon of interest. In our example, we focused on the overall aspects of the phenomenon and suppressed all the internal details, such as the itinerary of the travel or the procedure followed by the `Authorizer` to decide to OK an expense account.

In our example, we find that the role of `Traveler` may be played by any member of the staff. The role of `Authorizer` may be played by any manager, and the roles of `Bookkeeper` and `Paymaster` are played by Bill and Joe. We will have to consider if objects may play multiple roles, and decide if it is OK for a manager to authorize his or her own travel. The result is formally recorded textually in a role/ responsibility list, as shown in Figure 7.13.

We have here given the role definitions in textual form using extracts of the OOram language defined in Appendix A. We do not recommend a tabular form, because your role descriptions should be as complete as possible.

7.2.5 Determine the Work Process

Process diagram shows sample dataflow with associated actions

Through conversation and observation, we build our understanding of the actors, their responsibilities, their collaborators, and their information processes. We describe the work flow in a *process diagram*, as illustrated in Figure 7.14.

In Figure 7.14, the roles are represented as super-ellipses drawn at the top of the diagram. The rectangles shown below the appropriate role symbols represent tasks performed by the roles. Text appearing in angle brackets <> represents a pseudo operation. Parallelograms represent data that flow between the tasks. Data usually change ownership during the transfer and the column is irrelevant. The dataflow follows the arrows connecting the symbols.

Postpone classification

The roles are archetypical objects idealized in the context of the current area of concern. High complexity or repeated patterns are warnings that submodels should be factored out.

Data carried by messages between objects

Objects can interact only through messages in our object model. Data must therefore be carried from one role to another as parameters to appropriate messages. If a role needs several data items before it can perform a task, the role must store the received data as attributes until all data have arrived and the task can be performed. (The message which finally releases the task is frequently called a *trigger* in the literature.)

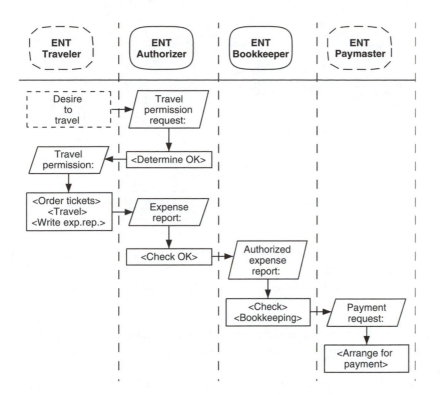

Figure 7.14

**Expense-
Account**
process view

We have stipulated that a list of roles is *documented* before the description of the work processes. The list is usually best *created* as a by-product of describing the work processes. The two sections are thus created concurrently.

Iterate!

7.2.6 Determine the Collaboration Structure

Based on the information in the process diagrams, and on our general understanding of the work processes, we draw a role collaboration view as shown in Figure 7.15.

The collaboration view may be annotated with role descriptions as illustrated in Figure 7.16.

7.2.7 Determine Interfaces

Associate a list of all the messages that a role may send to a collaborator with the corresponding port. A process view shows a sample process; the interfaces must include all messages shown in these views. Study the resulting interfaces, and add

*Determine the
messages that
may be sent
from each port*

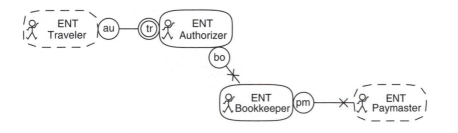

Figure 7.15

**Role
collaboration
view for the
travel expense
process**

Figure 7.16

**Role
collaboration
view annotated
with role
descriptions**

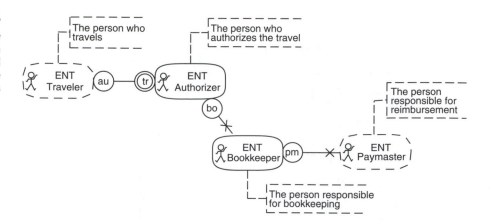

messages that seem to be missing to make them nicely rounded representations
of the role functionality.

*Two interface
notations*

The role collaboration view can be annotated with the permitted messages as
illustrated in Figure 7.17. The interfaces are often too large to conveniently fit
onto the diagram, or you may want to describe more details about message parameters and their types. You then describe the interfaces textually, as shown in
Figure 7.18. The language is an extract of the OOram language described in Appendix A.

The OOram language interface specification can optionally include the parameter types. The specification in Figure 7.18 is particularly interesting because the
parameters define relations between this model and the information model. The
parameter of the first message must, for example, reference an object which plays
the INFTravelPermission role in the Travel Expense Information Model.

Figure 7.17

**Role
collaboration
view annotated
with message
interfaces**

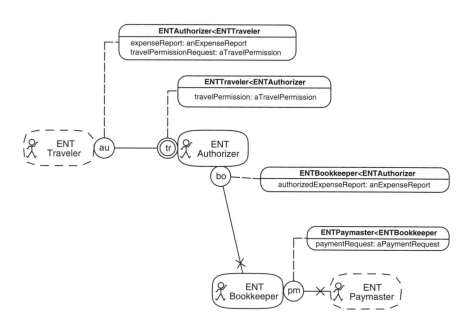

interface 'ENTAuthorizer<ENTTraveler'
/* *Read as "ENTAuthorizer from ENTTraveler"* */
    message synch 'travelPermissionRequest:'
        explanation "*Request authorization of submitted travel plan.*"
        param 'aTravelPermission' **type** 'INFTravelPermission' **::** 'Travel Expense
        Information Model'
    message synch 'expenseReport:'
        explanation "*Request reimbursement of submitted expense report.*"
        param 'anExpenseReport' **type** 'INFExpenseAccount' **::** 'Travel Expense
        Information Model'
interface 'ENTTraveler<ENTAuthorizer'
    message 'travelPermission:'
        explanation "*Travel authorization granted.*"
        param 'aTravelPermission' **type** 'INFTravelPermission' **::** 'Travel Expense
        Information Model'
interface 'ENTBookkeeper<ENTAuthorizer'
    message synch 'authorizedExpenseReport:'
        explanation "*Request reimbursement of submitted expense report.*"
        param 'anExpenseReport' **type** 'INFExpenseAccount' **::** 'Travel Expense
        Information Model'
interface 'ENTPaymaster<ENTBookkeeper'
    message 'paymentRequest:'
        explanation "*Reimburse the specified account.*"
        param 'aPaymentRequest' **type** 'INFPayRequest' **::** 'Travel Expense
        Information Model

Figure 7.18

Interfaces for the enterprise model, informal textual form

7.3　INFORMATION MODEL

The enterprise model described what people do to achieve a certain purpose. It also described the information that was the subject of the messages, but it did not define the information semantics or representation. We will now create a detailed model of this information.

The information model is derived from enterprise model

The information model describes the universe of discourse of the enterprise model, i.e., its message parameters and role attributes. You begin by listing all relevant parameters and attributes in the enterprise model. Then define an information model role for each of them and determine the relationships between them. Extend it into a complete model of the world of information as it is perceived by the user community.

You will need to choose an appropriate modeling paradigm: choose a relational database if a passive data repository is satisfactory; choose an object-oriented database if data behavior is an essential part of the information model.

Some information may be handled manually

Some information—such as travel permissions—may be handled informally, either orally or through informal media such as memos or electronic mail. The travel expense report itself is frequently required to be on a formal business form or data record, and contains fields for different kinds of information:

1　Traveler's name and ID.

2　Purpose of travel.

3　Authorizer name and ID.

4　Permission date.

5　Itemized specification of expenses.

6　Gross amount.

7　Advance payment.

8　Net amount.

Focus on computer-based information

9　Authorization date.

An early decision is to choose the information that will be represented in an information system and concentrate further work on this subset. Our choice is to focus on the ExpenseAccount itself.

Creating the information model

We will now develop a model of the ExpenseAccount information. Our suggested information-modeling process consists of creating the views listed below. This is just one of the many possibilities, and you will have to develop your own process to suit your own circumstances. And as usual, your work process will be iterative even if your documentation has to be sequential.

1　*Area of concern*—the scope of the information model.

2　*Semantic view*—also the foundation of a possible relational model.

3　*Role list view*—the information entities and their attributes.

4　*Collaboration view*—shows the data structure.

5　*Interface view*—definition of desired behavior.

The semantic view is most relevant when we consider the information model in conjunction with the enterprise model. Behavior will be added later to enable

Figure 7.19
Area of concern

The area of concern is modeling the information contained in travel expense accounts. We will focus on the expense account itself and will not model details about the input and output in the user interfaces.

the information model to respond to requests from the tools that are described in section 7.3. The main iterations are thus between the *enterprise model* and the semantic view of the *information model,* and between the *task/tool/service* model and the collaboration view of the *information model.*

7.3.1 Area of Concern

The area of concern shown in Figure 7.19 reflects our change of focus from enterprise to information.

7.3.2 Semantic View

We will encounter a number of information concepts when we interview users and build the enterprise model. It is a good idea to create and maintain a semantic view of this information, to help us understand the phenomena under study and to establish the precision and consistency needed for automatic data processing purposes. Figure 7.20 shows a semantic view of the information model.

7.3.3 Role List View

The roles are derived from the semantic view and optionally elaborated with attribute information. The diagram in Figure 7.20 may also be annotated with the role semantics, but it is usually better to describe the list textually, as shown in Figure 7.21. We have elected to omit the attribute type specification; this is optional according to the OOram language defined in Appendix A.

We usually postpone the formal typing of the attributes to a later stage in the process, but we may include type information here when it is known.

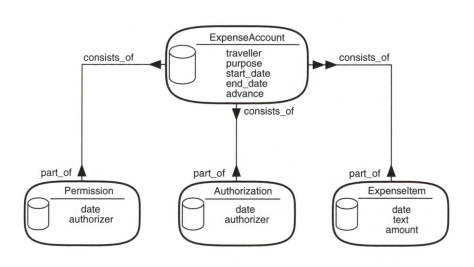

Figure 7.20

Semantic view of information model

Figure 7.21

The roles of the information model

role 'ExpenseAccount'
    explanation *"The master object representing an expense account."*
    attribute 'traveler'
    attribute 'purpose'
    attribute 'start_date'
    attribute 'end_date'
    attribute 'advance'
role 'ExpenseItem'
    explanation *"A specified cost."*
    attribute 'date'
    attribute 'text'
    attribute 'amount'
role 'Permission'
    explanation *"A permission to travel."*
    attribute 'date'
    attribute 'authorizer'
role 'Authorization'
    explanation *"A disbursement order."*
    attribute 'date'
    attribute 'authorizer'

7.3.4 A Hybrid Solution with a Relational Database

A database may improve the management of travel accounts

The relational database technology is a mature technology, and is ideally suited for the storage and retrieval of simple data records. We recommend that you use it wherever it is applicable.

For example, most of the expense account information will ultimately end up in the accounting department's data processing system. The enterprise might simplify its archiving function, and save some paper shuffling, if the traveler could enter the account data directly into the system, and the authorizer could read the account on a screen and authorize it by a keystroke.

The design of a relational database for storing expense accounts can be done by any of the popular database design methodologies. One possible structure is indicated in Figure 7.22.

A personal assistant may improve the creation of travel accounts

To those of us who never get the sums right, the expense account may be drafted in a spreadsheet. An even better solution would be a special expense account program which could help us fill in the different items, convert foreign expenses into our local currency, do the sums, and provide on-line information about the latest rules, regulations, and rates.

If the authorities insist that the accounts be submitted on the approved form, we could transcribe the spreadsheet results manually (as I had to do at a former employer). But we will discuss a better solution, in which we use objects to combine the behavior of the personal assistant with the data storage capabilities of the relational database. Object-oriented, direct manipulation user interfaces will be discussed in Section 7.3. They may be designed to print the official paper forms, to interact with relational databases, or to provide the interface between a user and an object-oriented information service.

Hybrid solution: An object can encapsulate a relational database

A relational database may be accessed from a program through what is known as an *application programming interface* (API). We can define objects with the message interface of our choice, and define the necessary methods to convert these messages to the appropriate API calls on the database.

A BUSINESS INFORMATION SYSTEM

Expense_Account table
expense_account_id
traveler_employee_id
travel_purpose
date_travel_start
date_travel_end
authorizer_employee_id
permission_date
authorization_date
advance

Employee table
employee_id
employee_name
department_id

Expense_Item table
expense_account_id
item_number
date
item_text
item_amount

Figure 7.22

**Possible
structure of
relational
information
model**

The simplest and most general solution is to define a message interface which essentially offers a database service, e.g., according to the SQL standard. This is illustrated in Figure 7.23a. A more sophisticated solution is to add an intermediate layer which offers a message interface relating to ExpenseAccount concepts, as illustrated in Figure 7.23b. The latter solution is more robust, because it isolates the database, its schema, and its constraints from the tool objects.

7.3.5 Collaboration View

Figure 7.24 shows a first iteration of the collaboration view of the information model. It is structurally similar to Figure 7.20; however, the lines of the semantic view denote conceptual relationships, while the lines of the collaboration view denote role accessibility and collaboration.

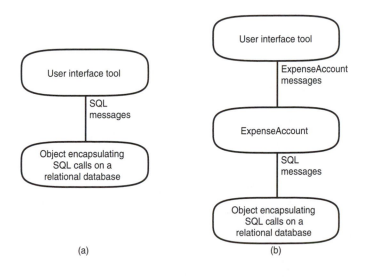

(a)   (b)

Figure 7.23

**Objects may
encapsulate a
relational
database**

Figure 7.24

Information model collaboration view

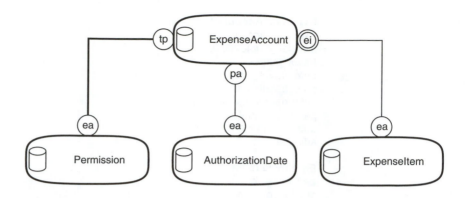

7.3.6 Interface View

Interface definitions The main behavior requirements for the information model will be derived from the task/tool/service models to be discussed in the next section. We may also want to add behavior associated with our travel expense regulations so that the system can provide default values and check against maximum values for different kinds of expenditures.

We will not discuss the detailed analysis of the information model behavior here; the work follows the same process as the analysis of the enterprise model, and you would be well advised to analyze both models simultaneously.

7.4 TASK/TOOL/SERVICE MODEL

An adequate solution for the information model is often available in the form of a relational database, but the lack of good information tools adapted to their users' tasks is still a problem. In this section, we will discuss the position of the tools in the architecture, and the characteristics of good tools. It should not be surprising that good user interfaces are object-oriented, making information appear as concrete objects that the users can manipulate directly on the screen.

Here, we will finally focus on the interface between the individual users and the computer-based information system. An information tool is a computer-based artifact employed by a user to perform one or more tasks. We study each of the user's tasks, in turn, with special emphasis on the appropriate information tools. Our job is that of a toolbuilder. Our goal is to create a pleasant and effective information environment.

A tool is an artifact

We have earlier recommended that you iterate between the different models, and even be prepared to reconsider the scope of the project. You should also include the tasks and tools in this iteration so as to find a good set of reusable tools. There is a many-to-many relationship between tasks and tools: a tool may be used in a number of tasks, and a task may employ several tools. There are two advantages in keeping a small number of tools: first, user familiarity with the tools increases proficiency and confidence, and reduces learning effort. Second, the investment in programming, documentation and maintenance goes down, while the quality goes up. The next best thing to using identical tools for different tasks is to use related tools which share user interface properties and code. The object inheritance property is an open invitation to your ingenuity for identifying related tasks and for devising families of similar tools.

Iterate!

We gave a simple model of human communication in Figure 2.4. Figure 7.25 shows a similar model describing the communication between a human user and a computer-based information system through an information tool. The tool presents and interprets data according to an implicit *tool information model,* while the user communicates according to his or her own mental model. Discrepancies will lead to communication errors in much the same way as between two humans.

Information tools are communication devices

The user has a mental model of the information handled in the task. The information system is based on an (object-oriented) information model that frequently is different from the user's model in scope, complexity, and precision. An important success criterion for a tool is that it provides the required filtering and transla-

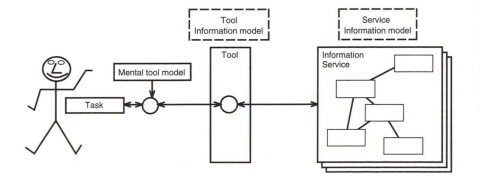

Figure 7.25

A person communicates with one or more computer-based Information Services through a tool

tion so that the user gets the illusion of working with a system that supports his or her mental model of the information.

The three-schema architecture of database systems serves this purpose: an *external schema* is tailored to the needs of particular users and provides a filtered view of the *conceptual schema*, which defines the information contents of the database. The third schema is the *implementation schema,* which defines how the information is actually stored in the computer. Object orientation gives us added freedom when defining the external schemas: algorithms in the tools can translate the concepts of the service information model into concepts more familiar to the user.

We have earlier described a situation concerning hydroelectric resource management, where two disciplines used the term *dam* to mean different things. Two solutions to this dilemma are open to the systems designer: we can force the disciplines to harmonize their terminology, or we can create tools that do the necessary translations so that the disciplines can retain their favorite terminology. Our technology permits both solutions. It is a management decision to select the one that best serves the needs of the enterprise.

7.4.1 Creating Task/Tool/Service Descriptions

Create task and tool descriptions

The tasks are extracted from the process diagrams, such as the example in Figure 7.14. We will now create a detailed task description as a precursor to designing a tool. The task description could consist of the following:

1 *Scope and goal* of the task.

2 *User work situation* describes the task in the context of the user's overall work situation. Task frequency and perceived importance are particularly relevant, since they determine the amount of specialized tool training that can be assumed.

3 *Input information* needed to perform the task.

4 *Trigger* that releases the task.

5 *Output information* that results from the task.

6 *Tool description* that specifies the tool to be used.

7 *Task scenario narrative* that describes how the task will be performed.

The tasks of our Expense- Account example

The tasks of our `ExpenseAccount` example are shown in the process view of the enterprise model in Figure 7.14. The tasks are as follows:

1 The `Traveler` role:
   - Prepare travel authorization request.
   - Prepare travel expense account.

2 The `Authorizer` role:
   - Process travel request and post answer.
   - Check and forward expense account.

3 The `Bookkeeper` role:
   - Check expense account, record accounts, and authorize payment.

4 The Paymaster role:

- Record amount to be added to next payment of salary.

We will now study possible tools to be used by the Authorizer for performing his or her task. This tool will be part of a personal information environment for persons playing the Authorizer role in the organization. We will describe two alternative tools. The common parts of the task descriptions are as follows:

Example task description: Authorizer process travel request

1 *Scope and goal.* The goal of this task is to determine if the proposed travel should be permitted. The Authorizer should estimate the value of this travel to the enterprise and check if the trip conforms to current plans. The Authorizer should also consider if funds are available in the budget for the proposed travel, and possibly arrange for additional funds if the situation warrants it.

2 *User work situation.* This task is but one of the numerous administrative tasks performed by persons playing the Authorizer role. In this case, it should be possible to perform it as a simple routine in a few minutes, and the training needed to master the tools should be minimal.

3 *Input information.* The information needed to perform the task is the travel request itself. Possible information items that could be useful to the Authorizer are the purpose of the journey, when it will take place, and the planned total cost. The Authorizer could also need access to the work plans for the indicated time period, to the budget, and to accounts showing current commitments.

4 *Trigger.* We assume that the Authorizer's information environment includes a task management facility. This task will then be added to the Authorizer's list of outstanding tasks so that he or she can select it for execution at her convenience. Since this task is but one of a large number of similar tasks, it is important that he or she not be required to spend any mental energy relating to this task outside the few minutes it takes to process it.

5 *Output information.* The authorization or rejection should be passed to the Traveler. This information shall also be stored, and should be retrieved automatically if and when the Authorizer receives an expense account for processing.

6 *Tool description.* We will discuss two alternatives below.

7 *Task scenario.* A first description is given under Task 1. More detailed scenarios will be given later.

7.4.2 User Interface Design

Interactive user interfaces come in different styles. The simplest, and oldest, is what I call the *guessing game interface*. The user types a command, followed by the appropriate parameters, and then hits ENTER. The computer checks its built-in list of permissible commands and either starts the appropriate application program or types a question mark, indicating that the user must make another guess.

It is hard to create good user interfaces

Two commands could support our example task:

```
display_travel_request    request_id
authorize_travel_request   request_id authorizer_id
```

Figure 7.26

Form-based
interface for the
authorization
task

Most users would prefer the *form-based interface*. The computer presents a form on the screen, and the user fills in the blanks before hitting the ENTER button. The user has to guess the syntax and semantics of the blanks, but the leader texts and possibly also default values make this interface much easier to use. A possible form for our sample task is shown in Figure 7.26.

*Making
information
appear concrete*

The goal of the object-oriented, direct-manipulation interface is to provide a visual presentation of the information in an intuitive and "obvious" manner, and to reflect a part of the user's mental model. The interface should permit the user to manipulate this information in the simplest way possible in accordance with the user's goals and tasks. *Information* is essentially an abstract notion. To my mind, the essential property of object-oriented, direct-manipulation user interfaces is that they make the information appear concrete: something the user can see, manipulate, and interact with. The following suggestions for good user interface design are adapted from a series of lectures presented by Bruce Horn to graduate students at the University of Oslo, Norway. These rules constitute the best advice I have ever seen on the subject. They appear here in print for the first time, with the permission of Bruce Horn and our gratitude:

1 *The design and implementation must have feedback.* The creation of user interfaces is a highly subjective endeavor, and I almost never get it right the first time. I therefore suggest that you create a prototype. Try it out yourself and let the users try it, improve it, and try it out again. Your empathy with the user is crucial. If you create a tool for a rote operation, the user may prefer a simple tool that leads him or her through a series of fixed steps. If you create a tool for a task requiring intelligence and creativity, the user may prefer a tool which makes the computer augment his or her intelligence. Use your own software in your own work if it is at all feasible. Your knowledge about its structure is likely to give ideas for improvement which would never occur to others.

2 *The principle of least astonishment.* The behavior of the system must follow the expectations of the users. Any exclamation of astonishment from a user must be considered a warning of poor design.

3 *See and point versus remember and type.* It is much easier to reference something you can see, via pointing, than to remember the name of something and type. This is the essence of direct manipulation: making the computer invisible—an extension of yourself—you point at an object and ask it to do some-

thing. Of course, not everything will (or should) have a name, so being able to see something and point at it may be the only way to specify it. In addition, one can select a group of objects from which to choose by describing them by analogy or by using a search specification, and then choosing the desired object by pointing.

4 *No modes.* Of course, computers have modes. Modes are just contexts in which the previous actions of the user change the meaning of current actions. However, in order to be acceptable, these modes must be either spring-loaded, such as a key or a button, or must be metaphorical, such as a paint tool. Modes are also acceptable when they are made apparent to the user, such as a cursor changing to a tool, or a window or pane that provides a particular modal function (drawing or text-editing panes, for example).

5 *Maintain user illusion of direct manipulation.* Maintaining this illusion is extremely important, and it affects decisions regarding implementation. It is critical that the attention of the user be focused on the computer's results. The *user-computer circuit* is the information flow from the user to the computer, and back again to the user. This circuit is maintained when the user is engaged and attending to the objects presented by the user interface:

- *Performance is critical.* If operations are too slow, the person is likely to wander off and break the circuit. Then we have the problem of the user rebuilding the contents of his or her short-term memory ("Where was I?").

- *Maintain closure.* With good performance in critical areas, we can maintain closure. Each operation is a closeable, atomic operation, such that the user need not remember a partial state. With small, atomic operations it is not necessary to provide a facility for interrupting the operation because the operation is self-contained, and the operation's length is short enough to maintain the user's attention.

- *Immediate feedback.* The illusion of information as concrete objects is enhanced by immediate feedback and suitable animation. You may, for example, highlight legal menu and palette operations in each context; animate spatial relationships, such as windows opening and closing; and show progress in long operations, such as printing.

6 *Handle errors gracefully.* The best approach is to design the interface so as to avoid possible error situations. Typing errors are avoided entirely if the user selects a visible object rather than typing its name, and if she selects a menu command rather than types text to a command line interpreter. Illegal menu commands should be disabled before the menu is opened. Unnecessary program restrictions, such as limited data buffer sizes, should be avoided. (A wise man once said that there are only three good numbers in data processing: *none, 1,* and *all.*)

If an error situation does occur, make sure you describe the error in user terms and explain what the user can do to take care of the problem.

7 *Support undo.* Undo is perhaps the most useful function in a direct manipulation user interface, because it allows experimentation, helps the user get out of dangerous situations, and helps support a positive mental attitude in the user since it permits the user to change his or her mind.

8 *Provide a help system.* When all else fails, it is important to allow the user to find the information needed on line, integrated with the system, rather than

forcing him or her to read the manual. A help system can answer questions such as "What is...?," "How do I...?," "What just happened?," and "Why was that an error?"

9 *Be creative.* Designing a user interface is a creative activity. It requires being able to look at several points of view simultaneously, and being able to try out conceptual ideas quickly. Creativity springs from rigor and imagination applied alternately—imaginative thought to create possible ideas, applied rigorously to the problem at hand to determine their suitability. "Rigor alone is paralytic death, while imagination alone is insanity" (Bateson).

...and above all, have fun.

7.4.3 A Simple Direct Manipulation Interface for Our Task Example

When we created the enterprise model in the previous section, we permitted ourselves to isolate travel expense account processing from all other processes taking place in the enterprise. The preceding task description tells us that this is a luxury we cannot afford when we consider the performance of the model's tasks. When the Authorizer processes a travel request, he or she has to consider three separate functions: expense account processing, budget and accounts, and planning.

The simplest solution, from the programmer's point of view, is to require the Authorizer to open three distinct and independent tools: a tool on budget and accounts, a tool on current plans, and a tool on the travel expense account. He or she can then perform the task as described under Task 1, transcribing information such as the planned total cost from one tool to another as required. A possible set of tools is sketched out in Figure 7.27.

Figure 7.27

Three distinct tools to serve the authorization task

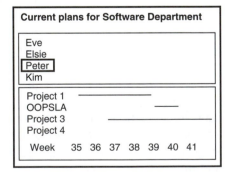

A possible scenario using these tools is as follows:

1 Open *Travel permission request* tool on a current permission request data set according to the rules of your information environment (e.g., point to a visual representation of the data set and give an open command).

2 Check the travel request purpose and determine that it is a reasonable request.

3 Open the *Budget and commitments* tool and the *current plans tool.* This may be done according to the relevant user manuals. Alternatively, the personal task manager could be part of a sophisticated process control system and provide direct access to these tools as described in a definition of the process.

4 Check the *Current plans* tool, and modify them if necessary to accommodate the proposed travel.

5 Check the budget and secure additional appropriations if necessary. Select the appropriate budget item and record the commitment.

6 Press the Authorize button in the *Travel authorization request* tool to transmit and record the travelPermission.

7.4.4 A Composite User Interface for the Manager to Determine Travel Permission

The tools described in the preceeding section were not integrated for the current task. The Authorizer had to select corresponding items in the different tools, create a new budget commitment and copy each amount from the TravelRequest into it.

We could consider creating a specialized tool for the travel authorization task. The decision to do so would depend on the potential savings and the cost of its creation. Automated aids such as VisualWorks from ParcPlace Systems makes it easy to create specialized tools, and future aids may well make it feasible for the users to create their own personal tools.

We will sketch out a possible tool in Figure 7.28 to illustrate the idea. A real-life tool would have to be based on a detailed study of the tasks, and should probably be more sophisticated.

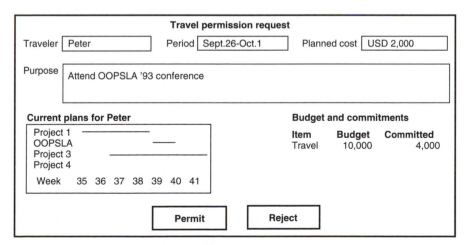

Figure 7.28

A simple tool integrated for the travel permission task

A possible scenario using this tool is as follows:

1 Open the specialized *Travel permission request* tool on a current permission request data set according to the rules of your information environment (e.g., point to a visual representation of the data set and give an open command).

2 Check the travel request purpose and determine that it is a reasonable request.

3 The appropriate budget and commitments items are automatically selected and displayed. Check them. A menu command opens a separate tool if corrective action is necessary.

4 The appropriate portion of the plans for the Traveler is automatically displayed. Check it. A menu command opens a separate tool if corrective action is necessary.

5 Check the budget and secure additional funds if necessary. Select the appropriate budget item and record the commitment.

6 Press the Permit button in the *Travel Permission* tool to transmit and record the travelPermission, and to record the budget commitment.

This single tool will be sufficient for most practical cases, and is clearly superior to the hodgepodge of windows needed in the previous solution. Note that this is an example of integration on Level 3 in Figure 7.5. The separation between different information services, which is so useful for the information-processing department, is uninteresting from the user's point of view and is hidden.

We will now create a role model of the tool shown in Figure 7.28. We begin with the area of concern in Figure 7.29.

The roles are specified in Figure 7.30 using the OOram language syntax defined in Appendix A. The Authorizer is the role representing any person who authorizes travel. We let a single role, Trav.Auth.Tool, represent the clusters of objects that implement the tool. This tool is a nice illustration of the two-dimensional nature of our architecture. It is an integrated tool that accesses three services. We represent each of them as a single role: an ExpenseAccountService, a PlanningService and a BudgetService. The ExpenseAccountService is the service described by the information model in Section 7.2. The description of the other services are left to your imagination.

We recognize that the tool and the service roles may be virtual. They will then be expanded into clusters of roles in a later stage of development.

<table>
<tr><td>Figure 7.29
Area of concern</td><td>The area of concern is an integrated tool for the authorization of a travel proposal in our enterprise</td></tr>
</table>

Figure 7.30
The roles
role 'TSAuthorizer' **explanation** *"The person who authorizes the travel."*
role 'TSAuthorizerTool' **explanation** *"The user interface system"*
role 'TSAccountService' **explanation** *"An object structure representing a particular expense account."*
role 'TSPlanningService' **explanation** *"A system representing the current plans for the enterprise"*
role 'TSBudgetService' **explanation** *"A system managing the enterprise budget"*

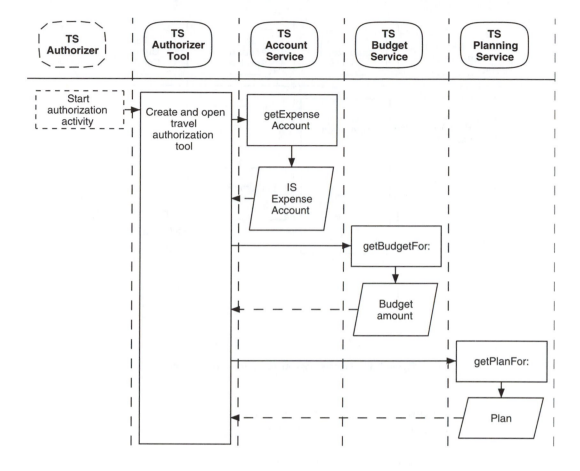

Figure 7.31   Process diagram: Open travel permission tool

We create two Process diagrams: one for the opening of the tool shown in Figure 7.31; and another describing a typical sequence of events when the Authorizer hits the PERMIT button, shown in Figure 7.32.

The top level collaboration view of Figure 7.33 follows directly from the basic tool model in Figure 7.25.

The stimulus messages are the available user commands, and each stimulus triggers an activity. We will not go into the detailed design of these activities here, but will indicate a likely set of typical message interfaces. They are shown graphically in Figure 7.34. We see that the diagram gets overloaded even in this simple example. The textual interface definition shown in Figure 7.35 is better, and it also invites the analyst to explain the message semantics. (Note that parameter typing is optional, and that we have included parameter types in this informal specification.)

We first met the user's tasks in the enterprise process view in Figure 7.14. We now find corresponding operations in the interface called TSAuthorizer-Tool<TSAuthorizer (AuthorizerTool from Authorizer). It is, therefore, possible to maintain formal threads from the human level in the enterprise model via the task/tool/service model to the information model.

Task/tool/ service model is closely linked to Enterprise and information models

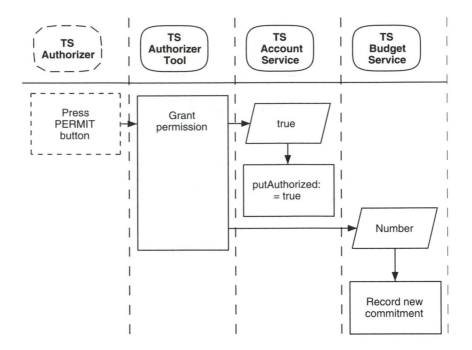

Figure 7.32   Process diagram: Grant travel permission

In many cases, the information model will be a first conceptual schema for a relational database. The service operations defined here will in simple cases be database queries and update specifications, and may conveniently be stored in suitable query objects. Nontrivial service functionality can be achieved by special travel service objects, as illustrated in Figure 7.23b, or the service can be implemented in an object-oriented database.

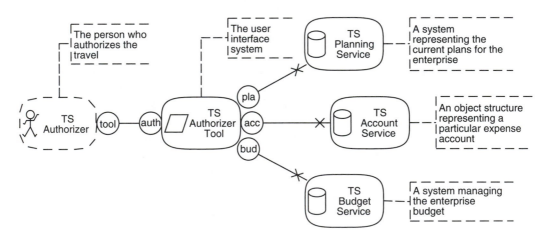

Figure 7.33   Interface collaboration view annotated with role responsibilities

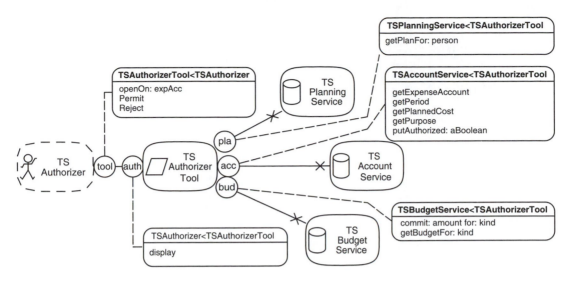

Figure 7.34   Interface collaboration view annotated with interfaces

interface 'TSAuthorizerTool<TSAuthorizer'
    message 'Permit' *"Permit the proposed travel."*
    message 'Reject' *"Refuse the proposed travel."*
    message 'openOn:' *"Create a new instance of the tool and open it on the specified ExpenseAccount."*
        param 'expAcc'
interface 'TSAccountService<TSAuthorizerTool'
    message 'getExpenseAccount' *"Return expense account information."*
        return 'INFExpenseAccount' **::** 'Travel Expense Information Model'
    message 'getPeriod' *"Return travel time period."*
    message 'getPlannedCost' *"Returned planned cost."*
    message 'getPurpose' *"Return purpose of travel."*
    message 'putAuthorized:' *"Set authorization if aBoolean = true, otherwise the travel is rejected."*
        param 'aBoolean' **type boolean**
interface 'TSBudgetService<TSAuthorizerTool'
    message 'getBudgetFor:' *"Return budget information."*
        param 'kind'
        return number
    message 'commit:for:' *"Allocate amount from budget."*
        param 'amount' **number**
        param 'kind'
interface 'TSAuthorizer<TSAuthorizerTool'
    message 'display' *"Read the currently displayed text."*
interface 'TSPlanningService<TSAuthorizerTool'
    message 'getPlanFor:' *"Return planning information."*
        param 'person'
        return 'Plan' **::** 'BasicTypes'

Figure 7.35   Interfaces

CHAPTER 8

Case Study: The Analysis and Design of a Real Time System

CONTENTS

8.1 Environment Model 213

    8.1.1 Determine the Area of Concern 213
    8.1.2 Identify Environment Roles and Stimulus/Response 213
    8.1.3 Determine Typical Message Sequences 214

8.2 Detailed Model 215

    8.2.1 Specify and Understand Objects and Roles 215
    8.2.2 Determine Typical Message Sequences 216
    8.2.3 Describe Roles as State Diagrams 216
    8.2.4 Determine the Interfaces 218

8.3 Implementation Examples 221

    8.3.1 Bridge to C++ 222
    8.3.2 Bridge to Smalltalk 223
    8.3.3 Bridge to SDL 224
    8.3.4 Bridge to Distributed Object Systems 226
    8.3.5 OMG/CORBA 227
    8.3.6 COM/OLE 228
    8.3.7 OOram Executable Specifications 229

This chapter is written for the specially interested programmer. It exemplifies the use of state diagrams. It also illustrates that role models are independent of implementation, by showing the transition from the models to traditional and distributed implementation environments.

We will now study a case in which the information is simple, but in which we have to ensure that the system behaves properly under all circumstances. The case we have chosen is a real time access control system, where a person identifies himself or herself through a card and code reader, and the system unlocks the door if the person is granted access. The example was inspired by a similar case in Braek [Bræk 93].

Work process includes precise modeling of behavior

Our suggested design process for solving the access control problem includes the specification of state diagrams to reflect our focus on behavior. There is a *state diagram* for each role; the diagrams are mutually dependent and must be consistent. The descriptions tend to be large and hard to modify, so we will postpone the specification of the state diagrams to a late stage in the design process. A scenario view is simpler than a set of state diagrams because it shows only the message sequences of a typical or critical case. We will use scenarios in the early iterations to keep the volume of the model small, and add state diagrams when the design is reasonably mature.

Processes should be tailored to each problem. It is therefore not surprising that our work process is different from the default process described in Section 2.4:

1 Determine the area of concern.

2 Identify environment roles and stimulus/response.

3 Specify and understand the roles.

4 Determine typical message sequences.

5 Describe roles as state diagrams.

6 Determine interfaces.

Iterate!

It is important to keep the early descriptions small so that they can be easily changed in accordance with our emerging understanding of the problem and its solution. As our models become firm, we will elaborate them with state diagrams and other details until we arrive at the final description.

We use virtual roles initially

Aggregation is a powerful technique for simplification. What we regard as a single role in one iteration may later be divided into a number of roles. We will here use aggregation in the form of a virtual role (Section 2.5): what appears as a single role in one description is really a shorthand for a cluster of roles in a more detailed description. Also, there is no object in the final system that corresponds to the virtual role.

We will show two iterations in this case study:

1 An *environment model*, showing the access control system as a single, virtual role.

2 A *detailed model,* showing a complete set of roles for the system objects.

8.1 ENVIRONMENT MODEL

We initially create a simple model showing the whole system as a single, virtual role.

The goal of our first iteration is to understand the system as seen from its environment. This iteration covers Steps 1, 2, and 4 in our suggested work process. We will bother neither with state diagram definitions nor detailed interface definitions at this early stage of the analysis.

8.1.1 Determine the Area of Concern

Figure 8.1 displays the area of concern for our study.

8.1.2 Identify Environment Roles and Stimulus/Response

We show the complete Control System as a single virtual role in this first modeling iteration; see Figure 8.2. This means that there will be no single object representing the whole system, but rather a cluster of interacting objects which we will later model as a cluster of roles.

The process starts when a person approaches the door and inserts his or her card to gain access. We represent the Person as an environment role, because it will send a stimulus message when the Person wants to open the door.

The Door is also an environment role, since the effect of locking and unlocking it is outside the scope of our area of concern. (The concept of *environment* was discussed in Section 2.5.)

> We want to design an access control system in which a person identifies himself with a card and a personal code to gain access through a door that is controlled by an automatic lock. The system supports any number of doors.

Figure 8.1

Area of concern

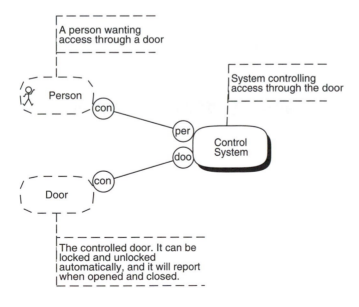

Figure 8.2

The system and its environment

8.1.3 Determine Typical Message Sequences

We consider two typical message sequences: one for successful access, shown in Figure 8.3, and one where the PIN-code has been rejected, shown in Figure 8.4.

Figure 8.3
Message sequence for successful access

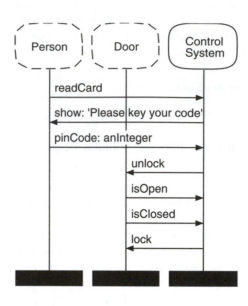

Figure 8.4
Message sequence for rejected PIN code

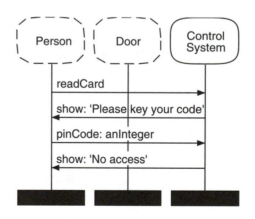

8.2 DETAILED MODEL

We elaborate the virtual role of the environment model and show details of the local part of the system.

In the second iteration, we will expand the `Control System` role, running iteratively through Steps 3–6.

The *area of concern* and the *environment views* are unchanged from the first iteration, and will not be repeated here.

8.2.1 Specify and Understand Objects and Roles

Using the hints of Chapter 2, we will identify the objects, distribute responsibilities, and specify the necessary roles of the detailed model.

There clearly must be some equipment at each access point, so that the `Person` can enter a card and PIN code. This equipment could also be used to store information about the people who are permitted access at that point, but this seems impractical if there are a number of controlled access points. We will define a `CentralUnit` that is responsible for managing all access rights.

We arrive at the collaboration view of the system shown in Figure 8.5 in a stepwise manner, moving back and forth between the collaboration view and the scenario view.

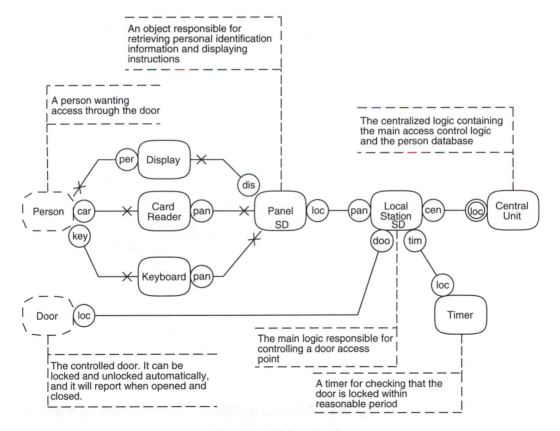

Figure 8.5 Collaboration view

In the scenario view, we expand on the message sequences of Section 8.1, distributing the message handling onto roles in the detailed model. This is documented in the next subsection. In doing this work, we benefited from using a CRC technique (Section 2.4).

8.2.2 Determine Typical Message Sequences

One or more scenarios may be specified; each describes a typical message sequence that implements an activity. When using a CRC card process, it is advantageous to record the scenarios at the termination of the CRC process, since the message sequences are not recorded on the cards. Figure 8.6 shows a scenario for a successful access activity.

8.2.3 Describe Roles as State Diagrams

State diagrams are suitable for formulating a detailed specification of role behavior without actually writing the code. We do not generally specify state diagrams

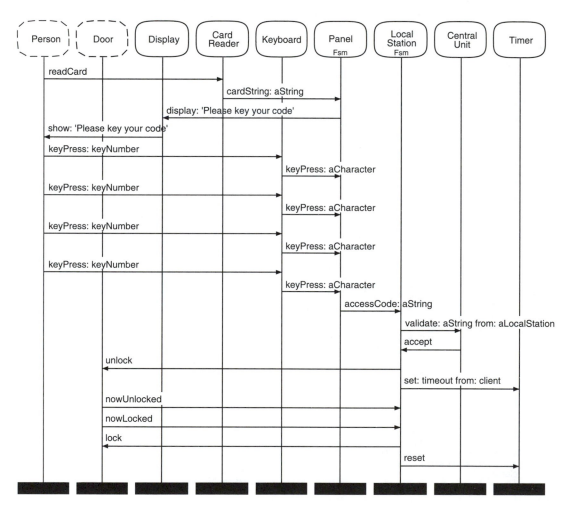

Figure 8.6 Successful Access Sequence

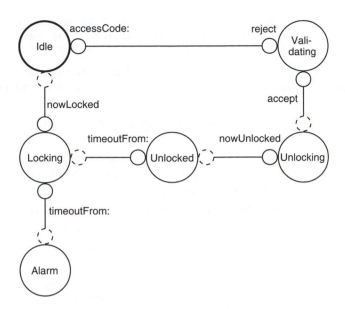

Figure 8.7

A State diagram for the **Local-Station** role

for our roles, but they are useful in certain cases—notably cases involving multiple message threads, such as are often found in telecommunications and real time systems.

As we have noted before, the volume of the description increases dramatically with the introduction of state diagrams, and you should use them only if you really need them, and then only at a late stage in the design process.

Use state diagrams sparingly and late in the process.

The theory and usage of state diagrams is a specialized subject which we will not attempt to cover adequately in this book. We will content ourselves with indicating how state diagrams may be defined in the context of a role in a role model, and refer you to the literature for further details [Bræk 93].

The state diagram for the LocalStation role is shown in Figure 8.7. The action to be performed on a transition from one state to another might be specified in pseudo code, in a programming language, or in a diagrammatic form. The state diagram is to be read as follows:

1 Idle state. The role is initially in the Idle state. It may receive one message (signal):

- accessCode: (received from Panel). Causes LocalStation to request a confirmation of the specified code from the CentralUnit, and wait for the answer in the Validating state.

2 Validating state. The role may receive an accept or reject answer from the CentralUnit:

- reject (received from the CentralUnit.) The request for access has been rejected. Causes LocalStation to display a suitable message on the Display and return to the Idle state.

- accept (received from the CentralUnit.) Causes LocalStation to send an unlock message to the Door and start a timer for the time the Door is permitted to be unlocked.

3 Unlocking state. The role is waiting for the Door to actually unlock. One message may be received. (We ignore the case when the Door does not respond, in this simple example.)

- nowUnlocked (received from the Door.) Causes LocalStation to start a timer for the time period that Door may remain unlocked, and to enter the Unlocked state.

4 Unlocked state. The role is waiting for the duration timeout to expire. It may receive one message.

- timeoutFrom: (received from the Timer.) Causes LocalStation to send a message to lock the Door, start the Timer for the period in which the Door must respond and enter the Locking state.

5 Locking state. The role is waiting for the Door to respond to the lock command. There are two possible messages that may be received:

- nowLocked (from Door.) This message signals that everything is okay, and that the role may enter the Idle state.

- timeoutFrom: (from the Timer.) The locking has been unsuccessful, possibly because the Person has prevented the door from closing and latching. Causes the role to go to the Alarm state.

- Alarm state. The role raises an alarm. The actions to be taken in the case of an alarm are not specified in this simple example.

The state diagrams for the other roles follow the same principles.

State diagrams and method specifications are usually alternative specifications of role behavior. The best choice depends on the particular application, and also on the implementation and runtime environments. Roles with state diagrams translate most easily to an implementation environment that also uses object states as a basic concept. In Section 8.3.3, we will show an example of such a state-oriented language.

When implementing a system directly in an object-oriented language such as C++ or Smalltalk, we are concerned with implementing the methods for the different messages that the objects are to receive.

Method must branch on the object state in state diagrams

State diagrams define an action to be triggered for each message (event) permissible in each state. A method may have to branch on the object state to select the appropriate action for execution, as shown in the method specification view of Figure 8.8. The figure shows a method specification view for the accessCode message sent from Panel to LocalStation. We have used the states given by the state diagram in Figure 8.7 to specify the method.

The message-passing is basically asynchronous. The different objects may therefore execute in parallel. Your final decision on parallelism must be accounted for in the implementation in accordance with the runtime environment.

8.2.4 Determine the Interfaces

The interfaces in Figure 8.9 are elaborations of the messages specified in the other views given in the previous sections. This textual view is written in the OOram language, which is defined in Appendix A. The language permits the specification of parameters and their types. We here show a reduced form which is particularly useful in the early stages of the modeling process and for overviews.

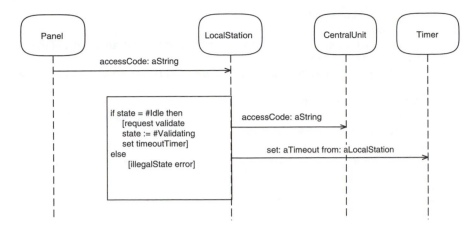

Figure 8.8

**Method speci-
fication view for
`Local-
accessCode:`**

interface 'CardReader<Person'
    message 'readCard' **explanation** *"Read my identity card."*
interface 'Panel<CardReader'
    message 'cardString:' **explanation** *"Accept the given String from the person's
identity card."*
interface 'Display<Panel'
    message 'display:' **explanation** *"Display the given String."*
interface 'Person<Display'
    message 'show:' **explanation** *"Read my displayed text."*
interface 'Keyboard<Person'
    message 'keyPress:' **explanation** *"The user has pressed the indicated key."*
interface 'Panel<Keyboard'
    message 'keyPress:' **explanation** *"Accept given character from person."*
interface 'LocalStation<Panel'
    message 'accessCode:'
        explanation *"A person requests access and has offered the identification
specified by aString, which is a coded combination of information from the identity
card and the received secret code."*
interface 'CentralUnit<LocalStation'
    message 'validate:from:'
        explanation *"Validate the given access code (aString) and return an
accept-message iff access granted, otherwise a reject-message."*
interface 'LocalStation<CentralUnit'
    message 'accept'
    message 'reject'
interface 'Door<LocalStation'
    message 'lock' **explanation** *"Lock the door."*
    message 'unlock' **explanation** *"Unlock the door."*
interface 'Panel<LocalStation'
    message 'display:' **explanation** *"Display the given String to the user."*

Figure 8.9

**Interfaces of the
detailed model**

(continued)

Figure 8.9

(cont.)

interface 'Timer<LocalStation'
    message 'set:from:'
        explanation *"Set the timer to the given timeout time, send timeout message at end of time period."*
    message 'reset' **explanation** *"Reset timer so that no timeout message will be sent."*
interface 'LocalStation<Door'
    message 'nowLocked' **explanation** *"The door has just been locked."*
    message 'nowUnlocked' **explanation** *"The door has just been unlocked."*
interface 'LocalStation<Timer'
    message 'timeoutFrom:' **explanation** *"The sending timer has reached timeout."*

8.3   IMPLEMENTATION EXAMPLES

A role model is basically independent of its implementation language. We will here indicate five alternatives: implementation in C++ and in Smalltalk; implementation in a distributed environment according to the standards laid down by the Object Management Group and by Microsoft; and an implementation in the form of an executable specification.

IN A NUTSHELL

We first will create an object specification view (in Figure 8.10) for the Access-Control system. It is very similar to the collaboration view of Figure 8.5, but the roles are now shown with heavy outlines to indicate that they have been promoted to object specifications.

Access control example

This object specification focuses on the local parts of the system. The CentralUnit is shown as an environment object, which means that we do not specify all of its characteristics. (It will for example, have additional functionality for setting and removing people's access rights and for handling alarms.) The other environment roles are the Person and Door roles, since they are outside the computer system.

The following sections illustrate the transition from the object specification to implementation in different environments:

1   An object-oriented programming language such as C++.

2   An object-oriented programming language such as Smalltalk.

3   A state-oriented language such as the System Description Language (SDL) that is commonly used in the telecommunications industry. (SDL is standardized, see [CCITT Z100].)

4   Distributed object systems based on standards created by the Object Management Group and Microsoft.

5   OOram executable specifications.

We will use LocalStation in the object specification shown in Figure 8.10 to illustrate these alternatives.

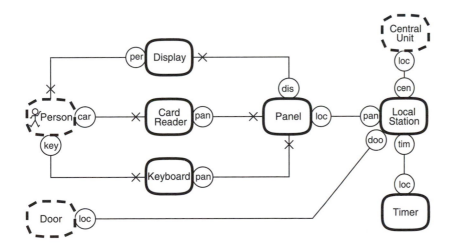

Figure 8.10

Access control system, object specification view

8.3.1 Bridge to C++

It is straightforward to derive a C++ class definition from an OOram object specification; in fact, it can be done automatically. Corresponding concepts are shown
in Table 4.1.

The default class definition defines a class for `LocalStation` and an instance
variable for each of its ports. The types of these variables are the names of the
classes implementing the collaborators, e.g., `Panel1`, `Door1`, `Timer1`,and
`CentralUnit1`.

C++ example

A C++ class definition corresponding to the definition of `LocalStation` given
in Figure 8.10 could be as follows:

```cpp
enum State {
  Unlocked,
  Locking,
  Alarm,
  LockTime,
  Idle,
  Validating,
  MaxValidationTime};
class LocalStation1;
class String;
class CentralUnit {
public:
  void validatefrom(const String&, LocalStation1*);
  void openDoorAlarm(LocalStation1*);
};
class Door {
public:
  void Lock();
};
class Timer {
public:
  void setfrom(State, LocalStation1*);
};
class Panel;
class Dictionary;
class LocalStation1 {
public:
  LocalStation1();
  ~LocalStation();
  State timeoutDictAt(State);
  void  accept();
  void  accessCode(const String&);
  void  nowLocked();
  void  nowUnlocked();
  void  reject();
  void  timeoutFrom(Timer*);
  void  dpsCaution(State, const String&);
  void  reset();
private:
      CentralUnit* cen;
      Door*    doo;
```

```
        Panel*    pan;
        Timer*    tim;
  static Dictionary* timeoutDict;
        State     state;
};
```

The member functions can be produced automatically. The body can either be taken from a method specification view, such as Figure 8.8, or it can be programmed manually. Two of the member functions for the LocalStation1 class could be as follows:

```
void LocalStation1::accessCode(const String& code)
{
 if(state == Idle)
 {
   state = Validating;
   cen->validatefrom(code, this);
   tim->setfrom(MaxValidationTime, this);
 }
 else
 {
   state = Validating;
   dpsCaution(state, " is illegal state");
   reset();
 }
}
void LocalStation1::timeoutFrom(Timer* timer)
{
 switch(state)
 {
  case UnLocked:
   tim->setfrom(timeoutDictAt(LockTime), this);
   doo->Lock();
   state = Locking;
   break;
  case Locking:
   cen->openDoorAlarm(this);
   state = Alarm;
   break;
  default:
   dpsCaution(state, " is illegal state.");
   reset();
   break;
 }
}
```

How the C++ implementation and runtime environment would deal with asynchronous behavior is not covered in this brief presentation.

8.3.2 Bridge to Smalltalk

It is straightforward to derive a Smalltalk class definition from an OOram object specification; it can be done automatically. Corresponding concepts are shown in Table 4.1.

Deriving a Smalltalk class definition from an OOram Object specification

A Smalltalk class definition corresponding to `LocalStation` is as follows:

Object subclass: #LocalStation1
    instanceVariableNames: 'cen doo pan tim '
    classVariableNames: ''
    poolDictionaries: ''
    category: 'AccessControl'

The methods of the class can be produced automatically, just as for C++. The body can also be taken either from a method specification view, such as Figure 8.8, or it can be programmed manually. Two of the methods for the `LocalStation1` class could be as follows:

LocalStation1 (LocalStation<Panel)
accessCode: aString
    " *A person requests access and has offered the identification specified* "
    " *by aString, which is a coded combination of information from the identity* "
    " *card and the received secret code.* "
    state == #Idle
    ifTrue:
        [state := #Validating.
        cen validate: aString from: self.
        tim set: MaxValidationTime from: self]
    ifFalse:
        [self dpsCaution: 'Illegal state: ' , state. self reset].

LocalStation1 (LocalStation<Timer)
timeoutFrom: timer
    " *The sending timer has reached timeout.* "
    state
        case: #Unlocked do:
            [tim set: (LocalStation1 timeoutDictAt: #LockTime) * 2 from: self.
            doo lock.
            state := #Locking]
        case: #Locking do:
            [cen openDoorAlarmFrom: self.
            state := #Alarm]
        otherCaseDo:
            [self warning: state , ' is illegal state'.
            self reset]

How the Smalltalk environment would deal with asynchronous behavior is not covered in this brief presentation.

8.3.3 Bridge to SDL

The OOram method is adaptable to different design and programming styles. Some clients in the telecommunications industry use the OOram method for early system analysis and top level design, and create their detailed designs and implementations in the standardized System Description Language (SDL) [CCITT Z100 and Bræk 93]. The clients use a version of the OOram method and tools that have been specialized with an SDL-like view on actions to simplify the transition from OOram role models to detailed design and implementation in SDL. An example of such an action specification is shown in Figure 8.11. The action is to be performed on the transition from the `Idle` state to the `Validating` state, which is in Figure 8.7

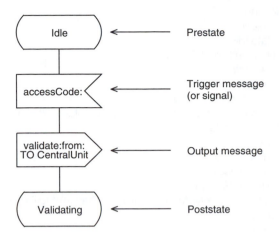

Figure 8.11
OOram/SDL diagram for **Local- Station >> accessCode**

Idle ← Prestate

accessCode: ← Trigger message (or signal)

validate:from: TO CentralUnit ← Output message

Validating ← Poststate

The actions associated with the message `timeoutFrom:` received from the timer are particularly interesting, because the action to be performed depends on the current state of the object, as shown in Figure 8.7. This is illustrated in Figure 8.12.

A message may trigger different actions

SDL has both a graphical and textual representation. The textual representation is called SDL/PR (SDL/Phrase Representation). It can be produced automatically from the OOram model. Objects in the object specification map naturally to SDL processes. An SDL/PR definition of the LocalStation process follows. The System and Block description levels in SDL have been omitted here for simplification. We have likewise omitted the variable declarations.

```
process LocalStation;
start;
        nextstate Idle;
        state Idle;
            input accessCode(aCode);
                output validatefrom(aCode,thisLocalStation)/* to CentralUnit*/;
            nextstate Validating;
```

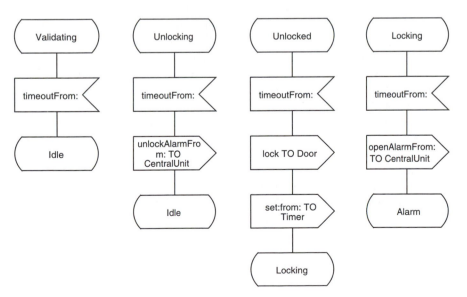

Figure 8.12
OOram/SDL diagrams for different actions in **Local- Station >>timeout- From**

```
        state Validating;
            input reject;
            nextstate Idle;
            input timeoutFrom(aTimer);
            nextstate Idle;
            input accept;
                output unlock/* to Door*/;
                output setfrom(unLockTime,thisLocalStation)/* to Timer*/;
            nextstate Unlocking;
        state Unlocking;
            input nowUnlocked;
            nextstate Unlocked;
            input timeoutFrom(aTimer);
                output unlockAlarmFrom(thisLocalStation)/* to CentralUnit*/;
            nextstate Idle;
        state Unlocked;
            input timeoutFrom(aTimer);
                output lock/* to Door*/;
                output setfrom(lockTime,thisLocalStation)/* to Timer*/;
            nextstate Locking;
        state Locking;
            input nowLocked;
            nextstate Idle;
            input timeoutFrom(aTimer);
                output openAlarmFrom(thisLocalStation)/* to CentralUnit*/;
            nextstate Alarm;
        state Alarm;
            input nowLocked;
                output doorLockedFrom(thisLocalStation)/* to CentralUnit*/;
            nextstate Idle;
    endprocess LocalStation;
```

8.3.4   Bridge to Distributed Object Systems

The separation in the *why*, *what*, and *how* abstractions of objects (Figure 1.13) makes the OOram method ideally suited for the analysis and design of distributed object systems. The method separates an object's interfaces from its internal behavior. The implementation of an object can be done in different ways, and objects having the same interfaces can have different implementations.

OMG/CORBA, from the Object Management Group, and COM/OLE, from Microsoft, are two approaches to distributed object systems. Both are based on a strict separation between interfaces and implementations of objects.

In the following, we will continue to use the AccessControl example to describe how the OOram model maps onto the interface description languages of OMG/CORBA and COM/OLE. We will show how the separation of role, interface, and implementation in the models matches the similar separation of interface and implementation for distributed objects.

The OOram concepts are easily mapped onto the concepts of the Interface Definition Language (IDL) of OMG/CORBA and COM/OLE as shown in Table 8.1.

Table 8.1

Mapping from
OOram concepts
to the concepts of
CORBA IDL and
Microsoft IDL

OOram	CORBA IDL	MS IDL
Role model	—	—
Role, object specification	Interface	Interface
Port	—	Interface reference
Interface	Interface	Interface
Message	Request	Message
Implementation class	Implementation class	Implementation class/ factory
Method	Operation, method	Method
Attribute	Attribute	Property
Derived model	Derived interface	Derived interface
Base model	Base interface	Base interface

8.3.5 OMG/CORBA

The Object Management Group (OMG) was established in 1989 with the goal of creating industry guidelines and object management specifications to provide a common framework for application development. The basis for the work is the Object Management Architecture. The Common Object Request Broker Architecture—CORBA—is the basic infrastructure that supports interaction between distributed objects in the architecture.

The interfaces of objects are described through an interface definition language (IDL). The object model underlying CORBA is based on a strict separation between the interfaces and implementations of objects. The CORBA standards are concerned only with the interfaces of objects. The implementations are totally hidden, which allows for implementations in different languages, both with and without implementation inheritance.

The interface descriptions in CORBA IDL are easily derived from the OOram object specification. An interface description of LocalStation in CORBA IDL could be as follows:

Deriving a CORBA IDL description from an OOram Object specification

```
module AccessControl {

    interface LocalStationFromPanel {
      void accessCode(in string aCode);
    };

    interface LocalStationFromDoor {
      void nowLocked();
      void nowUnLocked();
    };

    interface LocalStationFromCentralUnit {
      void accept();
      void reject();
    };
```

```
interface LocalStationFromTimer {
  void timeOutFrom(in Timer aTimer);
};
```

```
interface LocalStation: LocalStationFromPanel, LocalStationFromDoor,
                LocalStationFromCentralUnit,
    LocalStationFromTimer {

    readonly attribute CentralUnit cen;
    readonly attribute Door doo;
    readonly attribute Panel pan;
    readonly attribute Timer tim;
    };
};
```

As there is a standard mapping from CORBA IDL to C++ and Smalltalk, it is possible to automatically derive a language-specific equivalent to an interface described in IDL.

Both OOram and CORBA support inheritance of interfaces. OOram synthesis specifications can easily be mapped onto CORBA interface descriptions.

8.3.6 COM/OLE

The Microsoft Component Object Model (COM) is Microsoft's foundation for distributed objects. Microsoft Object Linking and Embedding (OLE) Integration technology is built on top of COM. In COM, all applications interact with each other through collections of functions, called *interfaces*. COM defines a standard way to lay out virtual function tables in memory (for each of several platforms), and a standard way to call a function in a table. All OLE services are realized as COM interfaces.

Compared to OMG/CORBA, this is a top-down approach to distributed objects that initially has provided services in a local environment, with plans to provide a distributed infrastructure in the future.

Deriving a
Microsoft IDL
description
from an OOram
Object
specification

The idea behind a component-oriented architecture is that it is possible to implement the components in different programming languages. The binary interface standard that strictly separates interfaces from implementations makes it easy to support implementations written in different languages.

The interface descriptions in Microsoft IDL are easily derived from the OOram object specification. The concepts map as shown in Table 8.1.

COM/OLE
example

An interface description of LocalStation in Microsoft IDL could be as follows:

```
interface IUnknown
{    HRESULT QueryInterface();
     ULONG  AdRef;
     ULONG  Release;
};
```

```
[  uuid(AF3B752C-89D0-101B-A6E4-00DD0111A658),
   version(1.0) ]
   interface ILocalSPanel: IUnknown {
   void accessCode([in] string aCode);
   };
```

```
[  uuid(AF3B7521-89D0-101B-A6E4-00DD0111A658),
   version(1.0)  ]
    interface ILocalSDoor: IUnknown {
      void nowLocked();
      void nowUnLocked();
    };

[  uuid(AF3B7522-89D0-101B-A6E4-00DD0111A658),
   version(1.0)  ]
    interface ILocalSCentralU: IUnknown{
      void accept();
      void reject();
    };

[  uuid(AF3B7523-89D0-101B-A6E4-00DD0111A658),
   version(1.0)  ]
    interface ILocalSTimer:IUnknown {
      void timeOutFrom([in] Timer *aTimer);
    };

[  uuid(AF3B7524-89D0-101B-A6E4-00DD0111A658),
   version(1.0)  ]
interface LocalStation:
{  CentralUnit *get_cen();
   Door *get_door();
   Panel *get_pan();
   Timer *get_ tim();
   };
```

A common feature between OOram models and Microsoft COM specifications
is the support of several interfaces for one object; i.e., a communication port can
have several interfaces.

8.3.7   OOram Executable Specifications

We have stressed the importance of early prototypes and exploratory programming. Like the Norwegian farmer Peter Amb said in an entirely different context:
"We may have our heads in the clouds, but we keep our feet firmly planted on
the ground."

Executable specifications make the abstract OOram descriptions real. They
have the attractive property of puncturing fancy abstract constructs and exposing
the real problems.

Executable specifications make the models real

Executable specifications are useful for checking program designs and any
other kind of model at an early stage. In forward engineering, we start from a
model and create an executable specification to study the model in more detail.
In reverse engineering, we start from an exploratory or real program that specifies
some desired functionality, and create a model to find and define appropriate
high level architecture and concepts.

OOram executable specifications are written in an object-oriented programming language, and the detailed techniques to be used for forward and reverse
engineering depend on the chosen language. In principle, we have three ways of
satisfying ourselves that the program logic conforms to a given design expressed
in a role model:

Checking correspondence between program and model

1 The program code could be analyzed by a suitable algorithm and compared with the role model information. This is a difficult research problem, and is probably not feasible in the general case.

2 We could implement the specifications in a new, high level language which has been designed so that the code could be mapped on to the OOram concepts. This is an interesting alternative which we are currently exploring.

3 We could monitor the execution of typical and dangerous cases, and record all message interaction, with current object states and message details. The recording can be compared automatically to the relevant role models, and illegal messages can be flagged.

Monitored execution gives important insights

We have chosen the last solution because it provides the designer with important insights into the operation of his design and because it is applicable in all cases.

This variant of executable specifications is called monitored execution. A *monitored execution* collects a trace of all messages being passed between the observed objects.

Facilities for monitored execution can take many forms. The Taskon experimental facility automatically produces three reports: An *object collaboration report*, an *execution scenario report*, and a *textual trace report*.

We have created an executable specification for part of the `AccessControl` example, and have run a number of monitored executions under different conditions. The object specification view, for the example, is shown in Figure 8.13, and the results of an execution are described in the following pages. We show all the collected information in our example, but would want to show a filtered subset in more complex situations.

The environment roles `CentralUnit`, `Panel`, and `Door` are marked as object specifications, because we implement them as dummy classes for testing purposes.

The object collaboration report shows all observed objects and their interaction paths

The object collaboration report shown in Figure 8.14 is similar to a collaboration view, but we use rectangles rather than super-ellipses to emphasize that we are displaying an object structure rather than a role structure. There is one rectangle for each observed object, and one port symbol for the start of each observed interaction path. Associated with each port are the messages actually sent through that port. We show only the messages observed from port 15; similar message lists are associated with all the other ports.

We notice that a `Timer` is associated with the `Door` object. This `Timer` was not part of the design, but had to be added to the dummy `Door` implementation to simulate the time taken by the various door operations, such as the time that the door is kept open.

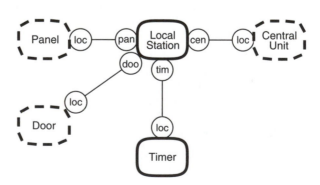

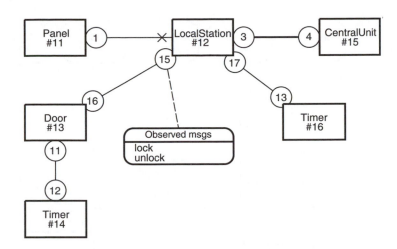

Figure 8.14

Object collaboration report for successful access example

The execution scenario report shown in Figure 8.15 uses a notation similar to that of a scenario view. The actors are the observed objects, and the interactions are the observed message interactions.

Light arrows in the execution scenario report indicate messages that conform to the role models; heavy arrows indicate nonconformance. As expected, all interactions with the Timer are marked as nonconforming.

The textual trace report shown in Figure 8.16 displays all of the information that has been collected, but it makes for hard and boring reading. It is, however, useful for studying details in the execution, such as parameter and return values.

The trace is interpreted as follows:

Line 01   Shows the name of the test.

Line 02   Identifies time and date of the execution.

Line 03   Identifies the version of the program being executed.

Line 05   Shows a message send.
The syntax of a message report is as follows:

```
sender object >> message name ( message parameters ) >>
receiver object
```

For example, line 5 is to be read:

The object Panel#11 sends
    the message named accessCode:
    with a String parameter: 'personIdentAndCode'
    to the object LocalStation#12

Line 11   Shows a program trace. The programmer may insert informative messages in his code. These messages are preceded by TRACE in the report.

Line 12   Shows an illegal message send. Message sends are checked against the port interfaces specified in the role models. If a message is not in accordance with the role model, the report line begins with the symbols)--. The messages in lines 12, 15, 17, and 18 are examples of nonconformance. They are all caused by a Timer

Figure 8.15

**The execution
scenario report
shows all
observed message
interactions in
time sequence**

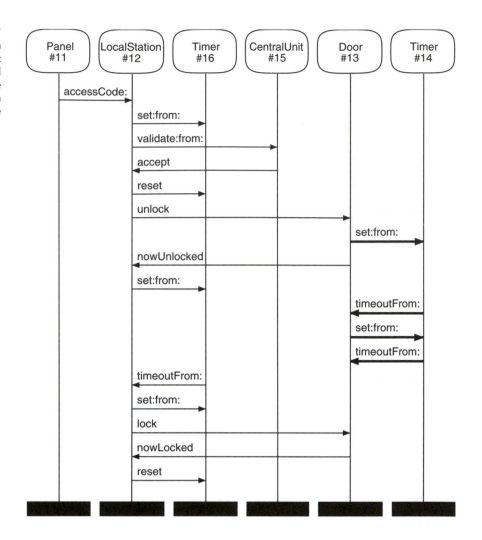

used in the dummy Door implementation to make it appear to open and close at determined times.

Not shown   Runtime errors are reported with a line beginning with CAUTION; the execution continues if at all possible.

Not shown   Message return values (Smalltalk messages always return a value) are given on the following line if different from the receiver object. The return value is preceded by the keyword RETURN:

```
RETURN return value
```

```
01   OK test
02   TASKON/OOram Monitored Execution, 12 April 1994 at 3:45:24 pm
03   program version e15-t10
04
05   Panel#11 >> accessCode: ('personIdentAndCode') >> LocalStation#12
06   LocalStation#12 >> set:from: (1 {LocalStation#12}) >> Timer#16
07   LocalStation#12 >> validate:from: ('personIdentAndCode' {LocalStation#12})
                          >> CentralUnit#15
08   CentralUnit#15 >> accept () >> LocalStation#12
09   LocalStation#12 >> reset () >> Timer#16
10   LocalStation#12 >> unlock () >> Door#13
11   TRACE-Door#13: Lock released at 3:45:31 pm
12 )-- Door#13 >> set:from: (2 {Door#13}) >> Timer#14
13   Door#13 >> nowUnlocked () >> LocalStation#12
14   LocalStation#12 >> set:from: (5 {LocalStation#12}) >> Timer#16
15 )-- Timer#14 >> timeoutFrom: ({Timer#14}) >> Door#13
16   TRACE-Door#13: Door opened at 3:45:33 pm
17 )-- Door#13 >> set:from: (2 {Door#13}) >> Timer#14
18 )-- Timer#14 >> timeoutFrom: ({Timer#14}) >> Door#13
19   TRACE-Door#13: Door closed at 3:45:35 pm
20   Timer#16 >> timeoutFrom: ({Timer#16}) >> LocalStation#12
21   LocalStation#12 >> set:from: (2 {LocalStation#12}) >> Timer#16
22   LocalStation#12 >> lock () >> Door#13
23   TRACE-Door#13: Lock activated at 3:45:37 pm
24   Door#13 >> nowLocked () >> LocalStation#12
25   LocalStation#12 >> reset () >> Timer#16
```

Figure 8.16

The textual trace report gives complete description of all interactions

CHAPTER 9

Case Study: The Creation of a Framework

CONTENTS

9.1 Step 1: Identify Consumers and Consumer Needs 237

9.2 Step 2: Perform a Cost-benefit Analysis 238

9.3 Step 3: Reverse Engineering of Existing Programs 239

  9.3.1 Container-Component Hierarchy 242
  9.3.2 Model-View-Controller 249
  9.3.3 Mouse and Keyboard Input 254
  9.3.4 Main Input Role Model 255
  9.3.5 TranslatingSensor Initialization Model 255
  9.3.6 The Scroller Role Model 257

9.4 Step 4: Specify the New Framework 259

9.5 Step 5: Document the Framework as Patterns Describing how to Solve Problems 260

  9.5.1 Pattern 1: The Tool 260
  9.5.2 Pattern 2: Fixed Proportion Tool Layout 261
  9.5.3 Pattern 3: Flexible Tool Layout 262
  9.5.4 Pattern 4: The Controller 263
  9.5.5 Pattern 5: The Model Object 263
  9.5.6 Pattern 6: The View 264

9.6 Step 6: Describe the Framework's Design and Implementation 266

9.7 Step 7: Inform the Consumer Community 271

This case is about low level programming. We will create a reusable framework written in Smalltalk, but the principles presented should be equally applicable to other programming languages.

This case study illustrates the creation of frameworks. We illustrate how a complex construct can be hidden in a framework so that the application programmer can apply it safely and simply while retaining the power to create arbitrarily sophisticated solutions.

The case we have chosen is the work we have done to adapt the visual parts hierarchy of Objectworks release 4.0 to our requirements. This seems to be work which never ends: We keep finding better concepts and solutions that reduce the burden on the application programmer and increase product quality. We have flattened several years of iterative development into a single step in the case study, and have even included an improved scheme for the changed update construct that we were exploring while this chapter was being written.

Guide to the case study
We presented a general process for creating frameworks in Section 5.3. The process is reflected in this case study report, where you will find the following subsections:

1 Identify consumers and consumer needs.

2 Perform a cost-benefit analysis.

3 Perform reverse engineering of existing programs.

4 Specify the new framework.

5 Document the framework as patterns describing how to solve problems.

6 Describe the framework's design and implementation.

7 Inform the consumer community.

We have attempted to keep the presentation within reasonable bounds, and have omitted many design and implementation details. We hope that what remains is still sufficiently substantial to convince you of the need for information hiding and the ability of our technology to satisfy this need.

9.1   STEP 1: IDENTIFY CONSUMERS AND CONSUMER NEEDS

In this case, the consumers were ourselves, and our needs were dictated by market pull for full color and integration with the platform's windowing system.

The consumers of this framework case study were the system developers at Taskon. When we first heard of Objectworks\Smalltalk release 4.0, we had developed a large system product consisting of some 1,500 classes, 37,000 methods, and some 300,000 lines of Smalltalk code running under Objectworks\Smalltalk release 2.5. The code was very compact, incorporating extensive reuse, and a typical runtime image consisted of more than a quarter-million objects.

An important part of the product was its sophisticated editors. Our editors were based on the MVC framework found in earlier releases of the Objectworks\Smalltalk library, but with substantial extensions to satisfy the needs of our editors.

Objectworks\Smalltalk release 4.0 provided a number of improvements that were sorely needed by our customers, and we decided to adapt it as quickly as possible.

Release 4.0 represented major improvements

From our standpoint, the most dramatic changes were the entirely new class hierarchy for managing windows and their parts. The big question was how the modified class library would influence our system. To answer this question, we established a project to create an OOram framework which modified and extended the visual parts of release 4.0 to make it satisfactory for our purposes.

We wanted to create sophisticated user interfaces quickly, simply and safely. This implies that we wanted to push as much of the problem's complexity as possible into the framework, that we wanted a small surface area between the framework and the application, and that we wanted the programmer to retain full control over the model functionality and the layout of the editors in the window. Specifically:

Simple, yet powerful user interface development

1 We wanted all the new capabilities of the new release.

2 We wanted to retain the functionality of our existing editors, because we liked them, and so did our customers.

3 We wanted to reduce the burden on the application programmer by significantly reducing the surface area between the framework and its derivatives.

4 We wanted to define the surface area between the framework and its derivatives so that the framework could be improved without threatening the derivatives.

5 We wanted to consider the automatic enforcement or checking of framework constraints to improve the quality of the derivatives.

9.2   STEP 2: PERFORM A COST-BENEFIT ANALYSIS

IN A NUTSHELL

*Benefit: Our
customers
wanted it*

*Benefit: Our
programmers
wanted it*

*Benefit: We
needed to
improve our
MVC
framework*

*Cost:
Designing a
new framework*

We wanted to combine the added functionality with a reduced number of editor glitches.

When we first gained access to Objectworks release 4.0, the decision to adopt it was trivial: our customers wanted its color capabilities and its closer integration with the platform windowing system, and they wanted it immediately. So we had no choice but to convert our programs to the new release as quickly as possible; cost was really not an issue.

In addition, our application programmers appreciated that the new architecture made their task easier, and wanted us to adapt to the new release because they believed it would make them more efficient (removing some of the hassle, but none of the fun).

The phenomenon covered by the visual parts hierarchy is of central importance to our business because it permeates all our task-oriented tool products. Certain aspects of the changed update construct had continued to cause difficulties even after several stages of improvements. (The solution presented here includes an even later revision, which our application programmers hope will finally prove to be the ultimate solution.)

We estimated that reverse engineering of release 4.0, forward engineering, design, and implementation of a new framework would take 8 person-months. Retrofitting the new framework in existing program products to make them compatible with release 4.0 would take another 12 person-months.

Resource estimation is very difficult with extensive reuse

I frankly find it extremely difficult to estimate the time needed for such programming projects. It is much like estimating the time needed to solve a crossword puzzle. I have an idea about where I am, where I want to be, and the things that need to be done to get there. Most problems are benign and are solved with the estimated effort. Some problems just disappear on closer scrutiny, but this is more than offset by the few problems which prove to be really hard.

It seems to me that there are only three ways of making firm project commitments: either keep the goal fixed, with time and resources flexible; keep time and resources fixed, with the detailed specifications of the goal flexible; or make the bureaucracy surrounding the project so large that it completely dominates the unknown, creative part.

In our case, the work was harder than expected, and the available time and resources were fixed due to commitments to customers. We were forced, therefore, to go through several iterations, even if in this presentation we pretend that there has been only one.

9.3   STEP 3: REVERSE ENGINEERING OF EXISTING PROGRAMS

Reverse engineering of our existing programs was very enlightening, and helped us identify a number of powerful object patterns.

IN A NUTSHELL

The third step was to do a reverse engineering analysis of the new visual parts hierarchy of Objectworks\Smalltalk release 4.0. We also did reverse engineering on all our editors, and determined how they could be reimplemented under the new framework. We found that while the new solution was a great step forward, there were still some glitches for which we had to create our own solutions.

The goal of the reverse engineering step was to understand how release 4.0 managed windows, with all their different subareas. We first browsed through the class library, and found that classes and methods were consistently and well commented. We studied the class hierarchy: Figure 9.1 shows the inheritance relation-

Third step: Reverse engineering

The class hierarchy was not helpful

```
Object
-   Controller
-   -   ControllerWithMenu
-   -   -   ParagraphEditor
-   -   ScrollbarController
-   -   StandardSystemController
-   -   WidgetController
-   DisplaySurface
-   -   Window
-   -   -   ScheduledWindow
-   InputSensor
-   -   TranslatingSensor
-   -   WindowSensor
-   InputState
-   Model
-   -   PopUpMenu
-   -   ScrollValueHolder
-   -   ValueModel
-   -   -   PluggableAdaptor
-   -   -   ValueHolder
-   -   -   -   TextCollector
-   Screen
-   SharedQueue
-   VisualComponent
-   -   VisualPart
-   -   -   CompositePart
-   -   -   -   BorderDecorator
-   -   -   DependentPart
-   -   -   -   View
-   -   -   -   -   AutoScrollingView
-   -   -   -   -   -   ComposedTextView
-   -   -   -   -   -   -   TextCollectorView
-   -   -   -   -   BooleanWidgetView
-   -   -   -   -   -   ActionButton
-   -   -   -   -   -   LabeledBooleanView
-   -   -   -   -   Scrollbar
-   -   -   Wrapper
-   -   -   -   TranslatingWrapper
-   -   -   -   -   LayoutWrapper
-   -   -   -   -   -   BoundedWrapper
-   -   -   -   -   -   -   BorderedWrapper
-   -   -   -   -   ScrollWrapper
```

Figure 9.1

A part of the Smalltalk class hierarchy

Figure 9.2

System Transcript

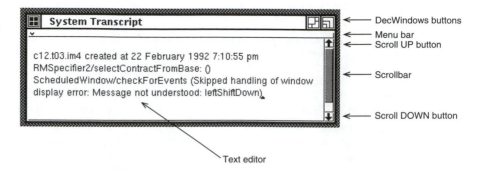

ships between the classes we have found to be most relevant to our study. (The relevant classes are shown in bold type.) We must admit that the hierarchy did not help us understand the design of a window and its parts. We clearly needed to study how the objects collaborated in an actual window, and not how their classes were related in the class hierarchy.

Dissecting a Transcript window

In the best Smalltalk tradition, we next tried to understand the new design by analyzing a concrete example. We first tried to investigate a program Browser, but found it far too complex for our purpose. So we selected the System Transcript, which is the simplest window of all. The System Transcript is a text editor in which programs can write messages to the user, and in which the user can type simple commands. Its appearance on the screen is shown in Figure 9.2.

The title bar at the top, with its resizing and other buttons, is managed by the platform windowing system (DecWindows in this case) and is not represented as a Smalltalk object. Our interest focused on the contents of the window—the menu bar, the scrollers, and the text editor itself.

We activated the System Transcript window, typed a program interrupt command, and inspected its object structure. We found a large number of interconnected objects, and extracted the ones that our experience indicated were of interest to our study. The result is shown in Figure 9.3.

Each object is shown as a rectangle annotated with its identifier and class name. Circles denote instance variables; collections are denoted by double circles. They are annotated as follows:

c	Controller	m	Model
cp	Component	s	Sensor
cps	Components	v	View
ct	Container	w	Window
ds	Dependents	ws	Window sensor

Separation of concern

Even though it was greatly simplified, the object structure of Figure 9.3 was still quite formidable. This did not surprise us, since even the simple Transcript window is quite sophisticated. We decomposed the Transcript functionality, and created a role model for each of its functions. (See Section 2.5.)

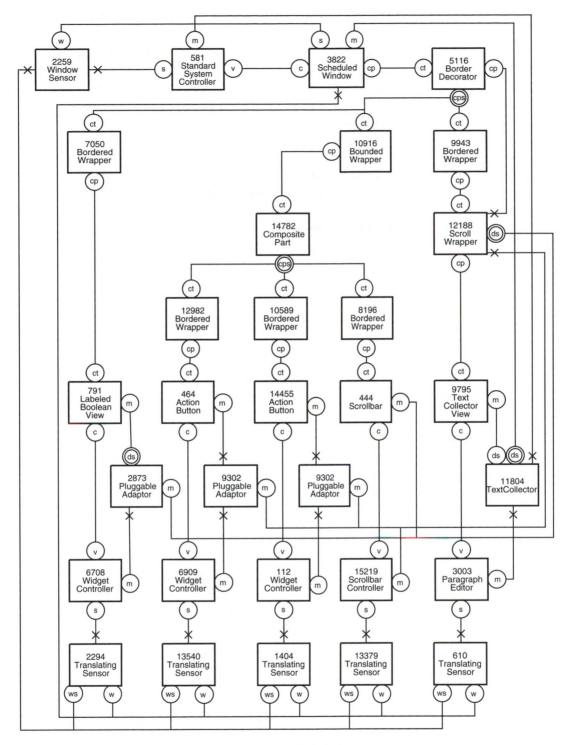

Figure 9.3   The main objects controlling the behavior of the transcript window

Some of the functions performed by the objects of Figure 9.3 will be described in the following subsections:

1 *Container-Component hierarchy* describes how the window is subdivided into smaller areas called *Visual Parts*.

2 *Model-View-Controller* describes the coordination between the objects that represent information, the objects that display the information, and the objects that take commands from the user.

3 *Mouse and keyboard input* describes how the stream of user input events is directed to the appropriate object.

4 *The scroller role model* describes how a large presentation can be scrolled so that different portions of it are made visible on the screen.

9.3.1 Container-Component Hierarchy

Container-Component is a prevalent construct

The organizing principle for windows is that a VisualPart object is responsible for a rectangular area within the window. A Container is a VisualPart which delegates this responsibility to other VisualParts, called Components. The principle is recursive: a Component object may also play the role of Container and further delegate responsibility for subareas to other Components.

We find ten instances of the Container-Component relationship in Figure 9.3; they are shown as arrows in Figure 9.4.

In Figure 9.4, the third object from the left in the top row is the 3822-ScheduledWindow object. It is the root of the visual component hierarchy, and forms the container for the BorderDecorator object.

The 5116-BorderDecorator object is the Component of the ScheduledWindow, and also the Container of three Components: the 7050-BorderedWrapper object, which is responsible for the menu bar area; the 10916-BoundedWrapper object, which is responsible for the area containing the scrollbar and scroll buttons; and the 12188-ScrollWrapper, which is responsible for the text editor area. Each of these Components act as Containers and delegate their responsibilities to other

Figure 9.4

Ten instances of the Container-Component relation

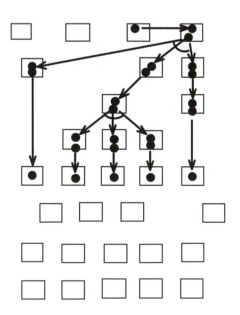

CREATION OF A FRAMEWORK

Components recursively, down to leaf Components such as 9795-Text-CollectorView.

Figure 9.5

Area of concern

The Container-Component construct explains the visual parts tree structure by focusing on a typical *parent-child* pair.

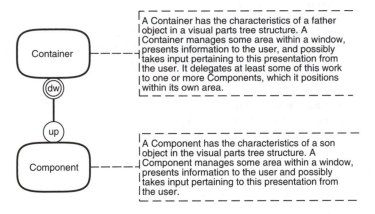

Figure 9.6

The roles and their respon-sibilities

A Container has the characteristics of a father object in a visual parts tree structure. A Container manages some area within a window, presents information to the user, and possibly takes input pertaining to this presentation from the user. It delegates at least some of this work to one or more Components, which it positions within its own area.

A Component has the characteristics of a son object in the visual parts tree structure. A Component manages some area within a window, presents information to the user and possibly takes input pertaining to this presentation from the user.

Figure 9.7

Stimulus/response

All messages can be stimulus messages.

The most interesting parts of this role model are the message interfaces. Most relevant objects play both roles. The role model helps us segregate the messages that are sent *down* the component hierarchy from the ones that are sent *up*. The most important messages are illustrated in Figure 9.8.

The message interfaces

Figure 9.8

Simplified interfaces for the Container-Component construct

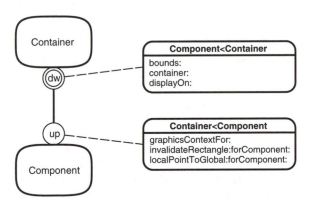

Figure 9.9

Textual interface view

```
interface 'Container<Component'
    explanation "We require that the Container should accept
these messages in any sequence. This means that it is the
responsibility of the Container to be prepared for any and all of
these messages after it has sent the container:-message to the
Part."
    message 'graphicsContextFor:'
        explanation "Return aGraphicsContext for set up for
aComponent."
        param 'aComponent'
    message 'invalidateRectangle:forComponent:'
        explanation "Invalidate the Rectangle aRectangle.
Propagate a damage rectangle up the containment hierarchy. This
will result in a displayOn: aGraphicsContext being sent to the
receiver."
        param 'aRectangle'
        param 'aComponent'
    message 'localPointToGlobal:forComponent:'
        explanation "Convert aPoint in coordinate system of aPart
to a point in the window's coordinate system."
        param 'aPoint'
        param 'aPart'
interface 'Component<Container'
    message 'bounds:'
        explanation "An actual bounding rectangle is being
asserted, aRectangle is in the coordinate system of the Part. The
bounds: message originates at the top of a hierarchy (usually a
ScheduledWindow) and is passed down to each VisualComponent.
ScheduledWindows send bounds: to their single component when
opened or resized. CompositeParts uses thiese messages to do
layouts of tiled components. BoundedWrapper uses the newBounds
rectangles as the actual bounding rectangles. Many
VisualComponents do nothing. Do not send a changedBounds: message
back up the hierarchy in response to this message."
        param 'aRectangle'
    message 'container:'
        explanation "The Part is being placed in containment
hierarchy inside of aContainer."
        param 'aContainer'
    message 'displayOn:'
        explanation "Display the receiver on the given
GraphicsContext, which is set up for the receiver's coordinate
system."
        param 'aGraphicsContext'
```

Using synthesis to recreate part of the object structure

Implementation comments

Figure 9.10 illustrates how the design of the Transcript window can be considered to be composed of repeated applications of this base model.

Whenever there is a change in the data, the window (or parts of it) has to be redisplayed. There are basically two mechanisms for doing this in a component: *invalidation* and *direct display*. Invalidation is illustrated in the scenario of Figure 9.11, and direct display is illustrated in the scenario of Figure 9.12. Sketches of the corresponding programs are given below.

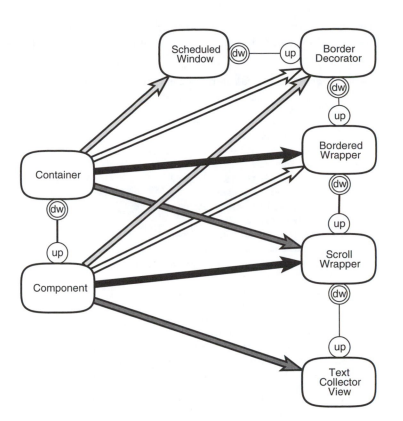

Figure 9.10

Repeated applications of the Container-Component model in the transcript structure

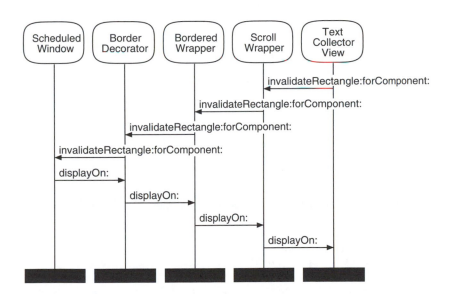

Figure 9.11

Scenario of display through invalidation

*Invalidate*The message `VisualPart>>invalidateRectangle: aRectangle` causes an event in the window which is equivalent to a display event from the platform windowing system:

```
01 aTextCollectorView invalidateRectangle: aRectangle repairNow:
aBoolean
02 . aScrollWrapper
        invalidateRectangle: rect1
        repairNow: aBoolean
        forComponent: aTextCollectorView
03 . . aBorderedWrapper
        invalidateRectangle: rect2
        repairNow: aBoolean
        forComponent: aScrollWrapper
04 . . . aBorderDecorator
        invalidateRectangle: rect3
        repairNow: aBoolean
        forComponent: aBorderedWrapper
05 . . . . aScheduledWindow
        invalidateRectangle: rect4
        repairNow: aBoolean
        forComponent: aBorderedWrapper
If aBoolean is FALSE, the following will take place some time in the
future. If it is TRUE, the following will take place immediately.
06 . . . anEdgeWidgetWrapper displayOn: aGraphicsContext
07 . . . . aTextCollectorView displayOn: aGraphicsContext
```

The above is the general algorithm. It gives all of the parts in a composite window the opportunity to display themselves within the specified `Rectangle` (which is transformed appropriately on its way up and down the hierarchy.) The alternative algorithm (Figure 9.12) is usually simpler and faster, and is suitable when it is known which parts need to be displayed.

Figure 9.12

Scenario to get `aGraphics-Context` for local display

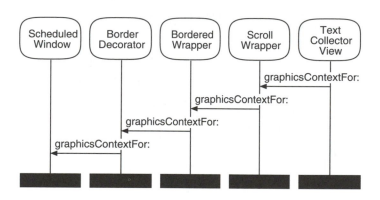

```
01 gc := aTextCollectorView graphicsContext
02 . aScrollWrapper graphicsContextFor: aTextCollectorView
03 . . aBorderedWrapper graphicsContextFor: aScrollWrapper
04 . . . aBorderDecorator graphicsContextFor: aBorderedWrapper
05 . . . . aScheduledWindow graphicsContextFor: anEdgeWidgetWrapper
06 gc
07   paint: aTextCollectorView backgroundColor;
08   displayRectangle: damageArea;
09   paint: aTextCollectorView foregroundColor.
10 aTextCollectorView displayOn: gc
```

CREATION OF A FRAMEWORK

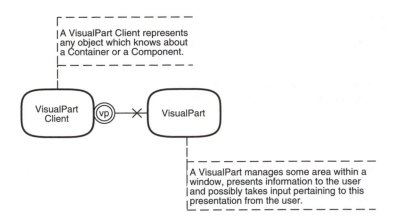

Figure 9.13

A **Visual-Part-Client** collaboration view

Note that in the previous case, ScheduledWindow cleared the area before asking for the display; in this case it is the responsibility of TextCollectorView to clear any garbage from the affected area (lines *06–09*) before displaying (line *10*).

In lines *01–05,* GraphicsContext is created and provided with the proper value for coordinate translation. GraphicsContext forms the link to the underlying platform window system, which does the actual rendering on the screen. It can work only if it is created on DisplaySurface or one of its subclasses, such as ScheduledWindow.

Containers and Components share an interface containing the messages that they may receive from any object. We define VisualPart as a common role, and VisualPartClient as its general client, as shown in Figures 9.13 and 9.14. The textual interface view is shown in Figure 9.15.

Additional interface to VisualParts

Notice the pair of almost identical messages in the VisualPart<VisualPart-Client interface and the Container<Component interface—graphicsContext and graphicsContextFor: aComponent. We need the second form because the responsibility for providing the proper coordinate translation rests with the Container. A composite Container such as the BorderDecorator will provide different translation parameters for its parts, and must know the identity of the relevant part. Our convention is that graphicsContext returns a GraphicsContext setup for the receiver, while graphicsContextFor: is used to request a GraphicsContext for one of the receiver's Components.

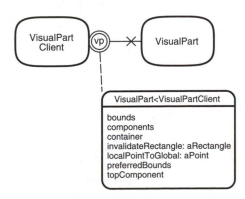

Figure 9.14

VisualPart< VisualPart-Client graphical interface view

Figure 9.15

VisualPart<
VisualPart-
Client textual
interface view

```
interface 'VisualPart<VisualPartClient'
    message 'bounds'
        explanation "Return a Rectangle that represents the Component'
        actual bounding rectangle on the screen in the Component's
        coordinate system."
    message 'invalidateRectangle:'
        explanation "Invalidate the Rectangle aRectangle. Propagate a
        damage rectangle up the containment hierarchy. This will result
        in a displayOn: aGraphicsContext being sent to the receiver."
        param 'aRectangle'
    message 'localPointToGlobal:'
        explanation "Convert a point in local coordinates to a point in
        the top windows coordinate system. Forwarded to the receiver's
        container."
        param 'aPoint'
    message 'preferredBounds'
        explanation "Return a Rectangle, which is the preferred bounds
        of the receiver in the receiver's coordinate system."
    message 'topComponent'
        explanation "Return the top component in the receiver's
        hierarchy. If the receiver is not in a hierarchy answer the
        receiver. (Taskon comment: This are very questionable semantics.
        The protocol of the usual topComponent (ScheduledWindow) is
        different from the protocol of an arbitrary Component. We have
        modified the specification to return aScheduledWindow or nil)."
    message 'components'
        explanation "Return a Collection containing the receiver's
        components. Answer an empty Collection if this is a leaf node."
    message 'container'
        explanation "Return the receiver's container, or nil."
```

The composite
does not tell us
anything new

We could easily create a composite of the Container-Component model and
the Client-VisualPart model; the result of this synthesis is the derived model
shown with white roles in Figure 9.16. This model is substantially more complex
than the two base models, and does not give us any new information. We will
normally not create the derived model, but leave the synthesis of individual roles
to the implementation stage.

Figure 9.16

A derived
Container-
Component
model created
by synthesis

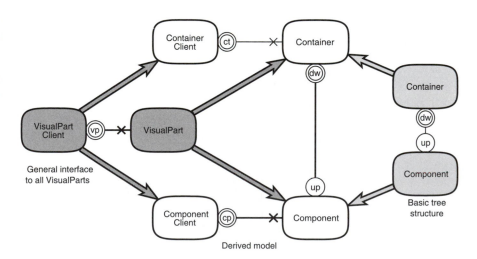

9.3.2 Model-View-Controller

The earliest example of an object-oriented framework was the Model-View-Controller (MVC) framework, which I created when I was working with Adele Goldberg as a visiting scientist at the Xerox Palo Alto Research Center in 1978–79. It was later improved by Goldberg and her staff, and is now a powerful part of Objectworks\Smalltalk [Gold 83].

The Model-View-Controller framework

In Smalltalk-76, the forerunner to Smalltalk-80, the idea was to let objects represent some information of interest to the user, and also to present this information on the screen and let the user edit it. This very powerful paradigm is the basis of the intuitively pleasing object-oriented user interfaces so popular today.

This concept proved inadequate when I wanted to use Smalltalk-76 to create a system for production control in shipbuilding. The information represented in the system was the production schedule, with its activities and resources. The user would want to see and manipulate it in many different forms: as a network of activities, as a chart showing each activity as a bar along the time axis, and as a business form presenting activity attributes as texts that could be edited.

I needed multiple presentations

A natural consequence of this was to tear the original object apart, so that one object represented the information, one was responsible for the presentation and one for capturing input from the user. The first was called the *model* object, the second was called the *view* object and the third was called the *controller* object. This gave one the freedom to have many different presentations and input facilities for the same object, and even to have several views of a given model on the screen simultaneously.

The object-oriented, direct manipulation user interface gives the user an illusion of working directly with (apparently) concrete information objects. The MVC breaks this illusion when the user displays several views on the same information object simultaneously. This is fortunately of no concern to the professional planner who is manipulating different views of the same plan, even in the manual systems.

Flexible mapping of MVC roles to objects

There have been many discussions in professional forums about the wisdom of the MVC scheme. Would two objects be sufficient (editor and model), or should the original idea of a single object doing all three jobs be retained? With role modeling, this is not an issue. We can map roles onto objects in any way we please, and the three roles of Model, View, and Controller can be mapped onto three, two, or one objects according to the merits of the problem.

If required, we can retain the valuable user illusion of concrete information objects by the simple expedient of constraining the user interface so that it only shows one view of each information object at the time.

Figure 9.17 shows the five instances of the MVC triad in the Transcript of Figure 9.3. Four of them manage the menu bar, the up-scroll button, the scrollbar, and the down-scroll button. The fifth one is farthest to the right: here, 11804-TextCollector plays the role of model, 3003-ParagraphEditor plays the role of controller, and 9795-TextCollectorView plays the role of view.

Figure 9.17

Five instances of
the MVC
construct in the
transcript of
Figure 9.3

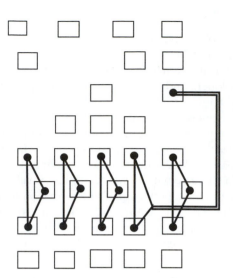

We will now present a role model of MVC as it is implemented in Object-
works\Smalltalk release 4.0. We concentrate on the general mechanism, ignoring
the specializations for the Transcript text manipulation.

Figure 9.18

Area of concern

> The MVC paradigm is fundamental to all Objectworks\Smalltalk thinking about
> dividing responsibility between objects. The basic idea is that we want a clear sep-
> aration between the representation of knowledge, called the *model*, and the means
> provided for a user to inspect and manipulate this information in the *view* and *con-
> troller*, respectively.

Figure 9.19

Environment
model

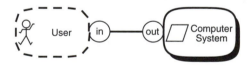

Figure 9.20

Stimulus/
response

Stimulus	Response	Comments
User>>anyInputCommand	System>>anyPresentation	The nature of the input and output is determined in the derived models

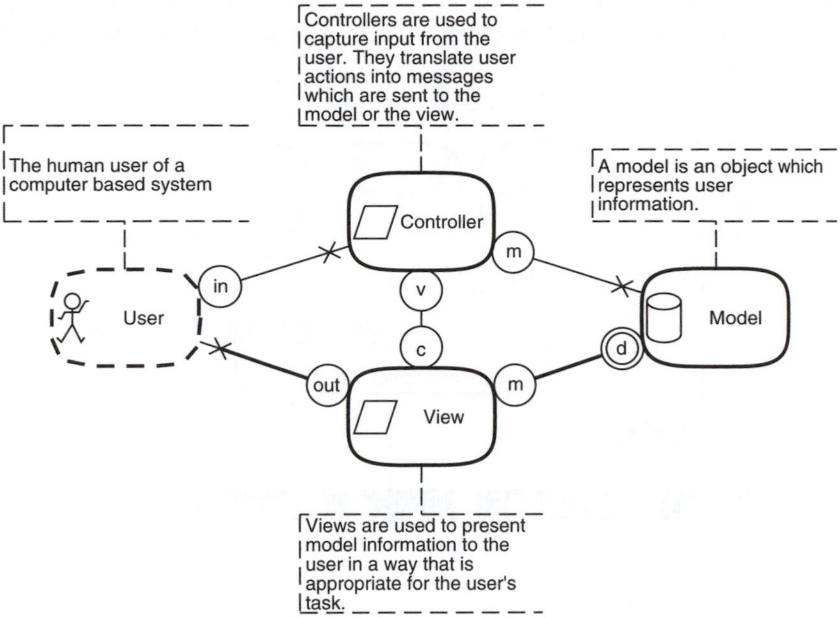

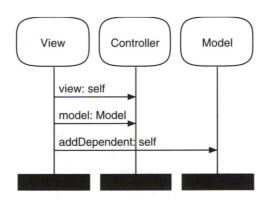

Figure 9.21

Collaboration model

The Model knows about any number of Views; they are called *dependents* and are the only relations that should exist from Model to View. Views and Controllers come in pairs. Each View knows about exactly one Controller, and each Controller knows about exactly one View. The View and the Controller know the same Model, but the Model does not know the Controller.

Figure 9.22

Scenario:
View and
Controller
setup

When a `View` is associated with a `Model`, it reports this fact to the `Model` by sending it the message `addDependent: self`. The `Model` remembers this until the `View` is released.

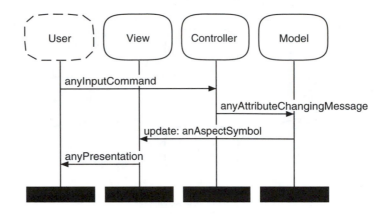

User input is handled as follows:

1 The user gives a command using the keyboard, the mouse, or a menu. This is captured by the `Controller`.

2 The controller transforms the input into messages it sends to either the `View` or the `Model`. The actual messages will be specified in various specializations of this `Model`, such as the text editor in the Transcript.

3 Any method in the model object that changes its attributes sends the message `self changed: anAspectSymbol`. The `Symbol` represents the aspect of the model which is changed.

4 The model method for `changed: anAspectSymbol` sends the message `update: anAspectSymbol` to all dependents (the `Views`). This is implemented in class `Object`, so any `Object` can be a `Model`. This is implemented somewhat more efficiently in the class `Model`, so it is often sensible to let model classes be subclasses of `Model`.

5 The View has several options when it receives an `update` message. The simplest is to ignore the `AspectSymbol` parameter and simply redisplay everything. This may take a long time and lead to an annoying flashing of the screen.

6 A better scheme is to restrict redisplaying to the cases when it is needed, as indicated by `anAspectSymbol`. More information is sometimes needed to limit redisplaying further, and there are different variants of the update message which facilitate this.

MVC roles designed to be specialized This sequence of events is controlled by the MVC framework, even if the command in Step 1, the message to the Model in Step 2, the nature of the model modification in Step 3, and the nature of the information requested by the View in the last Step are determined in the derived Model specializing the framework.

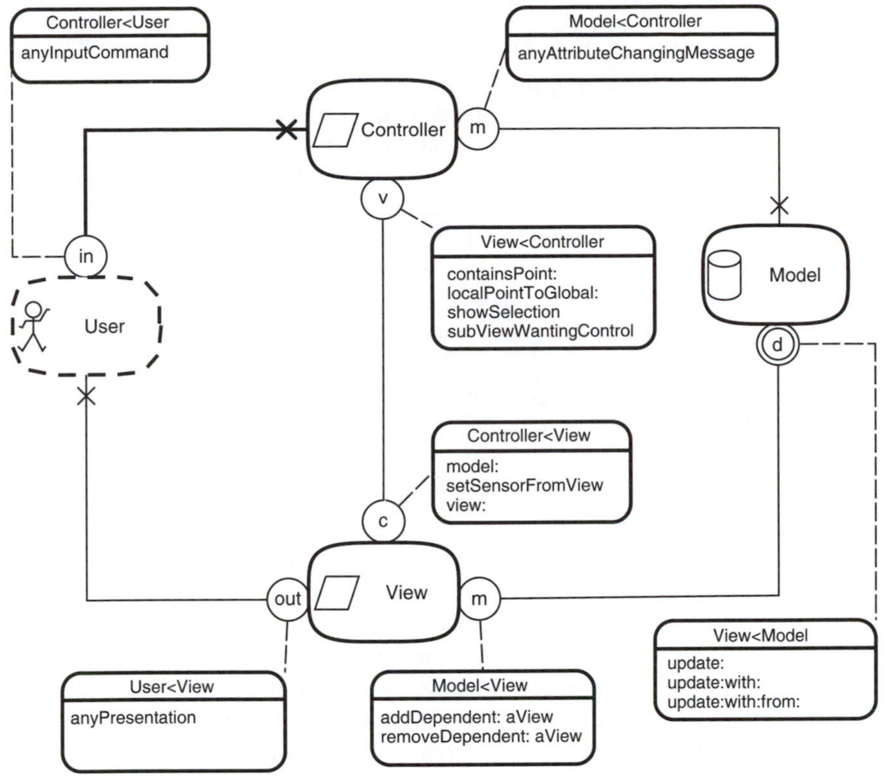

Figure 9.24
Some important messages

MVC useful

There are strong programming arguments for separating the model and the view. We find that many views are reusable by widely different models. This is mainly true for general views, such as Text, List, and Tree views, but to a lesser extent it also applies to more application-oriented views.

The value of separating the view and the controller is not as evident. There are examples of views being associated with different controllers, but much of the same functionality could be achieved by suitable configuration facilities. Smalltalk is a single inheritance language, and Controller and View benefit from having different class hierarchies.

We have not seriously considered merging the view and controller roles because we see no reason to reprogram our editors. We would reconsider the question if we were to design a new system library from scratch.

The strongest argument for separating model and view is based on user convenience. We use the MVC extensively in all our task-oriented tools, including our OOram tools and our document preparation tools. I find that I frequently use multiple presentations of the same information, and I believe the same applies to other users. The separation between the concepts of *model* and *view/controller* is very valuable from a user's point of view, and I miss it sorely when at times I have to use systems without it.

9.3.3 Mouse and Keyboard Input

Input management

All inputs from the keyboard and the mouse enter the Objectworks\Smalltalk image through an interrupt-driven process, which is an instance of class `InputState` (not shown in Figure 9.3). Each window has one instance of `WindowSensor` (2259-`WindowSensor` in our Transcript) that holds a `SharedQueue` of input events. The `InputState` places received input events into the `WindowSensor` queue of the currently active window. Every `Controller` holds an instance of `TranslatingSensor`, and asks this sensor for an input event whenever it needs one. The five instances of this construct in the `Transcript` are illustrated in Figure 9.25.

We will now discuss two role models that explain these input facilities. We will see that the models give a nice overview of the phenomena which would be hard to get by studying the classes.

There are two different chains of objects in Figure 9.3 which are of interest to our current discussion: one chain of visual component objects goes from top to bottom—3822-`ScheduledWindow`, 5116-`BorderDecorator`, 9943-`BorderedWrapper`, 12188-`ScrollWrapper`, and 9795-`TextCollectorView`. Another chain of objects go from bottom to top, such as 3003-`ParagraphEditor` (aController), 610-`TranslatingSensor`, 2259-`WindowSensor`. There are similar chains for the menu bar and the scroller buttons.

One of the responsibilities of the objects of the down-chain is to keep track of the coordinate transformations between the window's coordinate system and the coordinate system of the `TextCollectorView`, as described in Section 9.3.1. We will build on this functionality in the *TranslatingSensor initialization model*.

Main input role model

The first model is the *main input model*, which describes how the keyboard and mouse input is made available to the `Controller` (Figure 9.26). The second model is the *TranslatingSensor initialization model*, which describes how the `TranslatingSensor` is set to provide the required coordinate transformations.

Figure 9.25

Five instance of keyboard and mouse input construct

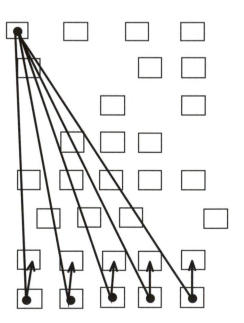

9.3.4 Main Input Role Model

All the five instances of the input construct highlighted in Figure 9.25 are represented by the three input roles of Figure 9.27.

Figure 9.26

Area of concern

This model describes the objects employed to let `Controllers` read mouse and keyboard inputs.

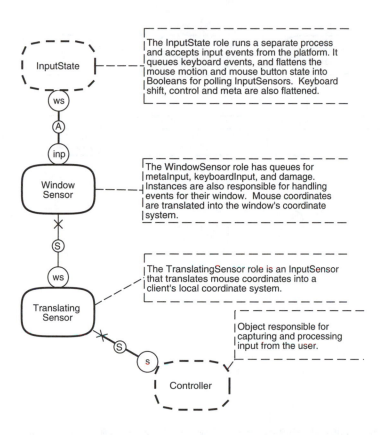

Figure 9.27

Collaboration view of main input model

The InputState role runs a separate process and accepts input events from the platform. It queues keyboard events, and flattens the mouse motion and mouse button state into Booleans for polling InputSensors. Keyboard shift, control and meta are also flattened.

The WindowSensor role has queues for metaInput, keyboardInput, and damage. Instances are also responsible for handling events for their window. Mouse coordinates are translated into the window's coordinate system.

The TranslatingSensor role is an InputSensor that translates mouse coordinates into a client's local coordinate system.

Object responsible for capturing and processing input from the user.

9.3.5 TranslatingSensor Initialization Model

Figure 9.28 describes the area of concern for this model, while Figures 9.29 and 9.30 show its collaboration and scenario views, respectively.

Figure 9.28

Area of Concern

The area of concern is to initialize the `TranslatingSensor` coordinate transformation of cursor positions. It uses parts of the `Container-Part` role model, to do so, as illustrated in the collaboration view and the scenario.

Figure 9.29

**Translating-
Sensor**
initialization
collaboration
view with
important
messages

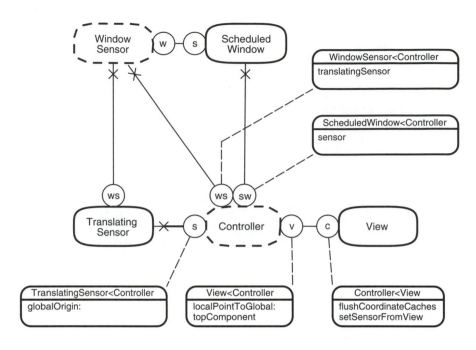

Figure 9.30

Scenario:
**Translating-
Sensor**
initialization

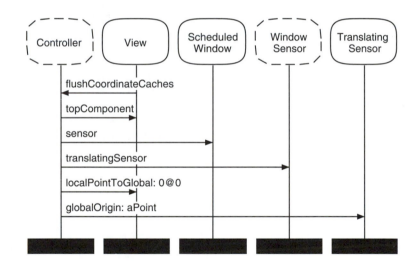

An interesting feature of this interaction is the central position of the `Control-ler`. The `Controller` asks the view for its `topComponent`, and gets a temporary port to the `ScheduledWindow`. It then asks the `ScheduledWindow` for its `sensor`, and gets another temporary port to the `WindowSensor`. It can then finally ask the `WindowSensor` for a new `translatingSensor`, which it can give the required co-ordinate transformation and install.

We see that the `Controller` knows a great deal about the complete structure of objects. This is generally not a good idea, because it makes it hard to change the structure. I think I would have preferred to let the `Controller` ask the `View` for a new `TranslatingSensor` and let this request pass up the `Container-Compo-nent` chain.

Ports are by default implemented as instance variables, but the Controller's sw *and* ws *ports are in this case implemented as temporary variables. They still have to be shown as* Controller *ports in the role model, because the* Controller *sends messages through them.*

9.3.6 The Scroller Role Model

Scrolling is needed when the rectangle allocated to a View may be insufficient to *Scrolling* show all of its contents. One instance of the scrolling construct appears in the transcript in Figure 9.31. Scrolling takes place when the user pushes the up- or down-scroll button, or slides the scrollbar slider. All three are implemented as specializations of MVC. We will show the design of the scrollbar as an illustration. The 12188-ScrollWrapper in Figure 9.3 is the model object; 444-Scrollbar is the view object; and 15219-ScrollbarController is the controller object. The corresponding role model is shown in Figure 9.32, which also shows the synthesis relationship between this model and the basic MVC model.

The message flow which takes place when the user moves the scrollbar is illustrated in the scenario in Figure 9.33:

1 The activity starts when the User moves the scollbar (scrollAbsolute).

2 The ScrollbarController senses this movement. It computes the relative displacement in model coordinates (mapToDataSpace:, dataExtent). The ScrollbarController notes the displacement of the scrollbar. It then sends the scrollVertically: message to the ScrollWrapper.

3 The ScrollWrapper scrolls itself by changing its coordinate transformation. (The ScrollWrapper also redisplays itself and its component. This display is done with the new transformation, and the contents appears scrolled. This is not shown in the scenario.)

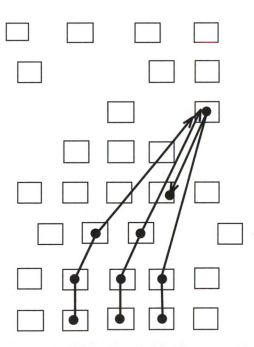

Figure 9.31

One instance of the scrolling construct

Figure 9.32

The Scrollbar role model is derived from MVC

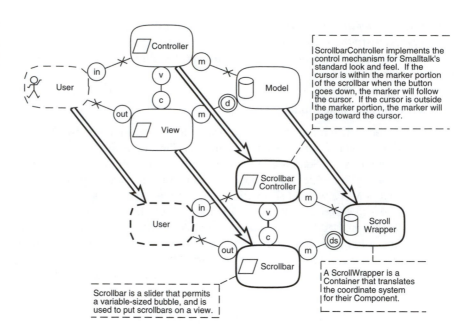

ScrollbarController implements the control mechanism for Smalltalk's standard look and feel. If the cursor is within the marker portion of the scrollbar when the button goes down, the marker will follow the cursor. If the cursor is outside the marker portion, the marker will page toward the cursor.

Scrollbar is a slider that permits a variable-sized bubble, and is used to put scrollbars on a view.

A ScrollWrapper is a Container that translates the coordinate system for their Component.

4 *The* Scrollbar *(view) redisplays itself.* The scrollbar position must be updated regardless of the cause of the stimulus causing the scrolling action. This is taken care of by the changed update mechanism: Whenever the ScrollWidget changes its scroll offset, it sends a changed message to itself which causes an update:with:from: message to be sent all dependents, including the Scrollbar. The Scrollbar then computes new values for the size and position of its slider from the visibleExtent, dataExtent, and scrollOffset of the ScrollWidget so that it can redisplay itself.

Figure 9.33

Scenario: Scroll vertically, using scrollbar

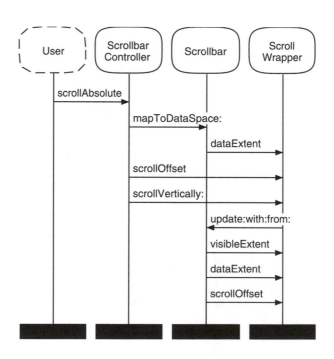

9.4   STEP 4: SPECIFY THE NEW FRAMEWORK

The new framework was specified to combine functionality that had been supported by different frameworks in the past.

IN A NUTSHELL

We want a single framework

In the past, we have provided separate frameworks for the visual component functions, much as we have described them in the reverse engineering report. Each framework is reasonably simple, but the sum is quite formidable, so that the creation of new editors has been a job for experts.

We now want to explore if the frameworks can be combined into a single framework which is so simple to use that even a novice Smalltalk programmer can program a new editor with ease and confidence.

The general requirements of Section 9.1 can be augmented by some specific technical issues:

1 *Model-View-Controller.* We need to improve the standard MVC solution to ensure safe synthesis in all situations.

2 *Change management.* We have recurring problems in managing the redisplay, caused by changes in the underlying information. We sometimes lose a required redisplay, and the screen sometimes flashes unnecessarily because of multiple redisplays. The new framework should offer a simple mechanism such that the application programmer does not need the intricacies of changed-update as part of his active competence.

3 *Configurability.* We have a large number of different editors (view-controller pairs) and want to be able to reuse them as leaf components in any component hierarchy. It should, for example, be possible to use a drawing as a table cell, and a table as a drawing element.

4 *Coordinate transformations.* It is hard to think in several coordinate systems simultaneously. The application programmers should be required to think only in terms of the application's coordinate system.

5 *Scrolling.* Scrolling is a fairly complex operation, involving many objects, and should be highly optimized. We want scrolling to be part of the internal details of the framework so that application programmers can always get it and never need to construct it. All visual components should be scrollable at the discretion of the application programmer, and it should be possible to configure scrolled components within other scrolled components.

9.5 STEP 5: DOCUMENT THE FRAMEWORK AS PATTERNS DESCRIBING HOW TO SOLVE PROBLEMS

IN A NUTSHELL

We assume the pattern user to be an expert

In this step, we give a number of patterns that describe how a consumer can apply the Tool framework.

We assume the reader of the patterns to be thoroughly familiar with the solution technicalities. This is in accordance with Alexander's patterns (Section 5.2.1), which are short and to the point. The patterns give sufficient information for the expert reader; the nonexpert can study the solution logic of Step 6 to become one.

An example is our use of the terms *actualBounds, virtualBounds,* and *changeParameter* in the patterns given below. They will be explained in Section 9.6, where generalists will find a first level of explanation.

We here give six sample patterns which relate to the Tool framework. The Tool pattern builds on smaller patterns, and the Tool framework builds on smaller frameworks. We describe the following patterns:

1 The `Tool`.

2 The Fixed Proportion Tool Layout.

3 The Flexible Tool Layout.

4 The `Controller`.

5 The `Model Object`.

6 The `View`.

9.5.1 Pattern 1: The Tool

When to use

A tool is a constituent of the user information environment and appears as a coordinated set of editors within a rectangle on the screen.

You use this Tool framework when the following conditions are satisfied:

1 You want to create a new tool.

2 None of the tools available in the library are satisfactory.

3 The new tool cannot be generated automatically by available scripting facilities.

Problem

Application programmers should be able to create new and sophisticated tools quickly, simply, and safely. The application programmer should have full control over the functionality of the models, views, and controllers, but the application should inherit the framework's handling of input, coordinate transformation, scrolling, transactions, change management, and selection.

Solution

To create a new tool, you create a new class as a subclass of `Tool1` and override certain methods, using the following steps:

1 Define your tool class to inherit from `Tool1`.

2 Define all your views, but do not worry about their sizes or positions yet. By convention, this is done by overriding `Tool1>>createSubviews`. Each view is added to the tool by the following construct: `self addView: yourViewIn-`

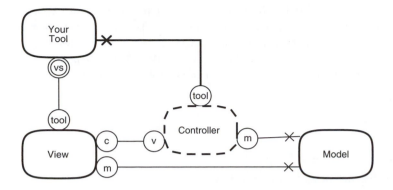

stance as: tileKind withName: viewName. yourViewInstance is an instance of your view class initialized with the appropriate controller and model. viewName is a Symbol identifying the view to this tool. tileKind is one of the following:

- #bounded : The view size on screen is determined by the tool.
- #unbounded : The tool will endeavor to make space available for the view's virtual bounds.
- #scrolling : The contents of the view will be scrollable.

3 Specify the layout of the views within the tool. Patterns 2 and 3 provide two ways for doing this.

4 Specify tool-defined menus, if any.

- Controllers can ask the tool for the yellowMenu with the following message, which either returns a menu or nil: self menuFromTool.
- Construct the selector for the Tool method from the corresponding view name as shown below. Write the corresponding method so that it returns a menu or nil: #<viewName>Menu, e.g., #editorMenu.

5 Specify coordinated selection, if any.

- Controllers report selection changes to the tool by the expression: self hasSelected: (Collection of aModelObject).
- Construct the selector for the Tool method from the corresponding view name as shown below. Write the corresponding method to handle the selection: #<viewName>HasSelected:, e.g., editorHasSelected: (aCollection of aModelObject).
- The tool may force selection in an editor by sending self viewNamed: viewName select: (Collection of aModelObject).

Use Pattern 2 to specify simple, proportional layouts, or Pattern 3 for full freedom in layout specification. See also Patterns 4, 5, and 6.

9.5.2 Pattern 2: Fixed Proportion Tool Layout

You use this pattern when your tool layout is defined by simple proportions. This pattern is one of the alternative specifications of the layout of Pattern 1. *When to use*

The application programmer should be able to simply specify the layout of a tool in terms of the available screen area. *Problem*

Solution Consider the tool's actual bounds to be the unit rectangle (0@0 corner: 1@1), and specify the outer boundary of each view with its borders and possible scrollbars as rectangles relative to this. The `actualBounds` of the views will automatically be recomputed whenever the tool's `actualBounds` is changed.

Specify the position origin and corner of each view as follows:

```
self
    viewNamed: viewName
    relativeLayout: aRelativeRectangle
    scrollHorizontal: hBoolean
    scrollVertical: vBoolean
```

The views are described in Pattern 6.

9.5.3 Pattern 3: Flexible Tool Layout

When to use You use this pattern when you want a complex layout of the views within a tool. This pattern is one of the alternative specifications of the layout for Pattern 1.

Problem The application programmer should have powerful and flexible facilities for specifying the layout of a tool in terms of the available screen area and other criteria.

Solution Override the `Tool1` method `suggestedWidth:height:` which is called every time the tool is to be allocated a new `actualBounds` and when other conditions have changed.

The suggested width and height specify the space that will be made available to the tool, `nil` values indicate that the container will adapt to whatever value you choose (e.g., by scrolling).

This pattern gives you full control at the cost of writing a somewhat complex method.

Specify the layout of the views within the tool by overriding `Tool1>>suggestedWidth: wIntegerOrNil height: hIntegerOrNil`:

1 Default `virtualBounds` for the tool is the `Rectangle` enclosing its components, but you may set a different value after you have completed the layout by using: `self virtualBounds: aRectangle`.

2 Resize and position each view. The views may be handled in any sequence, and the position and size of a view may be made dependent on the `virtualBounds` of other views after they have been positioned (all geometry in the following messages are in the tool's coordinate system):

   • You must offer the view an opportunity to resize itself:

```
self
    viewNamed: viewName
    suggestedWidth: wIntegerOrNil height: hIntegerOrNil.
```

   • You must position the view:

```
self
    viewNamed: viewName
    origin: originPoint
```

The views are described in Pattern 6.

9.5.4 Pattern 4: The Controller

You use this pattern when you want user command activities to be performed *When to use*
within a transaction. Views redisplay themselves once, at the end of a transaction
when the model is in a consistent state.

    This is the default pattern for controller objects which you use in Pattern 1.

The Controller is responsible for handling all user input. This pattern gives it *Problem*
added responsibility—to ensure that all activities that lead to model attribute
changes are performed within a transaction.

All commands that change one or more model attributes must be executed within *Solution*
a transaction. The transaction should be activated as close to the user interaction
code as possible:

```
TransactionManager
    inTransactionDo: [<code modifying model attributes>]
```

    `TransactionManager` is a global variable, the sole instance of class
`TransactionManager1`.

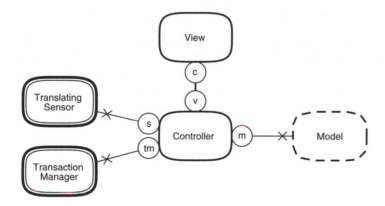

    Other patterns may be made which specialize this one, but we will not discuss
them here.

9.5.5 Pattern 5: The Model Object

You use this pattern when you want to program model objects and none of its *When to use*
existing specializations are appropriate. This is the default pattern for model objects which you use for Pattern 1. The corresponding programs are parts of the
Tool framework.

Views send messages to the model to obtain the current values of its attributes, *Problem*
and may cache the results on the screen or in a variable. It is the responsibility of
the model to inform its views whenever messages will return a new value.

Capture model attribute changes and map these changes to the externally avail- *Solution*
able interrogation messages.

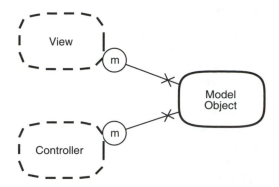

Define your new model class as a subclass of Model1. Then do the following:

1 Program the model functionality.

2 All methods which modify one or more object attributes should send this message:

```
self
    changedAttributes: (Array of attribute names)
    areas: aCollectionOfRectanglesOrNil
```

The default attribute names are the instance variable names, but you may select any names which reflect the model semantics, as long as you map them to the corresponding message selectors in changeParameterAssociations.

3 Define the following private class method, which associates the name of each attribute in your class with the selectors of messages whose return values depend on the attribute:

```
changeParameterAssociations
  " Associations between change attributes and method selectors. "
  ^(super changeParameterAssociations)
      add: <attributeNameSymbol>
        -> #(<list of message selectors>);
    <repeat for all attributes of this class>;
  yourself.
```

The Taskon Browser text command generateChParAssociations creates a default method which you must check carefully.

The Taskon Quality Checker will flag implementations of changeParameterAssociations which are missing or which do not mention all attributes specified in the changedAttributes:areas: methods.

4 TransactionManager allChangeInitializations must be executed to make the changeParameterAssociations take effect.

Other patterns may be made which specialize this one, but we will not discuss them here.

9.5.6 Pattern 6: The View

When to use   Use this pattern when you want to program view objects and when none of the framework's specializations are appropriate. This is the default pattern for view objects which you use for Pattern 1.

The view caches information it has obtained from the model, usually in the form *Problem* of a picture on the screen. The view receives the message `update1:` toward the end of the transaction if the model has changed. Make sure that the view is updated exactly as needed and no more.

The `ChangeHolder` parameter has accumulated information about all the model *Solution* changes that have occurred in a transaction. The `ChangeHolder` also accumulates information about required redisplays. These accumulated changes are merged and performed at the end of the transaction.

Make your `View` class inherit from `View1`. Override `update1`, and determine required redisplays and possible changes to the `virtualBounds` from the current `viewChangeHolder`:

1 Send the following message if you want to order a redisplay:

    self changeHolder invalidate: damageRectangle

2 Send the following message if you want to change the `virtualBounds` of the view:

    self virtualBounds: aRectangle

3 Send the following message if you want the accumulated change information to take effect without waiting for the end of the transaction:

    self commitChanges

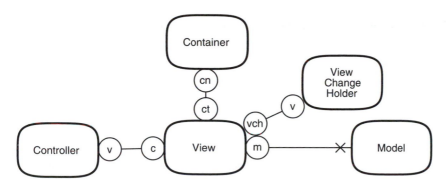

Other patterns may be made which specialize this one, but we will not discuss them here.

9.6 STEP 6: DESCRIBE THE FRAMEWORK'S DESIGN AND IMPLEMENTATION

IN A NUTSHELL

This step gives background technical information aimed at the application programmer who wants to use the Tool framework. We describe the overall design of the framework, and briefly discuss the rationale behind some of the design choices.

A striking feature of any window is the number of rectangles that must be considered. Figure 9.34 shows the most important ones in the Transcript. We clearly need precise definitions and consistent notation if we want to avoid getting confused.

Synonyms and homonyms

We studied the code of release 4.0 to determine the vocabulary used to describe all these rectangles. We found bounds, clippingBounds, clippingBox, compositionBounds, and insetDisplayBox. We suspected that all denote the area actually allocated to a component by its container. They are, therefore, synonyms or at least closely related concepts.

We also suspected that preferredBounds denotes the area required by a component, but some methods seemed to merge the bounds, compositionBounds, and preferredBounds, making *bounds* a homonym:

VisualPart>>bounds
  ^container == nil
      ifTrue: [self preferredBounds]
      ifFalse: [container compositionBoundsFor: self]

CompositePart>>compositionBoundsFor: aVisualComponent
  ^aVisualComponent preferredBounds

Our main rectangles

It is quite likely that we did not fully understand the ideas behind the visual component hierarchy, but we felt a strong need for some precisely defined words which we could use consistently throughout the framework. We defined the following three notions:

1   virtualBounds. The rectangular area required by a visual part. All visual parts must at all times be able to supply their virtualBounds. A container may ask its components for their virtualBounds, but we explicitly prohibit a component from asking the same of its container, to avoid infinite recursion. (virtualBounds is roughly equivalent to preferredBounds.)

2   actualBounds. The rectangular area allocated to a component by a container. A component without a container has actualBounds = (0@0 corner: 0@0). A component may at any time ask its container for its actualBounds, so the component need not remember it. It is, therefore, dangerous and meaningless for a container to ask its components for its actualBounds.

3   dataBounds. The rectangular area occupied by the data in a model object. This attribute is defined only where appropriate.

Our main classes of visual parts

VisualPart2 is the superclass of all our visual part classes. An extract of the class hierarchy is as follows:

VisualPart2

1   SimpleContainer2 defines a subroot in the visual part hierarchy that holds at most one component.

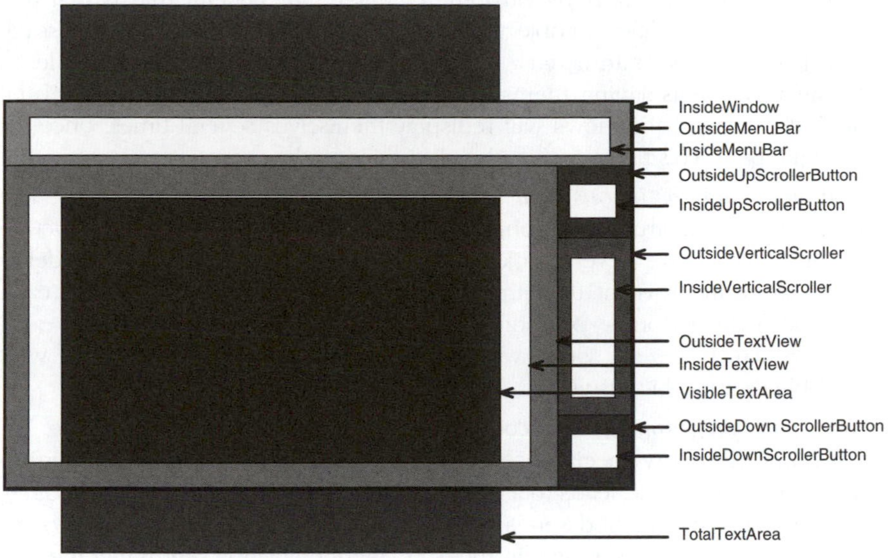

Figure 9.34

Rectangles in the transcript window

InsideWindow
OutsideMenuBar
InsideMenuBar
OutsideUpScrollerButton
InsideUpScrollerButton
OutsideVerticalScroller
InsideVerticalScroller
OutsideTextView
InsideTextView
VisibleTextArea
OutsideDown ScrollerButton
InsideDownScrollerButton
TotalTextArea

- `View2` is the Taskon `View` superclass; all Taskon views should be subclasses of this or an equivalent. `MarginTool1`, multi-media tree editor, is shown in Figure 12.5.
- `Tile2` defines the only visual parts which are responsible for coordinate transformations. A `Tile` positions its component within its container, transforms the relevant parameters, and returns values of the messages being passed up and down the visual hierarchy chain.
  - `BoundedTile2` defines a `Tile` whose `virtualBounds` is identical to the `virtualBounds` of its part.
  - `UnboundedTile2` defines a `Tile` whose `virtualBounds` is the area allocated by its `Container`. (A larger Part will be clipped.)
  - `ScrollingTile2` defines a `Tile` which is able to vary its coordinate transformation to effect scrolling of its component.
- `EdgeWidget1` is the common superclass for all edge widgets, such as scrollers and menu bars. The `EdgeWidget` plays the roles of both `Controller` and `View`, while a scrollable component such as a `ScrollingTile` plays the role of model.
  - `Scroller1` defines horizontal and vertical scrollbars.
  - `ScrollerButton1` defines the up, down, left, and right scroll buttons.

2 `CompositeContainer2` defines a subroot in the visual part hierarchy that holds any number of named components. `Tool2` defines CompositeContainers that manage one or more views which may be decorated with possible `Widgets` for menu and scrolling, and which are laid out in a reasonably stable pattern within the `Tool`'s `actualBounds`. Subclasses define specific tools.

The standard MVC changed-update mechanism works nicely in simple cases when the model consists of a single object and the user command leads to the modification of a single attribute. But the mechanism may cause difficulties in more complex situations:

Standard MVC unsafe

1   *Multiple displays for multiple attribute changes.* Our general rule is that any method which modifies an object should also send the `self changed` message This leads directly to an `update` message being sent to all views, which leads to the views redisplaying themselves. If the user command leads to several attribute changes, the views will redisplay themselves several times, once for each attribute. This takes time and is disturbing to the user.

2   *The model may be inconsistent in the middle of a modification activity.* The model may be a structure of objects such as a doubly linked list. A structure change will involve several objects and several methods, and the model is likely to be inconsistent until the modification activity is completed. If each method that performs part of the structure modification sends a `self changed:` message, the views will try to display an inconsistent model, with possibly catastrophic results.

3   *The model programmer loses control when sending an* `update` *message.* We have, in certain very special cases, found it convenient to program a chain re-action: user command leads to a model `change`, which leads to a view `update`. The view `update` method sends a new attribute modification message to the model. This is a new stimulus in the MVC model which is sent while the system is busy performing the previous activity. (This is exactly what we defined as unsafe synthesis in Chapter 3.)

Improved parameters to the changed-update messages

In the basic changed-update construct, the nature of the change is communicated from the model to the view through a `Symbol` parameter. We have tried various conventions about the choice of `Symbols`, but we often have ended up with special choices based on our knowledge about the exact needs of the views. We did not like this, because we wanted to maintain maximum independence between the model and the view.

This led us to reconsider the exact nature and purpose of the changed-update construct. We made the following observations:

1   *The universe of discourse is the message set.* The universe of discourse between the view and the model is the set of messages that the view employs to retrieve information from the model.

2   *The view caches model information.* The view caches model information and needs to be told about model changes so that it can update the caches. (The most common form of cache is in the display memory which controls the display.)

3   *The view needs to know the messages that return a new value.* The real meaning of an `update` message is that the model tells the view that "one or more of my messages will now return a different value." The view programmer needs to know which messages have been affected so that he or she can take appropriate action.

4   *The model knows which attributes have been changed.* We tried to let the model programmer specify the list of affected selectors as a parameter to the `self changed:` message, but this was almost impossible to maintain correctly when new messages were added to the model's interface. We therefore decided to let the parameter to `changed:` be a list of affected *attributes*, where an attribute may be anything the model programmer decides to consider as such. (The choice of attribute names is invisible outside the class.)

5   *changeParameterAssociation maps attributes to messages.* The view wants to see message selectors; the model wants to report the names of changed attributes. We clearly need to create a map between the two. Attempts to create this map automatically have all failed, and we require the application programmer to enumerate all attributes and to associate the affected selectors with each attribute. This is done in the private class method `changeParameterAssociations`.

The form of the `changeParameterAssociations` method has been chosen so as to make it easy to write and check the mappings. A special initialization method, `Object allChangeInitializations`, transforms this information into a `Dictionary` which is optimized for fast look-up. (This `Dictionary` is stored in an `Object` class instance variable called `changeAttributes`.)

6   *Damage areas.* We also considered adding a general parameter, the nature of which could be decided by the programmer. But this brought us right back to the original difficulties. Reverse engineering of our current solutions has shown that we need only one special parameter, namely the areas affected by the change in the attribute.

The `damageAreas` parameter is meaningful if the model semantics include a sense of geometry. The effects of an attribute change may then be limited to certain areas within the area covered by the model. We cannot quite decide if this is a profound truth about changed-update or if it is just a hack, but we have included it in our design anyhow.

7   *The* `ChangeHolder`. We finally created a new class for the parameter to the update message. The central feature is that the view can ask this parameter if specified selectors are affected by the current change, but it also holds information about the originating model object and the associated damage areas, if any.

8   *Models and views have* `ChangeHolders`. Every model object has a `ChangeHolder` where information about model changes is accumulated. Every view object has a `ChangeHolder` which holds information about interesting model changes and outstanding view operations.

The `Tool` object controls the layout of the `Tool`'s editors (view-controller pairs) and coordinates their behavior. This object has been a rover in our architecture. We have tried letting a controller play the `Tool` role, and we have tried letting the `Tool` object be a separate object outside the `VisualPart` hierarchy. Our current solution is to let the `Tool` be a `Container` object, because it is responsible for an area of the screen and manages a number of `Components`. A general role model showing the `Tool`'s position in the `VisualPart` structure appears in Figure 9.35.

The Tool *object is part of the visual component hierarchy*

We have introduced transactions to solve the problems with views trying to display inconsistent models, and with multiple, redundant display operations. Transactions also control the persistent storage of model objects, but this does not belong to our current discussion.

Activity phases controlled by transactions

Transactions are controlled by the `TransactionManager`, the sole instance of the class `TransactionManager1`. Only one transaction can be active at any time; there is no nesting. The activity is performed as a block in the `TransactionManager`; it is called by the `Controller` as described in Pattern 4. A transaction rearranges the actions of a user command activity into four phases:

1   *Model change.* One or more messages from a controller cause the model objects to modify their attributes. The methods that do the actual modifications

Figure 9.35

VisualPart
architecture
showing the
position of the
Tool role

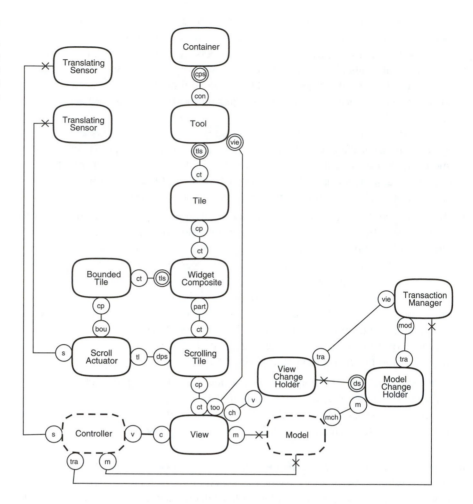

report this by sending the message self changedAttributes: attributeList damage: areaList. The information is temporarily accumulated in the model object's ChangeHolder.

2 *View update.* The components in the visual component hierarchy receive an update1 message in prefix order, starting with the ScheduledWindow in the root. All relevant information is available in the view's ChangeHolder when it receives the update1 message. The application programmer must override this method and do whatever is needed:

- Changes to the view's virtualBounds must be reported to its container by self changedBoundsFrom: oldBounds.

- Required display operations are stored in the ChangeHolder where they are retained until the next phase: self changeHolder invalidate: aRectangle.

3 *View display.* The visual component hierarchy is traversed to ensure the display of required areas once and once only.

9.7   STEP 7: INFORM THE CONSUMER COMMUNITY

In this case, the consumers are ourselves, but we still need a systematic informa-tion and training program.

IN A NUTSHELL

In our case, the main part of this step consisted of a number of short seminar and discussion groups. In addition, the Tool framework documentation was given to every programmer and also made available electronically.

The Taskon programmer's procedures were modified to check conformance with the rules of the framework. While nonconformance is permissible in special cases, programmers are encouraged to follow the framework as closely as possi-ble.

CHAPTER 10

Organizing for Software Productivity

CONTENTS

10.1 An Industrial Approach to Software Production 274

10.2 Large-scale Production of Intelligent Network Services 281

10.3 Large-scale Production of Customized Business Information Systems 285

This chapter is mainly written for the software manager or business person who is willing to consider new ways to create and deploy software.

10.1 AN INDUSTRIAL APPROACH TO SOFTWARE PRODUCTION

IN A NUTSHELL

Software life cycle models tell us what happens to a piece of software and when it happens. We will expand our interest with a third dimension: who makes it happen?

We believe that the people who contribute their skills to the creation and deployment of software should be organized in a value chain. The guiding principle should be that while the qualifications of people on different layers will be different, the individual qualification requirements should be realistic in terms of a large and distributed organization plan. The professionals performing the tasks on each layer should be supported by a combination of technologies, procedures, and tools.

We must organize properly to realize reuse potential

One of the great promises of object orientation is reuse, but we must organize ourselves properly to realize its potential. We present the idea of a value chain: a person creates something that is of value to somebody else, who creates something that is of value to somebody else, and so on, up to the end user, who applies software to perform a valuable task.

On each layer, there are people who employ the results created by the people on the layer below, and who provide results for the people on the layer above. The technology and techniques applied at each layer must be tailored to the personnel who populate it, their goals, tasks, working conditions, preferences, and areas of competence.

Different value chains for different kinds of software are likely to emerge as the industry matures. We expect to find a marketplace with a network of suppliers, each specialized to cater to a particular clientele.

The challenge to the software manager and businessperson is to find good answers to two questions: What will be *our* role in the future software industry? How do we get from here to there?

We will not pretend that we have the final answers to either of these questions, but we have worked on them for more than ten years. In this chapter, we give a report on a structure for the telecommunications Intelligent Network services industry, and also a report on how to organize the creation and deployment of business information systems.

Extend the life cycle model with an actor dimension

Software life cycle models are commonly used to describe the important events in the life of a piece of software. A model may, for example, distinguish between *system specification, design, implementation, testing, installation,* and *maintenance.* There are many variants of this model, but most of them have one thing in common: they describe the software life cycle from the point of view of the program developer. Just consider the apparently innocent word *maintenance.* It covers both bug-fixing and minor software improvements. Bug-fixing could involve a *user* who discovers a software irregularity, a *systems operator* in the user organization who passes a bug report to the vendor's *customer support person,* who reports the bug to the *head of the software development team,* who allocates it to a *responsible programmer,* who fixes the bug and returns a program patch along the same path.

We want to extend the traditional life cycle model to describe all the people and all the activities that contribute to the final value to the end user.

What, when, who

We could say that traditional life cycle models have two dimensions: *what* and *when.* We will extend the models, with *who* as a third dimension. This permits us to describe the software life cycle not only from the programmer's point of view, but also from the point of view of other people, such as the provider of reusable components, the distributor, and the end user.

The relationships between the people on the different layers are *producer-consumer* relationships, because the *raison d'être* of the people on one layer is to produce value for the people on the layer above them. We call the layers along this dimension a value chain, as illustrated in Figure 10.1. Each layer is populated by a team with defined responsibilities and skills. Each team builds on the results from the team below it and provides value to the team above (Figure 10.2).

We will first describe the characteristics of a single layer, and then discuss the nature of the whole value chain.

Figure 10.2 shows a generic specification of an abstract layer. The layer has its own tasks, work processes, and production facilities. The work processes can be formal or informal, according to the culture and preferences prevalent on that layer. The layer specification must be augmented by the special requirements associated with a concrete layer.

We need an effective work process

A set of production facilities will be available; these facilities will include work process guidelines that separate the total work into manageable tasks, techniques to perform these tasks, and computer-based tools that help actors to perform the

Supported by production facilities

Figure 10.1
The value chain

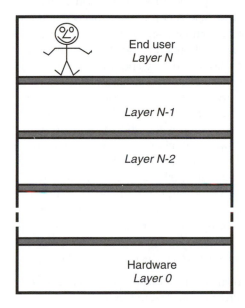

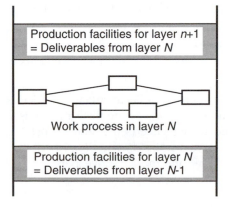

Figure 10.2

A layer in the value chain gets value from below and provides value to the layer above

tasks. The facilities of a given layer must be adapted to the interests and qualifications of the actors of that layer.

People form the most essential part of a layer

The actors populating a given layer have unique responsibilities, and corresponding competence and interests. The production facilities for the actors on every layer in the value chain should be designed at least as carefully as we design the end user systems. The current tendency to try and provide a common environment that satisfies all needs will result in solutions that are too complex to satisfy anybody. The guiding principle should be that the qualifications of the actors on the different layers must be realistic in terms of real people. Their goals, qualifications, tasks, and production facilities must all be in harmony.

The deliverables constitute the product

A layer creates a certain kind of value. The products delivered from one layer constitute the libraries and other production facilities employed on the layer above it. The success criterion of the people populating the layer (the supplier) is the satisfaction of the consumers on the next layer up. The actors who populate a layer must, therefore, understand the qualifications and requirements of their clients.

There should be firewalls between layers

An important principle in our architecture is that we assume actors to be hostile, sometimes by intent, but usually by ignorance of details which are of no interest to them. The production facilities for any layer must, therefore, be secure: it must be hard or even impossible for an actor on a given layer to threaten the integrity of the layers below it. A corollary to this is that the production facilities for a certain layer must be complete, in the sense that they must enable the actors to do everything they are authorized to do. Procedures and techniques are used at the discretion of the actors, and they should be given maximum freedom to exercise their ingenuity and creativity. If at all possible, security should be automatically enforced in the tool portion of their production facilities.

We will need different value chains

We now change our perspective from the individual layer to the value chain as a whole. Our first observation is that the value chain must be adapted to its purpose. We do not know the number of different value chains that will be needed, but we will need at least one for each of the main software categories, such as business information systems, telecommunications systems, real time control systems, and computer-aided design systems. We also expect that there will be variants of these value chains dependent on their commercial organizations: the interaction between companies are of a different nature than the interaction between teams within the same company.

There are several issues which need to be clarified:

1   What is the essential structure of the value chain? A linear list as shown in Figure 10.1? A tree structure? A directed graph?

2   How is a value chain created? By design? By evolution and natural selection?

3   Who creates the value chain? Do the actors on the various levels create the production facilities for the actors on the layer above them? Or will the basic structure and tools be created by "production engineers" who are outside the value chain?

The linear value chain

The term *value chain* implies a linear structure, which is the simplest structure imaginable. Our main reason for wanting this structure is that we want people to work in a homogeneous, integrated environment that is tailored to their needs and preferences (we stress that this does not imply that the work should be mindless or even routine; even the most creative person in the world will be more

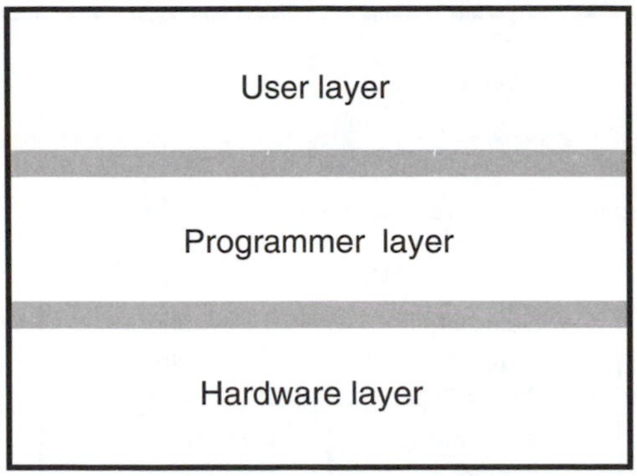

Figure 10.3
Early value chain

User layer

Programmer layer

Hardware layer

effective if he or she works in an environment that stimulates his or her creativity and simplifies mundane tasks).

In a linear value chain, the supplier on the layer below can be responsible for the complete production facility. Alternatively, a production engineer could create the production facility and integrate it with the supplier's layer. The former alternative is closer to an artisan's model of operation, while the latter is closer to an industrial model.

As an example of a linear value chain, consider the situation when I first started programming in 1958. The value chain was then as illustrated in Figure 10.3. I was the programmer, and since I programmed in binary, I based my work entirely on the computer's hardware capabilities, which were made available through a well-defined instruction repertoire. The user, my customer, loaded and started the program, and was then in the environment I had defined. Even though the computer had been built by my colleagues, there was no practical way for me to change its specifications. Similarly, the use of the program did not give the user access to its internal construction.

A simple, linear value chain

This scheme had obvious advantages. If the user interface and program functionality were well chosen, the learning burden of the end user was reduced to the bare essentials. Similarly, the interface between the programmer and the hardware was very simple; the instruction repertoire of the early computers was small and easy to learn.

The disadvantage to the user was that he or she was limited to running one program at a time. If the user needed the functionality of more than one program, he or she would have to quit one before running another, and it was hard to obtain a synergy effect by intermixing the functionality of several programs. The disadvantage to me as a programmer was the limited power of the hardware instruction set, and also that I had to do everything myself. This severely limited the functionality of the programs that it was feasible to create.

We get a tree-structured value chain when the work on a given layer is to be based on the results from several sublayers. This is the situation for most programmers today, who have to relate to a myriad of different facilities from different suppliers. Figure 10.4 illustrates that the situation is radically different from the good old days, but it must be admitted that it empowers us to create programs that could not be imagined in the 1950s. In Figure 10.4 "Programming language support" denotes the combination of programming language, compiler, loader, program libraries, editor and debugger. The term is repeated in several places to

The tree-structured value chain

User layer				
Application programmer layer				
Programming language support	Data communication system	Database system	Operating system	Windowing system and GUI library
	Programming language support	Programming language support	Programming language support	Programming language support
Hardware layer	Hardware layer	Hardware layer	Hardware layer	Hardware layer

Figure 10.4 Example of current value chain

The directed graph value chain

indicate that the creators of the different libraries do not necessarily use the same language or even the same hardware.

Real value chains usually take the form of an acyclic, directed graph. We made Figure 10.4 into a tree by cheating: some of the partitions in the hardware layer would almost certainly be shared among several partitions on the programming support layer. Our nice, simple model of Figure 10.1 has now changed into the complex picture of Figure 10.5, where the actors on one layer build on the results from several suppliers on the layer below.

Value chains created by design?

As an engineer, I tend to think that a value chain should be the result of careful analysis and design rather than the result of an arbitrary happening. This is indeed the case for the initial value chain we created for Intelligent Network Services in cooperation with the Norwegian Telecom that we describe below.

For each class of systems, we could consider the complete value chain from the hardware through the end user facilities. The purpose is to process end user data, and we try to understand the kind of people who will be most effective on each layer. We then exploit all available technologies to select those which will be most effective for each layer.

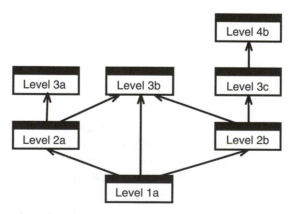

Figure 10.5 Directed graph value chain based on extensive reuse from several sources

ORGANIZING FOR SOFTWARE PRODUCTIVITY

Real life business is not as simple as this. Networks of organizations evolve under the influence of many pressures. Market pressure is the current fashion, but financial, political, technical, and even moral pressures influence business evolution. The software business is no exception, and fragments of value chains are appearing spontaneously all around us: operating system vendors try to entice application programmers to build on their results; repository builders encourage providers of CASE (Computer-Aided Software Engineering) tools to standardize on their products. Consultants and authors of newsletters try to make order out of chaos, and try to influence vendors and users to use a common vocabulary and to adhere to some common, high level architecture.

Value chains created by natural selection?

When we first worked on the initial system for Intelligent Networks, we assumed that the people on one level would be totally responsible for the production facilities of the people on the layer above them. But then a member of the project asked the very pertinent question: What is *our* role in this? We are not part of the chain, yet we design and implement it. This led to the idea of *production engineering*, which covers the design and implementation of value chains. This includes the chain architecture as well as choosing the appropriate technology for the different layers, specifying the work processes, choosing the production facilities, and installing them. This is illustrated in Figure 10.6. We have now reverted to the simple, linear, value chain model, because we believe it to be the duty of the production engineers to create the illusion of a linear chain, even if they integrate systems and products from several vendors to implement a production facility.

Production engineers create the value chain

No single enterprise controls all layers in the value chain. Most of us build on products delivered by our vendors, and many of us deliver products to customers in another enterprise. We can still think in terms of value chains, and organize our little parts to the best of our abilities. We can also influence our environment through user groups, industry associations, development consortia, etc.

The focus on people and responsibility which is embedded in the idea of value chains has proven useful in a number of situations. We have found that very complex problems are greatly simplified when we add the third dimension (people) to the life cycle model. The following subsections describe but two examples.

Create your own value chain

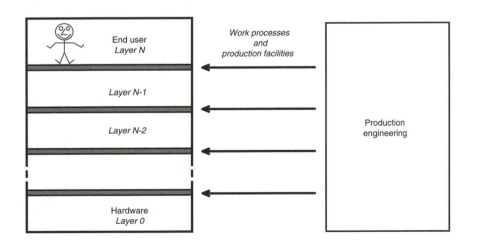

Figure 10.6

Role of the production engineers

There are two opposing forces. One which makes the producer tend toward specialization, another which makes the consumer want general suppliers:

1 People must specialize to be the best in what they do, so they will tend to focus on a small part of the value chain.

2 Customers do not like to deal with lots of vendors, so they will prefer to buy everything from one company.

The solution could be that some vendors create specialized products, while other vendors specialize in production engineering, and integrate these products to deliver complete production environments. Large programming shops can have their own production engineers and deal directly with the specialized product vendors.

If you believe that value chains can help you better organize your work, you may consider the following activities as part of your initial studies:

1 Identify all the people or organizational units involved, and describe the layers of the value chain. The top layer will be the ultimate end users of your software; that is the layer where value is created outside the realm of software. The bottom layer will likely be some purveyor of hardware or basic software, such as operating systems, communication systems, and database services. Also include suppliers of computer-aided software engineering tools. Make sure to include all layers, such as layers for distribution, installation, training, and service.

2 Describe the nature of the work performed in each layer and the success criteria of their actors.

3 Describe the kind of people who will be most effective on the different layers. You would expect to find extroverted people near the top of the chain because of their close relationship to the end users. The people near the bottom of the chain are likely to be introverted, more concerned about computational details than the happiness of users.

4 Select suitable technology to support the work on each layer, and specify the work processes and the production facilities. Be sure to be open-minded when you select the technology; a simple duplication of master objects may be more appropriate than sophisticated technology such as automatic program generators.

10.2   LARGE-SCALE PRODUCTION OF INTELLIGENT NETWORK SERVICES

IN A NUTSHELL

This section has been written for the interested layman, so we do not apologize to the telecommunications expert for glossing over the hard problems or for explaining principles that are well known to him or her.

Our aim is to illustrate how different reuse technologies are appropriate on different layers of practical value chains.

The telecommunications industry is expanding its product offerings with a number of new *Intelligent Network* (IN) services, such as Universal Personal Telephone, which makes it possible to find a person wherever he or she is; Call Forwarding, which makes it possible to redirect incoming calls to alternative receivers; and many others. Our study was based on an elaborate life cycle model. We identified six actors and mapped the activities of the life cycle model onto these actors to create a six-layer value chain. We found that the actors were very different in competence and outlook, selected appropriate technologies for each layer, and sketched out possible production facilities. We were pleased to discover that every one of the reuse technologies described in Chapters 5 and 11 was applicable on at least one layer.

A blueprint for an industry

The result was a blueprint for a major industry. We believe its general pattern shows the future of the software industry, and that a viable Intelligent Networks Industry could be based on our model. But study the following pages and judge for yourself.

We will report the results of the first iteration briefly in this chapter and more thoroughly in Chapter 12. This iteration was performed in 1993 and reported with a paper and demonstration at the TINA conference of that year [Ree 93]. The next iteration took place in 1994–95; its results were not ready in time to be included here.

A large number of different Intelligent Network services have been proposed, and some of them have already been made operational by operators. We list a few to give you an idea of their nature:

IN provides sophisticated telecommunications services

1   *Advice of charge.* The paying user is informed of usage-based charging information.

2   *Alternative billing.* A user can bill a call to a number other than the calling number.

3   *Automatic call distribution.* Incoming calls are distributed to several operators according to a selectable algorithm.

4   *Call forwarding.* Incoming calls are redirected, either unconditionally or depending on load, time of day, etc.

5   *Conference calling* allows multiple users to participate in a single conversation.

6   *Freephone* (800 numbers). The call is free for the caller and paid for by the called party.

7   *Televoting.* Call a number to cast your vote for your favorite hit tune or whatever.

8   *Universal personal telecommunication.* One telephone number will reach you wherever you are in the world.

9 *Video on demand (VOD).* Order your favorite movie to be screened—where you are and when you want it.

10 *Virtual private network.* A private communication network with its own, independent numbering scheme. It is technically implemented in the public network, but logically separated from it.

IN will be one of the world's major industries

The construction and deployment of IN services is going to be a very large operation. There will be a large and expanding number of available services: the total system complexity will be staggering, and many organizations employing people in different capacities will be involved in its creation and operation.

A first separation of IN into two distinct domains has been suggested in Vestli [Vestli, Nilsen 92]; this is illustrated in Figure 10.7. The *Switching Domain* encapsulates the network functions offered by the traditional telecommunications systems, and the *Service Domain* encapsulates all the Intelligent Network services functionality. This is a client-server architecture, where the Service Domain is a client of the Switching Domain. The interfaces between client and server are defined in terms of high level operations, independently of the concrete switch design. Service Domain software is, therefore, portable in the sense that it can operate against a range of different switches.

An elaborate life cycle model

Norwegian Telecom has proposed an Intelligent Network service life cycle model to the EURESCOM [Vestli, Nilsen 92]. The model has more phases than most other life cycle models, but a short reflection convinces us that all are needed if we want to support a very large number of users and encourage extensive software reuse:

1 *Analysis.* Analysis of the subscriber's requirements, producing a specification of the service as seen by the user.

2 *Specification.* Refinement of the specification. It should preferably be written in a formal language for later (automatic) verification of programs.

3 *Design.* Design of the service software: extensive reuse of existing solutions is envisaged.

4 *Implementation.* Production of a complete program that satisfies the specification, including new and reused software.

5 *Installation.* The new service software is installed in the distributed communication system to achieve acceptable speed and capacity.

6 *Activation.* The service is made available to selected users.

7 *Invocation.* A user sends a request for the execution of the service to the network.

8 *Execution.* The service has been invoked and initialized, and is now executing.

9 *Deactivation.* The service is made unavailable to selected users, i.e., it can no longer be invoked by those users.

Figure 10.7
The intelligent network

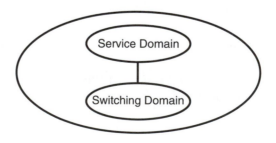

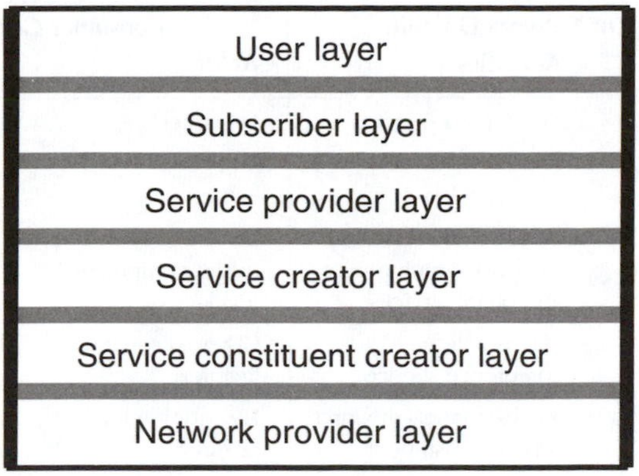

Figure 10.8
IN value chain

User layer
Subscriber layer
Service provider layer
Service creator layer
Service constituent creator layer
Network provider layer

10 *Deinstallation.* The service is removed from the network and can no longer be used.

Many different individuals and enterprises will be involved in the creation and invocation of IN services. Typical examples are subscribers and end users, public telecommunications administrations, *teleshops*, and independent software houses. These individuals and enterprises will, as a body, be responsible for supporting the complete IN services life cycle.

Many different actors

We have analyzed the life cycle model and identified six actors who can be organized in a six-layer value chain, as shown in Figure 10.8.

Identify the value chain

1 *User layer.* The user wants to use available services, and who is responsible for selecting and invoking a service.

2 *Subscriber layer.* The subscriber purchases a set of services on behalf of one or more users, pays for them, and is responsible for making the services available to his or her users.

3 *Service provider layer.* The service provider has a license for activating IN service software for specified subscribers. We think of the service provider as the corner teleshop where consumers can buy regular services, but it could also be a professional customer consultant who sells specialized services to advanced corporations.

4 *Service creator layer.* The service creator has a license for defining IN service software and installing it in the telecommunications network. The service creator will currently be a public telephone authority (PTA), but our model is open for several commercial service creator companies.

5 *Service constituent creator layer.* The service constituent creator has a license for producing software building blocks which may be configured into IN services. These software building blocks, called *service constituents*, are the reusable components used by the service creator to create service software.

6 *Network provider layer.* The network provider provides the basic communications facilities used by the IN services.

Table 10.1 suggests an analogy to a similar value chain in the consumer industry.

We will discuss the layers of the value chain in more detail in the case study of Chapter 12.

Table 10.1

IN versus consumer goods value chains

Intelligent Network Domain		Consumer Goods Domain	
Actor	**Activities**	**Actor**	**Activities**
User	Conducts a meeting by videoconference	Daughter	Listens to a stereo system
Subscriber	Buys a video-conference service	Father	Buys a stereo with CD player
Service provider	Sells videoconferences and other services	Audio equipment retailer	Sells CD player and other audio equipment
Service creator	Makes a video-conference service	CD player manu-facturer	Makes CD players
Service constituent creator	Makes a video mixing service constituent	Laser unit manu-facturer	Makes laser components for CD players and other uses
Network provider	Makes hardware video mixers available in the network	Electronic compo-nents manufacturer	Makes electronic compo-nents for lasers and other uses

10.3   LARGE-SCALE PRODUCTION OF CUSTOMIZED BUSINESS INFORMATION SYSTEMS

IN A NUTSHELL

One of the themes of this book is that object orientation enables us to create customized software which is adapted to the tasks and preferences of individuals. The tasks and preferences of professionals vary widely. Therefore, we need to organize a great number of different tools and an even greater number of configurations of tools into coherent information environments.

We cannot possibly hope to produce all the different information environments through traditional software development projects, and the use of shrink-wrapped software packages has its clear limitations. Therefore, we exploit object-oriented re-use technology to build a value chain for customized information environments for professionals. The main actors are the Tool Makers, who configure the different information tools; the Module Makers, who program configurable program components; and the Kernel Makers, who create the system architecture and common environment for the whole value chain.

We discussed the need for information environments for professionals in Chapter 7 in conjunction with task/tool/service models. We will also see the need for such environments on all the layers in the value chain for IN services. Douglas Engelbart first saw the potential in using computers to augment the human intellect and support human cooperation. He pioneered the mouse, the multiwindow screen, and a host of other ideas—some of them are commonplace today, and others will be commonplace tomorrow [Engelbart 62, Engelbart 67, and Engelbart 92].

Information environments for professionals

In the following, we will give a few examples to illustrate the personal augmentation part of Engelbart's ideas: business information systems for decision makers, experience-based information environments, and information environments for system designers. But it is important to realize that the essence of information environments are their uniqueness, since they should be tailored to the goals, needs, and preferences of the professional user.

Decision makers and other professionals need to harness both halves of their brains. They need logic and creativity; they need rational analysis of aspects that can be formalized, and an intuitive understanding of complex relationships that are beyond the reach of logic.

Business Information Systems support decisionmakers

A business information system is a system designed to provide a decision maker with customized access to information sources for exploration and analysis. The creation of such a system starts with analyzing the user's tasks to see how improved access to information can help the decision maker be more efficient.

We next search for information sources. We surprisingly often find that information which is essential to the decision makers cannot be derived from the information available in the enterprise computer systems. The essential information will then have to be provided by skilled personnel. We have in many cases had success with introducing the *Information Editor* as a new role in the organization; see Figure 10.9. This is a highly competent and responsible person who collates information from many sources, evaluates and interprets it, and presents the digested results to senior decision makers through the common information system. The work done by the information editor is not new; it is done informally in most organizations. The official introduction of the information editor makes the work visible, respectable, and repeatable.

```
                         ┌─────────────────────┐
                         │       Senior        │
                         │   decision maker    │
                         ├─────────────────────┤
       End user layer    │    Information       │
                         │      editor          │
                         ├─────────────────────┤
                         │  Basic information   │
                         │     provider         │
                         └─────────────────────┘
```

Experience-based information environments

I have met many managers of high technology enterprises who would like to capture and formalize the collective experience of the enterprise to make it less vulnerable to the vagaries of its experts, and to ensure that the enterprise as a whole learns from experience and does not repeat past mistakes.

Pipe maintenance intelligence

An example: A petroleum processing facility is composed of a very large number of pipes carrying a variety of fluids and gases ranging from the benign to the highly corrosive. The pipes have to be inspected at times to determine if they need to be replaced. Pipe inspection must be done during a planned process shutdown, which is costly and must be kept as short as possible. But a pipe failure can be dangerous to people and property, and leads to a very costly catastrophic process shutdown. There are clear benefits to be obtained if a systematic collection of pipe, inspection, and failure data could be made directly available to the pipe manager for exploration.

An information environment for a pipe maintenance manager helps the manager plan the pipe inspection operations. To do this, he needs to collate a great deal of information, and he would also benefit from automated means to identify the most vulnerable pipe stretches among the many thousands of stretches for which he is responsible. The tools have to be very flexible. The manager could, for example, suspect that pipes made from a certain batch of steel are causing trouble. Is this true, and if so, which of the afflicted pipes may need immediate attention?

The distinction between information environment categories is blurred

Is this experience formalization system a special business information system? We tend to define a business information system as a system which primarily collects data from many sources, presents accumulated views, permits exception monitoring and automatic triggers, and permits navigation in the information space. We regard the experience-based information system as all of this, but, in addition, there is usually a significant element of specialized algorithms, and possibly also decision support logic.

An environment for systems developers

A system developer's information environment could consist of the following components. They should all be fully integrated in a seamless fashion:

1 Tools giving access to a model structure which is shared with other developers.

2 Tools and a repository for programming and debugging.

3 Facilities for reuse of patterns and frameworks.

4 An advanced documentation tool which supports a free mixture of general elements, such as texts, drawings, and tables, together with special OOram report elements, and program source code.

5 Facilities for software quality assurance.

6 An electronic mail system which supports general e-mail, as well as the transfer of specialized system data.

7 A work process support system which helps people to cooperate without restraining their creativity, responsibilies, or initiative.

All kinds of information environments can be created

You would probably make a different list, and my list will probably be different a year from now. But this is immaterial to our argument: we start with goals, determine the kind of people who can best achieve them, and create a information environment which best supports these people in their preferred mode of working.

There is no value judgment in this; it is hard-nosed rationalism. Computers can be used to support the creative exploration of an information space as well as the repetitive (and mindless) entry of routine data. They can support free agents working voluntarily together towards a common goal, or command and strictly control people who work in a rule-based environment. They can be used to support *distributed decisions with central control,* in which a responsible person may delegate the performance of a job to other people while retaining control of selected boundary conditions.

We have organized the creation of information environments for professionals into a five-layer value chain, as illustrated in Figure 10.10. The five layers of actors are as follows:

1 The end users apply customized information environments to help perform their tasks. End users may also modify their information environments in various ways to adapt them to changing needs, to the extent that this is part of the layer's functionality.

    We frequently find it profitable to apply the principle of value chains to the end users' organization. The end user layer is then subdivided, e.g., as illustrated in Figure 10.9.

2 The tool maker is a customer consultant whose task is to empathize with end users, to provide their information environments, and to help them get maximum benefit from their tools.

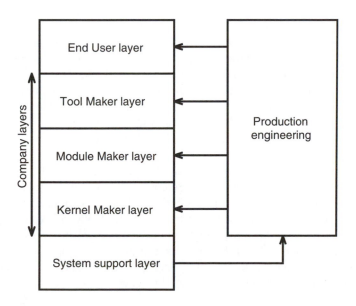

Figure 10.10
The value chain

A tool maker reuses the Taskon library of information models and work processes, configures and specializes functionality created by a module maker, generates user documentation, and makes the resulting systems available to the end users.

3   The module maker is an application programmer who specifies, designs, and implements new end user functionality.

The module maker reuses the available library of patterns and frameworks to achieve maximum results with a minimum of effort. The module maker also uses the company quality assurance standards and procedures to ensure that a new module conforms to standards and guidelines.

4   The kernal maker is a systems programmer who creates the library of reusable patterns and frameworks, the standards, and the guidelines. The kernel makers are also responsible for defining and maintaining the value chain with its associated procedures and tools; they are our production engineers.

5   The systems software suppliers are the vendors of operating systems, communication software, database management systems, compilers, and runtime systems for the different hardware platforms. They appear at the bottom of our value chain, but the vendors' value chains continue downwards.

Some of the systems software is less robust than we could desire and requires very specialized and detailed knowledge to make it run together with the rest of our software. This is one of the challenges that our production engineers have to face.

6   The production engineers are responsible for the methodologies for the upper four layers of the value chain.

Taskon's control of the bottom, system support layer is limited. We may sometimes select product and vendor, but often have to accept selections made by the client. The production engineers package the selected basic software within our development environment and, if possible, protect the module makers from its glitches and other peculiarities.

The business organization can be patterned after the value chain   The organization can be patterned after the value chain, as indicated in Figure 10.11. The tool makers are grouped in accordance with the end user business. This enables the company to reuse its understanding of the customers' requirements, as well as the appropriate technology. The module makers create application-oriented functionality, this functionality is often reusable for several categories of end users and, therefore, several tool makers. The kernel maker is responsible for generally reusable patterns and frameworks as well as procedures and production facilities. The kernel maker, therefore, can fill the function of production engineering, as well as the kernel maker layer in the value chain.

The Taskon fountain model   Our philosophy of system development is focused on reuse; we strive to increase our reusable assets so that we can meet new requirements with a minimum of new work.

Our life cycle model, shown in Figure 10.12, is called the Taskon fountain model: software production consists of spouting a column of specialized software from the pool of reusables; the end user drinks from this fountain to satisfy his thirst for solutions. The pool level rises when systematically collected experience is packaged as reusable facilities and components. The work needed to satisfy a given user requirement is given by the height of the production column; sophisticated requirements increase its height by lifting the top, while better reusable assets decrease its height by lifting the general level of the pool.

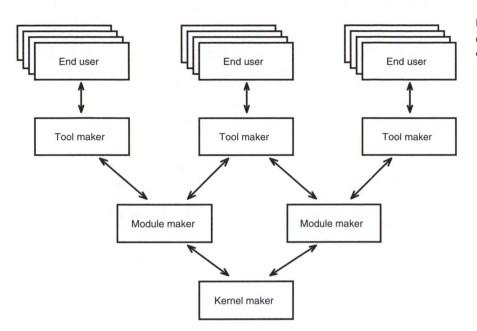

Figure 10.11
Company
organization

The life cycle model of Figure 10.12 is orthogonal to the organization model of Figure 10.11: the tool makers, module makers, and kernel makers all have their parts to play in the forward and reverse engineering parts of the fountain model.

System production activities aim at satisfying customer needs and generating revenue. The tool makers are in the front line: they determine user needs, instantiate and structure library objects, and preset initial parameters and other configuration data.

Production done by tool makers and module makers

If available functionality cannot satisfy the requirements, module makers program new functionality by building on functionality available in the library. Since we aim at multiple sales to related markets, the special programs constitute a very small part of the delivered system, typically ranging from zero to one percent. The module maker can focus on program functionality and robustness at the expense of generality and elegance, and he or she can frequently ignore questions of efficiency. Exploratory programming is ideal for this work, and is even used in the marketing phase to demonstrate the effectiveness of our technology.

The nature of the programming done in production activities leads to increased total system complexity; it is an entropy-increasing activity. If production is permitted to dominate for a period of time, there is a risk that the system will collapse under its own weight. The collapse will be clearly visible to everybody, because it will manifest itself by a sharp and increasing rate of system bugs. Attempts at fixing bugs can make the system worse, because the complexity makes it humanly impossible to fix one bug without introducing new ones. The module maker will, therefore, alternate between forward and reverse engineering: forward engineering when creating products, and reverse engineering when simplifying the programs and creating reusable components.

The collection of experience aims at increasing the value of our reusable assets and is an investment. The module makers do reverse engineering on their ad hoc solutions, look for generalizations and powerful abstractions, study feedback from users, and create improved application modules designed for reuse and specialization.

Experience collection done by module makers and kernel makers

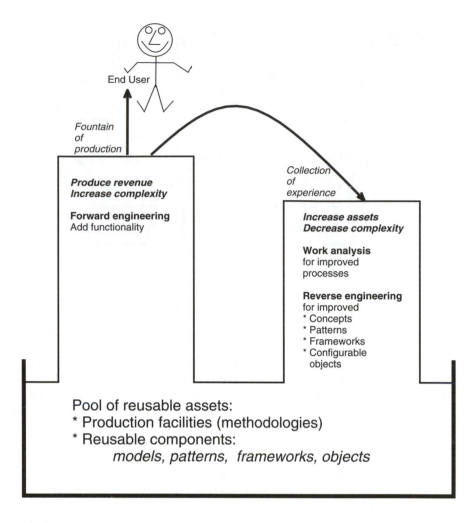

Figure 10.12
The fountain model for reuse

Kernel makers study all bug reports and gripes to identify trouble spots in our technology, do reverse engineering on the application modules in a search for simplification and common solutions, and create improved basic patterns and frameworks. They are also alert to stumbling stones in the production process and search for improved processes and tools.

The ultimate goal of the experience collection activities is to simplify the production process and make it more efficient. The experience-collecting activities lead to reduced system complexity; they are entropy-reducing activities. If the experience-collecting activities are allowed to dominate, system functionality may become inadequate to satisfy market needs, and the revenue stream may dry out. This is a sad situation, even if the system is nice and clean and the programmers are having great fun.

Job rotation essential
All of our organization models in this chapter are considered to be *role models*. The production engineers and the actors of the value chain layers are *roles* which must be mapped onto real persons. We believe there should be many-to-many relationships between roles and people. Specifically, we believe that people should alternate between production work and experience collection, between revenue creation and investment.

There is no limit to the number of dirty programs a keen production programmer may be willing to create to satisfy an urgent user requirement, but it helps if the same person from time to time cleans up other people's code and learns the hard way what kind of trouble is caused by dirty code.

There is no limit to the time a keen experience collector can spend on finding elegant solutions to a fictive problem, but it helps if the same person from time to time must produce end user functionality within strict time limits, learns what kinds of assets improve effectiveness, and how irrelevant are fancy solutions to nonexistent problems.

We simply believe that all programmers benefit from taking their own medicine: being the end users of their own software, using their own reusables, cleaning up their own production.

You may well ask if this is applicable to large organizations having hundreds of programmers. We believe it is, for two reasons: One is that it seems hard for a methodology section of a large programming organization to make front-line programmers adopt their wonderful components, processes, and tools—a certain interchange of people might help the transfer. The second is that the development of reusable assets is by nature a slow and painstaking process. A person who is working exclusively in that area will not understand the humble-tumble of front-line programming, and will be hard put to create the optimum production facilities. *Does it scale?*

So if you consider the layers of the IN value chain in Figure 10.8 or the information environment value chain of Figure 10.9, the best way to ensure that each value chain constitutes an organic whole is to let people play multiple roles. Not simultaneously, because the activities having the nearest deadlines will then be given priority, but alternately, so that people get varied experience over time.

When I first entered the programming field in the late 1950s, we tried to persuade a shipyard that it should invest in computer-aided design. On one memorable occasion, the yard management had to decide if they were to spend their scarce investment resources on a new welding machine or on a computer for the new systems. Simple arithmetic showed that the welding machine would pay for itself in one year, while nobody knew if and when the computer would pay its way. Fortunately for us, management made a good decision and bought the computer. *Management's challenge is to hit the right balance between production and investment*

The management of today faces the same kind of problems when they allocate scarce resources. Should they enter into a contract with customer X which will generate a known cash flow and satisfactory profit, or should they invest the same resources in an improved, low level framework which is invisible to management and customers alike? It would be nice if we could apply a formula to compute return on a proposed investment in reusables. We are sorry to admit that we do not have a good solution, and that resource allocation to investment and production activities are based more on intuition than rational computations. But we have some experience of schemes which do not work, at least not for us. We have examples of reusable components which have never been used, and we have on one occasion been precariously near the brink of total system collapse. We make sure our collective experience, bad and good, is made known within the company so that we all can learn from it.

We believe that the creation of reusable components cannot be part of production, because of the insurmountable clash between the goals and time schedules of the two kinds of activities. We believe that the creation of reusables cannot be an isolated operation, because it can then take off on a tangent. We believe that the creation of reusable components cannot be controlled by production (e.g., by production paying for them), because we lose the long-term considerations that should dominate the investments.

Investment decisions are currently dominated by people who alternate between both types of activities, who understand the needs of production and the potential for improvement in the reusables. We are searching for work processes that will make the benefits of appropriate reusables more visible, and that will quantize the cost of difficulties caused by inadequate methodologies and libraries.

The Taskon vision We will end this chapter with the Taskon vision for software development: study user requirements on a basis of experience from studying similar users; model user information by reusing models for similar users; specify tools which are adapted to the users' tasks; create systems without programming by duplication and conceptual modeling; if new functionality is required, create new software by marginally extending existing software. Reusable assets augment competent people to produce software which is cheaper, better-adapted to user needs, and more reliable than was achievable by using people alone.

Success depends on the ability to meet new challenges with existing components, producing high quality customized solutions in a short time, and at a marginal cost.

Dedicated and creative people will still be of paramount importance to the successful producer of software, but reusable assets will make them more effective.

CHAPTER 11

Advanced Reuse Based on Object Instances

CONTENTS

11.1 Introduction to Object Reuse 294

11.2 Runtime Configuration and Object Trading 295

11.3 The OOram Composition System 298

    11.3.1 The OOCS Schema Creator Layer 302
    11.3.2 List of Instructions: OOCS Schema Creation 302
    11.3.3 The Nature of OOCS Schemas 303
    11.3.4 The OOCS Type Implementor Layer 305

11.4 Object Duplication 309

    11.4.1 shallowCopy—Too Simple in Most Cases 311
    11.4.2 postCopy—A Default Duplication Algorithm 312
    11.4.3 structureCopy for the General Case 314
    11.4.4 deepCopy—A Dangerous Operation 316

This chapter is written for the specially interested reader. The technology presented is independent of role modeling, and constitutes an additional road to software reuse.

11.1 INTRODUCTION TO OBJECT REUSE

IN A NUTSHELL

We have discussed how to reuse models and classes through inheritance and specialization. We shall now see how we can compose a system from a pool of predefined objects. This technology is entirely different from the OOram role modeling technology. It is not as mature, but it has the potential to become the most important reuse technology of the future.

System creation by configuration

Encapsulation separates the external properties of an object from its internal implementation. Polymorphism permits different objects to use different methods for processing the same messages. These two properties, taken together, create an opportunity to construct object structures by composition. A large variety of systems can be constructed from a limited set of objects by connecting them in different ways. This is an object-oriented variant of *system creation without programming*—a methodology that has proven successful in the world of databases.

Many alternatives for selecting the class of new objects

An object is created and inserted in the collaboration structure by some other object. The selection of the appropriate class for a new object may be accomplished in many different ways, ranging from the simple and rigid to the complex and flexible. All of them have the common characteristic that they can be designed and implemented as general mechanisms that can be used by the application programmer according to simple rules.

As usual, there is no free lunch. Somebody has to decide on the kinds of structures to be supported, and somebody has to design the general interfaces that ensure that the different objects will fit together. It is hard to find the right balance between simplicity and power. The success of Lego bricks demonstrates that the benefits can be substantial.

In the following sections, we will present three different technologies for object reuse:

1 *Runtime configuration and object trading.* An object that needs a new collaborator asks a *trader* service to instantiate a suitable candidate. The trader holds a list of candidate objects. It manages a negotiation between the requestor and candidates to select acceptable candidates. It chooses the appropriate one, instantiates it, and installs it as a collaborator to the requestor.

2 *OOram composition system (OOCS).* A conceptual schema is a description of the world as seen by the end user community. Conceptual schemas have been applied to database design with great success. The database conceptual schema controls the composition of data in the database, and so forms a bridge from the users' mental models to the concrete data representation. It also forms a bridge from the data types to the users' mental models by specifying how the data are to be interpreted. We shall see that we can achieve similar results using objects.

3 *Object duplication.* New objects can be created by instantiating a class, or they can be created by the *duplication* of an existing object or object substructure. Both techniques are useful. Instantiation produces objects that are exactly as specified by the programmer. Duplication produces objects that reflect the history of the master object, and is useful when we want to accumulate specific information in a master before duplicating it. Object duplication may appear to be a trivial operation, and in many cases this is true. The duplication of a general object structure is an operation that is full of pitfalls, however, and we will discuss this problem in depth.

These object reuse technologies are described in the following subsections and illustrated in the case study of Chapter 12.

11.2   RUNTIME CONFIGURATION AND OBJECT TRADING

We often want to create user interfaces in which the user can navigate through an object structure and edit any chosen object. The challenge to the application programmer is to identify the type of the selected object, to select a suitable editor class, and to instantiate and install the selected class. This section gives you a general mechanism for creating a "dynamic matchmaker" which will achieve this goal and which you can use as a foundation when you want to create very powerful and user-friendly user interfaces.

IN A NUTSHELL

The position of the trading mechanism in our general model structure is indicated in Figure 11.1.

Two objects may be linked as collaborators if each behaves properly towards the other. We could, for example, have an information object and want to identify a suitable editor that can be linked to it. We frequently find we can use existing editors to edit new information objects. Similarly, a new editor class can often edit many existing information objects. The separation is particularly useful in the context of system configuration: a customer can buy and install a specific editor; it is then immediately available wherever it is applicable.

For example, a simple text editor can edit any object which understands the two messages `getText` and `putText`. A simple list editor can edit any object which understands `size`, `getElement (index)`, and `putElement (index, anObject)`. A simple graph editor can edit any structure of objects in which every object understands `getNeighbors`, `putNeighbor (anObject)`, and `removeNeighbor (anObject)`.

Several different editors may be applicable to the same information object. The information object could have a textual attribute, and a text editor could be used to edit it. The information object could also have an Array attribute, and a list

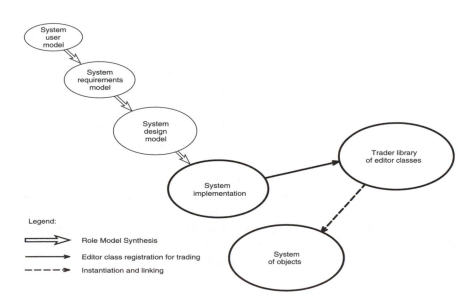

Figure 11.1

The trader identifies a suitable editor class and instantiates it

Figure 11.2

Collaboration view of trader mechanism

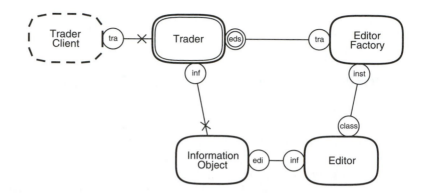

view could be used to present it. The information object could be the root of a tree structure, and a graphical editor could be used to present and edit the structure.

A powerful mechanism

An *object trading* mechanism separates the data from its presentation and editing: the data classes do not know the editor classes, and the editor classes do not know the data classes. There is a many-to-many relationship between editor types and data object types. An editor is capable of editing many different information objects, and an information object can be edited by many different editors.

The purpose of the trading mechanism is to select an editor that will cooperate properly with the information object,to instantiate the editor, and to link it to the information object.

The "master of ceremonies" is an object we call a *trader*. Any client object may ask it to provide an instance of an editor that is appropriate for a specified information object.

The objects participating in this mechanism play the five roles shown in Figure 11.2.

1 `InformationObject`. This role is played by any object which represents information that the user may want to see and possibly edit.

2 `Editor`. This object is responsible for the interface between the user and the designated information object.

3 `TraderClient`. This role is played by any object which knows an `InformationObject` and wants an editor for it.

4 `Trader`. This role is played by an object that is responsible for finding an editor for a given `InformationObject`. It is *immutable*, which means that it may not be specialized for different applications.

5 `EditorFactory`. This object is responsible for an editor class. It must be able to determine if an instance will be capable of editing a given `InformationObject`.

Two activities

There are two *activities* in the trading mechanism: `Initialization` and `Trading`. The `Initialization` activity must somehow instantiate the `Trader` object and load it with a list of `EditorFactories`. This list can be sorted in a priority sequence, so that the first acceptable editor will also be the default one. We have hard-coded a list of `EditorFactories` in our current implementation; it could alternatively be specified by the user or supplied through a configuration file.

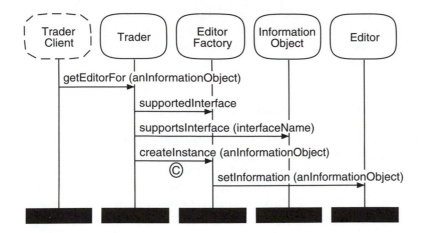

Figure 11.3

Activity for selecting and instantiating and editor

The Trading activity finds and instantiates an editor, given an `InformationObject`. One possible sequence of events is illustrated in the scenario of Figure 11.3:

1 `getEditorFor`. The `TraderClient` supplies the `Trader` with `InformationObject` and asks for a suitable editor.

2 `supportedInterface`/`supportsInterface`. The `Trader` traverses its `EditorFactory` list in priority sequence. It first asks an `EditorFactory` for the name of its required interface. It then asks the given `InformationObject` if it supports this interface. If the answer is `false`, the `Trader` continues the search.

3 `createInstance`. The first `EditorFactory` which answers `true` is asked to create an editor instance and to initialize it with the given `InformationObject` as the model.

4 `setInformation`. The `EditorFactory` creates a new editor instance and initializes it with the specified `InformationObject`.

A variant of this activity lets the `Trader` collect the names of all technically acceptable editors and invites the user to indicate his or her preference before the editor is instantiated.

Selecting the editor

In our first trader implementation, we presented a list of applicable editors to the user and invited him or her to select one of them. This proved exceedingly tedious, and we quickly created a second version of the trader which automatically selected a default editor and instantiated it. This proved too inflexible, and our third and current version normally selects a default editor automatically, but also has an escape command which lets the user select any applicable editor.

This description of the trading mechanism illustrates the separation of concern inherent in role modeling. The object that plays the `Trader` role in our system is a globally available object that plays a number of other roles, such as `Transaction Manager`, `Persistent Store Manager`, and `Clipboard Manager`. It would clearly

Objects typically play several roles

be confusing if we were to describe all of these roles simultaneously. We can also see that it is easy to discuss the trading mechanism in the context of all the participating roles, and it is nice to know that we can map these roles onto actual objects in any way we please.

11.3 THE OORAM COMPOSITION SYSTEM

IN A NUTSHELL

An OOram composition system (OOCS) controls the creation of object structures by composition. The idea is that given a seed object, an OOCS schema specifies the types of the objects that can be attached to it. One type is selected and instantiated, and the new object is attached to the seed. The composition proceeds by choosing new seed objects, selecting the type of a new addition, instantiating it, and attaching it to the growing structure.

System creation by composition

Figure 11.4 illustrates that we use a special work process when we create a system by composition. The *System User model* describes the system environment as in the normal programming case. The *System Requirements model* has been modified into an OOCS schema. An OOCS schema is not only a description of the world as seen by the end user community; it is also a precise and complete definition of the system. (It abides by the so-called 100% rule.) In this sense, the schema language is like a programming language. The difference is that the schema language builds on a few, simple notions which yield powerful leverage within its designated application area.

Database technology gives leverage through restricted structure

A database system provides a framework for representing information in the form of structured data. Its strengths and weaknesses are closely related to the way this is done. The first databases stored data in the form of trees; the relationships between data elements were all *consist of—part of* relations. Later, databases supported a general graph structure. They could be traversed along the

Figure 11.4

Models on all levels may be composed from simpler base models

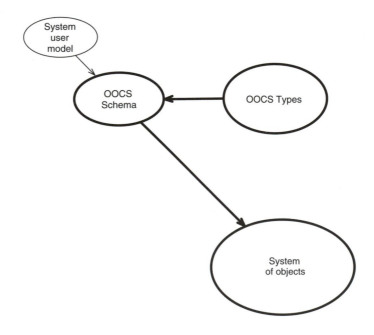

ADVANCED REUSE BASED ON OBJECT INSTANCES

My wife has been working as a database manager for a number of years. One of her reactions when helping me with this book was frustration. Database technology has been maturing slowly, so that she now can draw the conceptual schema of a new application on a computer screen and push a button. The finished program is generated correctly and automatically, and it works immediately, every time! No detailed coding, no intricate bugs to track down. She felt that object orientation would mean returning to the old days, when she spent most of her time coding and debugging, working through the night to find the last bug before system installation, and spending more nights fighting fires to keep the system operational.

Nobody should replace a mature technology with a new one without good reason. The new technology may be more fashionable, but pressing requirements that cannot be satisfied by the current technology should be the only acceptable reason. Psychologists claim that we only ask for things that we believe to be feasible [Aronson 72], and we must be careful to read *pressing requirements* as *real requirements*, not *perceived requirements*.

The second lesson is that to any informatician, it is traumatic to move outside the boundaries of an established conceptual framework with its mature tool support. But we must admit that any conceptual framework has its limitations and that the pressures of real requirements sometimes force us to exceed them. There are basically two ways to achieve this. One is to add special programs outside the conceptual framework: we could, for example, write special user interface programs which access the database without being part of it. The other way is to extend the conceptual framework so that the desired functionality is within its new boundaries.

relations, which could be of any kind. The current vogue is relational databases, where all data are organized in various *tables*.

A database system consists of the following parts:

1 A conceptual framework which defines the principles for database structuring. Examples: tree structure, graph structure, or tables. The conceptual framework also defines the types of the elements that can be stored in the structure. They are often collected in *records* that consist of a sequence of data items such as strings, numbers, dates, etc.

2 Means for specifying and recording the database schema. The schema defines the structure of the database and its elements in user-related terms.

3 Means for storing and managing data according to the rules and constraints specified in the schema.

4 Means for retrieving data from the database. This includes finding the required data and presenting them in a suitable form.

5 A program which manages the database at runtime.

Conceptual schemas are well known in the database community. They describe the semantic relationships between data items arising from relationships in the "real world" of the problem domain. A conceptual schema can be used to specify a customized information system, and programming in the traditional sense can often be avoided altogether.

Relational databases offer a small, fixed set of reusable data types

A conceptual schema specifies the system in terms of predefined data types; types such as `String`, `Date`, and `Number` are typically available. A `Person` could, for example, be defined as `{Name (String), Address (String), BirthDate (Date), GrossIncome (Number)}`. A `Person` is thus defined as a tuple of attributes; each attribute is specified by a name taken from the problem domain and a type selected from the predefined types. It is possible to specify more complex structures and impose constraints on these structures. A `Department` can be specified as having `Members` and a `Manager`. `Members` and `Managers` should be `Persons`, and the structure may be constrained so that there is at most one `Manager` per `Department` and the `Manager` is a `Member` of the same `Department`.

The set of available data types is fixed, and therefore is considered to be an integral part of the database system. We prefer to think of data types as reusable programs, because we can then establish an analogy to an object system with an extensible set of available types. The database system builder has created programs for these reusable types; and the application analyst uses them.

Extensible conceptual frameworks

Object technology seems very promising as a vehicle for extensible conceptual frameworks. We can add behavior to the static data of the conventional database. And we can replace the fixed domains of the database tables with object types, and thus get an extensible database system.

We should not get carried away by these possibilities. It is a sobering thought that the successful conceptual frameworks created over the past fifty years can be counted on one hand: the activity network, the database, and the spreadsheet come to mind. The successful introduction of a simple, powerful, and widely applicable conceptual framework is clearly not a routine matter.

Object-oriented database is not a candidate

Notice that we do not regard the object-oriented database as a viable competitor to the relational database. The object-oriented database is too general; it can be used to represent anything and cannot be used without low level programming. True competitors to the relational database will have to restrict their scopes to enable effective, high level system specification and generation tools. The object-oriented database has to add a conceptual schema layer to compete with the relational database.

Conceptual foundation for the object schema

The choice of a conceptual framework is critical to the success of a new composition system. Just as for database schemas, many different kinds of object schemas are conceivable.

We have practical experience with one possible choice that we call the *OOram composition system* (OOCS). The basic building blocks are objects that have the common characteristic that they can be linked together into different structures. These object structures are described generically in an OOCS schema in terms of an extensible set of object types called OOCS types. The "atom" of an OOCS schema is the OOCS entity, which associates a name taken from the problem domain with an existing OOCS type.

OOCS schema is a decision tree

The OOCS schema controls the composition of the system of objects in Figure 11.4. The schema is a kind of *decision tree*. Given an object, what are the types of the objects we may attach to it and what do the users call these parts? One of the possible types is selected, instantiated, and attached to the object structure.

This structure can, in principle, be any object structure. The general structure is realized as a tree with cross references. The tree is controlled by the OOCS schema, and the cross references are created algorithmically. For example, the schema creator can specify that the cells of a table should contain `Text` or `Pictures`. The final binding of each cell to an appropriate column and row is done programatically.

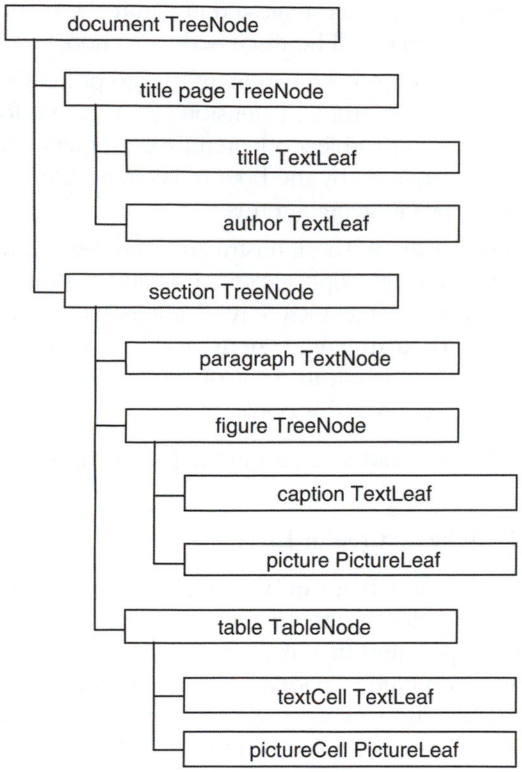

Figure 11.5
Simplified OOCS schema for a document

Let us consider a Document as an example of a problem domain, and let us model the Document as a structure of constituent parts as illustrated in Figure 11.5. OOCS entities in bold, OOCS types in italics. A document consists of a title page and sections; a title page consists of title and author, etc. This structure consists of 11 different entities. It is constructed from just four different object types: TreeNode, TextLeaf, PictureLeaf, and TableLeaf.

A dream

All living tissues are built from a family of chemical compounds called proteins. A protein is a complex molecule which is composed of amino acids. There are just 32 different amino acids, and all forms of life are composed from these 32 building blocks. (This is the chemistry aspect; we ignore a host of other aspects.) Now, consider that we might be able to create 32 different objects which we could use to compose data systems as varied as life itself!

The OOram composition system gives rise to a value chain with four layers, as shown in Figure 11.6 (value chains were discussed in detail in Chapter 10):

The OOCS value chain

1 *End user layer.* The end users create value when they add, retrieve, and remove objects in their OOCS system.

2 *OOCS schema creator layer.* The domain analyst who defines an OOCS schema may work according to the suggestions given in Chapter 7. The results will be expressed as OOCS schemas rather than as role models, and the imple-

mentation will be automatic, as suggested in Figure 11.4. The technical aspects of creating OOCS schemas will be discussed in Section 11.3.1.

3 *OOCS type implementor layer.* An important feature of the OOram composition system is that it is truly extensible. Extensions come in the form of new OOCS types. These are created by object-oriented programmers who base their work on the frameworks provided by the bottom layer. Section 11.3.2 describes the creation of OOCS types in general terms.

4 *Infrastructure creator layer.* The infrastructure needed to support the OOram composition system is quite sophisticated. It includes a module which exports a reusable framework to the OOCS type implementor, safe editors for the OOCS schema creator, a runtime system, and appropriate composition tools for the end users. The technical detail of this module is a specialized topic which is outside the scope of this book.

We will discuss the two middle layers in the following subsections.

11.3.1 The OOCS Schema Creator Layer

Figure 11.5 shows a structure that can be modeled using the OOram composition system. We saw that the eleven different entities of a document could be realized by only four OOCS types, and that alternative structures could be specified. But the notation used in the figure is inadequate for a complete OOCS schema specification, because there is no way to specify constraints as to sequencing and cardinalities. We will now describe a solution that actually works in practice.

We start with an application pattern (a list of instructions), before describing the nature of the OOCS schema in more detail (a logical map).

11.3.2 List of Instructions: OOCS Schema Creation

When to use It is appropriate to create an OOCS schema if the world as perceived by the users can be modeled as a structure of available OOCS type instances.

Problem The schema creator is to specify rules for how the end user can compose object structures from predefined types. The rules should be in the form of a decision tree: given an object in a partially completed structure, the rules should specify all permitted extensions.

Solution An OOCS schema is a generic specification of object structures. It associates the users' concepts with existing OOCS types, and forms a foundation on which the end users can build and manipulate object structure instances.

Figure 11.6
The OOCS value chain

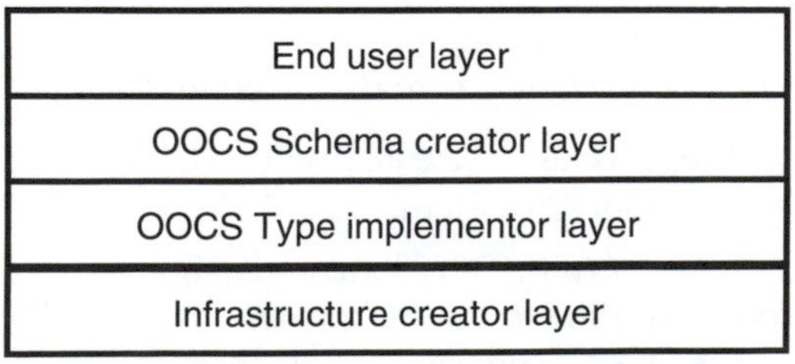

End user layer
OOCS Schema creator layer
OOCS Type implementor layer
Infrastructure creator layer

ADVANCED REUSE BASED ON OBJECT INSTANCES

You create an OOCS schema by following these operations (not necessarily in this sequence):

1 Identify the users of the OOCS schema: their goals, areas of competence, working habits, and preferences.

2 Identify the area of concern.

3 Analyze the user environment and information requirements.

4 Model the information as a tree of OOCS entities, giving them names that are meaningful to the users. Map each entity onto an OOCS type.

5 Inform the consumer community about the new system, motivate them to use it, train them, and make it available.

Necessary prerequisites are OOCS types for all entities; a schema editor that permits the specification only of legal structures; and the necessary runtime infrastructure, including OOram trading for editor selection and instantiation.

11.3.3 The Nature of OOCS Schemas

Objects are named, instantiated, and interconnected according to a generic object structure or *grammar* specified in an OOCS schema. The schema is in many ways an object-oriented parallel to the conceptual schemas used to describe relational databases. Both are used to model interesting information, and both obey the 100% rule, which means that a schema contains sufficient information for the automatic generation of the application program. But there are three important differences:

The OOCS schema

1 The relational model organizes information in a set of tables; the OOCS schema organizes information in an object structure.

2 The selection of available domains in the relational model is fixed; the set of available OOCS types is extensible.

3 The relational schema defines all legal data structures, and the database has to be restructured if the schema is changed. The OOCS schema controls object structure editing by defining legal object insertions and deletions. The object structure survives schema changes without restructuring.

Figure 11.7 is a semantic view of the OOCS schema elements, and Figure 11.8 shows an example OOCS schema. The schema elements are as follows:

1 The OOCS entity represents all objects that occupy a corresponding position in an object structure. An OOCS entity corresponds to a user concept and is given a user-defined name. A document object is at the root of Figure 11.8. A document contains titlePage, paragraph, figure table, and section. A figure contains caption and drawing.

2 The OOCS type represents the type of the objects that may occupy the position of the associated schema entity. It is an abstract way of specifying the class of these objects. The TreeNode OOCS type is mapped onto a class and instantiated to represent document, titlePage, figure, table, or section. (A TreeNode is an object which can play the role of node in a tree structure and which does not have any special attributes.) The TextNode OOCS type is mapped onto a class and instantiated to represent title, author, paragraph, or caption. (The TextNode class can be a subclass of the TreeNode class having a text attribute.)

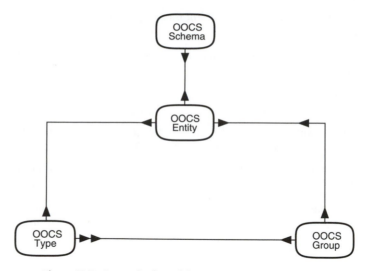

Figure 11.7 Semantic view of the OOCS schema notion

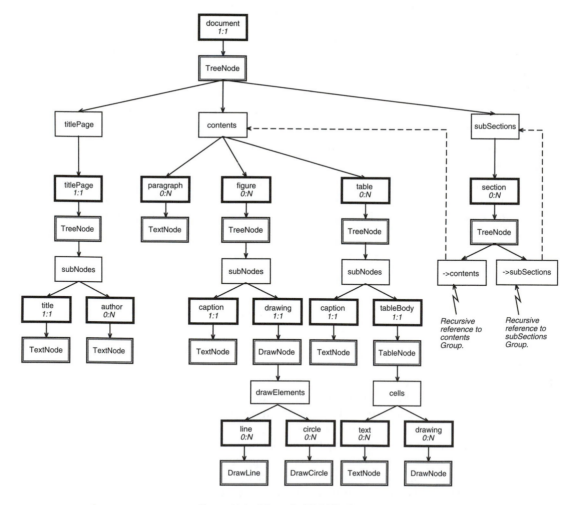

Figure 11.8 View of of OOCS schema

ADVANCED REUSE BASED ON OBJECT INSTANCES

3 The *OOCS group* provides the sequencing mechanism for the schema. The OOCS entities defined under each group can be inserted only *behind* the entities of the groups in front of it, and *in front of* the groups following it. In Figure 11.8, all `titlePage` objects will be in front of all `contents` objects, which will be in front of all `section` objects. OOCS entities defined under the same OOCS group can be inserted in any sequence. In our example, `paragraphs`, `figures`, and `tables` may be inserted in any order. `sections` can be inserted only after all the `contents`.

OOCS entities have a number of attributes which specialize the OOCS type. *Entity attributes* An important attribute is the cardinality, which it constrains the number of permitted instances and is displayed in the diagram as *minimum count : maximum count*. We must have exactly one `titlePage`, with exactly one `title`. We may have any number of `author` objects. `author` and `title` belong to the same group; `author` objects can therefore precede and follow the single `title` object. Notice that the schema controls editing operations and does not prescribe all permissible object structures. Modification of an entity cardinality will therefore influence only permissible editing operations, and will not affect existing object structures.

We have not shown other attributes here, but real systems will include attributes for setting default object values, for giving hints about the printing of the objects, etc.

Entity, type, and group objects may be specified as references to similar nodes *Recursive* somewhere else in the diagram; this permits the definition of recursive structures. *definitions* In our example, the `contents` of a `document` may be any mixture of `paragraph`, *permitted* `figure`, and `table`. The `section` group follows the `contents` group, and a `section` has a `contents` group followed by a new level of `subSection` group.

11.3.4 The OOCS Type Implementor Layer

An OOCS type is a building block that the end user may instantiate at his or her discretion, attach to an object structure, and edit. An OOCS type instance is illustrated in Figure 11.9. It is an object, or a cluster of objects, with a plug to attach it to a socket in the existing object structure. It may also have one or more sockets

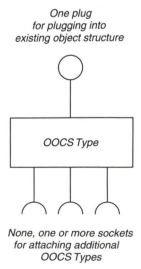

One plug
for plugging into
existing object structure

OOCS Type

None, one or more sockets
for attaching additional
OOCS Types

Figure 11.9

The OOCS type

for attaching additional OOCS type instances. Most of the common OOCS type functionality is captured in a framework, so that the application programmer can focus on the application-specific problems.

The problems   The following problems have to be solved:

1 *Semantic correctness.* The user should be able to construct a semantically meaningful object structure by successively selecting and instantiating user-defined concepts and attaching the instances to the object structure.

2 *Syntactic correctness.* The user should be allowed to attach only objects that will cooperate properly; program failures caused by improper object structures cannot be tolerated.

3 *Programming an OOCS type.* Each of the user-defined concepts must be associated with an existing class.

4 *Editor selection.* The user should be able to edit the attributes of the instantiated OOCS types.

Semantic Correctness

Two levels of semantic correctness   There are two levels of semantic correctness in the OOram composition system architecture:

1 *Human-level semantic correctness is the responsibility of the modeler.* On the human level, the OOCS schema should faithfully describe the notions of the user community. It is clearly the responsibility and *raison d'etre* of the OOCS schema creator to ensure that the model is correct in this sense.

2 *Technical-level semantic correctness should be enforced automatically.* On the technical level, semantic correctness means that the users' object structure should conform to the OOCS schema. The OOram Composition System infrastructure implements a somewhat weaker constraint: it checks all insertions and removals of OOCS type instances against the OOCS schema. This means that changing the OOCS schema does not cause changes in existing information. For example, if we were to modify the OOCS schema of Figure 11.8 so that the cardinality of the author entity was *1:1*, old documents with none or multiple authors would still be valid. But the user would not be allowed to create a new document without an author, and would not be permitted to remove the last author from an old document.

There are two reasons why we did it this way. One is that we do not know an algorithm that will intelligently transform an existing object structure to make it conform to the notions of a new OOCS schema. Another is that we do not want to rewrite history. Users may change their minds about their object structures, but the old structures were created under the old assumptions, and should be retained unchanged in the archives.

You may want a different solution   Our reasons may not be your reasons, and you may want a different solution. We believe that whatever the solution, the main responsibility for technical correctness should rest with the infrastructure creator, because the implementation of model conformance is a hard problem which should be solved once and for all.

Syntactic Correctness

A large subset of all object structures will operate without error. Their objects will receive messages as needed, and messages sent to collaborators will be handled correctly. We say that these systems are syntactically correct; the word *syntax* here alludes to the composition of OOCS type instances.

Syntactically correct programs do not crash

The plugs and sockets of Figure 11.9 are typed to ensure syntactic correctness. In our implementation, the OOCS types are given unique names, and the OOCS type implementor is fully responsible for ensuring that plugs and sockets with compatible names can be safely connected. Other schemes could be based on message signatures or mathematical descriptions of the interactions, but we have elected to keep our scheme as simple as possible.

A name denotes an OOCS type

Our OOCS types are organized in a type hierarchy so that a plug of a given type can be plugged into a socket with the same type or one of its subtypes. The OOCS types of the document example in Figure 11.8 are given in Figure 11.10 (the hierarchy is indicated by indentation).

```
TreeObject
    TreeNode
        DrawNode
    TextLeaf
    DrawElement
        DrawCircle
        DrawLine
    TableNode
```

Figure 11.10

Example OOCS type hierarchy

The OOCS type implementor must specify the types of the component's plug and sockets as part of the programming activity described in the next section.

Programming an OOCS Type

The OOCS type creator is responsible for the application-specific aspects of the component, and must write the appropriate programs. The infrastructure creator provides a framework which the OOCS type creator *must* specialize to create a specific component. Common functionality is defined in the base classes of the framework, and the framework also describes a typical work process and relevant constraints.

The OOCS schema assumes that all objects are organized within a tree structure. The role model is shown in Figure 11.11. We see that the root object of a

OOCS schema defines tree structure

Figure 11.11

Schema role model

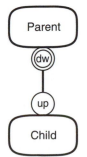

Figure 11.12
Schema base
model

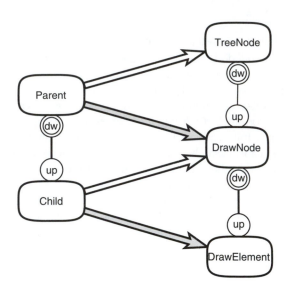

permissible structure must be able to play the Parent role; the leaf objects must be able to play the Child role; and all intermediate objects must be able to play both roles.

The interfaces on the dw (down) and up ports define messages for traversing the structure, for maintaining the two-way links when inserting and removing nodes, for duplicating a subtree, etc.

OOCS types
derived

All OOCS types are derived from the schema base model. The role model for a drawing application may, for example, be derived from the base model as illustrated in Figure 11.12. The base model is first used to synthesize the up plug of the DrawNode, and then applied again to synthesize the the relation between the DrawNode and its DrawElements.

OOCS type
implementor
must declare
socket types

The OOCS type creator writes a class for each OOCS type, and makes the type known in a class initialization message. He also declares the names and types of the sockets as exemplified in Figure 11.13. (SN denotes the schema group name, CT denotes OOCS type name).

Editor Selection

The infrastructure uses the object trading described in Section 11.2 to select and instantiate editors for the objects of different OOCS types.

The OOCS type implementor must make sure that a suitable editor is available for a new OOCS type. He or she may have to program a new one. This is a sep-

Figure 11.13
OOCS type
structure

```
TreeObject
      TreeNode
             SN subNodes     CT TreeObject
      TextLeaf
      DrawNode
             SN drawElements      CT DrawElement
      DrawElement
          DrawLine
          DrawCircle
      TableNode
          SN cells     CT TreeNode
```

arate activity which is basically an application of the tool framework described in Chapter 9, with a few extensions to ensure compatibility with the OOCS schema infrastructure.

11.4 OBJECT DUPLICATION

You may essentially create new objects in one of two ways: you can create a new instance of a class, or you can create a copy of an existing master object. While all instances of a class are created equal, the copy of an object will reflect the state of the master at the time of duplication. So if you want an object which is exactly as specified by the programmer, use instantiation. If you want an object which reflects information accumulated at runtime, use duplication.

IN A NUTSHELL

As computer programmers, we tend to focus on writing code for new programs. But we should not forget that the cheapest and safest way to produce a particular object structure is to copy a validated master. Figure 11.14 illustrates this. The master objects are first instantiated from the relevant classes and processed to give them the required attributes. They are later duplicated, and the copied objects are linked into the system of objects.

An alternative way of creating new objects

A facility for the duplication of selected material is an important part of almost all user interfaces. Duplication is also a powerful technique for the production of software; the PC revolution would be unthinkable without program duplication, packaging, and distribution. In the case study of Chapter 12, we argue that the instantiation, processing, storing, and duplication of master object structures will be an effective technique in the industrial production of customized software.

The problem

At first glance, duplication seems to be a simple and intuitively obvious operation. In any given situation, it will be quite clear what should be copied and what

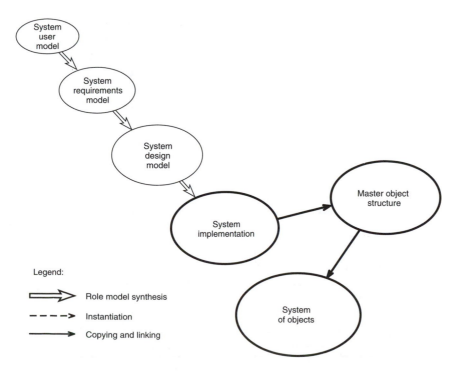

Figure 11.14

Structures of objects may be created by duplicating a master structure

should be left as it is. But this first glance is very misleading, because *copy* means different things under different circumstances—the difference being in how we handle referenced objects.

Just consider the copying of an array object containing pointers to a number of element objects. Do we want the copy to be another array object pointing to the same elements, or do we also want to copy the elements? And how do we want to copy the elements?

The general problem is illustrated in the object structure of Figure 11.15. Which objects should be copied together with the one in heavy outline? The answer clearly depends on the semantics of the object structure and the intentions of the user.

The solution   The duplication of object structures can pose serious problems to the programmer, and he or she may be hard put to create duplication programs that provide the "obvious" results in in all cases. This problem nicely illustrates both the power and the weakness of the distributed nature of object-oriented systems.

The power results from our ability to create programs that are valid for a wide variety of object structures, and that work correctly with any object as the selected

Figure 11.15

What should be the result of asking the heavily outlined object for its copy?

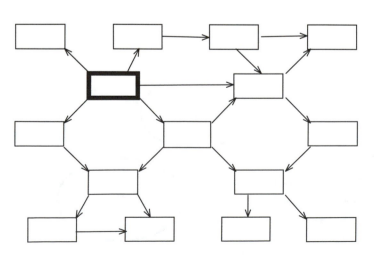

master. The weakness is that the algorithm will be distributed among the objects. There is no main program which sees and knows everything. Every object must be able to play the role of a master; every object must be able to play the role of a subobject that is to be copied together with the master; every object must be able to play the role of a copy; and every object must be able to play the role of an environment object which is to remain uncopied. Even seasoned programmers must be prepared for nasty surprises when a user attempts to copy an unexpected substructure.

We do not believe that a return to procedural programming will solve the problem, because the difficulties stem from the specification rather than the technology. We have traded the increased power of new technology for increased functionality, flexibility, and generality, and strained the programmers' capabilities to their limits.

No sane manager will ask a procedural programmer to create an algorithm that will copy an unspecified part of an unspecified structure. Even with object orientation, there is no magic. The only reason we can get away with such an open specification is that we can leave parts of the solution unspecified, to be filled in by the application classes, where the nature of the objects is known.

A framework candidate

We rephrase the problem as follows: *Can we create a framework that protects the application programmer (and the users) against nasty surprises?* The nasty surprises we have experienced all stem from unforeseen side effects. Our solution is that we let framework programs take care of the structural and interobject aspects of duplication, and leave the simple problem of duplicating individual objects to the application programmer.

Rephrasing the problem again, *we want to create a framework for the duplication of objects and object structures that limits the task of the application programmer to overriding specific methods where he or she needs to consider only one class at the time*. We have been through several cycles of solutions and nasty surprises, the surprises being caused by steadily more exotic problems. We will describe our current solution in Section 11.4.3, but we also will discuss some simpler algorithms which are useful in many common cases:

1 shallowCopy, which just copies a single object.

2 postCopy, which is a way to let each duplicated object recursively determine which of its instance variables should be copied.

3 structureCopy, which is our general algorithm for duplicating part of a structure of interconnected objects.

4 deepCopy, which recursively copies an object and all the objects referenced by its instance variables. This is a dangerous operation that we strongly advise you to avoid.

11.4.1 shallowCopy—Too Simple in Most Cases

The simplest case is shallowCopy. It creates a new object of the same class as the original which references exactly the same objects. This is illustrated in the Figure 11.16. (Heavy lines indicate the original structure; gray lines indicate the shallow copy.)

shallowCopy may cause bugs which are hard to track down. In the past, we have experienced trouble with Rectangle which used to have *shallowCopy* as its default *copy* operation. Rectangle objects have two instance variables, as depicted in Figure 11.16: origin, which is a Point object defining the upper left

shallowCopy of a Rectangle

Figure 11.16

shallowCopy
copies the object
and retains all
references
unchanged

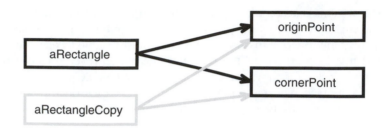

corner, and corner, which is a `Point` object defining the lower right corner. `shallowCopy` of a `Rectangle` master object yields a new `Rectangle` object which shares the origin and corner objects with the master. Do you see the possible problem?

A mysterious side effect

Consider that you have a window with a number of views. The bounds of each view within the window are stored as a `Rectangle` object. Open a new window as a copy of the first one. Rearrange the views of the copied window by modifying the x and y values of the origin and corner `Point`s of their bounds, e.g., by the code bounds `origin putXY (50, 25)`. The original window is also rearranged! Rearrange the views of the window copy by replacing the origin and corner `Point`s with new `Point`s, e.g., bounds `putOrigin ((Point new) putXY (50, 25))`. The original window is unchanged!

11.4.2 `postCopy`—A Default Duplication Algorithm

A simple recursive algorithm

A new duplication algorithm was introduced in Objectworks\Smalltalk version 4.0. It is similar to the default algorithm we have been using internally at Taskon for many years, and works satisfactorily in most cases. The idea is to create a `shallowCopy` of the original object, and then ask the copy to "do the right thing" with its own references.

The default copy method in class `Object`, the mother of all classes, is now as follows:

copy
    ^self shallowCopy postCopy

The method `postCopy` in class `Object` does nothing:

postCopy
    " *Finish doing whatever is required, beyond a shallowCopy, to implement 'copy'. Answer the receiver. This message is only intended to be sent to the newly created instance.*
        Subclasses may add functionality, but they should always do super postCopy first. "
    ^self

The application programmer overrides the `postCopy` method in the derived class. The responsibility of this method is to replace references to other objects with references to their copies wherever appropriate. Our `Rectangle` problem is

ADVANCED REUSE BASED ON OBJECT INSTANCES

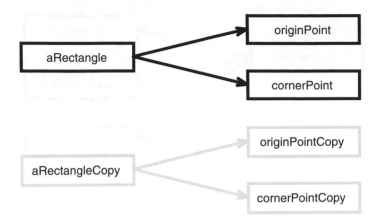

Figure 11.17

postCopy does
the right thing

now easily fixed, as shown in the following method. The result is illustrated in Figure 11.17. Heavy lines indicate the original structure; gray lines indicate the copy.

Rectangle (copying)
postCopy
```
        super postCopy.
        origin := origin copy.
        corner := corner copy
```

We will extend our example slightly to illustrate that an object may leave certain references unchanged. We color the Rectangle by extending the object with two variables: a variable holding a color index and a variable pointing to a Palette which holds an Array of colors. The Rectangle gets its color by asking the Palette for the color corresponding to its color index. We assume that the Palette should be shared by the master Rectangle and its copy. The result is illustrated in Figure 11.18, and the code is given below. Heavy lines indicate the original structure; gray lines indicate the copy.

We may not want to make a copy of all instance variables

Rectangle (copying)
postCopy
```
        super postCopy.
        origin := origin copy.
        corner := corner copy.
        palette := palette.
```

Notice the dummy statement, which does nothing with the reference to the Palette. This is a Taskon convention: every instance variable should be assigned a value in the postCopy method, to show that the programmer has considered it. If a new instance variable is added to a class, our automatic quality checker will flag that its postCopy method is incomplete. (The same applies to some other methods, such as initialize and release.)

The postCopy algorithm works fine if each object involved knows what to do with all its instance variables, but it is insufficient if a wider context is required to determine the right thing to do. We then have to use the structureCopy operation described in the next section.

Figure 11.18

postCopy will
not copy a shared
object

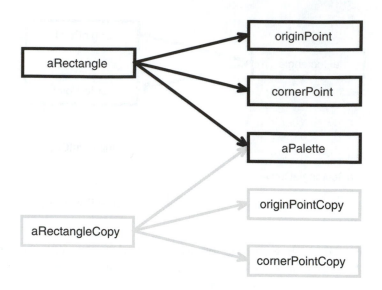

11.4.3 **structureCopy** for the General Case

Copying a part
of a directed
graph

This algorithm treats a directed graph roughly as a tree structure cross reference. It assumes that we know how to start from a given root object and traverse the structure to find all objects that should always be copied. It further assumes that with this knowledge available, we can identify the pointer variables that need to be modified. The algorithm is similar to postCopy, except that we now collect all copied objects before finalizing the operation.

Figure 11.19 shows an example. The subset of objects to copy depends on the selected root. We have selected object B, and want to copy objects D and E as well. We would have copied the whole structure if we had selected object A as the root, and only a single object if we had selected object D or E.

(The primary object to be copied is shown in heavy outline; the secondary objects which shall also be copied are shown in light outline; environment objects

Figure 11.19

Structure
duplication

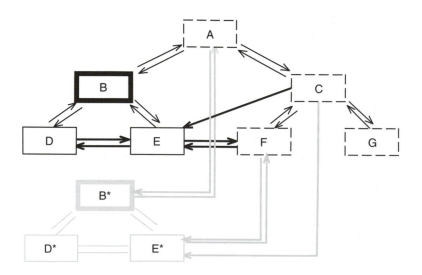

which shall not be copied are shown dashed. The duplicate objects and references are shown gray.)

The algorithm has two phases:

1 *Identify objects to be duplicated and create shallow copies.* Traverse the master structure of objects. For each object, create a `shallowCopy` and save it in a dictionary that associates each master object with its copy. In Figure 11.19, the dictionary associates objects B, D, and E with the corresponding copies B*, D*, and E*.

   The framework takes care of structure traversal, object duplication, and accumulation. The application programmer overrides the method `objectsToBeCopied`, which returns a `Collection` of instance variables that should always be copied if the receiver object is copied. For the example in Figure 11.19, the method will return (D, E) in object B and empty collections in objects D and E. The cross references are ignored in this phase.

2 *Complete the copy operation in each object in the context of the set of duplicated objects.* Each copied object is asked to fix its references given the dictionary of duplicated objects.

   The application programmer must override the method `completeDuplication`, which has one parameter: the dictionary of copied objects. This algorithm assumes that this information will be sufficient to determine what to do with the different references. There are three cases:

   - *Copied-to-copied.* The reference is replaced with a reference to the corresponding copy. For example, after the `shallowCopy`, object D* will have a reference to object E. This reference will be replaced with a reference to the corresponding copy found in the object dictionary, in this case E*. If this is a two-way pointer, we also inform the other object, so that it can establish the reverse pointer. This is consistent with Case 2, but implies that the method must tolerate that the reference has already been modified: e.g., object D* will establish both reference D*-E* and E*-D*. When we get to D*, it has to recognize this and do nothing.

   - *Copied-to-uncopied.* The reference is left unchanged. For example, after `shallowCopy`, object E* will have a reference to object F, which is left unchanged. If this is a two-way pointer, object E* must inform object F, so that the latter can establish the reverse pointer.

   - *Uncopied-to-copied.* This is the case where an environment object should have a pointer to the copy, but the copy does not know about it. In our example, object C should establish a pointer to E*, but neither E nor E* knows C. This case is not covered by the general framework. The application programmer has to take special action, presumably in the `completeDuplication` method of object B.

We could use this algorithm to duplicate the colored rectangle discussed in the previous subsection. The application programmer has to write the two duplication methods in the `ColoredRectangle` class:

Revisiting the colored rectangle

ColoredRectangle (copying)
addObjectsToBeCopiedTo: objectSet
    super **addObjectsToBeCopiedTo: objectSet.**
    objectSet add: origin.
    objectSet add: corner.

```
ColoredRectangle (copying)
completeDuplication: objectDictionary
        super completeDuplication: objectDictionary.
        origin := objectDictionary at: origin ifAbsent: [origin].
        corner := objectDictionary at: corner ifAbsent: [corner].
        palette := objectDictionary at: palette ifAbsent: [palette].
        colorIndex := colorIndex.
```

Two comments: both methods call the corresponding method in the super-class (using super ...) to give it a chance to do its part of the algorithm. The `completeDuplication` method has a very general format: the reference is replaced with a reference to the copy if it is defined; it is otherwise left unchanged. More specialized code may be needed if the semantics of the problem warrants it.

The application programmer need not override the framework methods

The main methods for structure duplication can be defined in the class `Object`, and need not be modified by the application programmers. We include a sketch of these methods for your perusal:

```
Object (copying)
structureCopy
        " A client sends this message to obtain a structured copy of the receiver. "
        | objectDictionary |
        objectDictionary := IdentityDictionary new.
        self collectDuplicatesIn: objectDictionary.
        objectDictionary values do:
                [:copiedObject | copiedObject completeDuplication: objectDictionary].


Object (copying)
collectDuplicatesIn: objectDictionary
        objectDictionary at: self put: self shallowCopy.
        objectSet := IdentitySet new.
        self addObjectsToBeCopiedTo: objectSet.
        objectSet do: [:subObject | subObject collectDuplicatesIn: objectDictionary].


Object (copying)
addObjectsToBeCopiedTo: objectSet
        ^self


Object (copying)
completeDuplication: objectDictionary
        ^self
```

11.4.4 deepCopy—A Dangerous Operation

An alternative is to use the deepCopy mechanism, which copies the object itself and all its collaborators recursively, as illustrated in Figure 11.20.

The recursive nature of deepCopy makes it unsuitable in many situations, and it can be quite devastating. Any circular object structure will lead to infinite recursion:

```
| arr |
arr := Array new: 1.
arr at: 1 put: arr.
arr deepCopy.
```

Our recommendation is that you never use deepCopy; use one of the other algorithms instead.

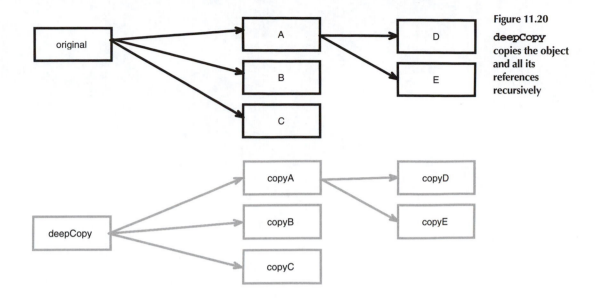

Figure 11.20
deepCopy
copies the object
and all its
references
recursively

CHAPTER 12

Case Study: Intelligent Network Services Organized in a Value Chain

CONTENTS

12.1   A Simple Case with an Extensible Solution   320

12.2   User Layer   326

12.3   Subscriber Layer   327

12.4   Service Provider Layer   329

12.5   Service Creator Layer   331

12.6   Service Constituent Creator Layer   334

12.7   Network Provider Layer   337

This chapter is written for the specially interested programmer. It illustrates the technical and organizational aspects of a specific value chain in some detail. We start by presenting a sample target system, and describe its objects and execution processes. We then discuss each layer in turn.

12.1   A SIMPLE CASE WITH AN EXTENSIBLE SOLUTION

IN A NUTSHELL

Providing telecommunication services is a very large operation having many actors. This case study describes a possible value chain and fills in details for a plain telephone service. We populate each of the six layers in the value chain and choose appropriate technology for each layer.

IN services were introduced in Chapter 10. We will now go into more detail. The value chain was shown in Figure 10.8, but we repeat it in Figure 12.1 for your convenience. The layers are as follows:

1 *User layer.* The user wants to use available services, and is responsible for selecting and invoking a service. The typical user wants to concentrate on his or her tasks, and should know a minimum of IN Service technology. Service interfaces should be as intuitive as possible, and provide only the functionality actually desired by each user.

   The work processes on the user layer are determined by the user's tasks and are outside the scope of this discussion.

2 *Subscriber layer.* The subscriber purchases a set of services on behalf of one or more users, pays for them, and is responsible for making the services available to his or her users. In private households, the subscriber is the user who enters into contract with the telecommunications provider and who pays the bills. In businesses, the subscriber will often be a facilities manager. The personal profile of the subscriber is similar to the user profile, but the professional subscriber may require somewhat more sophisticated facilities. The success criterion of the subscribers is that the users get to create *their* value, effectively, and effortlessly.

   The work processes on the subscriber layer are outside the scope of this discussion.

3 *Service provider layer.* The service provider has a license for activating IN service software for specified subscribers. We think of the service provider as the corner teleshop where consumers can buy regular services, but it could also be a professional customer consultant who sells specialized services to advanced corporations. The typical service provider is a sales clerk or customer consultant with fairly limited IN Service training, and should primarily be concerned with understanding customer needs and how they can be satisfied with available IN Service products. The success criterion is likely to be that as many users as possible use (and pay for) as many services as possible.

Figure 12.1
IN value chain

User layer
Subscriber layer
Service provider layer
Service creator layer
Service constituent creator layer
Network provider layer

INTELLIGENT NETWORK SERVICES

The main work processes on the service provider layer will be designed to support consulting and retail sales.

4   *Service creator layer.* The service creator has a license for defining IN service software and installing it in the telecommunications network. The service creator will currently be a Public Telephone Authority (PTA), but our model is open for several commercial service creator companies. The typical service creator should understand the realities of the marketplace and the needs of the service provider, and cannot be expected to be an expert in computer programming or the inner details of the IN technology. The success criterion is that the service provider constructs services that not only can be sold, but that actually will be used and create a revenue stream.

The main work processes on the service creator layer will involve collecting and analyzing market intelligence; specifying and defining products; and creating relevant documentation.

5   *Service constituent creator layer.* The service constituent creator has a license for producing software building blocks that may be configured into IN services. These software building blocks, called service constituents, are the reusable components used by the service creator to create service software. The typical service constituent creator is a computer programmer who specializes in some technical aspect of IN services. The service constituent creator will build on the results of the network providers and other service constituent creators, and will understand how these results can be applied to the problems at hand. The success criterion will be that the service creators can create all the services that are needed in the market, and that the service constituents are simply presented to the service creators, so that they can focus on the market and the products rather than the technology.

The main work processes on the service constituent creator layer will be crafted after some software life cycle model, such as the waterfall model or the spiral model [Boehm 88].

6   *Network provider layer.* The network provider is the party who provides the basic communication facilities used by the IN services. The network provider must also have facilities to control the integrity of the network and its services. The typical network provider person will be an expert in some aspect of communication switching technology. This is typically the responsibility of Public Telecommunications Authorities (PTAs). The network provider is, therefore, a large corporation possessing deep technical and commercial skills.

The main work processes on the network provider layer will be crafted to support the creation of very large, ultrareliable, distributed communication systems.

The actors' knowledge of Intelligent Networking technology varies from nothing, in the top layer, to expert, on the lower layers. Their interest in the subject varies correspondingly from the user, whose interests definitely lie somewhere else, to the network provider, whose professional life is centered on telecommunications technology. This must be reflected in the kind of facilities to be installed on the different layers, and hence also in the underlying technology. *Matching requirements to technology*

Seen from the perspective of a user, a service appears as something concrete which may be bought and used. Seen from the perspective of the IN system, a service is rather intangible; it is realized as a number of interacting objects. Some of these objects are specific to the service, while others are shared with other services. *No programming in four upper layers*

The specification of a computation, such as the execution of an IN service, is traditionally considered to be an exercise in computer programming. But computer programming is notoriously expensive, time consuming, and error-prone. This makes us take a much broader view, and we are actively searching for ways of specifying IN services that avoid programming. Possible means to achieve this without loss of flexibility are through parameterization of general objects, duplication of library objects and object structures, and instantiation controlled by conceptual schemas. When we do have to create new programs, the effort can be materially reduced by the proper application of frameworks and other reusable components.

What is programming?

Programming could be defined as the specification of a computation. System generation through parameterization, table-driven system generation, simple, application-specific visual generating tools, etc., would then all be classified as programming. We use *programming* in a more restricted sense, and limit it to mean the specification of a program in a programming language such as Eiffel, C++, or Smalltalk.

All reuse technologies needed for IN services

It was interesting and instructive to discover that all our reuse technologies found their proper places in the IN Service value chain. The highlights can be summarized as follows:

1 *User* and *subscriber layers*. If a service is appropriately designed, the two top layers may customize it by duplication and by supplying suitable parameters.

2 *Service provider layer*. The service provider specifies services for a customer in the form of a contract document. The document is edited on a syntax-directed editor controlled by an OOCS schema.

3 *Service creator layer*. The service creator specifies the universe of all possible services and combinations of services that may be sold by the service provider. The specification is in the form of an OOCS schema. The service provider defines the service entities and binds them to appropriate OOCS types. (Called *service constituents* in the IN community).

4 *Service constituent creator and network provider layers*. The service constituent creation and the network provider layers are the only layers involving programming in the traditional sense. Programming is minimized, however, through the application of frameworks. The deliverables are OOCS types.

An initial system

We will illustrate the nature of the IN value chain through a system that was demonstrated at TINA-93 [Ree 93]. The system was designed so that its operation could be demonstrated on a computer screen. The running system consisted of 18 objects—ridiculously simple in terms of telecommunications technology, but sufficient to illustrate how we match actors and technology in the IN value chain.

We will describe the operation of the running system in this section, and use it as a background for our subsequent discussion of the different layers.

The Plain Old Telephone service

The service in our initial system is what is affectionately known as POTS—Plain Old Telephone Service. *Person-A* wants to establish a telephone conversation connection to *Person-B*. It is the responsibility of the service to establish the connection between the parties. The service is dormant while *A* and *B* converse.

The service is again activated to take down the connection and arrange for charging when the conversation is complete. Our system focuses on the first phase: establishing the connection.

Our implementation separates POTS into two parts: an A service which is responsible for the calling end, and a B service which is responsible for the called end. This makes it possible to let the called party decide what to do with an incoming call: reject it, accept it, or direct it to specified equipment or to another user. We have implemented the following two service objects:

1   *Calling telephone service (Tel-A)*, which tries to establish a connection to *User-B*. The users are identified by their *userIDs* in the service domain, and the telephones are identified by their `accessPointIDs` in the switching domain.

2   *Called telephone service (Tel-B)*, which can accept or refuse the incoming request, forward the call to a third user, or route the call to one of a number of telephones associated with *user-B*. In the latter case, *user-B* may be thought of as a manager of several operators, for example, in a booking office. Each operator is characterized by a telephone with its own `accessPointID`, and *Tel-B* selects one of them to handle each incoming call.

A single object called *InvocationManager*, #102 `InvMngr`, is the main point of contact with the service domain for all users. This object delegates the management of each user's affairs to an *invocation analyzer* object associated with each user (#104 `Anlz-A` and #106 `Anlz-B`). Specifically, an invocation analyzer object holds a set of master service objects that represent all services available to its user.

Invocation manager and invocation analyzer are the main objects in the service domain

The public switched telecommunication network is an enormous distributed computer system; by direct dialing I can choose to connect to any one of some 200 million different B users. Many operators use equipment of different kinds, but all are interconnected into the one, coherent global communication system.

A virtual model of the switch for IN

The IN architecture (Figure 10.7) encapsulates this distributed and nonhomogeneous system and presents it to the service domain as a coherent service, accessible through common, high level interfaces.

One example of such an interface is a *network connection*, which enables an IN service object to order the interconnection of two or more access points in the switching domain. A network connection has one *connection point* and any number of *legs*; see Figure 12.2. Several telephones can be interconnected through legs which share a common connection point. A leg is an abstract wire with two termination points: the connection point and the socket in the wall which is identified by the `accessPointID` and is where you plug in your telephone.

The network connection point

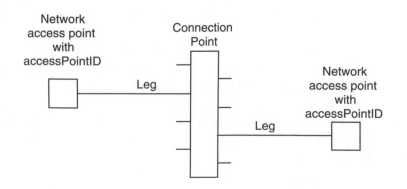

Network access point with accessPointID

Connection Point

Leg

Network access point with accessPointID

Leg

Figure 12.2

A network connection interconnects any number of network access points by legs which meet in a common connection point

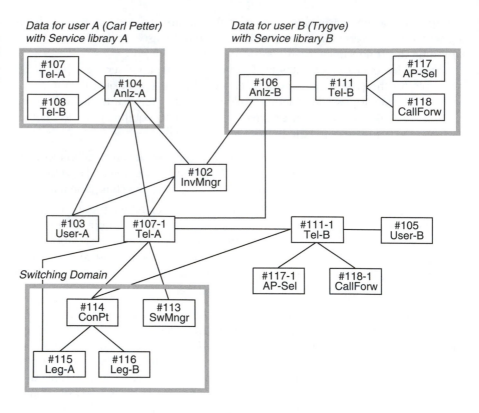

*18 objects in
the initial
system*

The initial object structure is shown in Figure 12.3. The users are represented by two user objects, #103 User-A and #105 User-B. #103 User-A is responsible for requesting a service (*Tel-A*) and initiating the invocation process, presumably through some user interface program inside the object. The #105 User-B object is responsible for accepting or refusing the requested call, as specified in the calling telephone service.

A typical invocation process is as follows:

1 The user object represents the user: think of it as an object which resides within the user's telephone. #103 User-A desires to establish a telephone service to User-B. It starts by asking the invocation manager #102 InvMngr for access to A's invocation analyzer. InvMngr returns a pointer to #104 Anlz-A.

2 #103 User-A then asks #104 Anlz-A for a calling telephone service. #104 Anlz-A checks its store of service objects, selects #107 Tel-A, installs a duplicate #107-1 Tel-A as the current active service object, and returns a pointer to this copy.

3 #103 User-A asks #107-1 Tel-A for a call to a user identified by its userID.

4 #107-1 Tel-A asks #102 InvMngr for access to the invocation analyzer of the user with the given userID, and gets a pointer to #106 Anlz-B.

5 #107-1 Tel-A asks #106 Anlz-B for its called telephone service. #106 Anlz-B checks its store of service objects, selects #111 Tel-B, installs a duplicate #111-1 Tel-B as the service object currently active for B, and returns a pointer to this copy.

Notice that the choice of calling service was done in an object belonging to A, while the choice of called service was done in an object owned by B. This permits detailed customization to the preferences of different users.

6 #107-1 Tel-A asks #111-1 Tel-B if it will accept a call. We assume the answer is YES.

7 #107-1 Tel-A asks the globally available manager of the switching domain, #113 SwMngr, for a connection point. The manager creates one, and returns a pointer to #114 ConnPoint.

8 #107-1 Tel-A asks #114 ConPt for a leg. #114 ConPt creates one, and returns a pointer to #115 Leg-A.

9 #107-1 Tel-A sets the accessPointID of user A in #115-Leg-A.

10 #107-1 Tel-A requests #111-1 Tel-B to establish a leg from #114 ConnPoint to the accessPointID of whichever telephone it wants to take the call.

11 #111-1 Tel-B is now free to select the called telephone in any way it chooses. In our initial implementation, #111-1 Tel-B may be initialized with any number of selectors, each selector containing a condition and an action. The condition can be on time of day, day of week, holiday/workday, etc. Two kinds of selectors provide two different kinds of actions: either selecting an access point belonging to user B, or forwarding the connection request to some other user. In Figure 12.3, only one selector of each kind is shown (#117 AP-Sel and #118 CallForw). The selectors are tested sequentially; the first with a satisfied condition will be activated. If none of the selectors are satisfied, a default telephone will be used.

12 If the call is to be completed by #111-1 Tel-B, #111-1 Tel-B uses its selected accessPointID and the connection point reference to establish a leg to the connection point.

13 The network connection in the switching domain is established, and the conversation can commence.

12.2 USER LAYER

IN A NUTSHELL

The user is the party who wants to use available services, and is responsible for the selection and invocation of a service. The invocation leads to the creation and installation of a copy of the relevant objects and the execution of the service. All remaining parameters must be bound by the user as part of the service invocation.

Current interfaces cumbersome

The cryptic codes to be used to activate current telephone services are printed on one of the first pages in the telephone directory. We have translated a few examples from our local telephone directory:

1 *Call Forward Unconditionally (CFU)*: wait for dialing tone, touch *21*, touch new number which is to receive call, terminate with #, wait for acknowledge tone, hang up. To cancel CFU: wait for dialing tone, dial #21#, wait for acknowledge tone, hang up.

2 *Call Forward on Busy (CFB)*: wait for dialing tone, touch *67*, touch new number which is to receive call, terminate with #, wait for acknowledge tone, hang up. To cancel CFB: wait for dialing tone, dial #67#, wait for acknowledge tone, hang up.

3 *Call Forward on no Reply (CFR)*: wait for dialing tone, touch *61*, touch new number which is to receive call, terminate with #, wait for acknowledge tone, hang up. To cancel CFR: wait for dialing tone, dial #61#, wait for acknowledge tone, hang up.

We would like to assume a simpler user interface: some of the users' telephones could have a switch with an associated warning light. A user leaving the office will throw the switch; this causes the warning light to come on and a CFU to a predefined number. When entering the office again, the user will return the switch to the off position, canceling the service and extinguishing the light. More advanced telephones could have a touch-sensitive screen that supported simple, yet powerful interaction with the user.

Invocation by trading and object duplication

In our initial system, an invocation analyzer object was allocated to each user. All services available to the user were stored in a library of master objects in the user's invocation analyzer object (encapsulated aggregation). The invocation analyzer was partially responsible for the following steps in the life cycle model:

1 *Activation.* The service is made available to the user by adding a service object to the set of services which is managed by the invocation analyzer object.

2 *Invocation.* The user's invocation analyzer object selects a suitable master service object in response to a request from the user (via some terminal equipment) or from a service object, duplicates it, and installs the copy for execution. Remaining open parameters, such as the new number which is to receive a forwarded call, must be bound before execution.

3 Object trading technology, described in Section 11.2, is used to assure that the selected service object is appropriate for the requesting client; object duplication is done according to the algorithms described in Section 11.4.

4 *Execution.* The selected service objects are responsible for service execution, but they are monitored by the invocation analyzer, which handles exceptions and service termination.

5 *Deactivation.* The invocation analyzer removes the service from its library of master service objects.

The user's production facility is defined by the subscriber. It consists of an (advanced) telephone which is permanently associated with the invocation analyzer object. The invocation analyzer object is loaded with objects for all services available to the user.

User production facilities

12.3 SUBSCRIBER LAYER

The subscriber purchases a set of services on behalf of one or more users, and is responsible for making the services available to them. The work of the subscriber involves selecting a desired service and making a copy of the relevant objects available to the user. Some of the service parameters may be bound as part of this process.

IN A NUTSHELL

We assume that the subscriber has a special terminal with bitmapped display, keyboard, and a pointing device. The subscriber could, for example, manage service availability to the individual users through a direct manipulation interface, as shown in Figure 12.4.

Possible user interface

This interface has one column for each user and one row for each available service. A cross in a cell indicates that the service is not available for the given user, presumably because the user's equipment does not support it. Other cells are touch sensitive: clicking in the cell causes the corresponding service to be activated (checked) or passivated (blank) for the given user. There is a *Customize* button for each service which may be customized through this interface. If the subscriber wants to customize a service, he clicks the Customize button, which causes a new interface to pop up. In this case, this interface will probably allow the subscriber to set the target for the switched CFU.

The subscriber is partly responsible for the activation and deactivation steps in the life cycle model. The subscriber is represented by an object in the IN system which holds an object for each of the services purchased by the subscriber. Applying the interface shown in Figure 12.4, the subscriber makes these services available to individual users.

Subscriber responsible for service activation and deactivation

1 *Activation.* A service is made available to the subscriber by adding a master service object to the set of service objects which is managed by the subscriber's management object. Some service parameters may be bound at this stage.

Figure 12.4

A possible subscriber tool

	User-1	User-2	User-3	User-4	User-5	
Switched CFU	+	✓	✓	✓		Customize
CFU					✓	
CFB			✓			
CFR	✓	✓	✓	✓		
Subscriber Service		+	+	+	+	

The service is later made available to the users by duplicating the service masters, binding parameters, and installing the copies as new masters in the users' service analyzer objects.

2 *Deactivation.* A service is made unavailable by removing the corresponding service objects from the subscriber manager object and the invocation analyzer objects of all the subscriber's users.

Subscribers were omitted from our initial system to keep it as simple as possible. You will, therefore, not find any subscriber objects in Figure 12.3.

The subscriber's production facilities

The subscriber production facility consists of some suitable equipment which supports the subscriber's tool, e.g., the one shown in Figure 12.4.

INTELLIGENT NETWORK SERVICES

12.4   SERVICE PROVIDER LAYER

IN A NUTSHELL

The service provider is an actor who is licensed to customize services and make them available to subscribers. The service provider selects services and service variants, and commands the instantiation of the necessary objects and their installation in the subscriber's management object (directly into the user's invocation analyzer object in our initial system, which does not have a subscriber layer).

The main responsibility of the service provider layer is to define subscribers and their services. An appropriate medium for this information is a *service contract document*, which may be printed (and signed), and which may be executed to cause the installation of the subscribers and their services in the service domain.

Possible user interface

The initial tool for creating this document is the *intelligent editor* shown in Figure 12.5. It permits the service provider to create any and all permissible service variants, but automatically prevents the creation of illegal combinations.

The tool in Figure 12.5 has two parts: The left margin gives a graphical representation of the structure. The rectangular symbols are OOCS entities; they represent the kinds of objects shown to the right. The small, black triangles represent *insertion points*, and indicate where the user can insert additional objects. An insertion point permits the insertion only of new objects which are appropriate at that point in the structure, as specified in the OOCS schema.

The tool edits a tree-structured model

The tool supports low level concepts such as text, graphics, and tables, as well as high level concepts such as IN services and access point selectors. A trading mechanism activates an appropriate editor when the user points inside one of the information objects in the right part of the tool. The tool permits *selective zooming*; the ellipsis after an object symbol indicates that the object presentation has been collapsed into a one-liner.

Figure 12.5 shows the editor when the service provider is defining the *Tel-B* service. The specification says that the network access points with IDs 222, 333, and 444 are to be selected in a round robin fashion Monday through Friday between 08:00 and 16:00. The hidden call forward selector specifies that all day

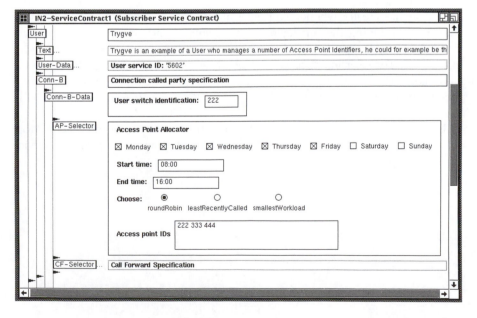

Figure 12.5
Editor for specifying the service contract document

Figure 12.6

Sample contract
document

The Teleshop
Date of issue: 22 September 1993
Subscriber Service Contract
Teleshop, Gaustadalléen 21, N-0371 Oslo 3 Norway.   Tel. + (47) 22 95 86 31

    Subscriber name: Manufacturer Inc
    Billing address: Drammensveien 1; Oslo
    Subscriber service ID: 56
    Subscriber Access Point IDs   #(111 222 333 444 555 666)

User: Carl Petter
Carl Petter is an example of a User who has a plain telephone connection,
he uses the Switch identifier 111.

Plain Old Telephone calling party specification
    Telephone A from Access Point ID: 111

Plain Old Telephone called party specification
    Telephone B from Access Point ID: 111

User: Trygve
Trygve has no Telephone A service, so he cannot place outgoing calls.

Plain Old Telephone called party specification
    Telephone B from Access Point ID: 222
    Access Point Allocation
        Weekday selection: #(#Monday #Tuesday #Wednesday #Thursday #Friday)
        Start time: 08:00
        End time: 16:00
        Choose: roundRobin
        Access point IDs: #(222 333 444 555 666)
    Call Forward Specification
        Weekday selection: #(#Saturday #Sunday)
        Start time: 00:00
        End time: 24:00
        Choose: roundRobin
        Forward Service IDs: #(5603)

Saturday and Sunday, incoming calls are to be forwarded to the user with userID 5601. In all other cases, the call is to be received in the default access point with accessPointID 222.

The service creator's production facilities

The service creator will need a powerful personal computer with suitable software for supporting the intelligent editor, printing, and administrative management of contracts, and automatic communication for operations such as service installation. The user interface, as described here, is based on the object trading technology described in Section 11.2. The service creator specifies a OOCS schema that defines all permissible services. OOCS schemas were discussed in Section 11.3.

A sample contract document

Figure 12.6 shows a sample contract document from the initial system. More work is needed to make it into something that could be used in a real IN service marketing operation.

12.5   SERVICE CREATOR LAYER

The service creator has a license for producing telecommunications service software to be made available for installation in the telecommunications network. The service creator creates an OOCS schema that defines a family of services, and possibly specializes their names and some service parameters to suit the service provider.

IN A NUTSHELL

The OOram Composition System (OOCS) was described in Section 11.3. Figure 12.7 shows the condensed OOCS schema for our system, and Figure 12.8 shows the extended schema. (Here, the name of the entity is on the first line. Cardinality constraints appear on the second line: minimum count : maximum count.)

The service creator specifies all permissible services

Figure 12.7 says that a document (i.e., a *contract*) consists of any number of Text objects, exactly one SubscrData object, and any number of User objects. The specification of a User consists of any number of Text objects, exactly one User-Data object, and any number of different services. The services offered here are Tel-A and Tel-B; each is specified with describing Text objects and certain attributes (Tel-A-Data and Tel-B-Data). Tel-B-Data may optionally be modified with one or more access point selectors (AP-Selector) or call forward selectors (CF-Selector).

Condensed OOCS schema shows service semantics

The expanded OOCS schema includes groups and types as shown in Figure 12.8. Groups, which are shown with thin outlines in the figure, control the legal sequence of objects, and also the total number of objects within a group.

Groups in expanded OOCS schema constrain cardinality and object sequence

There are three groups under ServiceContract: SubscrText, Subscriber, and User. This means that all subscriber texts must come in front of the subscriber data, which must come in front of all user definitions.

There are two entities under the group UserDef: Text and User-Data. The cardinality of Text is here 0:N, so there can be any number of Text objects. The cardinality of User-Data is 1:1, so there must be exactly one User-Data object. Since these two entities are in the same group, there may be any number of Text objects before or after the User-Data object. The cardinality of a group constrains the total number of objects in that group. So if cardinality of the User-Def group

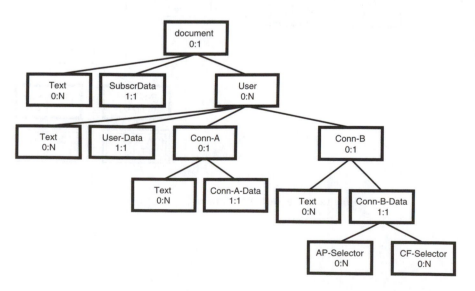

Figure 12.7

Condensed OOCS schema

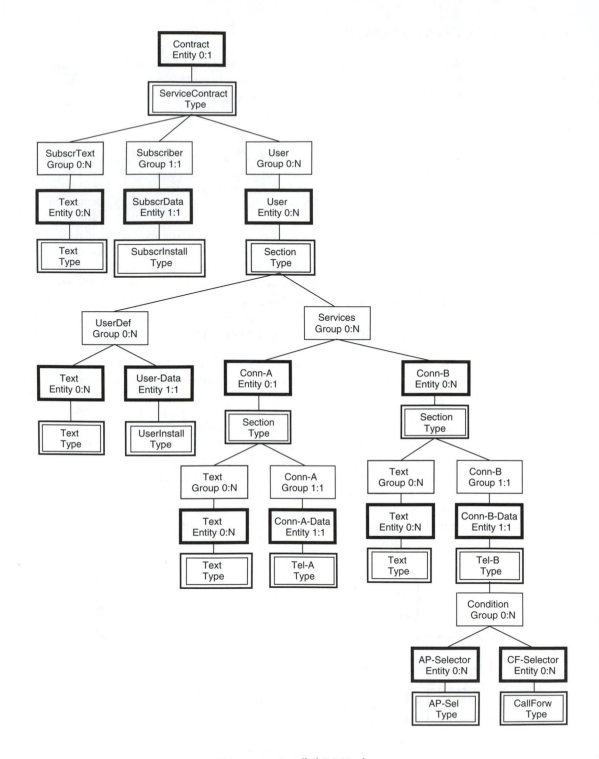

Figure 12.8   Detailed OOCS schema

had been 1:2, there could have been at most one `Text` object which could come before or after the `User-Data` object.

We need eight OOCS types to implement the schema of Figure 12.8: `Text`, `SubscrInstall`, `Section`, `UserInstall`, `Tel-A`, `Tel-B`, `AP-Sel`, and `CallForw`.

Types form bridge from OOCS schema to implementation

`Section` and `Text` are very general types which can be reused in a great many circumstances. The conditional types `AP-Sel` and `CallForw` are quite specific, but could conceivably be reused wherever we needed to select an `accessPointID` or a `userServiceID`.

The OOCS types are created in the next layer down by the service constituent creator. The service creator need only be concerned about their functionality, and can ignore design and implementation details. The tools will ensure that he or she can create only legal service specifications.

The service creator may define different OOCS schemas for different categories of service providers. One end of the spectrum could be the clerks in the corner teleshop who get to use a small schema, which just permits them to specify the simple services they learned in their training course. Another end of the spectrum could be a highly competent customer consultant who gets to use a very elaborate schema, that he knows how to exploit, to tailor advanced services to the needs of his sophisticated customers.

Several schemas can be defined

Objects seem to be eminently suitable as information carriers on the upper four layers because they remember specific values set to the service parameters:

1 The service creator specifies OOCS schemas, which define the services and all their permissible variants.

2 The service provider instantiates the service objects, sets certain parameters, and installs them in the subscriber's management object.

3 The subscriber duplicates the service objects, binds further parameters, and installs them with the user.

4 The user duplicates the service objects, binds remaining parameters, and installs them in the network for execution.

12.6 SERVICE CONSTITUENT CREATOR LAYER

IN A NUTSHELL

The deliverables from the service constituent creator layer are OOCS types—building blocks, which may be composed by the service provider under the control of OOCS schemas as specified by the service creator.

The OOCS type is implemented as a computer program that is created in the service constituent creator layer. We envisage extensive reuse. The most important reusable components are the framework service constituents.

Two kinds of service constituents

In the terminology of the IN industry, a *service* may be constructed from a number of *service constituents*. In our initial value chain, services are constructed both by composition and by inheritance, and have, therefore, two different kinds of service constituents: OOCS types and OOram frameworks. The relationships between them is shown schematically in Figure 12.9. Each box signifies a service constituent. Black arrows signify delivery of OOCS types to the service creator layer for schema composition; the open arrows signify synthesis relationships.

Deliverables from this layer are OOCS types

The deliverables from this layer to the service creator layer are *OOCS types*. They appear in the OOCS schema of Figure 12.8 as OOCS *types*, and their nature is discussed in Section 11.3.2.

Consider object #107-1 Tel-A in the sample object structure of Figure 12.3. This object appears as different roles in a number of descriptions:

A typical object plays many roles

1   It is a copy of the master object #107 Tel-A in Figure 12.3.

2   It is entity Conn-A-Data in the OOCS schema of Figure 12.8.

3   It is type Tel-A in the OOCS schema of Figure 12.8.

4   It is configurable according to the mechanisms used for schema composition.

Figure 12.9

The internal structure of the service constituent creator layer

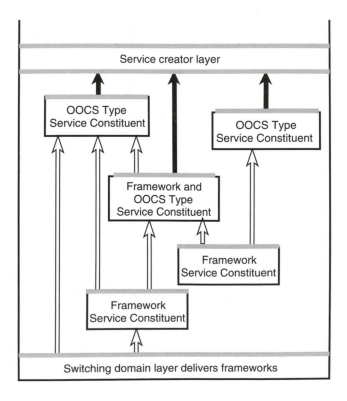

INTELLIGENT NETWORK SERVICES

5 The design of its service functionality is specified in a role model, POTS-A, which will be described briefly below.

6 It has a class which implements the calling end of a POTS communication channel.

7 It exploits the functionality of the switching domain by playing the role of Client to the Switch Connection framework, which is a deliverable from the network provider Layer.

A framework service constituent is usually described by several role models and object specifications, and the framework service constituent is a natural candidate for being packaged in a module.

Framework service constituents organized in Modules

A framework service constituent module may import one or more frameworks from other framework service constituent modules, and may export frameworks to other framework service constituent modules. On the top level, we find OOCS types that are used as building blocks in the schemas of the service creator layer.

The implementation of our tiny initial system consists of 38 application-specific classes with 314 methods, as shown in the program statistics in Table 12.1. There are only six modules: module Network is the deliverable from the network provider layer, and the others are organized in service constituent creator sublayers as shown in Figure 12.10 and described below. (A box signifies a service constituent. Black arrows signify delivery to the layer above; open arrows signify synthesis relationships within the service constituent creator layer.)

1 User. This module defines the experimental user interfaces. It does not export to the service creator layer because this part of the system is not configurable in our initial system.

2 Tel-A. This module defines the called part of POTS including the access point selection and call forward functionality. In a full-size system, these latter functions would be factored out into two separate modules to make them available for reuse.

3 Tel-B. This module defines the calling part of POTS, and is responsible for actually establishing the connection in the switching domain in our initial system. It imports the switch connection framework from the network provider layer.

4 Abstr-Tel. This module exports a mechanism which describes how the calling and called parts of the service interact in general terms. The mechanism is imported by the Tel-A and Tel-B modules.

5 Invocation. This module exports a framework, which defines the environment of the service objects.

6 Network. This module belongs in the network provider layer, and exports frameworks for switch connections and other switch services.

	Class count	Average inheritance depth	Methods count	Lines count	Change count
Demonstration system	38	4.66	314	988	101

Table 12.1

Program statistics for the application-specific classes

Figure 12.10
Module structure
in the initial value
chain

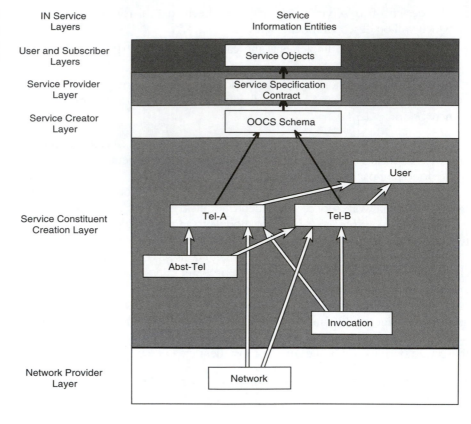

As the system is scaled up toward real size, and the service specifications are expanded into real services, it will be necessary to organize the service constituents in a large number of modules and to assign these modules to well-defined sublayers within the service constituent creator layer.

The real module structure must be carefully constructed

An effective architecture for the service constituent creator sub-layers with appropriate standards will create business opportunities for a rich variety of reusable patterns and frameworks.

12.7   NETWORK PROVIDER LAYER

The network provider layer presents the functionality of the actual switches in a unified, implementation-independent manner to the service domain software, and makes its functionality available to the service constituent creator in the form of one or more frameworks.

IN A NUTSHELL

The switching domain is implemented as a very large, very high capacity, very fast, and very reliable heterogeneous distributed real time system. Communication channels are established via paths through the switches between the users. Figure 12.11 illustrates how six users are interconnected through four switches in a conference connection.

The deliverables from the network layer

The purpose of the interface between the switching domain and the service domain is to hide the distributed nature of the communication network and to present a simple, abstract model of the network capabilities.

The deliverables from the network provider layer are a number of frameworks describing the offered functionality together with the corresponding implementation. We will give one example, the *connection control* framework.

One such framework is based on the connection control model, which was briefly described in Section 12.1. The distributed switches are abstracted into a single connection point, and each communication channel from a user to this connection point is abstracted into a *leg*. The *area of concern* is shown in Figure 12.12. The *collaboration view* in Figure 12.13. ConnUser may be specialized, i.e. synthesized with other roles. Leg and ConnPoint are immutable roles, i.e., roles that cannot be modified in the derived model. The symbol for immutable roles is a role symbol with a double boundary as shown in the figure.

The connection control model

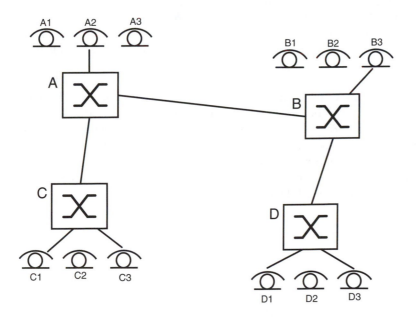

Figure 12.11

Simplified picture of how six users are interconnected through a conference connection

---

An abstract interface to the switching domain which offers connection functionality in an implementation independent form.

Figure 12.12

Connection control—area of concern

Figure 12.13

Connection control— collaboration view

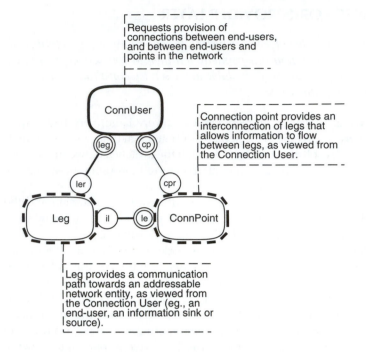

As seen from the service constituent layer, this model must permit the specialization of the ConnUser role through synthesis. The Leg and ConnPoint roles must be immutable because they cannot be modified in the derived models. The model will have been implemented in the network provider layer, and the class corresponding to ConnUser must be available for subclassing, while the other classes must be immutable. These constraints could, for example, be imposed by the compiler, or they may be checked by automatically analyzing the source code.

Frameworks hide switching domain details and protects integrity

We see that the complex realities of the switching domain are effectively hidden in the frameworks offered to the service constituent creators. This means that they can focus on their main goal, which is to create powerful service components, and do not need to worry about the complex technical details of the switches. We also see that the frameworks can help enforce various constraints that are needed to protect the integrity of the switching network. This is done by insisting that all access to the network is through validated classes, which may not be modified (subclassed) by the service constituent creator.

The OOram Language

The OOram technology has been developed around an object-oriented data base, and the preferred user tools have task-oriented, direct manipulation graphical user interfaces. It is nevertheless useful to define a textual form for all OOram model information, and this is the preferred form for some purposes, such as documenting interfaces and role attributes.

This appendix defines a first version of the OOram language. The language serves three purposes:

1　A summary of OOram concepts and the relationships between them.

2　A language for the precise documentation of OOram models.

3　An interchange language for communicating OOram models, e.g., through electronic mail and between different implementations of OOram CASE tools.

We present the lexical conventions of the OOram language in Section A.1, its grammar in Section A.2, and its scoping rules in Section A.3. The OOram semantics are defined in the main body of this book, particularly in Sections 2.5, and 3.3, and Chapter 6: We shall assume that the correspondence between the concepts defined there and the constructs of the language defined in the following will be clear from the chosen keywords, etc.

The examples and case studies presented in this book have been specified in the TASKON/OOram tools. The book itself has been written with the TASKON/OOram documentation tool, and the diagrams and other OOram views have been automatically created by the tools. Section A.4 contains an OOram language specification of the module, which forms the basis of Chapter 7, and Section A.5 is similarly the specification of a module which includes some of the models of Chapter 3.

A text describing an OOram model in the OOram language will be called an *OOram specification*.

A.1 LEXICAL CONVENTIONS

This section presents the lexical conventions of the OOram language, which define the structures of the tokens used, and the correspondence between a sequence of tokens and how it can be described by a string of characters.

The OOram language uses the ISO Latin-1 character set [ISO8859.1]. This character set is divided into alphabetic characters (letters), digits, graphic characters, the Space (blank) character, and formatting characters (CR, LF, FF, and TAB).

If the input character string has been parsed into a token up to a given character, then any following spaces, formatting characters, and comments (see below) will be skipped. Thereafter the next token is taken to be the longest string of characters that could possibly constitute a token.

Comments can occur anywhere between tokens. The characters /* start a comment, and it is terminated with the characters */. Comments do not nest. Comments may contain alphabetic, digit, graphic, space, and formatting characters. We recommend the convention that comments are printed in an italic font, but this has no formal significance.

The language uses the following kinds of tokens: separators, keywords, identifiers, string literals, and integer literals.

A.1.1 Separators

OOram specifications use the separator tokens shown in Table A.1.

A.1.2 Keywords

The words listed in Table A.2 are the keywords of the language. Upper- and lower-case letters are considered equivalent in keywords. For example, *module*, *Module*, and *MODULE* are all considered equivalent. We recommend the convention that keywords are printed in a **bold** font, but this has no formal significance.

A.1.3 Identifiers

An identifier token is a sequence of characters surrounded by single quotes, as in '...'. Within an identifier, the quote character must be doubled. All characters are significant, except that any sequence of Space and formatting characters counts as

Table A.1

OOram punctuation tokens

	( ) , :: <- >> \n

				Table A.2
boolean	data	deferred_synch	entity	**Keywords**
explanation	export	float	flow	
import	in	integer	interface	
interfaces	long_name	many	message	
module	none	number	object_specification	
one	param	port	process	
response_msgs	return	role	role_model	
scenario	semantics	state_diagram	states	
stimulus	string	synch	task	
transition	type	type_model		

Symbol	Meaning	Table A.3
::=	Is defined to be	**The symbols of**
|	Alternatively	**the OOram**
<text>	A normal nonterminal	**Extended Backus-**
<TEXT>	A nonterminal indicating a token of the given category	**Naur format and**
"text"	The text directly identifies a keyword or separator	**their meaning**
*	The preceding syntactic unit can be repeated zero or more times	
+	The preceding syntactic unit can be repeated one or more times	
{ }	The enclosed syntactic units are grouped as a single syntactic unit	
[ ]	The enclosed syntactic unit is optional—may occur zero or one time	

a single Space. In identifiers, uppercase and lowercase letters are considered to be different.

A.1.4   String Literals

A string literal is a sequence of characters surrounded by double quotes, as in "...". Within a string literal, the double quote character must be doubled.

A.1.5   Integer Literals

An integer literal is any sequence of digits, with a normal decimal value.

A.2   OORAM LANGUAGE GRAMMAR

The syntax notation used in this grammar is a variation of the Extended Backus-Naur format. Table A.3 lists the symbols used and their meaning. Two types of nonterminals are used: Those given with uppercase letters indicate that a token of this category should occur here. The others are normal nonterminals that are defined elsewhere in the grammar.

In an OOram specification, some occurrences of an identifier will serve to associate it with the entity described by the corresponding syntactical construct; other occurrences serve as references to entities described elsewhere. The occurrences of the former type are highlighted in the syntax below by giving the corresponding (normal) nonterminal in italics, e.g., *<rm_name>*. The association obtained in this way will have effect throughout the closest surrounding scoping construct in which the definition occurs. Exactly which constructs that qualify as scoping constructs is described in Section A.3.

```
        <specification> ::= <module>+

             <module> ::= "module" <module_name> <import_model>* <export_model>*
                          <rm_definition>*

        <module_name> ::= <IDENTIFIER>

        <import_model> ::= "import" <rm_name> "<-" <rm_name> "::" <module_name>

             <rm_name> ::= <IDENTIFIER>

        <export_model> ::= "export" <rm_name>

        <rm_definition> ::= <rm_kind> <rm_name> <node_descr> <rm_spec>*

             <rm_kind> ::= "role_model"
                          | "object_specification"
                          | "type_model"

           <node_descr> ::= [<long_name>] [<explanation>]

             <rm_spec> ::= "base_model" <rm_name> <inherit_map>*
                          | "interface" <interface_name> <node_descr> <interface_spec>*
                          | "role" <role_name> <node_descr> <role_spec>*
                          | "scenario" <scenario_name> <node_descr> <interaction>*
                          | "process" <process_name> <node_descr> {<task> | <entity> }* <flow>*

           <long_name> ::= "long_name" <STRING_LITERAL>

          <explanation> ::= "explanation" <STRING_LITERAL>

          <inherit_map> ::= <base_role_name> "->" <derived_role_name>

        <interface_name> ::= <IDENTIFIER>

        <interface_spec> ::= <type_dcl>
                          | <message_spec>

           <role_name> ::= <IDENTIFIER>

           <role_spec> ::= <attribute_spec>
                          | <stimulus>*
                          | <port_spec>
                          | <state_diagram_spec>

             <stimulus> ::= "stimulus" <scoped_message_name> [<explanation>] ["response_msgs" "("
                          <scoped_message_names> ")"] ["attributes_changed" "(" <scoped_attribute_names> ")"]

 <scoped_message_names> ::= <scoped_message_name> {"," <scoped_message_name> }*

  <scoped_message_name> ::= <message_name> ["::" <interface_name>]

 <scoped_attribute_names> ::= <scoped_attribute_name> {"," =
                          <scoped_attribute_name> }*

 <scoped_attribute_name> ::= <attribute_name> [ "::" <role_name> ]

        <scenario_name> ::= <IDENTIFIER>

          <interaction> ::= <role_name> ">>" <message_name> ">>" <role_name>

        <process_name> ::= <IDENTIFIER>

                <task> ::= "task" <task_name> <node_descr> "in" <role_name>
                          | "task" "stimulus" <task_name> <node_descr> "in" <role_name>
```

```
               <task_name>  ::= <IDENTIFIER>

                  <entity>  ::= "entity" <entity_name> <node_descr> "data" <data_list>

             <entity_name>  ::= <IDENTIFIER>

                <data_list>  ::= "(" <data_name> {"," <data_name> }* ")"

               <data_name>  ::= <IDENTIFIER>

                    <flow>  ::= "flow" <from_task> ">>" ">>" <to_task>
                             | "flow" <from_task> ">>" <entity_name> ">>" <to_task>

               <from_task>  ::= <task_name>

                 <to_task>  ::= <task_name>

          <base_role_name>  ::= <role_name>

       <derived_role_name>  ::= <role_name>

           <message_spec>  ::= "message" [<message_semantics>] <message_name> <node_descr>
                             <parameter>*

          <attribute_spec>  ::= "attribute" <attribute_name> <node_descr>  [ "type" <type_dcl>]

                <type_dcl>  ::= <base_type>
                             | <scoped_role_name>

               <port_spec>  ::= "port" <cardinality> <port_name> <node_descr> ["semantics"
                             <min_count> ":" <max_count> [<explanation>]] ["interfaces" "("
                             <interface_names>  ")"]

               <min_count>  ::= <INTEGER_LITERAL>

               <max_count>  ::= <INTEGER_LITERAL>

     <state_diagram_spec>  ::= "state_diagram" <state_specs> <transition>*

           <message_name>  ::= <IDENTIFIER>

               <base_type>  ::= "float"
                             | "integer"
                             | "boolean"
                             | "string"

        <scoped_role_name>  ::= <role_name> ["::" <rm_name>]

       <message_semantics>  ::= "synch"
                             | "deferred_synch"
                             | "asynch"

               <parameter>  ::= "param" <param_name> [<explanation>] ["type" <type_dcl>]
                             | "return"  [<explanation>] ["type"  <type_dcl>]

          <attribute_name>  ::= <IDENTIFIER>

             <cardinality>  ::= "none"
                             | "one"
                             | "many"

               <port_name>  ::= <IDENTIFIER>

         <interface_names>  ::= [<interface_name> {","  <interface_name> }*]

              <param_name>  ::= <IDENTIFIER>

             <state_specs>  ::= "states" "(" [ <state_name>  {"," <state_name>}*] ")"

              <state_name>  ::= <IDENTIFIER>

              <transition>  ::= "transition" <initial_state_name> <message_name> <action list> <next_state_name>

       <initial_state_name>  ::= <state_name>

              <action_list>  ::= "(" [ <action_name> { "," <action_name> }* ] ")"

             <action_name>  ::= <IDENTIFIER>

         <next_state_name>  ::= <state_name>
```

A.3   SCOPE OF IDENTIFIERS

As explained earlier, some occurrences of an identifier in an OOram specification serve to associate that identifier with the entity described by the corresponding language construct. This association will have effect throughout the closest surrounding scoping construct in which the definition occurs (also textually in front of the definition). Thus, from within its scoping construct an entity may be referenced directly by its identifier. By using scoped names, entities may also be referenced from outside their scoping construct. The scoped name x::y should be understood as the entity named x defined local to the scoping construct named y.

The syntactical units that qualify as scoping constructs are the following: Modules, role models, interfaces, messages, and roles. In the grammar, these constructs are identified by their initial keywords, and they are always nested as indicated in Figure A.1. In this figure we have also indicated what name types are local to the different scoping constructs. Note that the name of a scoping construct is itself local to the nearest enclosing scoping construct.

Local to one scoping construct, no two entities can be identified by the same name. However, local to two different scoping constructs the same names may be used, even if they are nested. A referencing occurrence of a name will always identify the entity with the name local to the nearest possible enclosing scoping construct.

When an OOram model is represented as a structure of objects, the different entities are identified by their object identifiers. The names that users assign to the entities help them understand the models, but have no formal significance.

If the model is used to generate code in a programming language, the names are used to generate identifiers in the selected programming language. The wise analyst will then use entity names that may be used unchanged as program identifiers to make the relationship between model and program as evident as possible. Our modeling tools support this by warning the analyst if a chosen name does not conform to the syntax and pragmatics of the chosen language. The tools will also warn the analyst about duplicate names which would cause compilation errors if used unchanged.

When an OOram model is represented as a string of characters, we could retain the object identifiers as the real identifiers of the different entities. These iden-

Figure A.1

The scope of the different OOram identifiers

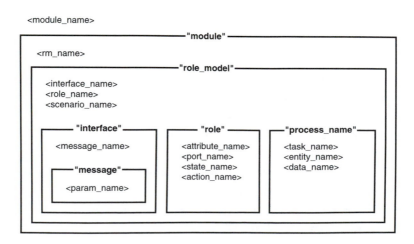

tifiers are typically quite unreadable to a human, and the OOram language is designed so that the entities are identified by their names. The kind of entity determines the scope of these names as illustrated in Figure A.1.

A.4 OORAM MODULE 'DEVELOPMENT OF A BUSINESS INFORMATION SYSTEM CHAPTER'

module 'Travel Expense case study'

    export 'Travel Expense Enterprise Model'

    role_model 'Travel Expense Enterprise Model'
        explanation "*The area of concern is the handling of travel expense accounts. We focus on the expense account itself, and do not model details about why the journey was made, nor how the traveler is reimbursed for his expenses.*"
        interface 'ENTPaymaster<ENTBookkeeper'
            message synch 'paymentRequest:'
                explanation "*Reimburse the specified account.*"
                param 'aPaymentRequest' **type** 'INFPayRequest' :: 'Travel Expense Information Model'
        interface 'ENTTraveler<ENTAuthorizer'
            message synch 'travelPermission:'
                explanation "*Travel authorization granted.*"
                param 'aTravelPermission' **type** 'INFTravelPermission' :: 'Travel Expense Information Model'
        interface 'ENTBookkeeper<ENTAuthorizer'
            message synch 'authorizedExpenseReport:'
                explanation "*Request reimbursement of submitted expense report.*"
                param 'anExpenseReport' **type** 'INFExpenseAccount' :: 'Travel Expense Information Model'
        interface 'ENTAuthorizer<ENTTraveler'
            message synch 'travelPermissionRequest:'
                explanation "*Request authorization of submitted travel plan.*"
                param 'aTravelPermission' **type** 'INFTravelPermission' :: 'Travel Expense Information Model'
            message synch 'expenseReport:'
                explanation "*Request reimbursement of submitted expense report.*"
                param 'anExpenseReport' **type** 'INFExpenseAccount' :: 'Travel Expense Information Model'
        role 'ENTTraveler'
            explanation "*The person who travels.*"
            stimulus 'travelPermissionRequest:' :: 'ENTAuthorizer<ENTTraveler'
                response_msgs ('paymentRequest:' :: 'ENTPaymaster<ENTBookkeeper')
                attributes_changed ( )
            port one 'au' **interfaces** ('ENTAuthorizer<ENTTraveler')
        role 'ENTAuthorizer'
            explanation "*The person who authorizes the travel.*"
            port many 'tr' **interfaces** ('ENTTraveler<ENTAuthorizer')
            port one 'bo' **interfaces** ('ENTBookkeeper<ENTAuthorizer')
         role 'ENTBookkeeper'
            explanation "*The person responsible for bookkeeping.*"
            port one 'pm' **interfaces** ('ENTPaymaster<ENTBookkeeper')
        role 'ENTPaymaster'
            explanation "*The person responsible for reimbursement.*"
        process 'ExpenseAccount Process diagram'
            task stimulus 'stimulus'
                explanation "*Desire to travel*"
                in 'ENTTraveler'
            entity 'travelPermissionRequest:'
                data (aTravelPermission)

task 'travelPermissionRequest:'
    explanation "*<Determine OK>*"
    in 'ENTAuthorizer'
entity 'travelPermission:'
    data (aTravelPermission)
task 'travelPermission:'
    explanation "*<Order tickets> <Travel> <Write exp.rep.>*"
    in 'ENTTraveler'
entity 'expenseReport:'
    data (anExpenseReport)
task 'expenseReport:'
    explanation "*<Check OK>*"
    in 'ENTAuthorizer'
entity 'authorizedExpenseReport:'
    data (anExpenseReport)
task 'authorizedExpenseReport:'
    explanation "*<Check> <Bookkeeping>*."
    in 'ENTBookkeeper'
entity 'paymentRequest:'
    data (aPaymentRequest)
task 'paymentRequest:'
    explanation "*<Arrange for payment>*."
    in 'ENTPaymaster'
flow 'stimulus' >>'travelPermissionRequest:' >> ('travelPermissionRequest:')
flow 'travelPermissionRequest:' >>'travelPermission:' >> ('travelPermission:')
flow 'travelPermission:' >>'expenseReport:' >> ('expenseReport:')
flow 'expenseReport:' >>'authorizedExpenseReport:' >> ('authorizedExpenseReport:')
flow 'authorizedExpenseReport:' >>'paymentRequest:' >> ('paymentRequest:')

role_model 'Travel Expense Information Model'
    explanation "*The area of concern is modeling the information contained in travel expense accounts. We focus on the expense account itself, and do not model details about the user interfaces.*"
    interface 'INFTravelPermission<INFExpenseAccount'
        message synch 'isPermitted'
    role 'INFExpenseAccount'
        explanation "*The master object representing an expense account.*"
        attribute 'travelerName'
        attribute 'travelerID'
        attribute 'travelPurpose'
        port one 'tp' **semantics** 1:1 "*Consists of*" **interfaces** ('INFTravelPermission<INFExpenseAccount')
        port many 'ei' **semantics** 0 : N "*Consists of*"
        port one 'pa' **semantics** 1:1 "*Consists of*"
        port one 'pr' **semantics** 1:1 "*Consists of*"
    role 'INFPayAuthorization'
        explanation "*A disbursement order.*"
        attribute 'date'
        attribute 'name'
        attribute 'ID'
        attribute 'signature'
        port one 'ea' **semantics** 1:1 "*Part of*"
    role 'INFExpenseItem'
        explanation "*A specified cost.*"
        attribute 'text'
        attribute 'currency'
        attribute 'rate'
        attribute 'value'
        port one 'ea' **semantics** 1:1 "*Part of*"
    role 'INFTravelPermission'
        explanation "*A permission to travel.*"
        attribute 'proposedCost'
        attribute 'authorizerName'

        attribute 'authorizerID'
        attribute 'authorizerSignature'
        attribute 'date'
        port none 'ea' **semantics** 1:1 "*Part of*"
    role 'INFPayRequest'
        explanation "*Authorization of payment.*"
        attribute 'date'
        attribute 'name'
        attribute 'ID'
        attribute 'signature'
        port one 'ea' **semantics** 1:1 "*Part of*"

role_model 'Task/Tool/Service model'
    interface 'TSAuthorizerTool<TSAuthorizer'
        message synch 'Permit'
            explanation "*Permit the proposed travel.*"
        message synch 'Reject'
            explanation "*Refuse the proposed travel.*"
        message synch 'openOn:'
            explanation "*Create a new instance of the tool and open it on the specified ExpenseAccount.*"
            param 'expAcc'
    interface 'TSAccountService<TSAuthorizerTool'
        message synch 'getExpenseAccount'
            explanation "*Return expense account information.*"
            return type 'INFExpenseAccount' **::** 'Travel Expense Information Model'
        message synch 'getPeriod'
            explanation "*Return travel time period.*"
        message synch 'getPlannedCost'
            explanation "*Returned planned cost.*"
        message synch 'getPurpose'
            explanation "*Return purpose of travel.*"
        message synch 'putAuthorized:'
            explanation "*Set authorization if aBoolean = true, otherwise the travel is rejected.*"
            param 'aBoolean' **type boolean**
    interface 'TSBudgetService<TSAuthorizerTool'
        message synch 'getBudgetFor:'
            explanation "*Return budget information.*"
            param 'kind'
            return type number
        message synch 'commit:for:'
            explanation "*Allocate amount from budget.*"
            param 'amount' **type number**
            param 'kind'
    interface 'TSAuthorizer<TSAuthorizerTool'
        message synch 'display'
            explanation "*Read the currently displayed text.*"
    interface 'TSPlanningService<TSAuthorizerTool'
        message synch 'getPlanFor:'
            explanation "*Return planning information.*"
            param 'person'
            return type 'Plan' **::** 'BasicTypes'
    role 'TSAuthorizer'
        explanation "*The person who authorizes the travel.*"
        stimulus 'openOn:' **::** 'TSAuthorizerTool<TSAuthorizer'
        port one 'tool' **interfaces** ('TSAuthorizerTool<TSAuthorizer')
    role 'TSAuthorizerTool'
        explanation "*The user interface system.*"
        port one 'auth' **interfaces** ('TSAuthorizer<TSAuthorizerTool')
        port one 'bud' **interfaces** ('TSBudgetService<TSAuthorizerTool')
        port one 'pla' **interfaces** ('TSPlanningService<TSAuthorizerTool')
        port one 'acc' **interfaces** ('TSAccountService<TSAuthorizerTool')

role 'TSAccountService'
    explanation "*An object structure representing a particular expense account.*"
role 'TSPlanningService'
    explanation "*A system representing the current plans for the enterprise.*"
role 'TSBudgetService'
    explanation "*A system managing the enterprise budget.*"
process 'OpenPermissionTool'
    task stimulus 'stimulus'
        explanation "*Start authorization activity.*"
        in 'TSAuthorizer'
    task 'openOn:'
        explanation "*Create and open travel authorization tool.*"
        in 'TSAuthorizerTool'
    task 'getExpenseAccount'
        explanation "*getExpenseAccount.*"
        in 'TSAccountService'
    entity 'ISExpenseAccount'
        data (expAcc)
    task 'getBudgetFor:'
        explanation "*getBudgetFor:*"
        in 'TSBudgetService'
    entity 'Budgetamount'
        data (expAcc)
    task 'getPlanFor:'
        explanation "*getPlanFor:*"
        in 'TSPlanningService'
    entity 'Plan'
        data (expAcc)
flow 'stimulus' >> >> ('openOn:')
flow 'openOn:' >> >> ('getExpenseAccount')
flow 'openOn:' >> >> ('getBudgetFor:')
flow 'openOn:' >> >> ('getPlanFor:')
flow 'getExpenseAccount' >>'ISExpenseAccount' >> ('openOn:')
flow 'getBudgetFor:' >>'Budgetamount' >> ('openOn:')
flow 'getPlanFor:' >>'Plan' >> ('openOn:')
process 'GrantPermission'
    task stimulus 'stimulus'
        explanation "*Press Permit- button.*"
        in 'TSAuthorizer'
    task 'Permit'
        explanation "*Grant Permission.*"
        in 'TSAuthorizerTool'
    task 'putAuthorized:'
        explanation "*putAuthorized: = true.*"
        in 'TSAccountService'
    entity 'true'
        data (aBoolean)
    task 'commit:for:'
        explanation "*Record new commitment.*"
        in 'TSBudgetService'
    entity 'Number'
        data (amount)
flow 'stimulus' >> >> ('Permit')
flow 'Permit' >>'true' >> ('putAuthorized:')
flow 'Permit' >>'Number' >> ('commit:for:')

APPENDIX A: THE OORAM LANGUAGE

A.5   OORAM MODULE 'SYNTHESIS'

module 'Some Synthesis Models'

    import 'Travel Expense Enterprise Model' **<-** 'Travel Expense Enterprise Model' **::** 'Work Environments'

    role_model 'BasicTree'
        explanation "*A role model describing a basic tree structure.*"
        interface 'Child<Mother'
            message synch 'preorderTraverse:' **param** 'aBlock'
            message synch 'postorderTraverse:' **param** 'aBlock'
            message synch 'getLeaves'
        interface 'Mother<Child'
            message synch 'getRoot'
        role 'Mother'
            port many 'dw' **interfaces** ('Child<Mother')
        role 'Child'
            port one 'up' **interfaces** ('Mother<Child')

    role_model 'ThreeLevelTree'
        explanation "*A role model describing a tree structure with three levels.*"
        base_model 'BasicTree'
            'Mother' -> 'Node'
            'Child' -> 'Leaf'
        base_model 'BasicTree'
            'Mother' **->** 'Root'
            'Child' **->** 'Node'
        role 'Root'
            port many 'dw'
        role 'Node'
            port one 'up'
            port many 'dw'
        role 'Leaf'
            port one 'up'

    role_model 'AirlineBooking'
        explanation "*Airline tickets are ordered by a booking clerk and paid directly to the travel agent. The traveler is to show the cost of the tickets on the expense report as an expense, and as an advance since the tickets were not paid by the traveler.*"
        interface 'ABTravelAgent<ABPaymaster'
            message synch 'payment:'
                 explanation "*Transmittal of payment.*"
                 param 'aCheque' **type string**
        interface 'ABBookKeeper<ABBookingClerk'
            message synch 'authorizedInvoice:'
                 explanation "*Pay this authorized ticket invoice.*"
                 param 'anInvoice' **type string**
        interface 'ABTraveler<ABBookingClerk'
            message synch 'ticketWithCost:'
                 explanation "*Transmitting the ticket(s) together with cost information.*"
                 param 'package' **type string**
        interface 'ABTravelAgent<ABBookingClerk'
            message synch 'orderTicket:'
                 explanation "*Reserve specified passages and issue ticket(s).*"
                 param 'ticketSpecification' **type string**
        interface 'ABPaymaster<ABBookKeeper'
            message synch 'paymentRequest:'
                 explanation "*Pay this invoice.*"
                 param 'anInvoice' **type string**

interface 'ABBookingClerk<ABTraveler'
  message synch 'orderTicket:'
    explanation "*Purchase ticket(s).*"
    param 'ticketSpecification' **type string**
interface 'ABBookingClerk<ABTravelAgent'
  message synch 'ticket:'
    explanation "*Transmittal of ticket(s).*"
    param 'aTicket' **type string**
  message synch 'invoice:'
    explanation "*Transmittal of invoice.*"
    param 'anInvoice' **type string**
role 'ABTraveler'
  explanation "*The person who travels.*"
  attribute 'costOfTicket'
  stimulus 'orderTicket:' :: 'ABBookingClerk<ABTraveler'
    response_msgs ('ticketWithCost:' :: 'ABTraveler<ABBookingClerk')
    attributes_changed ('costOfTicket')
  port one 'sec' **interfaces** ('ABBookingClerk<ABTraveler')
role 'ABBookingClerk'
  explanation "*Clerk responsible for managing the purchase of tickets.*"
  port one 'tr' **interfaces** ('ABTraveler<ABBookingClerk')
  port one 'ta' **interfaces** ('ABTravelAgent<ABBookingClerk')
  port one 'bk' **interfaces** ('ABBookKeeper<ABBookingClerk')
role 'ABTravelAgent'
  explanation "*A travel agent.*"
  port one 'cust' **interfaces** ('ABBookingClerk<ABTravelAgent')
role 'ABBookKeeper'
  explanation "*Responsible for accounting.*"
  port one 'pm' **interfaces** ('ABPaymaster<ABBookKeeper')
role 'ABPaymaster'
  explanation "*Cashier.*"
  port one 'ven' **interfaces** ('ABTravelAgent<ABPaymaster')
process 'AirlineBooking process'
  task stimulus 'stimulus' **explanation** "*Order tickets*" **in** 'ABTraveler'
  entity 'Travelspecification1' **data** ('ticketSpecification')
  task 'orderTicket' **explanation** "*Order tickets*" **in** 'ABBookingClerk'
  entity 'Travelspecification2' **data** ('ticketSpecification')
  task 'issueTickets' **explanation** "*Issue tickets. Prepare invoice.*" **in** 'ABTravelAgent'
  entity 'TicketsAndInvoice' **data** ('aTicket')
  task 'processTickets' **explanation** "*Process tickets and invoice*" **in** 'ABBookingClerk'
  entity 'TicketsAndCost' **data** ('tickets and cost information')
  task 'noteCost' **explanation** "*Note cost for later use*" **in** 'ABTraveler'
  entity 'Authorizedinvoice' **data** ('anInvoice')
  task "processInvoice' **explanation** "*Process invoice*" **in** 'ABBookKeeper'
  entity 'RemunerationRequest' **data** ('anInvoice')
  task 'pay' **explanation** "*Send payment*" **in** 'ABPaymaster'
  entity 'Payment' **data** ('aCheque')
  task 'receivePayment' **explanation** "*Receive payment*" **in** 'ABTravelAgent'
flow 'stimulus' >>'Travelspecification1' >> ('orderTicket')
flow 'orderTicket' >>'Travelspecification2' >> ('issueTickets')
flow 'issueTickets' >>'TicketsAndInvoice' >> ('processTickets')
flow 'processTickets' >>'TicketsAndCost' >> ('noteCost')
flow 'processTickets' >>'Authorizedinvoice' >> ('processInvoice')
flow 'processInvoice' >>'RemunerationRequest' >> ('pay')
flow 'pay' >>'Payment' >> ('receivePayment')

role_model 'DerivedTravelExpense'
  explanation "*The area of concern is the procedure for travel management including the purchase of tickets.*"
  base_model 'AirlineBooking'
    'ABBookKeeper' -> 'DTEBookKeeper'
    'ABTravelAgent' -> 'DTETravelAgent'

'ABBookingClerk' -> 'DTEBookingClerk'
'ABPaymaster' -> 'DTEPaymaster'
'ABTraveler' -> 'DTETraveler'
base_model 'Travel Expense Enterprise Model'
'ENTPaymaster' -> 'DTEPaymaster'
'ENTAuthorizer' -> 'DTEAuthorizer'
'ENTTraveler' -> 'DTETraveler'
'ENTBookkeeper' -> 'DTEBookkeeper'
role 'DTETraveler'
    explanation "*The person who travels.*"
    stimulus 'travelPermissionRequest:' :: 'ENTAuthorizer<ENTTraveler'
        response_msgs ('paymentRequest:' :: 'ENTPaymaster<ENTBookkeeper')
        attributes_changed ( )
    port one 'sec' **interfaces** ('ABBookingClerk<ABTraveler')
    port one 'au'
role 'DTEBookingClerk'
    explanation "*Clerk responsible for managing the purchase of tickets.*"
    port one 'bk' **interfaces** ('ABBookKeeper<ABBookingClerk')
    port one 'tr' **interfaces** ('ABTraveler<ABBookingClerk')
    port one 'ta' **interfaces** ('ABTravelAgent<ABBookingClerk')
role 'DTEBookKeeper'
    explanation "*The person responsible for bookkeeping. Responsible for accounting.*"
    port one 'pm' **interfaces** ('ABPaymaster<ABBookKeeper')
role 'DTETravelAgent'
    explanation "*A travel agent.*"
    port one 'cust' **interfaces** ('ABBookingClerk<ABTravelAgent')
role 'DTEPaymaster'
    explanation "*The person responsible for reimbursement. Cashier.*"
    port one 'ven' **interfaces** ('ABTravelAgent<ABPaymaster')
role 'DTEAuthorizer'
    explanation "*The person who authorizes the travel.*"
    port many 'tr'
    port one 'bo'
process 'ExpenseAccount Process diagram'
    task stimulus 'stimulus' **explanation** "*Desire to travel*" **in** 'DTETraveler'
    entity 'travelPermissionRequest:' **data** (aTravelPermission)
    task 'travelPermissionRequest:' **explanation** "*<Determine OK>*" **in** 'DTEAuthorizer'
    entity 'travelPermission:' **data** (aTravelPermission)
    task 'travelPermission:' **explanation** "*<Order tickets>*" **in** 'DTETraveler'
    task stimulus 'planTravel' **explanation** "*Order tickets*" **in** 'DTETraveler'
    entity 'Travelspecification1' **data** (ticketSpecification)
    task 'orderTicket' **explanation** "*Order tickets*" **in** 'DTEBookingClerk'
    entity 'Travelspecification2' **data** (ticketSpecification)
    task 'issueTickets' **explanation** "*Issue tickets. Prepare invoice.*" **in** 'DTETravelAgent'
    entity 'TicketsAndInvoice' **data** (aTicket)
    task 'processTickets' **explanation** "*Process tickets and invoice*" **in** 'DTEBookingClerk'
    entity 'TicketsAndCost' **data** (tickets and cost information)
    task 'noteCost' **explanation** "*<Note cost> <Travel> <Prepare expense account>*" **in** 'DTETraveler'
    entity 'Authorizedinvoice' **data** (anInvoice)
    task 'processInvoice' **explanation** "*Process invoice*" **in** 'DTEBookKeeper'
    entity 'RemunerationRequest' **data** (anInvoice)
    task 'pay' **explanation** "*Send payment*" **in** 'DTEPaymaster'
    entity 'Payment' **data** (aCheque)
    task 'receivePayment' **explanation** "*Receive payment*" **in** 'DTETravelAgent'
    entity 'expenseReport:' **data** (anExpenseReport)
    task 'expenseReport:' **explanation** "*<Check OK>*" **in** 'DTEAuthorizer'
    entity 'authorizedExpenseReport:' **data** (anExpenseReport)
    task 'authorizedExpenseReport:' **explanation** "*<Check> <Bookkeeping>*" **in** 'DTEBookkeeper'
    entity 'paymentRequest:' **data** (aPaymentRequest)
    task 'paymentRequest:' **explanation** "*<Arrange for payment>*" **in** 'DTEPaymaster'
flow 'stimulus' >>'travelPermissionRequest:' >> ('travelPermissionRequest:')

flow 'travelPermissionRequest:' >>'travelPermission:' >> ('planTravel')
flow 'planTravel' >>'Travelspecification1' >> ('orderTicket')
flow 'orderTicket' >>'Travelspecification2' >> ('issueTickets')
flow 'issueTickets' >>'TicketsAndInvoice' >> ('processTickets')
flow 'processTickets' >>'TicketsAndCost' >> ('noteCost')
flow 'processTickets' >>'Authorizedinvoice' >> ('processInvoice')
flow 'processInvoice' >>'RemunerationRequest' >> ('pay')
flow 'pay' >>'Payment' >> ('receivePayment')
flow 'noteCost' >>'expenseReport:' >> ('expenseReport:')
flow 'expenseReport:' >>'authorizedExpenseReport:' >> ('authorizedExpenseReport:')
flow 'authorizedExpenseReport:' >>'paymentRequest:' >> ('paymentRequest:')

References

[Alexander 77] Christopher Alexander: *A Pattern Language*. Oxford University Press, New York, 1977.

[Alexander 79] Christopher Alexander: *The Timeless Way of Building*. Oxford University Press, New York, 1979.

[E. Andersen 92] Egil P. Andersen and Trygve Reenskaug: *System Design by Composing Structures of Interacting Objects*. ECOOP '92, Utrecht, 1992.

[And 91] Jørn Andersen and Trygve Reenskaug: Operations on sets in an OODB. *OOPS Messenger*, **2**, 4 (October 1991) pp. 26–39.

[Aronson 72] Elliot Aronson: *The Social Animal*. W. H. Freeman and Company, San Francisco, 1972. ISBN 0-7167-0829-9

[Beck 86] O'Shea, T., Beck, K., Halbert, D., Schmucker, and K. J. Panel: The learnability of Object-Oriented Programming Systems. *SIGPLAN Notices, 21*, 11 (November 1986) p. 503.

[Beck 94] Kent Beck and Ralph Johnson: *Patterns Generate Architectures*. In: (M. Tokoro, R. Pareschi Eds) *8th European Conference on Object-Oriented Programming (ECOOP 94)*. Springer Verlag, 1994.

[Bent 86] See for example, John Bentley: Programming Pearls. *Comm. ACM* **29**,5 (May 1986) p. 364–369 and *Comm. ACM* **30**,4 (April 1987) p.384–290.

[Berr 93] Arne-Jørgen Berre: *An Object-Oriented Framework for Systems Integration and Interoperability*. PhD thesis, University of Trondheim, Norwegian Institute of Technology, 1993.

[Birt 73] G. M. Birtwistle, O.-J. Dahl, B. Myrhaug, and K. Nygaard: Simula Begin. *Auerbach/Studentlitteratur Lund,* 1973. ISBN 91-44-06211-7.

[Boehm 88] Barry W. Boehm: A Spiral Model of Software Development and Enhancement. *Computer,* (May 1988) pp. 61–72.

[Booch 91] Grady Booch: *Object-Oriented Design with Applications*. The Benjamin/Cummings Publishing Company, Redwood City, 1991.

[Booch 94] Grady Booch: *Object-Oriented Analysis and Design with Applications*. Second edition. The Benjamin/Cummings Publishing Company, Redwood City, 1994. ISBN 0-8053-5340-2

[Broc 94] Kraig Brockschmidt: *Inside OLE2*. Microsoft Press, Redmond, 1994.

[Bræk 93] Rolv Bræk and Øystein Haugen: *Engineering Real Time Systems. An object-oriented methodology using SDL*. Hemel Hempstead: Prentice Hall, 1993. ISBN 0-13-034448-6

[Car 85] L. Cardelli and P. Wegner: On Understanding Types, Data Abstracting and Polymorphism. *Computing Surveys* **17** (4) 471–522 (1985).

[CCITT Z100] *Specification and Description Language SDL*. Recommendation Z100. Geneva, ITU 1993.

[CCITT Z120] *Message Sequence Charts*. Recommendation Z120. Geneva, ITU 1993.

[Chambers 89] Craig Chambers, David Ungar, and Elgin Lee: An Efficient Implementation of Self, a Dynamically-Typed Object-Oriented Language Based on Prototypes. OOPSLA '89. *Sigplan Notices* **24**, 10 (October 1989).

[Chen 76] P. Chen: The Entity Relationship Model—Toward a Unified View of Data. *TODS* **1**,1 (March 1976).

[CORBA 91] *The Common Object Request Broker: Architecture and Specification*. Object Management Group Document Number 91.12.1, Revision 1.1 (Draft 10 December 1991).

[Coul 88] George F. Couloris and Jean Dollimore: *Distributed Systems—Concepts and Design*. Addison-Wesley, New York, 1988.

[Cox 87] Brad J. Cox: *Object-Oriented Programming. An Evolutionary Approach*. Addison-Wesley, New York, 1987. ISBN 0-201-10393-1

[Elmasri 94] Ramez Elmasri and Shamkant B. Navathe: *Fundamentals of Database Systems*. Benjamin/Cummings, Redwood City, 1994. ISBN 0-8053-1748-1

[Engelbart 62] Douglas C. Engelbart: *Augmenting Human Intellect: A Conceptual Framework*. Summary Report, Stanford Research Institute, on Contract AF 49(638)-1024, October 1962.

[Engelbart 67] William K. English, Douglas C. Engelbart, and Melvyn L. Berman: Display-Selection Techniques for Text Manipulation. *IEEE Transactions on Human Factors in Electronics* **HFE-8** (1) pp. 5–15 (March 1967).

[Engelbart 92] Douglas C. Engelbart: *Toward High-Performance Organizations: A Strategic Role for Groupware. Proceedings of the GroupWare '92 Conference*, San Jose, August 3–5, 1992, Morgan Kaufmann Publishers.

[Etzioni 64] Amitai Etzioni: *Modern Organizations.* Prentice-Hall, Englewood Cliffs, 1964, pp. 53–54.

[Ewing 92] Juanita Ewing: How to use class variable and class instance variables. *The Smalltalk Report* **1** (5) 13 (January 1992).

[Gabriel 94a] Richard P. Gabriel: Pattern languages. *JOOP* **5** 72–75 (January 1994).

[Gabriel 94b] Richard P. Gabriel: The failure of pattern languages. *JOOP* **5** 84–88 (February 1994).

[GaHeJoVli 95] Erich Gamma, Richard Helm, Ralph Johnson, and John Vlissides: *Design Patterns. Elements of Reusable Object-Oriented Software.* Addison-Wesley, New York, 1995. ISBN 0-201-63361-2

[Gazz 88] M. S. Gazzaniga: *Mind Matters.* Houghton Miffin, Boston, 1988. ISBN 0-395-42159-4

[Gold 83] A. Goldberg and D. Robson: *Smalltalk-80, The Language and its Implementation.* Addison-Wesley, New York, 1983. ISBN 0-201-11371-6.

[Gold 84] A. Goldberg: *Smalltalk-80, The Interactive Programming Environment.* Addison-Wesley, New York, 1984. ISBN 0-201-11372-4.

[HallFagan] Hall, Fagan: *General Systems, Yearbook of the Society for General Systems Research.* Ann Arbor, Michigan, Vols. 1–10, 1956–65.

[Hammer 93] Michael Hammer and James Champy: *Reengineering the Corporation. A Manifesto for Business Revolution.* Nicholas Brealey Publishing, London, 1993. ISBN 1 85788 029 3

[Harel 87] David Harel: Statecharts: a visual formalism for complex systems. *Science of Computer Programming* **8** 231–274 (1987).

[Helm 90] Richard Helm, Ian M. Holland, and Dipayan Gangopadhyay: Contracts: Specifying Behavioral Compositions in Object-Oriented Systems. *Sigplan Notices* **25** 10 (ECOOP/OOPSLA '90, Oct 1990).

[Hol 77] Erik Holbæk-Hanssen, Petter Håndlykken, and Kristen Nygaard: *System Description and the Delta Language.* Norwegian Computing Center publication no. 523. Second printing, Oslo 1977.

[IDEF0 93] *Software Standard Integration Definition for Function Modeling (IDEF0).* Federal Information Processing Standards Publication 183, 1993. Obtainable from National Technical Information Service, US Department of Commerce, Springfield, VA 22161.

[ISO8859.1] *Information Processing. 8-bit single-byte coded graphic character sets. Part 1: Latin alphabet no. 1.* International Standardization Organization, 1987.

[ISO9000] EN ISO 9000–1, *Quality management and quality assurance standards—Guidelines for selection and use.* ISO 9001, *Quality systems—Model for quality assurance in design/development, production, installation and servicing.* International Standardization Organization, 1994.

[Jacobson 92] Ivar Jacobson, Magnus Christerson, Patrick Jonsson, and Gunnar Øvergaard: *Object-Oriented Software Engineering. A Use Case Driven Approach.* Addison-Wesley, New York, 1992. ISBN 0-201-54435-0

[John 88] R.E. Johnson and B. Foote: Designing Reusable Classes. *Journal of Object-Oriented Programming,* **1** (2) 22–25 (June/July 1988).

[Johnson 92] Ralph E. Johnson: Documenting Frameworks Using Patterns. OOP-SLA '92. *ACM Sigplan notices,* **27** (10) 63–68 (October 92).

[KerPla 74] B. W. Kernighan and P. J. Plauger: *The Elements of Programming Style.* McGraw-Hill, New York, 1974. ISBN 0.07-034199-0

[Kleyn 88] M. F. Kleyn and P. C. Gingrich: GraphTrace - Understanding Object-Oriented Systems Using Concurrently Animated Views. OOPSLA-88. *Sigplan Notices* **23** (11) 191–205 (November 1988).

[Lieb 89] Karl J. Lieberherr and Ian M. Holland: Assuring Good Style for Object-Oriented Programs. *IEEE Software* 38-48 (September 89).

[Liskov 88] Barbara Liskov: Data Abstraction and Hierarchy. *SIGPLAN Notices* **23** (5) (May 1988).

[Love 93] Tom Love: *Object Lessons.* SIGS Books, New York 1993. ISBN 0-9627477-3-4

[Martin 87] James Martin: *Recommended Diagramming Standards for Analysts and Programmers: A Basis for Automation.* Prentice-Hall, Englewood Cliffs, 1987. ISBN 0-13-767377-9 025

[Nilsen 93] R. Nilsen J. Simons, and P. Dellaferra: *Object-oriented IN service provision.* TINA '93—The Fourth Telecommunications Information Networking Architecture Workshop, L'Aquila, Italy, September 1993. Proceedings from Scuola Superiore G. Reiss Romoli S.p.A.; Str. Prov. per Coppito km 0,300; 67010 Coppito (AQ); Italy.

[Nordhagen 82] Else Nordhagen: *Blaise, syntaksorientert programredigering av Pascal tekst i et Smalltalk system.* (Blaise, syntax-oriented programming in Pascal). MSc thesis, Department of Informatics, University of Oslo, 1982.

[Nordhagen 89] Else Nordhagen: Generic Object Oriented Systems. *Proceedings of Tools 89,* Paris, November, 1989, pp. 131–140.

[Nordhagen 95] Else K. Nordhagen: *The COIR Architecture for Flexible Software Components and Systems.* Research report no. 197 (1995), Department of Informatics, University of Oslo. ISBN 82-7368-108-4

[Oftedal 87] Gro Oftedal: *The use of remote applications from a Smalltalk work station.* M.Sc. thesis, Dept. of Informatics, University of Oslo, January 1987.

[Olle 88] T. William Olle, Jaques Hagelstein, Ian G. Macdonald, Colette Rolland, Henk G. Sol, Frans J. M. Van Assche, and Alexander A. Verrijn-Stuart: *Infor-*

mation Systems Methodologies. A Framework for Understanding. Addison-Wesley, New York, 1988. ISBN 0-201-41610-7

[Olsen 92] Grete Christina Olsen: *Objektorienterte databaser og rollemodeller.* (Object-oriented databases and role models). MSc thesis, Department of Informatics, University of Oslo, 1992.

[Oxford 86] *Oxford Dictionary of Computing.* Oxford University Press, Oxford, 1986. (ISBN 0 19 853913 4)

[Parnas 86] David Lorge Parnas and Paul C. Clements: A Rational Design Process: How and Why to Fake It. *IEEE Trans. on Software Engineering* **SE-12**, 2 (February 1986).

[Pfiff 64] John M. Pfiffner and Frank P. Sherwood: *Administrative Organization.* Prentice-Hall, Englewood Cliffs, 1964.

[Ree 73] Trygve Reenskaug: *Administrative Control in the Shipyard.* ICCAS Conference, Tokyo, 1973.

[Ree 77] Trygve Reenskaug: *Prokon/Plan–A Modelling Tool for Project Planning and Control.* IFIP Conference, North-Holland, New York, 1977.

[Ree 86] Trygve Reenskaug and E. Næss-Ulseth: Tender/One—An Environment for Tender Preparation. *Ninth International Cost Engineering Congress,* Oslo, 1986.

[Ree 87] Trygve Reenskaug: User-Oriented Descriptions of Smalltalk Systems. *Byte,* **6**, (8) 148–166 (August 1981); and G. E. Peterson: *Tutorial: Object-Oriented Computing, Volume 1: Concepts.* The Computer Society of IEEE, Los Alamitos, 1987, pp. 75–81.

[Ree 89] Trygve Reenskaug and Anne Lise Skaar: An Environment for Literate Smalltalk Programming. *Sigplan Notices* **24** (10) 337–345 (October 89).

[Ree 92] Trygve Reenskaug, Egil P. Andersen, Arne Jørgen Berre, Anne Hurlen, Anton Landmark, Odd Arild Lehne, Else Nordhagen, Eirik Næss-Ulseth, Gro Oftedal, Anne Lise Skaar, and Pål Stenslet: OORASS: Seamless Support for the Creation and Maintenance of Object-Oriented Systems. *JOOP* 27–41, (October 1992).

[Ree 93] Trygve Reenskaug: *The Industrial Creation of Intelligent Network Services.* TINA '93—The Fourth Telecommunications Information Networking Architecture Workshop, L'Aquila, Italy, September 1993. Proceedings from Scuola Superiore G. Reiss Romoli S.p.A.; Str. Prov. per Coppito km 0,300; 67010 Coppito (AQ); Italy.

[Rubin 92] Kenneth S. Rubin and Adele Goldberg: Object Behavior Analysis. *Comm. ACM* **35** (9) 48–62 (September 92).

[Rumbaugh 91] James Rumbaugh, Michael Blaha, William Premerlani, Frederick Eddy, and William Lorensen: *Object-Oriented Modeling and Design.* Prentice-Hall, Englewood Cliffs, 1991. ISBN 0-13-630054-5

[Skaar 82] Anne Lise Skaar: *Objektorienterte produktmodeller i DAK-system.* (Object-oriented product models in an CAD system). MSc thesis, Department of Informatics, University of Oslo, 1982.

[Soukup 94] Jiri Soukup: *Taming C++: Pattern Classes and Persistence for Large Projects.* Addison-Wesley, Reading, 1994. ISBN 0-201-52826-6

[Stenslet 82] Pål Stenslet: *Spørresystem basert på Smalltalk.* (Query system based on Smalltalk). MSc thesis, Department of Informatics, University of Oslo, 1982.

[Strou 86] Bjarne Stroustrup: *The C++ Programming Language.* Addison-Wesley, New York, 1986. ISBN 0-201-12078-X

[Verr 91] M. Verrall: *The Software Bus—its Objective: The Mutual Integration of Distributed Software Engineering Tools.* Proc. 5th Conf. on Software Engineering Environments, Aberystwyth, March 1991, Ellis Horwood, 1991.

[Vestli, Nilsen 92] Nilsen Vestli: The Intelligent Network Service Life Cycle. *Telektronikk* **2.92** (Norwegian Telecom Research, P.b. 83, 2007-Kjeller, Norway).

[Webster 77] We*bster's New Collegiate Dictionary.* Merriam-Webster, Springfield, 1977.

[WegZdon 88] P. Wegner and S. B. Z. Zdonik: *Inheritance as an Incremental Modification Mechanism or What Like is Like or Isn't Like.* Proc. ECOOP '88, Oslo, 1988, pp. 55–77.

[Weinb 71] Gerald M. Weinberg: *The Psychology of Computer Programming.* Van Nostrand Reinhold, New York, 1971.

[Weinb 75] Gerald M. Weinberg: *An Introduction to General Systems Thinking.* John Wiley, New York, 1975. ISBN O-471-92563-2

[Wheeler 92] John A. Wheeler, quoted by John Horgan in: Quantum Philosophy. *Scientific American,* 79 (July 1992).

[WiJo 90] Rebecca J. Wirfs-Brock, Ralph E. Johnson: Surveying current research in object-oriented design. *Comm. ACM* **33** (9) 113 (September 1990).

[Wirfs-Brock 90] Rebecca Wirfs-Brock, Brian Wilkerson, and Laureen Wiener: *Designing Object-Oriented Software.* Prentice-Hall, Englewood Cliffs, 1990

[Wirth 71] Niklaus Wirth: Program Development by Stepwise Refinement. *Comm. ACM* **14** (4) 221–227 (1971).

[Wynn 79] Elanor Herasimchuk Wynn: *Office Conversation as an Information Medium.* Ph.D. Thesis. Department of Anthropology, University of California, Berkeley, May 1979.

Where to Find Definitions of Important Terms

Systems

Environment   60
Models   33
System   36

Object Properties

Attribute   38, 58
Collaborator   39
Encapsulation   38
Identity   38
Instance variable   59, 108
Interface   58
Message   38
Method   39, 58
Polymorphism   39
State   59

OOram Technology

Activity   38, 84
Aggregation   80, 86
Base and derived roles, models   10, 80
Generalization-specialization   80
Implementation map   15
Module   173

Object pattern   9, 17
Object-subject relationship   80
Object, type, role, class   14
Perspective   60
Role model   9, 44
Stimulus message   38
Superposition   86
Synthesis   73, 80
   safe and unsafe   12, 85
The ten OOram views   60
Use case   65

Reuse

Engineering, forward and reverse   27
Fountain model for reuse   26, 290
Framework   17, 141
Incidental, planned reuse   135
Object   14
OOCS (OOram composition system:
   schema, entity, and type)   142, 300
Pattern   17, 141
Polymorphism   39
Trader   296
Value chain   275

Index

A

Abstract class   109
Abstractions
    How   14
    Is   14
    What   14
    Why   14
Action   36, 37, 59, 122, 168
Active competence   140
Activity   21, 38, 47, 62, 84
    Aggregation   86, 91
    Network   8
    Superposition   86, 90, 99
Actors   28, 186, 276
Aggregation   80
    Embedded   88
    Encapsulated   87
    Relation   159
Alexander   17, 143, 144
Analysis   39, 79
Andersen   85
Application programming interface (API)   196
Application programs   13
Area of concern   8, 45, 94, 185
    View. *See* View; Area of concern
Aronson   299
Association   159
Asynchronous   58, 65
Attribute   36, 37, 39, 57–59, 60, 88
Automatic code generator   120

B

Base
    Class   10, 43, 108
    Model   11, 73, 80
        RST   94
        XY   94
    Port   84
    Role   73, 80
    Role models   10
Beck   44, 54
Behavior   57
Behavior-centered approach   2
Birtwistle   2, 36
Boehm   125, 321
Booch   xv, 2, 20, 86
    method   20
Bræk   168, 212, 217, 224
Business process reengineering   184

C

C   102
C++   14, 20, 105, 106, 117, 129, 222
CCITT
    Z100   221, 224
    Z120   65
Chen   21, 159
Class   xv, 14, 43, 108, 116
    Diagrams   20
Class-responsibility-collaborator
    cards (CRC cards)   54

Clerk   6
Client-server   88
    architecture   179
Code sharing   79
Collaboration view. *See* View; Collaboration
Collaborator   39
COM   226, 228
COM/OLE   226
Common Object Request Broker Architecture
      (CORBA). *See* CORBA
Component   242
    Object Model (COM)   228
Composition   16, 294
Conceptual schema   200, 294
Configurability   112
Connection Point   323
Consumer Goods Domain   284
Container   242
    -Component Hierarchy   242
Controller   249
CORBA   37, 58, 226, 227
    IDL   227
    OMG   226
Cox   xv, 2, 104, 155, 173
Cunningham   44, 53, 54, 144
Current state   59

D

Dahl   36
Data
    -Centered approaches   2
    Stores   164
Decision maker pattern   149
Deliverables   3
Derived
    Class   10, 43, 108
    Model   11, 73, 80
    Port   84
    Role   73, 80
    Role models   10
Divide and conquer   10
Duplication   16, 294
Dynamically typed   130

E

Egoless programming   128
Eiffel   102, 120, 129
Elmasri   21, 159
Embedding   87

Encapsulation   38, 57, 87, 112, 294
End User   287
Engelbart   285
Engineer   288
Enterprise   178
Entity   159
    -relationship   2, 21
    -relationship (E-R) model   159
Environment   37, 60
    role   189
E-R. *See* Entity-relationship (E-R) model
Etzioni   55
EURESCOM   282
Executable specifications   13, 229
Execution Scenario report   231
Export   173
External collaboration view. *See* View; External
      collaboration
External schema   200

F

File Transfer Protocol (FTP)   48
Finite state
    Diagrams   22
    Machines   2
Fire walls   126
FORTRAN   105
Forward engineering   27, 40, 229
Fountain model for reuse   290
Frameworks   16, 17, 22, 153, 154
FTP. *See* File Transfer Protocol
Functional decomposition   2

G

Gabriel   145
Gamma   17, 144
Garbage collection   130
Gazzaniga   33
Generalization-specialization   80, 175
Goldberg   2, 36, 249

H

Hall   36
Hammer   184
Harel   20
Helm   17, 44, 144
Hierarchical
    Aggregation   86
    Decomposition   13, 86

Holbæk-Hanssen   36
Horn   202
Human communication   35

I

IDEF0   162
Identity   22, 38
IDL   226
Immutable   296, 337, 338
Implementation   13
    Description   141
    Schema   200
Import   173
IN services   320
Incidental reuse   133, 135
industrial   28
Information
    Editor   285
    Environments   178
    Hiding   38, 176
    Service   179
    Tool   199
Inheritance   43, 112
    Table   92, 93
    Collaboration View. See View; Inheritance
        Collaboration
Instance variable   41, 59, 108
Instances   108
Instantiating   108
Intelligent Network Domain   284
Intelligent network services   281
Interaction   65
    Diagrams   20
Interface   58, 121, 191
    Definition Language (IDL)   226, 227
    View. See View; Interface
Invocation Analyzer   326
ISO Latin-1   340
ISO9000   141

J

Jacobson   xv, 2, 21, 65
Johnson   17, 144

K

Kay   36
Kernel maker   288, 289
Kernighan   126

L

Late binding   58
Layer   274
Leg   323
Legacy system   179
Life cycle model   274
List of instructions   140
Logical map   141

M

Martin   64
Mechanism   17
Member functions   122
Mental interpreter   33
Message Parameters   88
Messages   38, 60
Method   38, 39, 47, 58, 84, 108, 122
    View. See View; Method
Methodology   3
Microsoft   228
Model   249
    Creation process   23
    Enterprise   181
    Information   181, 194
    Manifest   34
    Mental   33, 199
    Object   59
    System requirements   181
    System user   181
    Task/tool/service   181, 199
    Tool information   199
Modeling in the large: The OOram Module   173
Model-View-Controller   249
Module   20, 21
    Maker   288, 289
Monitored execution   230
Multiple inheritance   15
MVC   249

N

Naming convention   117
Network
    Connection   323
    Provider   283, 321
Next state   59
Nilsen   282
Nordhagen   85
Norwegian Telecom   282
Nygaard   36

O

Object   xv, 3, 14, 36, 37
   Attribute   38, 39
   -Based languages   15
   Collaboration report   230
   Diagrams   20
   Duplication   294
   Identity   22
   Linking and Embedding (OLE)   228
   Management Group   37, 226, 227
   Model. *See* Model; Object
   Modeling Technique (OMT)   20
   Pattern   17
   Specification   14, 116
   Structure duplication   142
   Trading   142, 294, 296
   Type   14
Objective C   129
Object-oriented
   Database   194
   Direct manipulation interface   202
   Framework   154
ObjectOry   21
Object-subject relationship   80
Objectworks\Smalltalk   237
OLE   226, 228
OMG   226, 227
OMG/CORBA. *See* CORBA; OMG
OMT   20
   Dynamic model   20
   Functional model   20
   Object model   20
OOCS   142, 298, 300
   Entity   300, 303
   Group   305
   Schema   142, 298, 300, 303
   Type   142, 300, 302, 303, 305
OOram
   Analysis   45
   Composition System (OOCS)   142, 294, 298, 300, 331
   Framework   141, 153, 154
   Interface   121
   Language   172, 206
     Inheritance specification   92, 94
   Method   xix, 3
   Modules   158, 173
   Role model   xvi
   Specification   340
   Technology   6

OOSE methodology   21
Organization   3

P

Parameter types   192
Parnas   24
Passive competence   140
Patterns   16, 17, 141, 143, 144
   language   143, 145
Perspective   60
Planned reuse   133, 135
Plato   44
Plauger   126
Polymorphism   39, 58, 106, 112, 294
Port   45, 84, 121
postCopy   312
Principle of minimizing risk   124
Process   3
   Diagrams   20, 22, 190
   Steps   52
   View. *See* View; Process
Production   288
   engineering   279
Programming   102
   approach
     Bottom-up   124
     Top-down   124
     Yo-yo   26, 124
   -in-the-large   173

R

Rational work organization   55
Records   21
Relations   21, 159
   Aggregation   159, 175
   Association   159
   Peer-to-peer module   175
   Subtype   159
   Use   159
Relational database   194
Relational model   21
Response   60, 62
Responsibility Driven Design (RDD)   21
Reusable assets   26
   building process   23
Reusable components   3, 16
Reverse engineering   27, 40, 229
Role   9, 14, 44, 45, 59, 60, 116
   Instances   45
   Model   xvi, 3, 8, 9, 44, 59

Model collaboration view. *See* View; Role
    model collaboration
Model synthesis   3, 10, 11, 80
Rubin   184
Rumbaugh   xv, 2, 20, 184
Runtime configuration   142, 294

S

Safe Synthesis. *See* Synthesis; Safe
Scenario   22, 47, 65
    View. *See* View; Scenario
Semantic correctness   306
Separation of concerns   xvi, 3, 10
Service   334
    Constituent   322, 334
    Constituent Creator   283, 321
    Creator   283, 321
    Domain   282
    Provider   283, 320
shallowCopy   311
Single inheritance   15
Smalltalk   14, 105, 107, 117, 120, 129, 223, 237
Soukup   143
State   59
    Diagram   20, 168
Statically typed   130
Stimuli   62
Stimulus messages   38, 47, 60, 85, 189
Stimulus/response   189
Stroustrup   2
structureCopy   314
Subclass   108
Subject of discourse   25
Subscriber   283, 320
Superclass   108
Surface area   155, 173, 237
Switching Domain   282
Synchronous   58, 65
    deferred   58, 65
Syntactically correct   307
Synthesis   11, 40, 71, 73, 78, 79, 80
    Collaboration view. *See* View; Synthesis
      collaboration
    Relation   73
    Safe   12, 70, 85, 165, 169
    Unsafe   13, 70, 85, 91, 165
    View. *See* View; Synthesis
System   36
    Description Language (SDL)   224
    Design model   25, 70

Development process   23
Implementation   70
Implementation model   25
of objects   300
Requirements model   25
Software Supplier   288
Transcript   240
User model   25, 70

T

Tables   21
Task description   200
Task/tool/service architecture   179
Taskon Fountain Model   288
Technology   3
TINA   281
Tool   179
Tool Maker   287, 289
Toolbuilder   199
Trader   294, 296
Trigger   38, 76, 190
Tuples   21
Type   14, 104
Type checking   122

U

Universe of discourse   25
UNIX   102
Unsafe synthesis. *See* Synthesis; Unsafe
Use case   21, 65
User   283, 320
    Information Environment   179
    interfaces   201

V

Value chain   16, 28, 274, 275
Variable   121
Vestli   282
View   9, 60, 249
    Area of concern   46, 60, 62
    Collaboration   9, 46, 61, 63, 95
    External collaboration   64
    Inheritance collaboration   92
    Interface   9, 61, 66, 99
    Method   9, 48
    Method specification   61, 68, 99
    Process   61, 157, 162, 163
    Role List   61, 158, 172
    Role Model Collaborative   9

View *(cont.)*
    Scenario 9, 61, 65, 97
    Semantic 61, 154, 157, 159
    State diagram 61
    Stimulus-response 60, 62, 95
    Synthesis 92
    Synthesis collaboration 73
Virtual 87
    roles 64, 189, 212
VisualPart 242
Vlissides 17, 144

W

Weber 55
Weinberg 128, 140, 187
Wirfs-Brock xv, 2, 21, 54, 184
Wirth 103

Work process 23, 52
    Enterprise modeling 184
    Framework creation 156, 236
    Information modeling 194
    Model creation 24
    Module architecture 174
    OOCS schema creation 303
    Pattern creation 146
    Real time system modeling 212
    System development 25
Wynn 186

Y

Yo-yo approach. *See* Programming; Approaches;
    Yo-yo